PORTRAIT OF DIVORCE

PERSPECTIVES ON MARRIAGE AND THE FAMILY
Bert N. Adams and David M. Klein, *Editors*

PORTRAIT

OF

DIVORCE

Adjustment to Marital Breakdown

GAY C. KITSON
with
William M. Holmes

THE GUILFORD PRESS
New York   London

© 1992 The Guilford Press
A Division of Guilford Publications, Inc.
72 Spring Street, New York, NY 10012

Printed in the United States of America

This book is printed on acid-free paper.

Last digit is print number: 9 8 7 6 5 4 3 2 1

Library of Congress Cataloging-in-Publication Data

Kitson, Gay C.
    Portrait of divorce: adjustment to marital breakdown /
Gay C. Kitson with William M. Holmes.
        p.   cm.—(Perspectives on marriage and the family)
    Includes bibliographical references and indexes.
    ISBN 0-89862-081-3
    1. Divorce—United States.   2. Divorce—Psychological aspects.
I. Holmes, William M. (William Michael), 1946–   II. Title.
III. Series.
    [DNLM: 1. Divorce.   WM 55 K62p]
HQ834.K57   1992
306.89—dc20
DNLM/DLC
for Library of Congress   91-35431
                                                                CIP

To
James T. Kitson
and to my parents,
Marguerite F. and Raymond E. Capouch

Acknowledgments

This book presents data from four studies of marital instability and divorce in order to present a comprehensive portrait of the divorce process. The project had its genesis when Marvin B. Sussman asked me to join him in a study of divorce adjustment. He initiated the longitudinal suburban study of divorce adjustment that is the major focus of this book. I was the coinvestigator and field director of that study, responsible for its day-to-day development and management. After Professor Sussman left Case Western Reserve University, I became the director of the research project. Because of the pressure of his other responsibilities, it became difficult for Professor Sussman to continue to work on the project. I am grateful to him for the opportunities he gave me and for the many important skills and lessons I learned from him.

William M. Holmes was also associated with this project in its later stages when he was at Case Western Reserve University. He subsequently wrote early drafts of Chapter 8, "The Economic Divorce," and Chapter 9, "Social Support in Divorce," and made helpful comments on initial drafts of some other chapters. However, as his responsibilities changed after he left the university, it was not possible for him to complete work on Chapters 8 and 9. I therefore wrote the final versions of these chapters and added some supplementary analyses. The chapters are based on Holmes's original work and are jointly authored.

Alan Booth read the manuscript in its entirety, and Robert Weiss, Sharon Houseknecht, Leslie Morgan, Benjamin Gottlieb, and the late Reuben Hill made helpful comments on earlier versions of some of the material that appears here. I appreciate the advice, counsel, and careful reviews of these chapters by the editors of the Guilford Perspectives on Marriage and the Family series, Bert N. Adams and David M. Klein. They have been unfailingly supportive and helpful. I am also grateful to Marie Sprayberry of Guilford Press for her careful copy-editing of the manuscript.

I talked with a number of persons in formulating ideas for these studies. Among them were Pauline Bart, William J. Goode, Helen J. Raschke, the late Max Rheinstein, John Scanzoni, Robert S. Weiss, Lenore J. Weitzman, and the late Robert F. Winch. Professors Weiss, Bernard L. Bloom, Helena Z. Lopata, and Colin Murray Parkes served as consultants for the marital transition study. During the long process of completing this project, it has also been sad to note the passing of two friends and colleagues, Julie A. Fulton and Gerald F. Jacobson.

I am grateful for the assistance of the following during the conduct of these studies: Karen Benson Babri, Raymond J. Balester, Gwendolyn Williams Biggins, Beth Ann Chase, Richard D. Clark, David S. DeGarmo, Melvyn C. Goldstein, Murray A. Goldstone, Marjorie E. Goodell, Marie R. Haug, Nancy Lawrence, James Peacock, Mary Joan Roach, Adrienne J. Schaffer, Barbara Klepak Shickmanter, Deborah Sitter, Jeanne L. Steinberger, Howard S. Sudak, Leslie Swift-Rosensweig, E. Jean Szucs, Rosemary Usman, Eugene S. Uyeki, Pamela J. Zbasnik, Randi F. Zeehandelaar, and Stephen J. Zyzanski. A large staff of interviewers did an excellent job of locating and recontacting subjects in an empathetic manner. A faithful, four-footed companion, Boswell Kitson, "assisted" in much of the writing.

The collection of data on the divorced sample and the married comparison group for the longitudinal suburban study was made possible by National Institute of Mental Health Grant No. 22575. The reconciliation survey and the county-wide omnibus marital status survey were supported by National Institute of Mental Health Grant No. 30782. The county-wide marital transition survey was supported by National Institute on Aging Grant No. 4561. National Institute on Aging Grant No. 6591 has also provided support. The Department of Sociology at the University of Akron has provided a congenial and collegial setting for the completion of this project.

I am extremely grateful to the divorcing persons we contacted, who were so willing to talk about their thoughts, feelings, and experiences concerning an often difficult period in their lives. Every effort has been made to protect their confidentiality. They hoped, as I do, that others will learn from their experiences in order to advance our understanding of the at least temporarily disorienting effects of ending a marriage.

Having been immersed in studying the topic of divorce for much of our marriage, I especially value my enduring bond to, and the support, patience, and encouragement of, James T. Kitson.

GAY C. KITSON
Shaker Heights, Ohio

Preface

This book takes a comprehensive approach to studying the process of divorce—its causes and its consequences. In the research that constitutes the principal focus of the book, a group of divorced persons has been followed longitudinally and compared with a matched sample of married people followed over the same time period. The events surrounding the decision to divorce and the changes that marital dissolution brought to the divorced subjects' lives are explored. The divorced have been followed from a description of the period of estrangement in their marriages through the divorce process and on to 2–3 years after the divorce, or about 4 years after the couples separated.

Data are also presented from three other studies completed in the same metropolitan area (Cleveland, Ohio), to provide more insight into the problem of marital separation and reconciliation and to examine possible changes in adjustment to divorce in the 1970s compared to the 1980s. These include a study of persons who filed for divorce but changed their minds and reconciled with their spouses; a county-wide omnibus survey of marital status, designed to assess separations before filing for divorce; and a second county-wide, longitudinal sample of divorced women.

In this book, adjustment to divorce is viewed as a multidimensional concept. A model of adjustment is advanced that attempts to link the long-at-odds "crisis" and "pathology" approaches to divorce adjustment. Measures designed for this study are presented to operationalize key concepts in the divorce process. These include measures of "attachment," "couples' growing apart," "hesitancy to divorce," "marital expectations," "marital complaints," "stigma," "satisfaction with the legal process," and "couple contacts." Social and psychological risk factors that distinguish the divorced from their comparison sample of the married are explored and linked to data on self-reported causes of divorce. Changes in adjustment to divorce are examined in detail, both cross-sectionally and longitudinally.

THE FRAGMENTARY NATURE OF DIVORCE RESEARCH

Despite the growth of research on divorce, many studies of divorce have presented a fragmented picture of divorce adjustment because of either the specificity of the topic covered, the narrowness of the study population, or the cross-sectional nature of the research. Studies have been done of individuals of low socioeconomic status, mothers with custody of the children, fathers with custody of the children, parents who keep in contact after the divorce, economic and legal issues in divorce, people seeking outpatient therapy, and so forth (e.g., Ahrons, 1981; Goode, 1956; Grief, 1985; D. S. Jacobson, 1978a, 1978b, 1978c; G. F. Jacobson, 1983; Kreisberg, 1970; Rosenthal & Keshet, 1981; Weitzman, 1985). Each of these studies has made a contribution, but questions have been left about how the topic studied interacts with other dimensions of the divorce process, how the missing components of the study populations cope with divorce, and what divorce adjustment looks like longitudinally. Relatively little is known about how men adjust to divorce compared to women, or about how blacks adjust compared to whites.

CHARACTERISTICS OF THIS RESEARCH

The research to be reported upon here has attempted to fill some of these gaps. It differs from other studies in having done *all* of the following things: (1) using divorce court records; (2) selecting a community-based sample; (3) using a married comparison sample; (4) using a multidimensional definition of adjustment; (5) developing a "loss" model of adjustment that attempts to link the "crisis" and "pathology" approaches to divorce adjustment; (6) introducing a series of measures designed to operationalize key concepts in the divorce process; (7) exploring gender differences in adjustment; (8) exploring racial differences in adjustment; (9) looking at the divorce process from estrangement to the establishment of new relationships; (10) examining social, psychological, legal, economic, and parenting issues in adjustment; and (11) doing all of these things on a longitudinal basis.

THE PLAN OF THIS BOOK

Among the questions to be explored in the following pages are the following:

1. How do those who divorce compare to those who do not in their social and psychological characteristics? Do the divorced have more risk factors that may predispose them to divorce than the married?

2. Can some of the factors that have contributed to the increase in the rate of divorce be identified? Is there a new type of divorce that reflects greater concern for marriage as an arena for personal fulfillment?

3. How long does it take individuals to adjust to divorce? Do men and women, blacks and whites differ in their patterns of adjustment?

4. What impact do social, legal, economic, psychological, and parenting issues have on adjustment?

5. How do people go about the process of reconstructing their lives after a divorce?

6. What social, psychological, and economic characteristics distinguish those who adjust well to divorce from those who adjust poorly?

7. Does a model that looks at divorce as an event involving losses add to our ability to understand adjustment, compared to a model that looks at divorce as a life event?

In Chapter 1, the background for today's mixed view of divorce is outlined. Society has traditionally regarded divorce as entailing moral, social, and/or psychological pathology. Relatively recent social and historical changes, however, have led to a shift in views of marriage: It is now seen as an intense, close relationship rather than a more instrumental, role-segregated partnership, and this shift has made marriage a more difficult relationship to sustain. A model of adjustment to divorce that attempts to integrate the pathology and crisis models of adjustment is outlined; this new model includes elements of loss and change.

Chapter 2 describes the four sources of study data that are reported upon in this book and indicates how the key elements of adjustment to be explored—subjective distress, attachment, self-esteem, and illness contacts—were measured.

Chapter 3 examines background characteristics of the suburban, reconciled, and marital transition samples, in order to address the issue of comparability of the samples. "Risk factors" that have been thought to make those who divorce at greater risk for marital dissolution are explored, as are attitudes about marriage and divorce.

Chapter 4 explores the process of relationship estrangement that precedes any formal steps to terminate a marriage. The discussion covers indicators of marital instability, such as dissatisfaction with the relationship; previous separations and attempts at reconciliation; and the timing of the divorce decision, including changes in the timing of the divorce process that have occurred since William Goode's (1956) landmark 1948 Detroit study of women's adjustment to divorce.

Chapter 5 looks at three meanings of the term "causes of divorce": legal definitions; social and psychological correlates of the decision to divorce; and the meaning of the divorce as seen by the divorced themselves (i.e., their self-described marital complaints). Changes in the nature of the complaints across time and within the present research are examined. The risk factors for divorce identified in Chapter 3 are linked to the self-described marital complaints of the divorced.

In Chapter 6, the psychological and physical health of male versus female and black versus white divorced and married persons is described, both cross-sectionally and longitudinally. The periods in the divorce process that the divorced reported to be most distressing are detailed. Data are presented to address the issue of whether adjustment has become easier in recent years as divorce has become a more common experience. The role that other life events occurring simultaneously with or subsequent to the divorce played in fostering or retarding adjustment is also described.

In Chapter 7, parents' perceptions of how the divorce affected their children are described. The characteristics of parents that led them to see positive, negative, or no changes in their children as a result of the divorce are outlined.

Chapter 8 examines the economic situation of the divorced both cross-sectionally and longitudinally, as well as in comparison to the married. Based on a constant-dollar formula, decreases in economic well-being for women over the past decade are noted, despite societal efforts to foster more equitable formulae for child support and the division of property.

Chapter 9 describes patterns of social support for the divorced. These include individuals and institutions from whom or which the divorced received help; the kinds of help they received; differences in patterns of help cross-sectionally, longitudinally, and in comparison to the married group; and the kinds of help that were more effective in reducing the distress of divorce.

Chapter 10 examines some of the changes that take place after a divorce occurs: differences in the behavior of others because of the change in marital status; the extent to which divorced spouses remain in contact after the dissolution of their marriages; attitudes toward the legal system; the extent to which the divorced find new partners; and the easier and harder aspects of adjustment, as perceived by the divorced.

Chapter 11 attempts to integrate the material presented in the earlier chapters, in order to determine which factors are associated with better and worse adjustment to divorce, both cross-sectionally and longitudinally for men and women and for blacks and whites. The relative utility of a model of adjustment to divorce that includes measures of loss, as opposed to a life events model.

Chapter 12 reviews the study findings, examines policy implications of the research, and looks toward next steps in divorce research.

Appendices A, B, and C present the questions that were asked of the married and divorced samples, the coding categories used for the adjustment measure subjective distress, and the categories used to code the marital complaints, respectively.

GAY C. KITSON
Shaker Heights, Ohio

Contents

What Do We Know about Divorce, and What Do We Still Need to Know?

I went into a store one time and I was looking at some beds for my son. I spoke to a salesman and he asked me, "Is this going to be cash or charge?" I said, "Well, I don't know yet," because I was thinking of starting some credit on my own. And he said, "Well, what does your husband do?" And I said, "I'm divorced." And he said, very cold, very distant, "Oh, well, I'm terribly sorry. Are you working?" I went back the next day and I got another salesman. And the same thing, "What does your husband do?" And I said, "I lost my husband six months ago." "Well," he says, "I'm sure we can work something out." Boy, I got all the sympathy in the world.

    —A divorced mother in her 30s, quoted by Weiss (1979, pp. 10–11)

A civilized divorce is a contradiction in terms.

    —Gavin D'Amato, the lawyer portrayed by Danny DeVito
    in the 1989 movie *The War of the Roses*

Perhaps then, the Bottom Line in 95% of the cases is that everyone loses in a divorce and that we should support people in their shaky relationships by helping them to resolve their own internal conflicts around intimacy through the insights provided in analytic treatment. . . . The American Family is being threatened with total extinction and needs our help desperately.

    —Friend (1983, p. 1)

It would be comforting to dismiss the quotations above as quaint statements about divorce from earlier, unenlightened eras. They are not. They reflect not uncommon views about and experiences of divorced persons in the present. Why? What is it about divorce that leads to discrimination against those who voluntarily choose to end their marriages, to an often acrimonious divorce process, and to the feeling of some laypersons and professionals that those who divorce are "sick"? Another curious finding about divorce is that divorced persons have repeatedly been shown to have higher rates of suicide and death from other causes, physical illness, mental illness, and even car accidents than married or single persons do, and often higher rates than widowed persons do. Why? What is it about divorce or about those who divorce that accounts for these startling findings?

Answers to such questions increase in importance at a time when, depending upon their age cohort, one-third, two fifths, one-half, or three-fifths of first marriages in the United States and a quarter of all remarriages are eventually likely to end in divorce (Cherlin, 1981; Glick & Norton, 1979; Bumpass, 1990; Norton, 1983; Norton & Moorman, 1987). Today, the ranks of the divorced cross virtually all social and age categories; they also include more couples who are white, more who are older, more who are middle- to upper-middle-class, and more who have children than was true in years past.

Although divorce has become more frequent, frequency has not necessarily made ending a marriage an easier event. For many persons, divorce is an experience about which they are extremely ambivalent, and such ambivalence can make adjustment more difficult. Even the worst marriage whose ending produces a sense of enormous relief was not all bad or always bad. Hardly anyone enters a marriage intending to end it. There is often a bittersweet quality to the marital breakup, with a lot of "What if . . ." and "If I'd only . . ." statements or thoughts. Such strong, contradictory feelings may make divorce one of the most devastating events that the majority of Americans are likely to experience.

Why is it that couples divorce? A long-standing explanation has been that those who divorce are less morally, socially, or psychologically "fit" than those who do not. But what does it mean about us or our society to make such statements today, when so many U.S. marriages are ending in divorce? If these assertions are true, the prophets of marital doom have underestimated the extent of the problem facing us. Divorce may be the harbinger of the disintegration not only of the family, but of all of our values and institutions—a sign of a "sick" society. Although this is possible, and some people hold this view, a less dramatic explanation is that a new type of divorce has developed. In this chapter, this new view of divorce and the factors that have led to its development are examined.

This discussion serves as a backdrop for the presentation of longitudinal data gathered on how men and women, and blacks and whites, in a large Midwestern metropolitan area adjusted to the events of divorce and the changes it brought to their lives. Their replies are, in many cases, compared to those of a comparison group of married persons selected from the same city blocks as the divorced. The divorced are followed from their description of the period of estrangement in the marriage through the divorce and on to 2–3 years after the divorce, or about 4 years after the couples separated. Data are also presented from three other studies, in order to clarify possible changes in adjustment to divorce in the 1970s compared to the 1980s, and to provide more insight into the problem of marital separation and reconciliation.

A NEW TYPE OF DIVORCE?

Some of the increase in the divorce rate appears to be a result of the evolving nature of the society—the result of a shift in the meaning of marriage as life has become more urban and industrial (Burgess & Locke, 1953; Goode, 1963; Parsons & Bales, 1955). As a consequence, the marital "ante" has been raised, and more individuals expect more from marriage than ever before. Heightened marital expectations are the result of increased financial security, greater leisure, and years of singing the praises of companionate marriage. With material needs more easily met, especially for women through their own labor force participation; the compressing (and even, if couples choose, the suppressing) of childbearing and child rearing; and the possibility of 40, 50, or 60 years of marriage, the marital focus has shifted. A marriage is increasingly assessed in terms of the ability of the partner or relationship to foster the individual's or couple's growth. Such evaluations are subject to an even more idiosyncratic metric than the assessment of occupational achievement, parenting, or housekeeping skills. A partner can easily be found wanting when the focus of the relationship is on more fragile, less easily met needs, such as affection, empathy, understanding, and companionship.

To suggest that a new type of divorce accounts for much of the increase in the divorce rate is not to ignore the role of more traditional social and psychological factors in producing divorce, or the importance of such influences in making divorce adjustment difficult. As the subsequent discussion indicates, numerous factors—such as premarital pregnancy, marrying young, dissimilar social backgrounds for marital partners, mental illness, and a family history of divorce—have been implicated as precipitants of divorce. Furthermore, divorce occurs in a social and historical context that is an amalgam of views about the sanctity and inviolability of the marriage contract. Even if there has been a change in attitudes about the reasons for maintaining a marriage, these long-standing and often negative societal attitudes continue to play a role in how others view the divorced and how the divorced view themselves. The pages to come examine some of the reasons for the public's continued concern about divorce. Such concern signifies the importance and fragility of the institutions of marriage and the family in our society. After all, if marriages were less important and more easily maintained, there would not be a need for so many legal and social safeguards against their disintegration.

THE COMPLEXITY OF DIVORCE

Divorce is a complex social and psychological event. Few other commonly occurring events influence so many spheres of a person's life: legal, social, psychological, economic, and (for those with children) parental (Bohannan, 1970, 1985; Goode, 1956; Waller, 1930/1967; Weiss, 1975). These changes are often preceded by an alienating period of increasing estrangement between the partners as one or both move toward the decision to divorce. Not only are the process of estrangement and the social, legal, psychological, economic, and parental changes themselves upsetting; they are also frequently accompanied by further anger, disappointment, and hurt fueled by continued wrangling with the ex-spouse and the negative reactions of others to the divorce. These complex interrelationships, which constitute the focus of this book, are outlined in the following sections.

Estrangement

For many couples, deciding to end their marriages is a process of escalating levels of discontent, including frighteningly fierce arguments that may become physically violent (O'Brien, 1971; Wallerstein & Kelly, 1980), or lengthy, increasingly alienating silences during which hurts and wrongs continue to pile up. For some individuals, the divorce decision comes with the shock of the apparently sudden, unexpected announcement by the partner that he or she is filing for divorce. Divorced persons often report that this period during which the pros and cons of continuing the marriage are weighed is the most distressing part of the divorce process (Albrecht, Bahr, & Goodman, 1983; Chester, 1971; Chiriboga & Cutler, 1977; Goode, 1956).

The partner's taunts and the epithets of this often extended period of increasing estrangement can take a long-lasting toll on self-esteem and self-worth. The sting of being called or made to feel stupid, worthless, thoughtless, hateful, unloving, ungrateful, unfeeling, and/or undesirable is not easily removed. Some of the charges hit close enough to home to make it hard for a person to sort out the ones to "own." Others confirm the person's worst unspoken fears about the self.

Legal Issues

Perhaps as much a sign of the social importance of marriage as any of its other characteristics is the fact that the decision to end a marital relationship requires civil approval through the involvement of the courts. Today, for spouses who have decided that their relationship is no longer viable, such approval seems simply a formality. It was not too many years ago, however, that in many jurisdictions in the United States it was uncertain whether a couple would be allowed to divorce (Blake, 1962; Wheeler, 1974). Not until 1970 in California was it possible for a couple in the United States to divorce simply because of "irreconcilable differences" or the "irretrievable breakdown" of their relationship. Before then, one party to the divorce had to be legally "innocent" of any wrongdoing, and the other legally "at fault." Depending on the state, from 1 to 10 or 12 legal grounds were admissible reasons for a divorce. These grounds were often interpreted quite literally, but as attitudes about divorce began to change, grounds became more broadly interpreted in the United States and in other Western societies (Blake, 1962; R. Phillips, 1988; Riley, 1991; Stone, 1990). An adversarial legal system, it was said, contributed to the acrimony and length of the divorce process. Starting in the early 1970s, nonadversarial, no-fault divorce, or "dissolution of marriage" (see Chapters 2 and 5), became available; all states now have some form of no-fault divorce, sometimes coupled with fault-based divorce and sometimes as the sole means of ending a marriage (Freed & Walker, 1988).

Nevertheless, even with the legal process simplified through the introduction of no-fault divorce provisions, divorcing spouses can wrangle over the division of assets, custody of the children, and alimony and child support payments, making these legal necessities a continuing arena for hostilities. Such hostilities are still so common that states are increasingly introducing legislation requiring mediation before couples appear before a judge, in those cases in which couples cannot agree upon a settlement (Emery & Wyer, 1987b).

The Social Divorce

Like a pebble tossed into a smooth pond, the ramifications of a divorce ripple through a couple's social network. Some of the changes are results of the shifting situation, interests, and values of the divorced. Other changes may result from the discomfort of the still-married with their friends' divorce (Miller, 1970). For example, many social engagements for the married involve couples, and the divorced may find themselves at loose ends in these settings. Divorced women report being viewed suspiciously by their married women friends as potential homewreckers, or becoming the object of passes from their married male friends. Acquaintances of the couple may feel that in a divorce, friends, like property, have to be divided into "his" and "hers." Still others are reminded of the fallibility of their own relationships by the divorce. The "There but for the grace of God go I" school of thought takes hold: "They seemed like such a happy couple. If it happened to them, what about us?" of "If he could make the break, why can't I?" Such feelings of discomfort and threat can lead to distancing from the divorced persons. Out of sight may be out of mind.

Friendships and social ties are not the only other relationships strained by a divorce. Divorce also often produces a break in the extended family with the loss of in-laws, who, even more readily than friends, take sides (Spicer & Hampe, 1975). Even one's own relatives who disapprove of the split may make continued contact or even moral support difficult.

The Economic Divorce

With finite resources, it is difficult for a formerly married couple to split into two economic units (Espenshade, 1979). Many of the tangible assets of married life, such as chairs, tables, and beds, do not stretch far enough to furnish two households. Furthermore, with the increase in the number of working wives, many couples have become accustomed to living on two incomes. Even with two incomes, the loss of income induced by the divorce is not evenly distributed. Data from the University of Michigan Panel Study of Income Dynamics indicate that before the marital split, 80% of the household income in divorcing families was produced by the male head (Weiss, 1984). Women's educational and occupational training has, for the most part, qualified them for low-paying jobs (Bane, 1979; Brandwein, Brown, & Fox, 1974). The economic dislocations produced by divorce are such that today many female-headed single-parent families produced by divorce are living in or near poverty (McLanahan & Booth, 1989).

The Parental Divorce

Much of the literature on divorce reports on the problems experienced by children when marital disruption occurs. These include depression, school problems, and even difficulties in later relationships as adults

(Hetherington, 1989; Jacobson, 1978a, 1978b, 1978c; Krantz, 1988; Kulka & Weingarten, 1979; Levitin, 1979; Wallerstein & Blakeslee, 1989; Wallerstein & Kelly, 1980). A growing body of data also suggests that some of these children's problems result from the inability of their parents, in the throes of their own turmoil, to recognize the children's distress and to keep them uninvolved in the continued hostilities between the ex-spouses (Wallerstein, 1983).

As indicated by the focus on divorced women with children in many studies, it has been assumed that children are at least an added problem and often a liability in adjusting to a divorce (Colletta, 1979; Goode, 1956; Kreisberg, 1970). Such studies may, however, confuse the very real financial problems experienced by women with children with the children's impact on their parents' adjustment. Two or more cannot live as cheaply as one, but to the extent that adjustment is not contingent on financial resources, two or more may be able to adjust better than one alone. Both Brown, Felton, Whiteman, and Manela (1980) and Weiss (1979) report that many custodial parents feel that their children provide a reason and a need to keep going, despite the fact that the parents themselves are feeling rotten. What is less clear is what it is like for a noncustodial parent (generally the father) to have less contact with or even to lose contact with his children. Some epidemiological data suggest that males have greater difficulty adjusting to divorce than do females (Riessman & Gerstel, 1985). Part of this difficulty may stem from the even more substantial role changes required of divorced men than of divorced women. They generally leave the family home, are less practiced in household skills, and have less contact with their children.

The Psychological Divorce

Research on life events has fairly conclusively established that many life transitions, including divorce can have an adverse effect on physical and psychological health (Dohrenwend & Dohrenwend, 1981; Elliott & Eisdorfer, 1982; Wheaton, 1990). The dynamics of divorce mean that a person may be pulled in different directions: "Should I stay or should I go?" "How could she leave me?" "It's a relief to have this over." "Maybe we should have tried longer." "How am I going to cope?" "How am I going to make ends meet?" "What about the kids?" "How could she pick that man to date?" The tumbled mix of feelings of anger, regret, relief, anxiety, longing for the partner and for what was, desire for revenge, and jealousy make the process of psychologically withdrawing from a marital relationship a complicated one for many people.

Negative social attitudes about marital dissolution may exacerbate the effects of these changes on the divorced. As has been discussed, the threat that marital dissolution represents to others explains in part why the divorced are so often treated badly. But how did divorce develop such a bad reputation? The following section examines some of the foundations for these negative attitudes about the divorced.

DIVORCE AS DEVIANCE

Although acceptable reasons for seeking a divorce and the frequency with which it occurs vary cross-culturally, the option of divorce has been almost universally recognized as a regrettable necessity (Goode, 1963; Lee, 1977; Murdock, 1950; Murstein, 1974; Stephens, 1963). But if it is a virtually universal option, why then are the divorced so often discredited, or, to use Goffman's (1963) phrase, "stigmatized"? Part of the answer seems to be that divorce is viewed as deviance.

To be "deviant" can mean that a person's behavior is infrequent, unacceptable, or upsetting to his or her group as a whole or to a powerful minority. One of the consequences of being defined as deviant is that the abnormal, infrequent, or immoral characteristic used to label the person may so overpower others that it becomes his or her only defining characteristic, often following the person through life (e.g., "the former mental patient"). The same thing can happen to the divorced: "Why, I didn't know she was divorced," or "Well, you know, this is a second marriage for him," as if this chain of events somehow explains or accounts for the person's behavior.

One possible explanation for such reactions is that divorce represents a threat to others in the society. Efforts to contain divorce have often used informal social control through family involvement and pressure. For example, through such devices as "bride-price" and dowries, the couple's families make a financial investment in the continuity of the relationship (Goode, 1963; Murdock, 1950; Stephens, 1963). Control was also encouraged when marriage was seen, as it has been for much of its history, as a kinship matter—a set of ties between families who arranged marriages for their members (Goode, 1962, 1963; Murstein, 1974). Even when love and free choice of marital partners became a more common basis for mate selection, the parental encouragement of such choices among people of similar social characteristics was another effort at ensuring family control.

Divorce as Moral Pathology

Christianity, building on Judaic tradition, was a major institutional impetus to the development of many of our current attitudes about divorce (Blake, 1962; Chester, 1977). The early Christian church introduced the idea of marriage as an indissoluable, monogamous union that was the only acceptable arena for sexual intercourse (Rheinstein, 1972). A long struggle ensued to replace the early notion of marriage as a dissolvable union with that of its indissolubility (Halem, 1980; Murstein, 1974; R. Phillips, 1988; Rheinstein, 1972). New forms of marital regulation were developed through church courts. Originally, desertion and a wife's adultery (and sometimes a husband's adultery, if other issues such as rape, bigamy, or cruelty were involved) were considered the only grounds for obtaining a divorce. It was out of this ecclesiastical system that the notions of guilt and innocence that still haunt much of current thought about divorce developed. The marital stakes were high, for it was the innocent or wronged party who was free to remarry, while the transgressor was punished by not being allowed to remarry. The parties therefore became adversaries, with each attempting to establish his or her innocence. The decision was such a difficult one that civil courts were established "to relieve ministers of the delicate task" (Rheinstein, 1972, p. 23).

How did such church and civil machinations contribute to the view of the divorced as devaint? That those in power defined divorce as unacceptable focused additional social pressure on transgressors of the marital rules. As noted above, one definition of "deviance" is infrequent behavior. The guilty party to the divorce was unable to remarry and was therefore singled out as abnormal. The immorality that this represented was a failing presumably produced by some flaw in character.

Kai Erikson (1966) has described, through the use of "crime waves" in 17th-century New England, how a behavior defined as deviant helps to reinforce the resolve and sense of rightness and righteousness of the rest of the group. The same holds for divorce. Holding the divorced up as shameful persons with whom it was unfit to be associated reaffirmed the sense of purpose, resolve, and probity of the married. This was especially useful to the authorities in a period in which they were attempting to establish the principle of indissoluble marriage. Thus, the treatment of divorce as deviance may have served (and may still serve) a useful purpose for the rest of the society or for certain powerful minorities within it.

The force of the efforts to contain divorce and the early use of adultery as an acceptable reason for divorce indicate that sexuality plays a role in forming attitudes about marital dissolution. Adultery, though present in virtually all societies, has generally been condemned because of the threat it produces to the stability of the family (Murdock, 1950). Sexual impulses are so powerful that they are often dealt with through denial of their presence or projection of one's own desires onto others who are without the moral fiber of the reluctant (and perhaps envious) beholder. When giving free play to sexual impulses outside of marriage is viewed as morally and socially unacceptable, this increases the intensity of the reaction of those who break the rules.

As industrialization and urbanization increased, the interdependence of family members and the role of the extended family lessened (Goode, 1963; Winch with Blumberg, Garcia, Gordon, & Kitson, 1977). Individuals had freer choice in selecting their marital partners. These changes meant in some societies that divorce became more frequent as there was less pressure from the extended family for continuing a relationship; they meant in other societies, such as Japan, that divorce rates went down as family pressure to terminate relationships lessened (Goode, 1963; Kumagai, 1983; Yuzawa, 1990). The social dislocations produced by industrialization, migration, and urbanization were blamed for producing a decline in the importance of the family. In the United States, divorce was possible in the colonial era (Riley, 1991). Divorce rates, although still quite low, began to go up in the states in the 1800s. For example, 7,380 divorce decrees were granted in 1860, for a rate of 0.3 divorces per 1,000 population; by 1880, 19,663 divorces were reported, for a rate of 0.4 divorces per 1,000 population; by 1900, 55,751 divorces were reported, for a rate of 0.7 per 1,000 population (Jacobson with Jacobson, 1959).

In the period immediately after World War II, divorce rates in the United States were high (3.5 per 1,000 population in 1945) and then went down, with the low of 2.1 per 1,000 population occurring in 1958. After a period of fairly steady but unspectacular increases in the number of divorces, the divorce rate began to increase in the 1960s.[1] The rate of 3.5 divorces per 1,000 population was not reached again until 1970 and has been exceeded every year since then. The divorce rate did not begin to level off until the mid-1970s, with the peak to date occurring in 1979 and 1981 at 5.3 divorces per 1,000 population. From 1982 to 1986, the divorce rate fluctuated between 4.9 and 5.0 per 1,000 population. In 1987 it dropped to 4.8 and to 4.7 in 1988 through 1990 (National Center for Health Statistics, 1989, 1990b, 1991). Although estimates are declining somewhat, demographers continue to predict high lifetime rates of divorce for those who have recently married with 40% to 60% of these marriages anticipated to eventually end in divorce. (Bumpass, 1990; Norton, 1991; Norton & Moorman, 1987).[2]

Divorce as Social Pathology

It was during the period of social change in the 1800s that the view of divorce as social pathology came into prominence—that is, the view that those who divorce are socially deviant (Halem, 1980; O'Neill, 1973). This view held that inadequate social conditions produced faulty child rearing, which in turn made certain individuals, as adults, bad candidates for sustaining a marriage. Variants of this view still surface periodically, as indicated by the influential Moynihan (1967) report, which described the high divorce rates among blacks as a product of social disorganization; by the more recent concerns of the Moral Majority; and even by the heavy research focus on correlates of divorce proneness (Kitson, Babri, & Roach, 1985; Kitson & Raschke, 1981; Price-Bonham & Balswick, 1980; White, 1990). If divorce is a social problem, presumably more can be learned about the conditions under which it occurs. The problem can then be "fixed," and divorce can be avoided altogether.

Divorce as Psychological Deviance

In the early 1900s, a new explanation for the cause of divorce developed—a view still emphasizing individual deviance, but one cloaked in psychological rather than moral terms. This was that those who divorce are somehow flawed in personality structure, and that these neurotic flaws produce an inability to live intimately with another. Later examples of this approach are illustrated by books by psychiatrist Edmund Bergler with the titles *Unhappy Marriage and Divorce* (1946) and *Divorce Won't Help* (1948), and by the quotation at the beginning of this chapter from an editorial by psychiatrist Claire Friend (1983). According to this view, individuals who divorce are no better off than if they continued in their marriages, because they carry their neurotic interaction patterns with them into other relationships unless they undergo psychiatric treatment (preferably, in earlier years, psychoanalysis). These characteristics, it is said, are what make adjustment to divorce so difficult.

In a review of the literature on the relationship between marital status and mental disorder, Bachrach (1975) called this approach "selectivity theory." According to selectivity theory, some persons with physical or mental disabilities are less likely to marry; if they do marry, they are less likely to remain married or to remarry after divorce. Thus, "healthier" people are selected into marriage.

Such psychopathological views have played an important role in determining what should be done about "the divorce problem." They helped to produce reconciliation courts, required counseling for those wishing to divorce, and assessments of the fitness of divorced parents for becoming the custodians of their children (Group for the Advancement of Psychiatry, 1980; Halem, 1980). Although psychological pathology may sound less repressive than social or moral deviance as the cause for divorce, it still considers a divorced person as somehow flawed (Litwak, 1955). As Halem (1980) notes, whether a person is viewed as immoral, abnormal, or psychologically ill, "the assumption lingers that divorce in some way is connected to or results from a defect or weakness in one or both partners" (p. 3). The ascendancy of the view of divorce as psychological pathology was furthered as psychiatry began to replace religion and the law as a new form of social control. What was formerly considered to be morally or legally deviant was now defined as a product of illness (Conrad & Schneider, 1980; Freidson, 1970; Lasch, 1977.)

DIVORCE AS ROLE ADAPTATION AND CRISIS

In reaction to the various views of divorce as pathology, researchers began to look at divorce in different ways. Such views developed out of several circumstances. First, divorce researchers, many of whom had been divorced themselves, felt that the perspectives available to examine divorce did not "fit the facts" as they knew them.[3] Second, increasing numbers of people were divorcing, and it did not seem possible that they could all be psychiatrically disturbed. These personal and social conditions called for new explanations.

Role Adaptations

In 1948, toward the end of the brief period of high divorce rates after World War II, William Goode (1956) initiated a landmark empirical study of adjustment to divorce called *After Divorce*. In a court-records-based sample of Detroit metropolitan area mothers aged 38 and under, Goode defined adjustment as being able to adapt to the various roles with which a divorced person was faced. Relatively few divorce studies have taken this approach since Goode's work (see, e.g., Raschke, 1977).

For a decade or so after the publication of Goode's work on divorce, little research focused directly on the topic of divorce adjustment. Much of what was learned about divorce was based on secondary analyses of data collected for other purposes, or focused on "causes" or correlates of the decision to divorce (for reviews, see Bachrach, 1975; Levinger, 1965, 1976). As divorce rates increased in the 1960s and 1970s, divorce itself began to become a primary topic of interest (for reviews, see Kitson & Raschke, 1981; Price-Bonham & Balswick, 1980).

Crisis

Another, more widely used approach looked at divorce as a crisis to which individuals adjusted (Hill, 1958; Waller & Hill, 1951). In the growth of psychological services after World War II, it became apparent that people experienced a number of events that produced dislocations in their customary ways of thinking and acting. These included birth, death, job loss, promotion, moving, marriage, and divorce. Many of these crises, it was thought, resolved in a fairly short period of time; however, it was also believed that short-term psychological counseling could aid this process. This model of commonly and less commonly occurring life events as crises, or stressors, began to be applied specifically to the study of divorce (Weiss, 1975) and to clinical work with divorced persons (Wiseman, 1975).

In assessing the impact of life transitions, researchers have developed lists of commonly occurring life events and have asked subjects to rank these events in terms of how much adjustment they think the events require. In a list of 43 events, Holmes and Rahe (1967) found that divorce was ranked second (behind the death of a spouse) as the event requiring the greatest amount of adjustment. In a list of 101 events compiled by Dohrenwend, Krasnoff, Askenasy, and Dohrenwend (1978), divorce ranked as the fifth most difficult event to which to adjust (behind death of a child, death of a spouse, physical illness, and going to jail). Such scales, however, may be as much a reflection of the public's view that an "unwilled" event should be more distressing and evocative of sympathy and support than a "willed" one. As Zena Blau (1973) has noted, divorce is a willed event, as opposed to the death of a spouse, which is unwilled. Others may think that if a person chooses to end a relationship, the difficulties he or she is likely to experience will be fewer in number than if the relationship ends prematurely by death. This ignores partners' ambivalent feelings about divorce and their ex-spouses, as well as the fact that both partners are rarely equally interested in divorcing; one is the leaver and one the left, or as Hennon (1983) has noted, "the dumper" and "the dumpee."

What this crisis, stress, or life events approach often ignores is that divorce is not "an" event, but a series of events. It is a process that often does not move quickly to a conclusion. In fact, for those with children, the ties can continue through a lifetime. Researchers who initiated longitudinal studies in which divorce was conceptualized according to a variant of this model found, to their surprise, that the changes associated with and adjustments to divorce kept occurring in their subjects' lives for longer than they had expected (Bloom, Hodges, Kern, & McFaddin, 1985; Wallerstein & Kelly, 1980).

Thus, neither of the two major views of divorce adjustment accurately reflects the reality of divorce. The first view is that pathology in one or both partners explains adjustment difficulties, but this seems too global a prescription to explain the situation of many divorced persons. According to the second view, divorce is a crisis, but divorce adjustment does not appear to be as easy or rapid as this approach would suggest. This book presents an attempt to tie these views together into a loss-based model of adjustment to divorce. The following section explores this view in greater detail.

DIVORCE AS FAILURE AND LOSS

Aspects of Failure in Divorce

The long-standing and still lingering societal disapproval of divorce obscures, and in some cases complicates, what happens when a husband and wife voluntarily end their marriage. For example, another important characteristic of deviance is that the person others consider deviant is also a product of the culture that has produced these views, and he or she often knowingly or unknowingly shares them. This mechanism comes into play in a marital breakdown. For an adult, to be partnered, if not married, is the norm. As a result, marriage is an important part of a person's social identity (Hart, 1976) and is seen as a sign of maturity, normality, and success. Generally, people become invested in their social identities and relish the sense of normality that these identities accord them. Being married is an important piece of a person's social identity. Thus, in the eyes of others—and, more importantly, in one's own eyes—divorce is often a failure in a major role. To have chosen so badly, to have been so unaware of what one was getting into, or to have stayed so long in a relationship after it turned out to be bad, is perceived at best as a sign of bad judgment.

In addition to the stigma attached to being divorced, other characteristics of marriage make its ending hard. Virtually no one marries with the intention of divorcing. To have a relationship that is entered into with such high hopes end, whether with a bang or a whimper, is not easy. Here are two people who have entered each other's life, as Erving Goffman (1959) has called it, "backstage." They have seen each other literally and figuratively naked, with stubbly beards, no makeup, bulges, bumps, stretch marks, bad breath. Each knows the other's vulnerabilities, and as the relationship has deteriorated, each has probably used this knowledge to hurt the other.

More importantly, in this most intimate of relationships, the person going through a divorce has been found wanting, undesirable, and unacceptable. No matter how successful or how respected a man or woman is in the wider community, the person who supposedly knows him or her best has thought, looked, considered, and concluded, "I can't take it any more. This person, this relationship, isn't for me." For the average person, that conclusion is not an easy one to reach, nor is it easy to accept that one's spouse has made it. At the least, it may leave a residue of nagging self-doubts; at its worst, it can be a devastating indictment of one's worth and an appalling indication of the ease with which one can be deceived or misled. Divorced persons talk of being "burned" and "wary" of new relationships. For some, a basic sense of trust has been so badly violated that it takes time to rebuild their sense of confidence in themselves and in others.

So, to have failed at the normative task of marriage can be personally shameful and mortifying, regardless of the frequency with which others divorce, the reasons for the divorce, or the acceptance accorded the divorce by others. It is not that those who divorce dislike marriage; rather, they think so well of it that they refuse to accept a bad one. The majority of divorced persons remarry, with remarriage estimates ranging from five out of six divorced men and three out of four divorced women (Cherlin, 1981) to a more recent estimate, for divorced women, of two out of three remarrying (Norton, 1991).

In addition to societal pressures, there are interpersonal pressures on relationships. In the past, marriage was a family matter: The kin group often had an important stake in the decision about whom to marry and where the couple would live. Because the couple often lived with or near kin, kin could fill needs for support and encouragement, even if a spouse could not. Today, however, many couples live away from kin. This forces spouses to rely on each other for succorance and emotional support in ways married persons did not have to do in the past. Such emotional needs are fragile and hard to meet, and people are easily offended if they are not met. The present-day ideal of a good marriage produces a standard against which a person can compare his or her relationship with those of others, and, more importantly, can assess his or her *ability* to relate. So, from this perspective, to divorce is to fail not only in the eyes of others, but also in one's own eyes. One's own contribution to this failure of what is considered normal, adult behavior is hard to accept or even to admit. As a result of denial and projection of a person's own feelings onto the other, anger and blame for the failure of the marriage may be heaped at the feet of the spouse.

To add even more to the volatile marital mix, life expectancy has lengthened at the same time that more is expected of marital partners, making the commitment of "till death us do part" an endurance contest. In earlier centuries, even when there were more pressing forces such as economics and familial ties holding couples together, long marriages were a rarity. The life span was shorter, women died in childbirth, and infectious diseases took their toll. Now, with fewer external forces to keep a couple together, compression of child rearing into fewer years because of more effective contraceptive techniques, and a greater demand for marriage to focus on harder-to-meet affectional needs, marriages are expected to last longer. Spouses spend more years alone, together. In one sense, with such high hopes riding on having a good marriage for 40, 50, or 60 years, the wonder is that so many husbands and wives are able to grow, change, accommodate, and nurture each other well enough to choose to stay married, rather than that so many fail to do so.

The Longevity of Attachment*

Ironically, the dislocations that divorce can produce may accentuate the importance of another characteristic of intimate relationships that makes their ending difficult. This is "attachment," the emotional bonds of ease, comfort, and security that have developed between marital partners. Attachment theory has expanded from its original emphasis on the development of affectional bonds in children to an exploration of attachment in adults (Bowlby, 1977a, 1977b, 1980; Bowlby & Parkes, 1970; Marris, 1974; Parkes, 1972, 1975, 1982, 1986; Weiss, 1975, 1976, 1979, 1982). Attachment helps explain the anomalous situation in divorce, in which an individual is apparently grieving over the loss of someone of whom he or she is often simultaneously glad to be rid.

*Parts of this section are reprinted from "Attachment to the Spouse in Divorce: A Scale and Its Application" by G. C. Kitson, 1982, *Journal of Marriage and the Family, 44,* 379–393. Copyright 1982 by the National Council on Family Relations. Reprinted by permission.

Attachment behavior is persistent, learned behavior that begins to develop in infancy (Bowlby, 1969, 1973). It is specific and focuses on a small number of individuals in a clear order of preference. Once established, attachment may continue to a significant degree even when a relationship is no longer rewarding, because the predictably familiar is preferred over the strange. Part of the continuing tie between ex-spouses is based on the intensity and variety of emotions and experiences that they have shared in establishing, maintaining, and breaking up their relationship. The development of affectional bonds produces a complex model of the self and environment in which attachment figures provide a sense of security, comfort, and well-being. "All's right with the world" and with the self when the attachment figure is present or at least physically and emotionally available.

Bowlby (1969, 1973) maintains that there is a biological basis for attachment in animals and humans. In situations of alarm, seeking out others is a natural reaction that enhances the possibility of obtaining protection. In adults, attachment behavior is therefore especially likely to occur when they are "distressed, ill, or afraid" (Bowlby, 1975, p. 293). Ironically, the changes produced by the decision to divorce may induce the need for the familiar and previously comforting attachment figure of the former spouse. This is especially true in the face of the contradictory emotions and memories that the end of the marriage may engender—the good times, the bad times, continuing affection and regard, anger, anxiety, hurt, hatred, longing, and disbelief.

When the bonds of ease, comfort, and security that attachment figures provide for each other are disrupted, even in a relationship that has gone sour, individuals may react with separation anxiety (Bowlby, 1969, 1973, 1980) or separation distress (Parkes, 1972; Parkes & Weiss, 1983). This includes restlessness, searching behaviors to locate the lost person, tearfulness, depression, and sleeplessness. Because psychological distress is considered a normal outgrowth of loss (Freud, 1917/1963; Lindemann, 1944; Parkes, 1972; Simos, 1979), the distress many divorced persons experience may have a basis in attachment. This distress may be heightened by the lingering sense of social disapproval and stigmatization of those who divorce. Some divorced persons may be especially vulnerable to the normal distress associated with divorce because of previous mental illness or experiences of loss, such as the death of a parent or parental divorce. They have felt or tried to fend off this welter of feelings before, and it is hard to face them again. Adjustment to the divorce may be exacerbated by memories of these past events or unrecognized links to them.

The physical and mental health disturbance produced by what has variously been called "bereavement," "grief," "loss," and "loss of attachment" (Goode, 1956; Marris, 1974; Parkes, 1972; Simos, 1979; Waller, 1930/1967; Weiss, 1975) may help to account for the often-reported high rates of mortality and morbidity that the separated and divorced experience. These include death, physical and psychological illness, accidents, suicide, alcoholism, and outpatient and inpatient psychiatric care (Bachrach, 1975; Blumenthal, 1967; Briscoe, Smith, Robins, Marten, & Gaskin, 1973; Ensel, 1986; Gove, 1972a, 1972b, 1973; Gurin, Veroff, & Feld, 1960; Kisker & Goldman, 1987; McCormack, 1985; Mergenhagen, Lee, & Gove, 1985; Rosengren, Wedel, & Wilhelmsen, 1989; Rushing, 1979; Smith, Mercy, & Conn, 1988; Somers, 1979; Verbrugge, 1979; Veroff, Douvan, & Kulka, 1981).

The Loss Model

Although divorce is thought of as *an* event, it actually entails a pileup of events, each of which may contribute to a wrenching series of losses: loss of a once and perhaps still presently loved partner, loss of friends and family, loss of status, possibly loss of one's children, and sometimes loss of financial security. It takes time to recover psychologically from such losses—more time than might be expected. For those whose vulnerability has been increased by previous experiences of loss and disappointment, divorce may be an especially difficult event to face. It is a key hypothesis of this book that looking at the losses involved in divorce will enhance understanding of the divorce process to a greater extent than will looking at divorce simply as a response to a serious life event. The approach to be explored here attempts to link the pathology approach and the crisis or life events approach to divorce adjustment.

WHAT CONSTITUTES "ADJUSTMENT" TO DIVORCE?

Although adjusting to divorce from a spouse has been likened more or less to the grief process when a spouse dies (Blau, 1973; Bohannan, 1970; Goode, 1956; Waller, 1930/1967; Winch, 1971), the implications of this statement for divorce adjustment have only recently begun to be explored (Brown et al., 1980; Jacobson, 1983; Kitson, 1982; Kitson, Babri, Roach, and Placidi, 1989; Kitson, Graham, & Schmidt, 1983; Kitson & Roach, 1989; Kitson & Zyzanski, 1987; Petiet, 1982; Riessman, 1990; Roach & Kitson, 1989; Weiss, 1975, 1976, 1979, 1982). In each event, the emotional ties to the once-significant partner are broken, and the individual must adjust to the loss. As has been seen, these losses include not only a person but also a position in society, and often, for women, economic security. The social, psychological, and economic losses and changes produced by this shift in status are not adapted to without difficulty.

To consider distress a predictable response to such losses shifts the focus for explaining the high rates of physical and psychological disturbance experienced by divorced persons from pathology to an understanding of the issues that make some persons especially vulnerable to distress. As in adjusting to the death of a spouse, such factors may include emotional illness and previous losses that complicate adjustment to the new changes brought about by the divorce (Parkes & Weiss, 1983). For others, divorce adjustment may be difficult because of the ambivalence the divorced experience about the loss of their spouses, the public disapproval, the private sense of failure, and the seemingly bewildering feelings of attachment to persons from whom they are simultaneously glad to be parted.

The issue of what constitutes "adjustment" to divorce has often been glossed over. Although there is a general sense of what is meant by the term, there is little consensus about how to define it empirically. Nevertheless, by using phrases such as "She's adjusting well," "He's coping poorly," or "They're having a hard time," it is acknowledged that certain kinds of events or experiences may create some sort of disturbance in customary ways of thinking or acting. It is seen as normal, perhaps even expectable, for people to be upset as they struggle to assimilate the changed situations they are facing and attempt to establish a new sense of equilibrium. Some definitions of adjustment to divorce focus on the process of "re-equilibrating," as illustrated by Albrecht et al.'s (1983) focus on "individuals having to deal with the problems of reestablishing order and continuity to a life that has been disrupted (often severely) by a divorce" (p. 119). In their research, adjustment was defined by having individuals provide a self-assessment characterizing their experience as difficult or easy. Another approach is epitomized by Bloom, Asher, and White's (1978) review article, which reported upon physical and psychological symptoms that are frequent among the divorced. As noted earlier, Goode (1956) looked at adaptations to the various roles with which a divorced person has to cope. Raschke (1977) has also defined adjustment as experiencing few problems and a low level of stress as divorced persons incorporate new roles. Spanier and Thompson (1984) have defined adjustment as "characterized by a stable and resilient pattern of life, separate from the previous marriage and partner and based on anticipation rather than memory" (p. 103).

Some of these definitions, however, ignore the multidimensional nature of divorce adjustment and the likelihood that certain aspects will be easier and others harder. To have adjusted, a person must have sufficiently mastered the social, psychological, and economic events facing him or her that he or she is able to go about the tasks—and pleasures—of daily life without difficulty. Thus, "adjustment" is defined here as "being relatively free of symptoms of psychological disturbance, having a sense of self-esteem, and having put the marriage and former partner in enough perspective that one's identity is no longer tied to being married or to the former partner." Such a definition assumes that a person has been able to put enough psychological distance between himself or herself and the divorce to be able to move ahead with his or her life. This does not mean that divorce-related problems and issues will not continue to arise, but that an individual will be able to deal with these in a relatively straightforward manner. In the pages that follow, the social, psychological, and economic adjustments that those who decide to end their marriages experience are explored, both cross-sectionally and longitudinally.

CONCLUSION

In this chapter, the social and historical background to the current status of divorce and divorce adjustment has been presented. Marriages are more commonly viewed today as dissolvable unions than they were in previous eras. This is the result of a shift toward urban, industrial life in which the hold of the kin group on individuals has lessened. At the same time that individuals are more isolated, marital expectations have been heightened to focus more on companionate marriage. This very emphasis (in the face of one's inability to attain such an ideal) can help to foster distress in divorce.

Divorce is a complex phenomenon involving a period of estrangement, legal issues, changes in social networks, economic issues, parenting issues, and psychological adjustment. Divorce today still carries the baggage of earlier views of divorce as moral, social, and psychological deviance, which can increase distress for those choosing to end their marriages. Those who are divorced are seen as somehow flawed. Adjustment to divorce has also been examined as role adaptation and response to a crisis. Each of these views probably has some truth to it, but each still provides only a partial view. An alternative view of divorce is presented in this book: Adjustment to divorce is seen as a response to loss and change, the end of a once and still possibly meaningful relationship. That loss is easier or harder for people to adjust to, depending on their characteristics and previous experiences. Adjustment itself is seen as being relatively free of symptoms of psychological disturbance, having a sense of self-esteem, and being able to put the end of the marriage in enough perspective that one's identity is no longer tied to being married or to the former spouse.

NOTES

1. The high divorce rate after World War II has been attributed to the dislocations produced by the war and postwar adjustment. Many couples married with short courtships and then spent long periods apart in very different, often difficult, circumstances. After the war they reunited, only to discover that they no longer had much in common. Taking a longer view, Cherlin (1981) states that it was the period of decline in divorce rates in the 1950s that was the abnormality in the United States. These were people who grew to maturity during the Great Depression, lived through the war period, and then savored stability in relationships. Aside from this period, divorce rates have been increasing in the United States since population-based data on divorces were first collected, and as M. Schultz (1984) indicates, even earlier (1810–1860).

2. The divorce rate per 1,000 population is the "crude" rate. The more accurate indicator is the "refined" divorce rate, the number of divorces per 1,000 married women aged 15 and older. The crude rate is used in the text for comparisons with data from the 1880s. To illustrate the difference in the methods, the refined rate for 1945 was 14.4; for 1958, 8.9; for 1971, 15.8; for 1979, 22.8 and for 1987, 20.8 per 1,000 married women 15 and over (National Center for Health Statistics, 1990a).

3. There is also a tendency for those who have experienced a divorce to feel that their responses were not like those of others. They generally feel that their own responses were better, and that they are therefore not like "those other people" who divorced. "Those people" may have psychological problems, poor parents, or bad parenting styles, but these factors are not believed to represent the observers' experience.

People use a number of defenses, such as denial and projection, to cope with an event that many members of society find distasteful or completely unacceptable. It is sometimes hard to admit that one's experience was not all that good, or that the event engendered a number of negative feelings about oneself, one's partner, or one's parents. It is even harder to allow such thoughts and feelings into consciousness. This leads to a defensiveness about the experience: "It wasn't so bad," "It wasn't like that for me." Although such observations and experiences have contributed to a broader, more accurate view of the divorce process, they also illustrate the power that the experience of divorce has for people, sometimes years after the event has occurred.

How the Divorced and Married Were Studied: Methods of Sampling and Measurement

I would emphasize the need of research with divorced couples. It is relatively costly in time and labor, but has distinct advantages.
—Researcher Lewis Terman in 1939, quoted by Locke (1951, p. 2)

In this chapter, the four sources of survey data to be reported upon in this book are described, as are certain key measures. The data were all collected in Cuyahoga County, Ohio—metropolitan Cleveland. The four data sources were as follows: a longitudinal suburban survey of divorced persons and of a married comparison group; a study of persons who filed for divorce but changed their minds and reconciled with their spouses; a county-wide survey of marital status; and a county-wide sample of divorced women that was part of a study comparing adjustment to widowhood and divorce.

DATA NEEDS FOR RESEARCH ON DIVORCE

Certain kinds of data are needed to answer questions about the ways in which the divorced are similar to and differ from the married; to explore possible historical changes in the process of divorce; and to examine changes over time in the attitudes and behaviors of the divorced as they adjust to the breakup of their marriages.

Sampling Issues

In exploring such issues, the first requisite is, obviously, a sample of divorced persons, preferably one representative of the population in which divorce is on the increase. As the divorce rate increased in the

22

1960s and 1970s, social class differences in the characteristics of those who divorced became less striking. Previously, divorce was more likely among those with low-status occupations, little education, and low income (Kitson et al., 1985; Kitson & Raschke, 1981; Levinger, 1965, 1976; Price-Bonham & Balswick, 1980; Raschke, 1987).[1] In the 1970s, although those of lower social status still accounted for more of the divorces that occurred, the percentage increase in divorce was greater among higher-status groups. As Norton and Glick (1979) noted, "The important conclusion that can be drawn from these trends is that the recent increase in divorce has been pervasive with regard to social and economic level but that socioeconomic differences in divorce are now smaller than they used to be" (p. 14). Because of these changes, settings for research are needed in which divorce has become more frequent, in order to assess the factors associated with the changing distribution of divorce. A sample of suburban communities fits this need.

Types of Samples

To be most useful, a second characteristic of divorce data is that reactions to divorce should not be collected from volunteers or from persons selected from clinical settings. The reactions of individuals in therapy, or of volunteers who may have stepped forward for study because of their greater concerns about their divorces, can bias the results toward the more distressed or toward those with more extreme attitudes. For example, separated and divorced persons are generally more likely than those of other marital statuses to be hospitalized for mental illness and to seek outpatient psychotherapy (Bebbington, 1987; Rushing, 1979; Somers, 1979). It is less clear just how common psychological distress is among those who divorce, whether or not that distress leads to the seeking of professional help.

Useful information can be gained from samples of patients or volunteers, but there are unknown biases to these sources. Data collected from a community-based sample is a method of putting such data into a broader context. Such data might come from a probability sample of the community in which those who are divorced are compared to those who are married. This approach can produce problems in estimating the effects of divorce if some persons have been divorced for long periods of time, whereas others have remarried or are only recently divorced. Despite such problems of interpretation, probability samples are representative of the population from which they are drawn.

Another type of representative sample is based on divorce court records. Where such records are public information, as is true in much of the United States, this is the best method of selecting a representative sample of persons who have recently filed for divorce (Kitson & Raschke, 1981; Kitson et al., 1982). The date of filing serves as a common reference point for comparing the length of time it takes couples to decide to divorce and for variations in postdivorce adjustment patterns. If desired, a specialized sample of divorced persons can be selected for study on the basis of information available in the records, such as age, number of marriages, presence or absence of children, and community of residence. Divorce court records also have the advantage of providing demographic background information with which to compare the characteristics of individuals who have agreed to participate in the survey and individuals who have refused, in order to determine what (if any) biases there are in the final group of subjects surveyed. In the studies to be reported upon here, three samples of persons drawn from divorce court records and one probability sample have been used.

Longitudinal Data

A third sample characteristic needed to address the issues that constitute the focus of this research is that the divorced group should be followed for an extended period of time, in order to determine how they adjust. If coping with marital separation and divorce is a process, and if the losses and changes involved in adjusting to divorce represent a stressful life event or crisis, then the heightened distress of the early stages of divorce should decrease with time. But if distress does decrease, does it do so at similar rates for men and women, or for blacks and whites?

Curiously, despite the social, psychological, and economic magnitude of the divorce experience, there have been relatively few longitudinal studies on how people go about adjusting to the losses and changes involved. The studies that have been carried out to date include those by Ahrons and Wallisch (1987), Ambert (1989), Bloom, Hodges, et al. (1985), Chiriboga, Catron, and Associates (1991), Hetherington (1987), Hetherington, Cox, and Cox (1976, 1985), Spanier and Thompson (1984) (and, using the same sample, Furstenberg & Spanier, 1984), Wallerstein and Blakeslee (1989), and Wallerstein and Kelly (1980). These studies differ from the data to be presented here by being based on small samples (Ambert's work), consisting in whole or part of volunteer participants (Bloom et al.'s, Hetherington's, Wallerstein's, and Spanier & Thompson's work), focusing on parents who maintain contacts with their ex-spouses (Ahrons & Wallisch's work), and sometimes focusing on parents and their children (Hetherington's and Wallerstein's work). The only one of these studies based completely on a court-records-based sample is Chiriboga et al.'s work; however, subjects were restricted to having been married a minimum of 6 months and separated 8 months or less, and they were only interviewed twice (with the second interview 3½ years after the first).

To assess the issue of changes in adjustment most appropriately, a cohort of divorced persons should be followed—not just those who remain single, but those who remarry as well. There is, for example, increasing evidence to suggest that because of the complexity of the resulting family structure; remarriage itself may constitute a stressor that affects adjustment (Ganong & Coleman, 1986; Roberts & Price, 1985–1986; Sager et al., 1983). Much research on divorce is cross-sectional, often looks at either one gender or the other, and only rarely examines differences in adjustment by race. Cross-sectional data also mean that it is only possible to report the association or correlation of variables, not "causality"—that is, which variable is likely to have "caused" or produced the other variable. Longitudinal data make it possible to begin to sort out issues of cause and effect.

Comparison Group

A fourth consideration is that a comparison group of married persons matched to the divorced on social and community background factors is needed to determine what, if any, characteristics and experiences are unique to those who have divorced versus those who have not. With the use of a comparison group matched on basic characteristics, any differences that occur between the divorced and married may then more accurately be attributed to the divorce process. Without such a comparison group, the standard against which to assess "good" or "poor" adjustment is not clear.

A number of divorce studies have employed no comparison group against which to examine the response of the divorced (Ahrons & Wallisch, 1987; Goode, 1956; Wallerstein & Kelly, 1980). In these cases, either clinical assessments or intragroup comparisons have been made. Thus, the divorced "look worse" than some ideal or typical clinical or community norm, or some of them adjust "less well" than others, with no indication of how the whole group stacks up in comparison to the general population. Although Kraus (1979) maintains that single, never-married persons are the most appropriate group against which to compare the divorced, the control group most generally used is the married. Marriage is the societal norm. Virtually all adult Americans have at one point been married. In addition, the vast majority of divorced persons do not aspire to remain in the single status, but choose to remarry or repartner; in fact, at any given age they are more likely to remarry before a single person of the same age married for the first time (Glick & Norton, 1979). Using the married as a control or comparison group means that variations from the "adjustment" levels of the married will suggest the relative risk associated with being divorced. This is the approach taken in the research reported in this book. The divorced sample has been compared to a sample of married people drawn from the same city blocks as the divorced.

Studying Couples

Although the quotation from Terman at the beginning of the chapter has been selected for its emphasis on the costliness in time and labor (and, one might add, expense) in doing survey research on the divorced, it also points out a fifth potential characteristic of divorce research: studying couples. Some studies have collected data from divorced couples (Ahrons & Wallisch, 1987; Ambert, 1989; Fulton, 1979; Hetherington et al., 1976; Jacobson, 1987; Masheter, 1991; Wallerstein & Kelly, 1980). However, with the exception of the Hetherington and Wallerstein studies (which used convenience samples), in each case only a subset of couples agreed to be interviewed; the agreement rates ranged from 81.2% for Ambert's Toronto convenience study to 17.2% in Masheter's Connecticut research.[2]

Data collected from each spouse before a divorce decree have also, in the past, left researchers open to the possibility of subpoena because they did not have the guarantee of privileged communication that physicians, lawyers, therapists, and members of the clergy have had with their patients and clients. Although there are no known instances in which research data collected about one divorcing partner (e.g., information about dating, sexual activities, mental health status, drinking, or drug use) were subpoenaed for use, this was a possibility until recently. Recent rulings do give researchers some immunity from prosecution in protecting the confidentiality of their data. The Public Health Service Act (1988) provides protection against disclosing the identity of subjects.

There are substantial statistical problems involved in the use of couple data as well, because the partner data are not independent (Thompson & Walker, 1982). There is likely to be overlap or correlation in replies of couples, but the degree of overlap varies from couple to couple. A variety of techniques have been tried to handle this problem statistically, such as difference scores, combined means, and so forth, but the solutions are generally unsatisfactory.

In the research to be reported upon here, men and women from the same couples were not interviewed. This was done because of concerns (although they were thought to be minimal) about not being able to maintain the promised confidentiality of data, should the information obtained be subpoenaed in a contested divorce. There were also concerns about the ability to obtain permissions from both spouses for interviews so soon after the divorce petition was filed; about how to handle the data when the partners' replies did not agree; and about the thorny statistical issues involved in the analysis of couple data from a subsection of the sample. Finally, the focus in this research was and is on how individuals, not couples, adjust to the breakdown of their marriages. The decision to interview only one divorced person per couple also meant that more marriages could be examined.

REPLICATING STUDY RESULTS

Selecting a representative sample helps put study results in context. If the sample is without biases, others in the community with similar characteristics will be likely to respond in a similar manner if they are also questioned. Such samples also increase confidence that the findings will be representative of people in other communities who are like those being studied. But, given the cumulative nature of science, the vagaries of chance, and the difficulties of controlling for all the sources of error that can creep into a study, another key element in research is replication: Has another study using similar research methods found similar results? Replication provides added assurance that the results of a study are not simply attributable to chance or to special characteristics of a certain community, group of respondents, or time period. When study findings are similar, even given differences in settings, subjects, and time periods, this suggests that the findings are indeed providing an accurate portrait of the topic and types of people being studied.

As noted earlier, this book presents data from four different studies, collected over a 12-year period in metropolitan Cleveland, Ohio. Where there are similarities in study results, such replication increases confidence in the generalizability of the study findings to other settings like the Cleveland area. Those instances in which there are differences in results suggest the need for careful scrutiny of the factors that may account for the differences.

Differences Between Then and Now?

Because all of the data to be reported upon were collected from the same metropolitan area, with similar research methods used in the three court-records-based studies, important sources of error (differences in community and methods) have been minimized. But, with comparisons planned among data collected in 1974–1979, 1980, and 1985–1986, an alternative explanation for any observed differences in results is that the times at which the data were collected differed. This argument would state that the times have been changing so rapidly that the study findings are not relevant to the present day.

In response to this potential criticism, the impact of time is likely to be minimal. The differences in the dates of interviews were not so great as to involve substantial cohort effects. Furthermore, replies to items about positive and negative affect (Bradburn, 1969), two of the dependent variables on which the samples are compared, are not likely to have varied much simply as a function of time.

Further support for the likelihood of minimal differences in well-being based on differences in the date of interviewing comes from Veroff, Douvan, and Kulka (1981). In comparing two sets of nationally collected cross-sectional data obtained 19 years apart, they noted, "There is remarkable consistency in the way men and women respond to questions about their well-being in 1957 and 1976. *Overall, changes are small, often there is not change at all*" (p. 542; italics in the original). Although the measures of well-being used by Veroff et al. differed from those used here, the underlying concepts are similar. As a result, few differences in results by time period are anticipated.

Much of the current knowledge about divorce and remarriage is based on data that were collected or began to be collected in the 1970s and early 1980s (Ahrons & Wallisch, 1987; Bloom, Hodges, et al., 1985; Chiriboga et al., 1991; Hetherington, 1989; Wallerstein & Blakeslee, 1989; Weitzman, 1985). One could argue, with justification, that a new generation of studies is needed to compare research findings. Nevertheless, the implicit or explicit assumption of these various studies is that there has been little change in the processes of divorce adjustment over this period. It is possible to test this assumption here because several sets of data are available.

The particular value of the 1974–1979 longitudinal suburban divorce study is that it looks in detail at changes in adjustment over time in ways that no other study has done. Such data provide a fuller picture of the social and psychological features involved in divorce adjustment.

Potential Biases Because of the Study Location?

A series of studies based on data collected in a Midwestern, urban, racially mixed, metropolitan area still leaves open the question of whether similar findings would be obtained in the South, the Far West, or in rural areas. Confidence in the setting for the study is enhanced because in its demographic characteristics such as age, sex, and level of education, Cuyahoga County, Ohio, is representative of the aggregate 248 urban areas as defined by the U.S. Bureau of the Census. The county is also similar to other large Eastern and Midwestern areas in terms of women's labor force participation (for more on these points, see Breslau, Salkever, & Staruch, 1982). These characteristics increase the likelihood that the study findings are representative of other divorced and married persons in the United States.

A WORD ON THE TERMS USED

Although the words "divorce" and "divorced" are used to describe people in these studies, some of the persons surveyed obtained a "dissolution of marriage" through the no-fault divorce provisions available in Ohio. Others, by contrast, obtained divorces through the adversarial, fault-based system of divorce that prevailed in the United States up to the early 1970s and still exists as an option in many jurisdictions such as Ohio. The term "divorced" is used to cover all the subjects, regardless of the legal route taken to end their marriages. The terms "divorced" and "divorcing" also include those who had not yet received their divorces or dissolutions at the time of the first interview, but who were still awaiting the legal ending of their relationships.

To distinguish the married comparison group from the subjects who divorced, the terms "married" and "divorced" are used. Obviously, those who are separated or divorced were at one point married. The term "married" is used here, however, to distinguish those who were members of intact families throughout the study period, as opposed to those who ended their marriages.

THE SAMPLES

Of the four studies to be reported upon, three were based on divorce court records and the fourth was based on a random sample of residents of Cuyahoga County. The primary source of data for the analyses that follow is a longitudinal study of nonwhite (primarily black) and white suburban Cleveland men and women who filed for divorce. These subjects were interviewed three times over a 5-year period between 1974 and 1979. A comparison group of married persons drawn from the same city blocks as the divorced was interviewed twice. These data provide answers to questions about changes in adjustment over time and about the differences and similarities of divorced and married persons. The second source of court-records-based data is a cross-sectional study based on interviews conducted in 1980 with samples of men and women who had filed for divorce but withdrawn their divorce petitions in 1974–1975 and in 1977–1978. These data provide a window into a subset of marriages, some of which appeared to be quite disturbed, but which remained intact. This study illustrates that even with the increases in divorce rates, there is still a reservoir of married couples living in some degree of marital distress. The third court-records-based data source, the marital transition study, is based on interviews conducted in 1985 and 1986 with a county-wide divorce-records-based sample of women. This sample was stratified by age into those under and over age 45, and was matched by age, race, and median income of census tract to a sample of women selected from the death certificates of their husbands who died from natural or accidental causes (Kitson & Zyzanski, 1987). The divorcees constitute the focus of study in this book, not the widows. The data from the reconciliation and county-wide divorce surveys help to establish whether the experiences of the suburban sample are similar to those of the wider population and whether the basic findings have changed over the past decade.

The final source of data—and the one not based on divorce court records—is a 1980 county-wide, multistage random survey of marital status, marital separations, reconciliations, and psychological health. These data indicate how many married individuals experienced marital separations without going so far as to file for divorce, and provide additional evidence for the relationship between marital status and health. The methods used to gather all of these data are described in greater detail in the following sections.

The Suburban Divorced Sample

The suburban divorced sample was drawn from the records of the Domestic Relations Division of the Cuyahoga County Court of Common Pleas. In order to be representative of those areas in which divorce rates have been on the increase, the study targeted upper-middle-class, middle-class, and working-class communities. Seven such communities were selected for study because of their racial, economic, and religious mix. Two of the study communities were listed in the 1970 census as having no black residents and in the 1980 census as having very few. The other communities were selected to maximize the number of Jewish and black middle-class subjects. The median income for black families in the study communities in 1970 was higher than that for blacks in the city of Cleveland, Cuyahoga County, or the United States as a whole. For the study communities, the 1970 figures ranged from $9,432 to $13,793; in 1980, they ranged from $11,916 to $39,673. For the city of Cleveland, Cuyahoga County, and the United States as a whole, the 1970 income figures for blacks were, respectively, $7,617, $8,005, and $6,308; for comparison in 1980, the figures were, respectively, $12,277, $18,009, and $16,841. (U.S. Bureau of the Census, 1972a, 1972b, 1972c, 1980). Because there were relatively few divorced persons on any given street at any one time, the communities from which the subjects were selected are not identified by name in order to preserve the anonymity of the respondents. As a further protection, identifying characteristics of subjects have been changed in quotations from those of the individuals surveyed.

Sampling Procedures

To avoid seasonal biases in filing rates, all divorce cases for the suburbs selected were drawn from the divorce records of the Domestic Relations Division of the Cuyahoga County Court of Common Pleas for 4 months: June 1975, a high-filing month; December 1974, a low-filing month; and March 1975 and September 1974, two intermediate-level months.[3] On September 23, 1974 (a Monday), Ohio divorce law was changed to include a no-fault provision. In order to include 1 month's worth of fault-based divorce actions only, the first month sampled actually lasted from August 26 to September 20, 1974.

In March 1975, a community-by-community count of the number of divorce filings for the county indicated that the 138 filings from the seven sample suburbs represented 18.3% of the total filings for the month ($n = 753$), not substantially different from the 17.7% of the county population the communities represented. In comparison, the city of Cleveland represented 53.8% of the filings for March 1975, and 43.6% of the population. The city of Cleveland, compared to the county, has more low-income and minority-group residents. Thus, if a county-based sample were used, more of the divorced would have been among lower-income, minority-group persons. The aim of the suburban study was to focus on the higher-status groups in which divorce was on the increase. The 568 cases selected for study represented 17.6% of the 3,227 cases filed for the 4 months selected.

Selection of Subjects and the Completion Rate

Trained interviewers were matched to the suburban respondents by race, by gender, and (where possible) by age. They were required to make at least four attempts to contact each subject. Alternately, the man or woman in each divorcing couple was selected for study, with no substitutions made for refusals. To be eligible for inclusion in the first set of interviews, the persons selected for study still had to be living in the four-county Cleveland standard metropolitan statistical area (SMSA) and to have obtained or still be in the process of obtaining a decree. As indicated in Table 2.1, 7.0% had moved out of the area. Another 19.5% were not interviewed because they had withdrawn or dismissed their divorce petitions.

Of the 421 people actually eligible for study, 203, or 48.2%, agreed to be interviewed; 113, or 26.8% refused. The remainder could not be contacted, had moved, or were dead or otherwise unavailable. For the 316 persons actually contacted, this constituted 64.2% who were interviewed and 35.8% who refused. Although low compared to response rates for other topics, this response rate for the suburban study is comparable to—in fact, superior to—that of most other court-records-based surveys of divorced persons. For example, the completion rate for a 1975–1977 San Francisco/Oakland, California court-records-based study of divorce was 33.3% (Chiriboga, 1982; Chiriboga, Roberts, & Stein, 1978), and that for a 1977 study based mostly on court records

TABLE 2.1. Response Rate for First Interview: The Suburban Divorced Sample

	%			
	Number of cases selected	All cases selected	Divorce obtained or pending in four-county SMSA	Contacted
Petition withdrawn or dismissed	107	18.8	—	—
Moved out of four-county area	40	7.0	—	—
Moved, no forwarding address	36	6.3	8.6	—
Other	8	1.4	1.9	—
Unable to contact	61	10.7	14.5	—
Refused	113	19.9	26.8	35.7
Interviewed	203	35.7	48.2	64.2
Total	—	100.0	100.0	100.0
(n)	(568)	(568)	(421)	(316)

in Centre County, Pennsylvania, was 22.9% (Spanier & Anderson, 1979; Spanier & Thompson, 1984). For more on response rates in divorce research, see Kitson et al. (1982).

More important than these comparisons with other studies is this finding: Difference-of-means and chi-square tests indicated that those interviewed in the suburban study did not differ significantly by gender, race, age, and median income of census tract of residence from those in the total sample population or in the sample of those located who obtained divorces. Subjects who refused did, however, differ significantly by race ($p < .01$), with more blacks than whites refusing to participate—a finding also reported by Brown et al. (1980). Because race is not recorded on divorce petitions, race was estimated from knowledge of residential patterns and other available information. To put the response rate for this longitudinal study in context, national surveys on less sensitive topics during the initial period of this study were reporting response rates in the 60–70% range (American Statistical Association, 1974).

Reinterviews

The divorced respondents were reinterviewed in 1975–1977, a year after obtaining their decrees, and 2–3 years later, in 1978–1979. To aid in relocating them, subjects were asked at each interview for the names and addresses of two people "who will always know where you live." After the initial interview, for which the subjects were required to live in the four-county Cleveland SMSA, respondents were reinterviewed wherever they moved (including Canada and the western United States). At the second interview, six subjects were interviewed by behavioral scientists in colleges or universities near their new locations; at the third, nine were so interviewed.

The Second Interview. Between the first and second interviews, an additional 15 divorce petitions were withdrawn or dismissed by the court. Because the study focus was on adjustment to divorce, these subjects were not reinterviewed. Of the 189 persons initially interviewed who obtained divorces, it was not possible to locate or make contact with 14.8% (Table 2.2). Of those respondents previously interviewed, 96.3% were reinterviewed. Only 6 persons, or 3.7%, refused to be reinterviewed. An additional 10 respondents who either could not be contacted previously or could not be located at the time of the first interview were located. Four of these new contacts refused to be interviewed, and 6 were added to the study. These people were given

TABLE 2.2. Response Rate for the Second and Third Interviews:
The Suburban Divorced Sample

Completion rates	Second interview		Third interview	
	n	%	n	%
Response rate for those interviewed at prior time				
Moved, no forwarding address	9	4.8	14	8.7
Unable to contact	12	6.4	13	8.1
Refused	12	6.4	10	6.2
Interviewed	155	82.4	124	77.0
Total	188	100.0	161	100.0
Refusal rate for those interviewed the previous time				
Refused	6	3.7	10	7.5
Interviewed	155	96.3	124	92.5
Total	161	100.0	134	100.0
Additional interviews (not interviewed previous time)				
Refused	4	40.0	9	40.9
Interviewed	6	60.0	13	59.1
Total	10	100.0	22	100.0
Refusal rate for all contacts				
Refused	10	5.8	19	12.5
Interviewed	161	94.2	133	87.7
Total	171	100.0	152	100.0

a combined interview that asked about demographic and other un-
changing background information (this information was obtained for
most subjects at the first interview) and then assessed their activities
and feelings at the second interview. This means that for some items at
the first interview there were a maximum of 203 responses, and for
others there were 209.[4] Adding the newly located respondents to the
other respondents resulted in an overall response rate for the second
interview of 94.2%, with 5.8% refusing.

   The Third Interview. At the third interview, 87.9% of those contacted
at the second interview were relocated (Table 2.2). For these persons,
the response rate was 92.3% with 7.7% refusing. An additional 22 respondents, who either refused or could not be contacted at the second
interview, were located at the third. Nine refused to be reinterviewed;
of these, 6 had also refused at the second interview. Thirteen combined second and third interviews were obtained, for a total of 133

third interviews. For all those contacted at the third interview, the response rate was 87.5%, with 12.5% refusing. The final sample constituted 63.6% of those initially interviewed. Comparisons of the distributions at the first and third interviews indicated that there were no statistically significant differences in losses by gender or race.

The interviews, which included a combination of fixed-choice and open-ended questions, took from 1 to 1½ hours to complete, for a total of approximately 3 to 4½ hours of interviews per divorced respondent (see Appendix A for the questions asked). Spot checks were made to ensure that the interviews were actually conducted. All of the data were independently coded by two coders, and all coding differences were reconciled. The data were then keypunched twice, the two versions were compared, and any discrepancies were reconciled. These steps helped to ensure that the data collected were accurately recorded. These same coding and data-cleaning techniques were also used for the reconciliation study and the county-wide marital transition study.

Lengths of Time between Key Events, and the Timing of the Interviews

Table 2.3 indicates the mean lengths of time between key events in the divorce process and the timing of the three interviews in the suburban divorce study. Separation rather than the date of filing is a better indicator of the effective end of a marriage, because many couples separate before filing. Information on date of separation is not available in Ohio divorce court records. Therefore, once the subjects were selected by date of filing, they were asked how long they had been separated. Twenty-three, or 11.1% were not separated from their spouses at the time of the first interview. The majority, however, separated before filing for divorce.

At the first contact with the subjects, the mean length of separation before the interview was 1 year. Some couples had been separated for a long time, and they therefore inflated the mean length of separation for the group. For example, one couple had been separated for a little over 8 years, and 15 others had been separated for 3 years or more. Both the median and the mode were 5 months. The divorce suits had been filed, on the average, 5.0 months before the interview, with the mode being 3.0 and the median 4.2 months. Because of the brief waiting period before a divorce can be granted in Ohio (30 days), 46.2% of the subjects had already received their divorce decrees by the time of their first interview.

By the second interview, the couples had been separated for an average of 2 years, with the median length of separation being 1½

TABLE 2.3. Events in the Divorce Process and Number of Months between Interviews: The Suburban Divorced Sample

Events in the divorce process	Number of months between events		
	Interview 1 (1974–1975): Time of filing	Interview 2 (1975–1977): 1 year after decree	Interview 3 (1978–1979): 2–3 years after decree
When couple separated			
Mean	12.0	24.2	50.6
Median	5.0	18.2	48.2
Mode	5.0	13.0	48.0
Range	1–97	8–11	36–110
(*n*)	(184)	(153)	(119)
When decree filed			
Mean	5.0	16.4	43.8
Median	4.2	14.8	43.8
Mode	3.0	12.0	39.0
Range	1–19	8–50	38–59
(*n*)	(208)	(167)	(130)
When decree granted			
Mean	—	11.7	39.1
Median	—	10.7	38.9
Mode	—	11.0	37.0
Range	—	2–47	24–52
(*n*)		(157)	(123)

years. This was, on the average, 1 year and 4 months after the divorces were filed, and about 11 months after the divorces had been granted.

At the time of the third interview, the differences among the mean, median, and mode were less, so the mean values have been used. On the average, the couples had been separated for 4 years, had filed for divorce 3 years and 9 months earlier, and had been divorced for about 3 years and 3 months. Thus, the study followed couples for an average of 4 years of their experience through the divorce process.

The Married Comparison Group

The distribution of the U.S. population is such that there are more people of lower than of higher socioeconomic status. Under these circumstances, if comparisons are made of the married and divorced from samples drawn from the general population, differences in social class, education, and occupation are likely to be found. These differences may indicate something about the distribution of divorce, but not about what distinguishes those at any given social class level who divorce from those who do not. If the married and divorced are not matched in demographic characteristics, it is difficult to determine whether any observed differences are due to the differences in social class or to those in demographic characteristics. If, however, a comparison group of married persons is successfully matched to the divorced, there should be little difference in background characteristics between the two groups. In this way, in groups that are otherwise similar, any remaining differences in social and psychological characteristics may indeed play a role in the decision to divorce or in divorce adjustment. It was for these reasons that the married and divorced samples were matched in the longitudinal study.

With the aim of producing samples similar in background characteristics, the comparison group of married persons was selected from the same city blocks as the divorced. Neighborhoods generally attract residents with similar characteristics. Using a neighborhood-based approach increased confidence that differences between the married and divorced groups would not simply be attributable to differences in background, but rather would be attributable to factors associated with marital status.

To further ensure sample comparability, two other characteristics were used for matching: gender and race. Thus, for example, for every divorced white female who agreed to be interviewed, a married white female was sought from the same city block. Sample replacement was used for persons who refused to participate and for inappropriate matches on marital status or race. Matching for the variables of gender, race, and marital status was time-consuming and expensive. It took 484 tries to obtain just 178 married subjects; because of the time and expense involved, it was necessary to stop at this point. As a result, 87.7% of the 203 separated and divorced respondents interviewed at the time of filing had a married match. Out of 278 married persons of the appropriate sex and race who were actually contacted for interview, 178, or 64.0%, agreed to be interviewed, and 100, or 36.0%, refused to participate.

The married sample was reinterviewed in 1978–1979 by telephone to assess changes in marital status and their current psychological status. One hundred and forty-two respondents were reinterviewed. The major category of loss consisted of 24 persons, or 13.5%, who moved without leaving a forwarding address. It was not possible to contact 4 persons (2.2%), and 2 (1.1%) had died. Of the 148 persons actually contacted, 142, or 95.9%, were interviewed and 6, or 4.1%, refused. Those reinterviewed constituted 79.8% of the original comparison sample. No statistically significant differences by gender or race were found between the married samples at the first and second interviews. At the second interview, four of the married subjects contacted had divorced, one was separated, and two were widowed.

The Other Samples

Although the key source of data in this book is the longitudinal suburban divorce study, data from several other Cleveland-area surveys are also reported upon. These studies are briefly described below.

The Reconciled Sample*

As subjects in the suburban divorce study were contacted, people who had reconciled with their spouses exhibited several striking characteristics that raised questions about whether these people were different from or similar to those who obtained their divorces. First, in indicating that they had reconciled and therefore did not want to participate in the research, some subjects said things like "I'm so happy that I don't want to talk about it," or "We're back together again, but I don't want to talk to you and upset everything." Replies like these raised questions about what such apparently fragile relationships were like.

A second impetus was that 23% of the divorce petitions filed in the suburban study were withdrawn or dismissed (Kitson, Holmes, & Sussman, 1983). This represents a substantial number of marriages that were in enough difficulty for the spouses to take the step of filing for divorce, but that did not appear in final divorce statistics. Such a large number of petition withdrawals and dismissals suggests an even higher rate of marital instability than is indicated by the estimated 1,175,000 divorces granted in 1990 (National Center for Health Statistics, 1991).

If the suburban Cleveland figure of 23% is used as a basis for a national estimate of petition withdrawals and dismissals, it means that an additional 350,974 petitions were filed and then dropped in 1990. This estimate is lower than that produced by using the 30% figure for petitions that did not go through in California in 1966 (Schoen, Greenblatt, & Mielke, 1975) or the 1972–1973 figure of 28% for Florida (Gunter, 1977). These two percentages would produce estimates, respectively, of 503,571 and 456,944 additional filings per year.

Furthermore, withdrawing a divorce petition or having it dismissed is not a random event. An analysis of court records showed that

---

*Part of this section is reprinted from "Couples Who File for Divorce but Change Their Minds" by G. C. Kitson and J. K. Langlie, 1984, *American Journal of Orthopsychiatry,* 54, 469–489. Copyright 1984 by the American Orthopsychiatric Association. Reprinted by permission.

petitions were more likely to be withdrawn or dismissed if the husband filed for the divorce, if fewer legal grounds were used for the divorce, if the spouses were similar in age, and if they had few or no minor children (Kitson, Holmes, & Sussman, 1983).

It also became clear that there was little research on the fate of people who enter the legal system because of marital disharmony and then leave (for one such study, see Levinger, 1979). Do these cases represent duplicate filings, do such couples stay reconciled, or do they subsequently obtain divorces? Finally, what are the characteristics and experiences of such people? Are they similar to or different from those who divorce? If marriages are so bad as to cause spouses to file for divorce, what distinguishes those who complete the divorce from those who do not?

It was decided to study reconciliations in the same seven Cleveland suburban communities in which the longitudinal study had been done, in order to have a group of persons with similar characteristics to whom to compare the reconciled. All 328 withdrawn or dismissed cases in the seven suburbs for the year of the original study, August 22, 1974, to August 21, 1975, were selected from the divorce court records. At the time interviewing began in January 1980, this meant that if the couples had resumed living together when their divorce petitions were withdrawn or dismissed, they could have been reconciled for as long as 5½ years. Because of concerns about recall of past events and attrition, a second census of all dismissed and withdrawn divorce cases for the seven study suburbs was done for the period August 22, 1977, to August 21, 1978. This produced another 272 cases.

As in the longitudinal divorce study, the male or female in each couple was alternately selected for study, with no substitutions for refusals. Interviewers were matched to respondents by race and, where possible, by gender. More of the cases that were available for study were withdrawn by the couple (67.3%) than were dismissed by the court (32.7%).

Out of the original 600 cases, 79, or 13.1% were found to be ineligible because the spouse selected to be interviewed had moved out of the SMSA or had died. Of those eligible to be interviewed, 183, or 35.1%, had moved and could not be located, and another 70 (13.4%) were located but could not be contacted. Thus, of the 521 spouses eligible for study, 268, or 51.4%, were contacted. Of these, 152, or 56.7% were interviewed and 116, or 43.4%, refused. Thus, losses and refusals in the reconciliation study were not significantly different from the losses, refusals, and overall completion rate in the longitudinal divorce study.

To assess the representativeness of the sample, the subjects were compared first to the remainder of the sample ($n = 449$), and second to the outright refusals ($n = 116$). Demographic information available upon the divorce petitions was used to make comparisons by gender of the subjects selected for study, date of petition withdrawal or dismissal, age, length of marriage, number of children in the household, and number of previous marriages. Measures were developed for race based on knowledge of the area of residence, and for income based on the median income of the census tract of residence. Among the eligible spouses who were contacted, there were no significant differences between respondents and outright refusers on any of the variables measured. Their respective distributions on most of the variables were nearly identical.

Several significant differences were apparent when respondents were compared to *all* nonrespondents. However, most of these differences appeared to be related to the propensity of the nonrespondents to move away or be difficult to locate. Nonrespondents were significantly more likely to be male and to be black (χ^2 for gender $= 5.7$, $df = 1$, $p < .05$; χ^2 for race $= 7.9$, $df = 1$, $p < .01$). Nonrespondents also tended to be about 2½ years younger on the average than the respondents, to have been married a shorter time (an average of 8 years vs. 11 years for the respondents), and to have fewer children. In fact, 40% of the nonrespondents had no children born to the study marriage, compared to 28% of the respondents. Thus, the findings of this study may be biased toward more "settled" families.

In the longitudinal suburban divorce study, there were few errors in the court records in the listing of the date of birth and date of marriage, and no cases in which respondents denied that court action was taken. However, since the reconciliation study explored new areas about which little was known, the accuracy of the records was reassessed. Respondents were asked whether their petitions had been withdrawn or dismissed, who filed, whether the suit was contested, and the dates of filing and of petition withdrawal or dismissal. These replies were compared to the court record data. In all cases, the agreement between the respondents and the court records was greater than 90%. As a result, information on the court records was used for the dates of filing and for petition withdrawal or dismissal, since it was likely to be more accurate than would the respondents' recall of specific dates 5 or more years earlier.

Of the 152 persons who were contacted for interviews, 3 claimed that they had never filed for divorce. The respondents were asked their birth date and date of marriage, and these were verified in the court records. It is therefore unlikely that errors were made in selecting the cases. It would appear that in some small number of cases of petition withdrawal or dismissal, individuals were unaware that their spouses had filed, were using denial to such an extent that they were no longer able to acknowledge or remember the event, or were embarrassed or otherwise unwilling to participate in the study and did not want to refuse outright.

In an effort to focus on reconciled couples who returned for more than a fleeting "one-night stand," a "reconciliation" was defined as living together again for at least a week after the petition was withdrawn or dismissed. The 33 individuals who indicated that they had not lived together for at least a week were asked an abbreviated version of the interview schedule. Where possible, data from these respondents are included in the analyses of the reconciled. The final sample of reconciled persons consisted of 119 respondents who had filed for divorce, had withdrawn or dismissed their divorce petitions, and had subsequently lived with their spouses for at least 1 week.

The Marital Transition Sample

In 1985 and 1986, a sample of separated and divorced women was drawn from the records of the Domestic Relations Division of the Cuyahoga County Court of Common Pleas. They were matched by age, race, and median income of census tract of residence to a sample of widows, who were drawn from the death certificates of their spouses. The divorced sample was not a random sample of divorcees in Cuyahoga County; instead, it was designed to match the characteristics of widows, in order to clarify how widowed and divorced women differ and are similar in their patterns of adjustment. Death of a spouse and divorce are two events that have been defined, as noted in Chapter 1, as theoretically similar.

To be eligible for interview, subjects had to have resided in Cuyahoga County at the time the divorce was filed and to be living in the four-county SMSA at the time of the interview. So that the impact of age on adjustment could be assessed, the samples were stratified into those aged 44 and under and those 45–62. Each of these age groups was further subdivided into those aged 18–34, 35–44, 45–54, and 55–62, to ensure that cases did not bunch into the middle years. Subjects were interviewed in their homes by interviewers matched by race, by gender, and (where possible) by age.

For the 419 eligible divorcees, the completion rate was 44.9%, with 188 agreeing to be interviewed. Another 134 (32.0%) refused; 57 (13.6%) could not be contacted despite repeated efforts; 39 (9.3%) moved without leaving a forwarding address; and 1 (0.002%) had died. For those divorcees actually contacted, the response rate was 58.3% and the refusal rate 41.6%. (For comparisons of the widowed and divorced samples in this study, see Kitson & Zyzanski, 1987; Kitson & Roach, 1989).

The data available on the court records indicated that there were no statistically significant differences in completion rate by age of the respondent, age of the spouse, or median income of census tract of residence. Race was not listed in the court records, but estimates of the racial composition of neighborhoods and other available information indicated that the completion rate did vary significantly by estimated race: Blacks were less likely to participate than whites, as was also noted in the longitudinal suburban divorce study and the reconciliation study.

The median length of time between the divorce filing and the interview was 5 months, and the mean was 5.4 months. Couples were twice as likely to have filed for a dissolution of marriage as for a divorce. Dissolutions comprised 66.3% of the cases and divorces 33.3%; there was one annulment (0.5%). At the time of the first interview, only 8.8% of the divorces and dissolutions were not granted, as compared to 53.8% that had not been granted in the longitudinal suburban divorce study by the time of the first interview. Although somewhat more of the suburban divorce interviews were completed earlier in the divorce process than in this study (the median divorce was filed 4.2 months prior to interview in the suburban study, compared to 5 months in the county-wide marital transition study), neither the increase in the number of dissolutions nor the increased rapidity with which decrees were granted appeared to be due to the age distribution of the marital transition sample. The differences would appear to represent real shifts in the legal process in northeastern Ohio between the mid-1970s and mid-1980s. At the second interview (13 months after the first) 156 divorced women, or 83.0%, agreed to be reinterviewed. The major category of loss consisted of those who could not be relocated.

The Marital Status Sample*

Research following a group of persons as they go through the divorce process provides a description of divorce adjustment, while research on those whose divorce petitions were withdrawn or dismissed reports on those who may have been ambivalent about the divorce decision. Court-records-based divorce and reconciliation data are able to describe those who felt that their marriages were in enough distress that they should enter the legal system. They do not, however, shed light on those who might have separated and subsequently reconciled with-

---

*Some of the material in this section is adapted from "Marital Discord and Marital Separation: A County Survey" by G. C. Kitson, 1985, *Journal of Marriage and the Family*, 47, 693-700. Copyright 1985 by the National Council on Family Relations. Reprinted by permission.

out resorting to legal action. The marital status survey was designed to look at marital separations that did not necessarily lead to filing for divorce, and to explore differences in psychological status by marital status.

Marital separation can be an informal arrangement between a husband and wife, not one marked by state intervention. In 1989, 4,383,000 persons, or 2.3% of the U.S. population, were separated from their spouses because of marital discord (U.S. Bureau of the Census, 1990). In some cases such separations are legalized. In others they are not, although the spouses may continue to live apart without ever obtaining a divorce, or at least may do so for many years. In what is assumed to be the majority of cases, separation is a step on the way to obtaining a divorce. The least researched aspect of marital separations involves individuals who separate from and then reconcile with their spouses without ever having filed for divorce.

To examine marital separations that were associated with marital discord but that might not have led to filing for divorce, data on marital history, demographic characteristics, and psychological status were collected as part of a 1980 omnibus survey of Cuyahoga County residents. In an "omnibus" survey, several investigators share the costs of a survey and common demographic data for the opportunity to ask certain questions of interest to them.

The sample was a multistage, random sample of adults 18 years of age or older. It was stratified on race, income, and housing type (single-family vs. multiple-family dwelling units). Because the strata were defined in proportion to the county population, it was not necessary to weight the data. Of the 1,600 cases selected for study, 1,101 were interviewed, for a completion rate of 68.8%. Although women, composing 60.3% of the sample, were overrepresented compared to the 1980 census figures for Cuyahoga County (54.0%), the sample was similar to the census figures on race and family income (see Kitson, 1985; U.S. Bureau of the Census, 1981, 1984).

The data from the four surveys described above provide different perspectives on the processes of marital separation, divorce, and post-divorce adjustment. The following section describes the way in which adjustment was operationalized.

DEVELOPING MEASURES OF ADJUSTMENT

Adjustment is best viewed as a multidimensional concept that cannot be adequately examined with only one set of items. As defined in

Chapter 1, it includes being free of symptoms of physical or psychological disturbance, having a sense of self-esteem, and having put the marriage and the former partner in enough perspective that a person's identity is no longer tied to being married or to the former partner. In the primary source of data to be explored, the longitudinal suburban divorce study, four scales were used to explore the concept of adjustment empirically: scales measuring subjective distress, attachment, self-esteem, and illness contacts.

Subjective Distress

Attempts to assess the psychological status of people living in the community are fraught with confusion and controversy. Measures of psychological status swing in and out of favor, with researchers continually expressing dissatisfaction with the scales developed. Although there is little consensus about what constitutes a good measure of psychological disturbance, certain symptoms commonly occur in many of the scales, such as anxiety and depression, which are particularly common among the divorced (Bloom & Caldwell, 1981; Briscoe et al., 1973; Jacobson, 1983; Waller, 1930/1967; Weiss, 1975). Because of the importance of this dimension in adjustment to divorce, items that assessed depression, anxiety, daily routine, leisure-time impairment, thoughts of suicide, and somatic concerns were selected from the Psychiatric Status Schedule (Spitzer, Endicott, Fleiss, & Cohen, 1970). The Psychiatric Status Schedule was originally designed to examine role functioning and signs and symptoms of psychopathology. It was developed in psychiatric inpatient and outpatient settings, and then was used to assess community samples as well.

The 22 items assessed here included the following feelings or behaviors: "anxiety," "sadness or depression," "fear of losing mind," "discouragement," "aimlessness," "poor appetite," "irritability," "phobias," "panic attacks," "obsessive thoughts," "sexual difficulty," "impairment in daily routine," "preoccupation with health," "hypochondriasis," "worrying a lot," "trouble sleeping," "impaired memory or forgetfulness," "poor money judgment," "difficulty making decisions," "suicidal thoughts," "consideration of suicide," and "suicide attempt." (See Appendix A for the specific wording of the items and Appendix B for the coding scheme.)

With the exception of the items assessing "sadness or depression" and "anxiety," which were scored 0, 1, or 2[5] the items were scored "no" or "yes" (0 or 1). Scores on the scale ranged from 0 to 24, with a high score on the scale indicating high distress. The alpha reliability of the scale was .70 for the suburban sample. For the married comparison group, the alpha reliability was .80. This same measure was used in the reconciliation study, where the alpha reliability of the scale was .79.

Positive and Negative Affect: Short Measures on Subjective Distress

In the short telephone follow-up interview with the married suburban comparison sample, the subjects were not asked the full battery of psychological status measures. Instead, the 10-item Affect Balance Scale was used (Bradburn, 1969). The scale is used as its two subscales, Negative Affect and Positive Affect, instead of as one scale (Cherlin & Reeder, 1975). These items were also asked of the divorced at all three interviews in the suburban study; in addition, they were used in the reconciliation study, the marital transition study, and the marital status survey. The scale measures an individual's sense of psychological well-being with "no" and "yes" answers, scored as 0 and 1, respectively. Sample items from the Positive Affect and Negative Affect subscales, respectively, are "During the past several weeks, have you felt that things have been going your way?" and "Have you felt depressed or very unhappy during the past several weeks?" The Negative Affect subscale was strongly correlated with the longer subjective distress measure in the longitudinal study (for the divorced, $r = .54$, $p < .001$; for the married, $r = .54$, $p < .001$). This means that the two measures assessed a similar domain of anxious and depressed feelings.

When compared to the other health status measures used, the subscales of the Affect Balance Scale had lower alpha reliabilities. For the divorced at the first interview, the reliability for the Positive Affect subscale was .63 and for the Negative Affect subscale was .55. For the married, the scores were .54 for Positive Affect and .47 for Negative Affect. In the reconciliation study, the alpha reliability for Positive Affect was a low .49, and for Negative Affect it was .70. In the county-wide survey of marital status, the alpha reliabilities were .61 for Positive Affect and .63 for Negative Affect; in the county-wide marital transition study, the scores for divorcees were .65 for Positive Affect and .69 for Negative Affect. These scores are similar to the reliabilities reported by Cherlin and Reeder (1975).

Because of their lower reliabilities, the subscales of the Affect Balance Scale are not major analytic tools in the chapters that follow. Even with their lower reliabilities, however, there are some advantages to using these subscales; these include their brevity, widespread use, and correlation with the longer subjective distress measure. Most importantly, these subscales provide a benchmark for assessing changes in psychological status across all four of the studies. This is useful as a check upon a basic assumption of the research: the comparability of results across time and studies, as well as the stability of the health status scores for the married. What if the scores for the married actually changed significantly between the two time periods, rather than, as posited, remaining the same? If this were true, there would be serious problems in comparing the initial interview scores for the married with data from a third interview for the divorced. What if health status scores were to vary from study to study?

The Positive Affect and Negative Affect scores for the suburban married comparison sample shed some light on this issue. First, there were virtually no differences between the mean scores for the married on either measure at the two testings, which were 3–4 years apart. The mean Positive Affect score was 3.6 at the first interview and 3.6 at the second. The Negative Affect scores averaged 1.0 at the first interview and 1.0 at the second. This indicates that although some married individuals may have experienced increased psychological difficulties over the course of the study period, their increases were offset by those whose troubles decreased or remained the same. Thus, the assumption of stability in the scores for the married is supported. These data, then, provide reassurance that the initial health status scores of the married can be compared to those of the divorced at the second and third interviews. As for the comparability of scores across time, data from the three companion studies address this issue.

Attachment

At the time the measures for this study were being developed, there were no empirical indicators of attachment in divorce available. (For more recent measures of attachment, see Berman, 1985, 1988; Brown et al., 1980; Brown & Reimer, 1984; Masheter, 1991.) As a result, the items for this study were developed according to the conceptual framework employed by psychiatrist Colin Murray Parkes (1972) to describe reactions to the death of a spouse and other losses. According to this model, continued attachment includes denial and disbelief at the end of the relationship, pining or preoccupation with the former spouse, guilt, anger, loss of normal patterns of conduct, and apathy.

A series of items that were thought to assess these concepts was developed. The divorced were asked to indicate on a scale from 1 ("not at all my feelings") to 5 ("very much my feelings") in what way the items expressed their feelings about the divorce. Nine items hypothesized to be assessing attachment were entered into a factor analysis with an orthogonal solution and a varimax rotation to determine whether they tapped a single dimension called "attachment."[6]

The results of the factor analysis indicated that the items did represent a unidimensional phenomenon. Eighty-two percent of the variance was explained by four items, producing an eigenvalue of 2.8. Four items with a consistent pattern of higher correlations were used to construct the attachment index. These items, with their factor score coefficients noted in parentheses, were as follows:

"I find myself wondering what my (ex-)husband/wife is doing." (.514)
"I find myself spending a lot of time thinking about my (ex-) husband/wife." (.259)
Sometimes I just can't believe that we're getting a divorce." (.117)
"I feel I will *never* get over the divorce." (.113)

The higher factor score coefficients for these items indicate that preoccupation with or pining for the spouse and disbelief are particularly important components in attachment.

Although in several earlier pages (Kitson, 1982; Kitson, Graham, & Schmidt, 1983) the attachment scale scores were transformed into z scores and multiplied by the coefficients developed in the factor analysis, in this book the raw scores are used. Scores for the scale ranged from 4 to 20, with a high score on the scale indicating high attachment. The use of the raw scores makes it easier to understand changes in the mean values of the scale across the interviews. Because the alpha reliability score was so high (.80), either scoring approach can be used.

Among adults, attachment seems easier to assess when a partner is absent. It is perhaps for this reason that many of the discussions of the concept occur in studies of divorce (Brown et al., 1980; Spanier & Casto, 1979; Weiss, 1975, 1976, 1979, 1982) and of bereavement (Parkes, 1972; Parkes & Weiss, 1983; Zisook & Shuchter, 1986). Although several authors have made a start on the difficult task of measuring attachment among the married (Henderson, Byrne, Duncan-Jones, Scott, & Adcock, 1980; Henderson, Duncan-Jones, Byrne, & Scott, 1980; Hirschfeld et al., 1977), at the time these measures were constructed it was not possible to develop a comparable measure for the married. Therefore, when comparisons on adjustment are made in this book for the married and the divorced, only the subjective distress, illness contacts, and self-esteem measures are used.

Self-Esteem

The third component of adjustment, self-esteem, was assessed using Rosenberg's (1965) 10-item Self-Esteem Scale. The items are scored on a 5-point scale, with 1 indicating strong agreement with the statements and 5 strong disagreement; scores range from 10 to 50. To avoid "response set," in which subjects develop a style of agreeing or disagreeing with all the items, half of the items in the scale are worded negatively. Thus, a subject who has high self-esteem should agree with five of the items (e.g., "I feel I'm a person of worth, at least on an equal basis with others") and disagree with the other five (e.g., "All in all, I am inclined to feel that I am a failure"). In computing the scale, the scoring of the negatively worded items is reversed so that a score of 1 equals 5, 2 equals 4, and so forth. *A high score on the scale indicates poor self-esteem.* The alpha reliability of the scale for the suburban divorced sample was .83, and for the married comparison sample it was .77. In the reconciliation study, the reliability was .79.

Illness Contacts

Although adjustment to divorce is generally treated as a psychological issue, epidemiological studies report that the divorced have higher rates of physical illness than do other marital status groups (Verbrugge, 1979). Physical illness was assessed in the present research by a three-item scale. The items asked about the number of times in the past year the subject was ill enough to have to stay in bed at least a day; the number of times the subject made visits to a doctor; and the number of times the subject was hospitalized for an operation or illness. Because the three items composing the scale varied in the number of categories they contained, the items were rescored so that the scale had a range from 0 to 15.[7] A higher score indicated more physical health problems. The scale had an alpha reliability of .70 for the suburban divorced sample and .57 for the married comparison sample.

Correlation of the Adjustment Measures

Table 2.4 displays the correlations of each of the adjustment items with the others across the three divorce interviews in the longitudinal suburban study. With correlations between .24 and .56, the subjective distress, attachment, and self-esteem measures were strongly and consistently related to each other. Those with a high number of symptoms of psychological distress also had high scores on the self-esteem and attachment measures. At the same time, although these items were significantly associated with one another, no one measure was so highly correlated with another as to suggest that the items were measuring the same phenomenon. As examples, only 5.7% of the variance was explained by a correlation of .24, and 31.4% by a correlation of .56.

TABLE 2.4. Correlation Matrix for Adjustment Measures (Subjective Distress, Attachment, Self-Esteem, and Illness Contacts): Suburban Divorced Sample at Three Time Periods

Adjustment measures	First interview (n = 201)				Second interview (n = 160)				Third interview (n = 129)			
	Subjective distress	Attachment	Self-esteem[a]	Illness contacts	Subjective distress	Attachment	Self-esteem[a]	Illness contacts	Subjective distress	Attachment	Self-esteem[a]	Illness contacts
Subjective distress	—	.42	.40	.25	—	.33	.56	.18	—	.40	.47	.18
Attachment		—	.24	.07		—	.39	.08		—	.30	.14
Self-esteem[a]			—	.03			—	−.04			—	.03
Illness contacts				—				—				—

Note. All correlations .25 and above are statistically significant at $p < .001$.
[a]High scores on the self-esteem measure indicated *low* self-esteem. See text.

This means that even for the larger correlation coefficients, substantially more than half of the variance was left unexplained. The only one of the adjustment measures with which illness contacts were significantly associated was subjective distress. This means that the variable of illness contacts generally contributed a unique amount of variance. These findings support the use of a multidimensional approach to assessing adjustment.

The wording and coding of other measures to be used in the pages that follow are described as the items are presented in the text. All of the questions in the suburban divorce study discussed in this book are displayed in Appendix A, with an indication of the time period at which they were asked.

CONCLUSION

In this chapter, the design and completion rates for the four studies to be examined in this book have been described. The samples for three of these studies were drawn from divorce court records in Cuyahoga County, Ohio (metropolitan Cleveland). The study that constitutes the focus of the majority of the analyses was a 4-year longitudinal analysis of adjustment to divorce in seven suburban communities, with a comparison sample of married persons matched by gender, race, and city block of residence to the divorced. A study of reconciliations, done in the same seven communities as the first study, examined persons who filed for divorce but then withdrew their divorce petitions or had them dismissed. A study of marital transition employed a sample of separated and divorced women, who were matched by age, race, and median income of census tract of residence to a sample of widowed women. Finally, data on marital status, marital separations, and psychological well-being were collected from a multistage, random sample of county residents. These different types of data should help to clarify different aspects of marital distress, separation, and post-divorce adjustment. The dependent variables for the study—subjective distress, attachment, self-esteem, and illness contacts—have also been described.

NOTES

1. Historically in the Western world, divorce was more common among the elite than among the poor. Glick (1957, p. 156) has called desertion "the poor man's divorce." In fact, it was so much a part of the conventional wisdom that

divorce was more likely among the wealthy than the poor that William Goode (1956), in planning his important 1948 study *After Divorce*, at first thought he had a biased sample of court records when he found more divorces among those in lower- than in higher-status occupational groups.

2. Determining the response rate in divorce research is difficult (Kitson et al., 1982). It is particularly difficult to do so for couple data. Some studies include data from one individual in a couple when the other spouse refuses to participate, while including data from both partners for another portion of the sample. Thus, Fulton (1979) reported that 33.7%, or 141 couples or 282 persons, out of her final sample of 560 agreed to be interviewed in a court-records-based Minnesota study. In a Wisconsin court-records-based study, Ahrons and Wallisch (1987) reported interviewing 98 couples, or 51% out of an estimated 198 eligible and locatable couples. These couples in turn constituted 52.2% of 379 couples deemed to be eligible solely on the basis of court records data.

Masheter (1991) received questionnaires from at least one partner in 226 couples in a Connecticut court-records-based study, but was able to collect data from only 39 couples, or 17.2% of the total. The 265 individual respondents in her study represented 39.0% of the 656 deliverable questionnaires. In a study requiring interviews with both divorced biological parents and their new partners, Jacobson (1987) located 1,879, or 32.3% of 5,828 potential couples in a Los Angeles court-records-based sample. Of these, 645, or 36.1%, qualified for the study. Of these in turn, 370, or 57.4% of the first set of couples, agreed to participate in the research; however, 82 of the second set of couples needed did not agree to participate, so that a total of 288, or 44.7%, of the 647 eligibles included interviews with all four family members required. In the best response rate for such research, Ambert (1989), in a metropolitan Toronto convenience sample, was able to interview at least one ex-spouse in 39, or 81.2%, of 48 couples. Some subjects had been married several times, so that multiple ex-spouses were interviewed for some.

3. In Ohio, the high-filing months in the summer are distinguished by more marriages in which there are children. It is likely that such couples may wait until the end of the school year to divorce.

4. With the additional cases, the overall response rate for the first interview was 49.6%, with a refusal rate of 26.8%. Of those 322 persons actually contacted, 64.9% responded and 35.1% refused.

5. Subjects who were "often sad or depressed" received a score of 1, and those who felt "depressed most of the time" received a score of 2. Those who were "often anxious or tense" received a score of 1, and those who felt "anxious or tense most of the time" received a score of 2.

6. The nine items were as follows:

> "Everything I have to do seems like an effort."
> "I find myself spending a lot of time thinking about my (ex-)husband/ wife."

"I'm feeling like myself again."
"Sometimes I just can't believe that we're getting a divorce."
"I find myself wondering what my (ex-)husband/wife is doing."
"I have no interest in anything."
"I'm angry at my (ex-)husband/wife."
"I do not feel any guilt about the divorce."
"I feel I will *never* get over the divorce."

These items were part of a larger set of questions developed to assess divorce reactions. These were theoretically defined as assessing attachment, with factor analysis used as a test of this hypothesis. Using factor analysis as a way of identifying items that fell together rather than of confirming theoretical notions, Thompson and Spanier (1983) took a different subset of these items to develop an 11-item scale assessing "acceptance of marital termination." Their approach does not seem an appropriate method of using these items.

7. The number of visits to a doctor was collapsed from six to five categories by combining category 6, those reporting the highest number of visits, with the next highest group. The number of times sick enough to be in bed was collapsed from six categories to five by combining those who reported six or seven times in bed with those reporting five separate times. Hospitalizations were recoded so that one hospitalization equaled 3, two equaled 4, and three equaled 5. Nineteen percent of the divorced reported one hospitalization, 2%, two hospitalizations, and 1% three or more. Twelve percent of the married reported a hospitalization in the past year.

C H A P T E R 3

Risk Factors for Divorce: A Comparison of the Study Samples

Marriage is a wonderful institution, but who wants to live in an institution?
—Groucho Marx quoted in Dickson (1981, p. 276)

This chapter examines background characteristics of the suburban, reconciled, and county-wide marital transition court-records-based samples, to address the issue of the comparability of these samples. If the groups are similar in their background characteristics, any differences in findings are likely to be related to differences in marital status or to the passage of time. The chapter also describes similarities and differences in the suburban married and divorced samples, to address the comparability of these two groups and to explore the issue of whether the divorced are "flawed" socially, psychologically, or morally by comparison with the married. According to one school of thought, those who choose to end their marriages have characteristics that make them "divorce-prone." Many comparisons of the divorced and married, however, are based on samples that differ in background characteristics. The present research has attempted to take these differences into account through the sampling procedures employed. Finally, attitudes about marriage and divorce in the suburban samples are explored.

DEMOGRAPHIC BACKGROUND CHARACTERISTICS OF THE COURT-RECORDS-BASED SAMPLES

Because of differences in the ways the samples were collected and differences in the time periods at which data were collected, it is important to determine how nearly comparable the three samples drawn from court records are. Because only women were surveyed in the county-wide marital transition study, the comparisons across studies displayed in Table 3.1 include only women. There were no statistically significant differences in the distribution of subjects by gender,

TABLE 3.1. Race, Sex, Family Social Class, and Respondent's Education: Court-Records-Based Samples

Demographic characteristics	Percentage of women replying in court-records-based samples				χ^2			
	Suburban divorced	Reconciled	Marital transition	Suburban-reconciled	Suburban-marital transition	Reconciled-marital transition
Race						
White	74.8	69.1	83.5			
Nonwhite	25.2	30.9	16.5			
Total	100.0	100.0	100.0	0.7, $df = 1$, n.s.	3.3, $df = 1$, n.s.	6.5, $df = 1$, $p < .05$
(n)	(107)	(68)	(188)			
Family social class						
Class I: Upper	10.5	3.1	8.6			
Class II: Upper middle	21.9	17.2	20.9			
Class III: Middle	35.2	34.4	29.4			
Class IV: Working	23.8	40.6	32.1			
Class V: Lower	8.6	4.7	9.1			
Total	100.0	100.0	100.1	7.7, $df = 4$, n.s.	2.7, $df = 4$, n.s.	5.0, $df = 4$, n.s.
(n)	(105)	(64)	(187)			
Respondent's education						
Ninth grade or less	1.9	2.9	4.3			
Some high school	12.1	7.4	13.9			
High school graduate	36.5	48.5	38.0			
Some college	28.0	27.9	23.0			
College graduate	12.1	1.5	11.2			
At least some post-graduate work	9.3	11.8	9.6			
Total	99.9	100.0	100.1	8.8, $df = 5$, n.s.	1.9, $df = 5$, n.s.	9.9, $df = 5$, n.s.
(n)	(107)	(68)	(187)			

race, family social class, as measured by the Hollingshead (1957) Index of Social Position,[1] or the respondent's level of education for the total suburban divorced sample or the reconciled sample. (For distributions on sex, race, and family social class for males and females in the reconciled and suburban divorced samples, see Kitson & Langlie, 1984.)

Despite the differences in the ways the subjects were selected for study as described in Chapter 2, the three samples were comparable on family social class position and the respondent's level of education. The differences in the racial composition of the suburban divorced sample and the county-wide divorced sample from the marital transition study were not statistically significant, but the distribution of women subjects by race did differ significantly for the reconciliation and marital transition studies: There were fewer nonwhites in the marital transition sample. Virtually all of the nonwhites in all three samples were blacks. The difference between the reconciled and the marital transition sample may have resulted in part from the fact that the latter was designed as a comparison group of divorcees for a sample of widows. Matching characteristics included race. The divorce rate is higher among blacks than among whites (Norton & Moorman, 1987). With fewer blacks remaining married, relatively fewer become widows; therefore, few black divorcees were selected as a comparison group for these widows. In any event, no comparisons are made in these chapters by race between the reconciled and county-wide marital dissolution samples, so this difference is not especially important.

These data indicate that any differences in findings across the court-records-based studies are unlikely to have resulted from differences in basic background characteristics, such as family social class or education of the respondents. This produces greater confidence that any observed differences or similarities in the samples were "real," not just the result of problems in sampling.

COMPARISONS OF BACKGROUND CHARACTERISTICS: THE SUBURBAN MARRIED AND DIVORCED SAMPLES

In this section, the married and divorced subjects in the suburban study are compared. The aim was to make the married and divorced samples comparable in their background characteristics; this goal was at least partly achieved. There were no statistically significant differences between the married and divorced samples on background characteristics such as sex, race, and family social class (Table 3.2). These data indicate that the married and divorced samples were quite similar in their basic demographic characteristics.

Table 3.2 also displays the distribution of background characteristics by race, because possible racial differences in divorce adjustment constitute one of the areas to be examined in some detail in the following chapters. There were no statistically significant differences between whites and nonwhites in the suburban divorced sample on any of the characteristics being examined, as measured by chi-square or by the more sensitive technique of a *t* test.

Although the married and divorced samples were similar in basic characteristics, there were some differences between the two groups. They varied on family income in the last year of marriage as measured by *t* test, with the married having higher incomes than the divorced, but the two groups did not differ by the less powerful statistical technique of chi-square. The study groups varied on length of marriage and age, with more of the divorced respondents having been married a shorter period of time and being younger. The mean age of the divorced was 33.1 years, with the median being 29.5; the average length of marriage was 7.7 years, and the median was 4.2. For the married, their mean age was 40.0 years and their median age 39.0; their average length of marriage was 14.7 years, with the median being 10.9. The similar social class position of the two groups and the relative youth of the divorced suggest that the divorced may have had a relative socioeconomic advantage over the married at the beginning of the study. In other words, the divorced had reached the same suburban neighborhoods as the married, who for the most part were older and presumably more settled; however, as indicated by their income, the economic situation of the divorced was somewhat more precarious.

The samples also differed on the number of children born to each couple and on the family's life cycle stage. Couples in the married sample had more children—a mean of 1.9, as opposed to 1.2, for couples in the divorced sample. The divorced were more likely to have no children or young children, and the married respondents were more likely to have at least one child over the age of 18 or all children over 18. Couples without children have generally been more likely to divorce, although this is less often true than it was previously (Levinger, 1976). To some extent, the relationship between childlessness and divorce is a result of the fact that divorces generally occur in the early years of a marriage, with the national median length of marriage at divorce being 6.7 years in 1970 and 6.9 years in 1986 (National Center for Health Statistics, 1989). Another contributing factor to the relationship between the presence of children and marital longevity seems somewhat less important today than it was in earlier years; this is a feeling of parental responsibility to maintain the marriage for the sake

TABLE 3.2. Demographic Characteristics: Suburban Divorced and Married Samples, and Divorced Sample by Race

Demographic characteristics	% replying Married (n = 178)	Divorced (n = 209)	χ^2 or t	% replying: Divorced by race White (n = 153)	Nonwhite (n = 56)	χ^2 or t
Sex						
Male	46.6	48.8		47.7	51.8	
Female	53.3	51.2		52.3	48.2	
Total	100.0	100.0	$\chi^2 = 0.2$, $df = 1$, n.s.	100.0	100.0	$\chi^2 = 2.1$, $df = 1$, n.s.
Race						
White	73.6	73.2		—	—	
Black	25.8	25.8		—	—	
Oriental	0.6	1.0		—	—	
Total	100.0	100.0	$\chi^2 = 1.2$, $df = 2$, n.s.	—	—	
Family social class						
Class I: Upper	10.7	8.9		10.7	3.8	
Class II: Upper middle	25.4	23.1		22.7	24.5	
Class III: Middle	29.4	31.0		30.0	34.0	
Class IV: Working	28.8	31.0		30.7	32.1	
Class V: Lower	5.6	5.9		6.0	5.7	
Total	100.0	100.0	$\chi^2 = 0.8$, $df = 4$, n.s.	100.1	100.1	$\chi^2 = 0.3$, $df = 3$, n.s.[a]
Income						
Under $4,999	3.4	4.7		2.8	10.2	
$5,000 to $9,999	11.5	20.2		19.4	22.4	
$10,000 to $14,999	24.7	25.9		26.4	24.5	
$15,000 to $19,999	27.6	22.3		22.2	22.4	
$20,000 to $29,999	20.1	19.2		21.5	12.2	
$30,000 and over	12.6	7.8		7.6	8.2	
Total	99.9	100.1	$\chi^2 = 8.0$, $df = 5$, n.s.	99.9	99.9	$\chi^2 = 2.7$, $df = 3$, n.s.[b]
(Mean, dollars)	($19,023)	($16,762)	$t = 2.3$, $df = 160$, $p < .05$	($17,257)	($15,306)	$t = 1.3$, $df = 191$, n.s.
(SD, dollars)	($9,887)	($9,271)		($9,040)	($9,874)	

(continued)

TABLE 3.2. Demographic Characteristics: Suburban Divorced and Married Samples, and Divorced Sample by Race (continued)

Demographic characteristics	% replying			% replying: Divorced by race		
	Married (n = 178)	Divorced (n = 209)	χ^2 or t	White (n = 153)	Nonwhite (n = 56)	χ^2 or t
Age of respondent						
Under age 20	0.6	1.9		2.6	—	
Ages 20 to 29	32.6	48.1		49.7	43.6	
Ages 30 to 39	19.7	25.0		22.9	30.9	
Ages 40 to 49	24.2	14.4		15.0	12.7	
Age 50 and over	23.0	10.6		9.8	12.7	
Total	100.0	100.1		100.0	99.9	
(Mean, age)	(40.0)	(33.1)		(32.8)	(34.0)	
(SD, age)	(13.7)	(10.4)	$\chi^2 = 16.1, df = 4, p < .01$ $t = 4.7, df = 384, p < .001$	(10.5)	(10.1)	$\chi^2 = 2.1, df = 3,$ n.s.[c] $t = 0.8, df = 206,$ n.s.
Length of marriage						
Less than 1 year	9.6	11.6		12.4	9.3	
1 to 4 years	18.1	40.6		38.6	46.3	
5 to 9 years	18.6	18.8		22.2	9.3	
10 to 14 years	13.6	9.7		5.9	20.4	
15 to 19 years	7.9	8.2		9.2	5.5	
20 to 24 years	6.8	5.3		5.9	3.7	
25 to 29 years	12.4	2.9		3.3	1.9	
30 or more years	13.0	2.9		2.6	3.7	
Total	100.0	100.0		100.1	100.1	
(Mean, years)	(14.7)	(7.7)	$\chi^2 = 42.7, df = 7, p < .001$ $t = 6.1, df = 382, p < .001$	(7.7)	(7.6)	$\chi^2 = 7.4, df = 4,$ n.s.[d] $t = 0.1, df = 205,$ n.s.
(SD, years)	(13.1)	(8.4)		(8.7)	(7.8)	

Number of children from this union

None	43.1	27.3	46.1	34.6
One	19.1	15.9	15.8	28.8
Two	21.6	25.0	20.4	25.0
Three	10.3	14.2	11.8	5.8
Four	2.9	10.8	3.3	1.9
Five or more	2.9	6.8	2.6	3.8
Total	99.9	100.0	100.0	99.9
(Mean, number)	(1.9)	(1.2)	(1.2)	(1.2)
(SD, number)	(1.4)	(1.7)	(1.4)	(1.6)

$\chi^2 = 20.7$, $df = 5$, $p < .001$ $\chi^2 = 6.0$, $df = 3$, n.s.[e]
$t = 4.4$, $df = 385$, $p < .001$ $t = 0.1$, $df = 207$, n.s.

Family life cycle stage

No children	19.0	31.0	36.2	16.7
All children under age 3	6.7	5.9	6.0	5.6
Preschoolers	5.6	13.8	11.4	20.4
Children in primary grades	22.0	19.7	17.4	24.1
Teenagers	8.4	11.8	11.4	14.7
Oldest child over 18 with others under age 18	8.9	20.4	9.4	9.3
All children over 18	8.4	20.8	8.1	9.3
Total	100.0	100.0	99.9	100.1

$\chi^2 = 28.0$, $df = 6$, $p < .001$ $\chi^2 = 6.2$, $df = 5$, n.s.[f]

[a]For calculation, Classes I and II were combined, as were Classes IV and V.
[b]T test based on grouped mean scores with the midpoint for "under $1,000" defined as $500 and the midpoint for the highest income category defined as $40,000.
[c]For calculation, the category "under age 20" was combined with "ages 20 to 29."
[d]For calculation, the categories "10 to 14 years" and "15 to 19 years" were combined into one category, and marriages over 20 years in length were combined into one category.
[e]For calculation, "three," "four," and "five or more" were combined into one category.
[f]For calculation, "all children under age 3" and "preschoolers" were combined into one category.

of the children. It is now often felt that children are better served if a bad marriage ends rather than continues for their sake—a sentiment reinforced by attitude data on this issue, to be reported upon later in this chapter. For whatever reason, the divorced in this sample were less likely to have children.

RISK FACTORS THAT PREDISPOSE TO DIVORCE?

This section explores a variety of characteristics that have been discussed as part of the divorce-as-pathology approach. According to this approach, those who divorce are morally, socially, or psychologically deviant, and these deviant characteristics are what make them more likely to divorce. Either in their rearing or in their beliefs and behaviors as adults, those who eventually divorce are thought to differ from those who do not (Halem, 1980). Despite much discussion of these characteristics, there have been relatively few empirical examinations of this thesis, in part because comparable samples of the married and divorced have rarely been available to explore these ideas. The distribution of a number of these characteristics is examined individually and then aggregated, to determine how many of the divorced and married subjects had characteristics that might presumably predispose them to divorce.

Research has suggested a number of characteristics that distinguish those who divorce from those who do not. Spouses who eventually divorce are more likely than those who remain married to come from different socioeconomic and ethnic backgrounds, so that they have less in common upon which to build a marital relationship (Goode, 1956; Levinger, 1976). Divorce is more frequent among those who marry at a young age (Norton & Moorman, 1987) or in haste, sometimes because of a premarital pregnancy (Bumpass & Sweet, 1972; Coombs & Zumeta, 1970; Furstenberg, 1976; Hampton, 1979; Norton & Moorman, 1987). As a result of such impetuosity, the spouses may not know each other well, may not otherwise have married each other, or may not have been able to complete their education and may therefore have lowered career opportunities. As a consequence, such a couple may have financial problems that also affect the marital relationship adversely.

Divorce is somewhat more likely among adult children of divorced parents (Bumpass & Sweet, 1972; Glenn & Kramer, 1985, 1987; Glick & Norton, 1979; Kulka & Weingarten, 1979; McLanahan & Bumpass, 1988; Mueller & Pope, 1977; Pope & Mueller, 1976). Coming from a family in which parental divorce occurred is thought to affect the life chances of the offspring, to color their perceptions of what a marital relationship is like, and to increase their willingness to end an unsatisfactory relationship. Those who divorce and remarry are also likely to divorce again. However, as Norton and Moorman (1987) note, redivorce rates show "signs of decline. Overall, the data suggest that in the future, the incidence of redivorce may be quite similar to the incidence of first divorce" (p. 13).

Those who divorce have also been less likely than those who stay married to belong to a religious denomination or to be active in religious activities—characteristics considered indicative of "unconventional behavior," such as choosing to divorce (Bumpass & Sweet, 1972; Glenn & Supancic, 1984). The divorced are also considered more psychologically troubled than the married, as indicated by higher rates of mental hospitalizations, affective disorders, and alcoholism (Bebbington, 1987; Bloom et al., 1978; Blumenthal, 1967; Briscoe et al., 1973; Rushing, 1979). Although it is possible that such illnesses are *consequences* of a troubled marriage, it has been suggested that psychological difficulties may be *precipitants* of a divorce.

Comparisons of the divorced and the married in the matched samples on these factors that have previously been implicated in the decision to divorce may indicate that the factors still hold true. On the other hand, the demographic similarities of the two groups may reduce the importance of these indicators, or, alternatively, the times may have changed sufficiently as to make many of these relationships no longer valid. Data on a series of individual indicators are examined, and then replies are summed across all the factors to determine whether the divorced differ from the married in the total number of these characteristics or in the frequency with which they exhibit them.

Homogamy

When two people who marry have similar, or "homogamous," social backgrounds, this is thought to make it easier for them to have or to develop common attitudes and values; in turn, this is thought to lead to greater mutual understanding and fewer arguments and disagreements. In the suburban study, the educational levels of the men and women in both the divorced and married samples differed significantly. Husbands had generally completed more years of education than their wives (for the divorced, $\chi^2 = 69.5$; for the married, $\chi^2 = 81.2$; for both, $df = 9$, $p < .001$). Men in the married sample had completed more years of education than men in the divorced sample ($\chi^2 = 16.4$, $df = 5$, $p < .01$). Women in the two samples had similar amounts of education. The two samples, however, did not differ significantly in the proportions of couples with educational differences. When the level of education differed for a husband and wife, a score of 1 was assigned. Among the divorced, 64.1% of the couples differed in educational attainment, and among the married the figure was 64.6%.

In both samples, the men came from families in which their fathers' occupational status was higher than that of their wives' fathers, but the divorced were no more likely to report different occupational statuses for husbands and wives than were the married. For the divorced in 73.7% ($n = 152$) of the couples, their fathers had dissimilar occupational backgrounds, whereas 75.7% ($n = 157$) of the married reported such dissimilarities.[2] When the spouse's father's occupational status was known, the distributions for the two groups were comparable, but the divorced subjects were significantly less likely than the married to *know* what the father-in-law's occupation was. Twenty-three percent of the divorced did not know what their spouses' fathers did for a living, whereas 14.0% of the married did not know ($\chi^2 = 4.3$, $df = 1$, $p < .05$). The inability of some of the divorced to answer this question suggests another characteristic of divorce-prone families—problems in communicating with and about in-laws, either because of dissimilar backgrounds or because of difficulties in getting along with them.

Marital History

The divorced were significantly more likely than the married to be in a second or later marriage. This was at least a second marriage for 30.1% of the suburban divorced sample, as opposed to 20.0% of the married comparison group ($\chi^2 = 5.0$, $df = 1$, $p < .05$). In 14.4% of the divorced couples one partner had been married previously, and in 12.9% of the couples both partners had been married before. By contrast, one partner had been married before in 10.2% of the married sample, and both had previously been married in 7.4%. For both the married and the divorced groups, almost all the previous marriages were ended by divorce or annulment rather than by death of a spouse.

Marital History of the Subjects' Parents

The two groups did not differ in the frequency of parental divorce before the respondents were aged 16, with 23.0% ($n = 161$) of the divorced reporting that either their own parents or their spouses' parents had divorced, as opposed to 23.6% of the married. (The divorced were asked this and some other background questions at the second interview, so that data are not available for the full divorced sample for some of these background items.) Even more parents in both samples had divorced after the respondents were aged 16. By the time of the interview, the divorce rate for the parents of the divorced couples had doubled to 47.2%. For 66 of the study couples, or 41.0%, either the husband's or the wife's parents had divorced or separated, and in 10 couples, or 6.2%, both sets of parents had divorced ($n = 161$). This compares to a lifetime divorce rate (up to the time of the interview) for the parents of the married sample of 36.5%, with divorces occurring for an additional 12.9% after the subjects were aged 16.

The two groups did not differ significantly in the proportions reporting that their parents' marriages were happy, with 44.6% of the married and 43.3% of the divorced reporting "very happy" parental marriages. "Somewhat happy" parental marriages were reported by 28.4% of the divorced and 34.1% of the married, with, respectively, 27.0% and 22.6% of the marriages considered "not too happy." These data do not support the previously reported likelihood of troubled family backgrounds for those who divorce, as measured by the stability or reported happiness of their parents' marriages. Compared to the national samples on which such conclusions have generally been drawn, the samples studied here were small. Even in such national studies, the tendency for intergenerational transmission of divorce has been small (Glenn & Kramer, 1985, 1987; Mueller & Pope, 1977; Pope & Mueller, 1976). The conservative conclusion to be drawn from the data examined here is that although they suggest no difference in parental divorce, larger studies indicate some slight tendency for the divorced to come from less stable homes than the married.

Premarital Pregnancy

The couples who filed for divorce were twice as likely (13.9%) as the married (6.7%) to have a child who was premaritally conceived—that is, a child whose birth date was less than 8 months from the date of the marriage, the length of time that has been traditionally used to indicate premarital conception ($\chi^2 = 4.7$, $df = 1$, $p < .05$). When only those with children from the study marriage were examined, as opposed to all couples in the samples, the differences were even more striking: 29 out of the 115 divorced women with children were premaritally pregnant (25.2%). Among the 128 married couples with children, this was true for only 12 women (9.4%).

Age at Marriage

The two groups did not differ significantly in the proportions who married at a young age. At least one of the marital partners was aged 19 or less for 23.4% of the divorced and 28.7% of the married. In this study population, then, although premarital pregnancy was more common for the divorced than the married sample, there were no differences between the two groups in age at marriage.

Ethnicity

The married and divorced samples did differ significantly in the degree to which they identified with ethnic groups. Among the divorced, 29.0% ($n = 155$) did not consider themselves and their spouses members of the same ethnic group, compared to 16.1% ($n = 142$) of the married ($\chi^2 = 6.9$, $df = 1$, $p < .01$). Ethnic differences included couples in which the partners belonged to different ethnic groups, as well as those in which one partner identified with an ethnic group while the other did not. The proportions reporting the same ethnic background for both partners were similar in the two samples (18.7% for the divorced and 19.0% for the married). Thus, as has been previously found as well, those who divorced in this survey were apparently less strongly tied to at least some traditional cultural values than were the married.

Religion

Traditionally, those who divorce are less likely than the married to belong to religious denominations, and more likely to attend church or synagogue services infrequently; when one or both partners belong to religious denominations, divorced partners are more likely to have different religious affiliations (Glenn & Supancic, 1984; Goode, 1956; Kitson & Raschke, 1981; Levinger, 1965, 1976; Raschke, 1987). These differences in religious indicators are felt to indicate less traditional attitudes among the divorced, including a willingness to view marriage as a dissolvable union.

The divorced in the suburban sample were significantly less likely than the married to consider themselves and/or their spouses members of religious denominations. Among the divorced, 35.9% were without a denomination, compared to 22.5% of the married ($\chi^2 = 8.2$, $df = 1$, $p < .01$). When a religious denomination was mentioned, there were few differences in affiliation in the two marital status groups. The married were only slightly more likely to report themselves as members of "main-line" Protestant denominations (Methodists, Episcopalians, etc.)[3]: with 29.7% who reported such affiliations, compared to 24.6% of the separated and divorced. The married were a little more likely to report being Jewish (8.0% vs. 4.5% for the divorced) or Catholic (29.7% vs. 24.6% for the divorced). None of these differences was statistically significant, however. Despite reports that those who divorce are more likely to be members of "fundamentalist" denominations (Bumpass & Sweet, 1972), the smallest religious difference in the two groups was for fundamentalists[4]: 16.0% of the married reported belonging to denominations grouped under this heading, compared to 15.1% of the divorced. Thus, although in general population studies Roman Catholics and Jews have been found to be less likely to divorce and fundamentalists more likely to do so, differences in divorce proneness by religious tradition are slight when community background is matched.

Although religious denomination per se was not associated with divorce, those who filed for divorce were significantly less likely than the married to report "very much" or "quite a bit" of influence of religious beliefs on their daily lives. Only 41.6% of the divorced reported such influence of religion, compared to 56.7% of the married ($\chi^2 = 9.0$, $df = 2$, $p < .05$). The divorced were significantly less likely to attend church "once a week or more" (26.4% vs. 46.5% for the married) and substantially more likely to attend church "infrequently or not at all" (21.4% vs. 5.8% for the married; ($\chi^2 = 28.0$, $df = 4$, $p < .001$). They were also more likely to indicate that they and their ex-spouses differed in their religious faiths: 49.7% reported different affiliations and 16.6% no affiliation, compared to 26.6% of the married with different affiliations and 9.6% with no affiliation ($\chi^2 = 32.4$, $df = 2$, $p < .001$). Lack of agreement on, or inability to compromise on, a common religious affiliation is another indicator of marital dissension. These data, then, support the commonly found association of religiosity and marital stability: Those who divorce are less active in organized religion than those who remain married.

Psychological Status

In addition to differing on certain social characteristics, the divorced also differed significantly from the married on background indicators of psychological status. They were more than six times as likely as the married to report having been hospitalized for mental illness at some point prior to the first interview. Among the divorced, 12.4% had been hospitalized, as opposed to 2.3% of the married ($\chi^2 = 13.7$, $df = 1$, $p < .001$).

Everyone was asked, "Have you ever made an attempt to take your own life?" The divorced were three times as likely as the married to have made a suicide attempt: 7.7% reported at least one such attempt, compared to 2.3% of the married ($\chi^2 = 5.5$, $df = 1$, $p < .05$). Differences in concerns about alcohol use were not significant. Among the divorced, 14.7% reported that others feared for their health because of the amount of alcohol they drank, whereas this was true for 10.2% of the married.

The survey did not ask about mental hospitalizations, suicide attempts, or problem drinking for the spouses, but each respondent was asked, "Did your husband/wife have any health problems during your marriage that affected his/her relationship with you?" The divorced were significantly more likely than the married to report that their spouses had problems that affected the relationship, either in a general way or sexually, socially, or economically. The divorced were substantially more likely than the married to consider these problems as involving mental illness, personality problems, or "nerves." Of the 55 divorced persons who said that their spouses had problems, 40.0% defined these difficulties as psychological problems, versus 14.8% of the 27 married persons who reported such problems. For the total samples, the figures for the divorced were 10.5% with psychological problems and 2.2% for the married ($\chi^2 = 10.6$, $df = 1$, $p < .001$). The divorced were also significantly more likely than the married to report that they themselves had health problems that had affected their marriages ($\chi^2 = 5.0$, $df = 1$, $p < .05$); of these respondents, 31.1% described their problems as chronic physical conditions, followed by 28.8% who mentioned psychological problems ($n = 45$). Among the married respondents who described problems of their own, chronic conditions were mentioned by 29.4% and psychological problems by 5.9% ($n = 17$).

When the four indicators of psychological status (hospitalization for mental illness, suicide attempts, problems with alcohol, and psychological problems of the spouse that affected the marriage) were summed, 35.2% of the divorced had at least one indicator of psychological problems, compared to 13.5% for the married; the mean number of indicators was 0.43 for the divorced and 0.17 for the married ($t = 4.7$, $df = 385$, $p < .001$). In these data, as was also reported in a court-records-based survey in St. Louis, Missouri with a community sample of the married (Briscoe et al., 1973), the divorced respondents had more psychological risk factors than did the married.

Although these data do suggest that the divorced were more psychologically distressed than the married, it is difficult to sort out cause and effect. Marital difficulties may precipitate a breakdown in psychological health, or psychological distress may be a cause of the marital breakdown. The most accurate way to assess this issue is to follow a group of subjects from the date of marriage to see how such events occur in the couples' marital history. Even this approach does not take into account differences that may have developed before marriage, however.

One clue in these data to the temporal ordering of events is that of the 24 mental hospitalizations reported for the divorced, over half (58.3%) occurred in the year immediately prior to the first interview. The number of these individuals who had also been hospitalized earlier as unknown; however, these data, coupled with the substantially lower number of hospitalizations that occurred within the year prior to the second interview (4 out of 159 reporting) and the year prior to the third interview (1 out of 131 reporting), suggest that the end of the marriage may have been a precipitant. In their more detailed analysis of psychological status, psychiatrists Briscoe and Smith (1973) concluded that the majority of those they studied who had affective disorders were reacting to the events surrounding the end of their marriages. But in their clinical judgment, in 40% of the cases the depressive symptoms were a cause of the divorce, not a result of it.

Risk Factor Scores

The risk factors explored thus far for divorce are summarized in Table 3.3. The data indicate that although the married and the divorced subjects lived in the same neighborhoods and had similar social class backgrounds, there were substantial differences between the two groups in characteristics that are considered risk factors for divorce. Out of 11 indicators listed, the divorced scored significantly higher than the married on 7 of them. The divorced respondents were more likely to have been divorced before, to have conceived their first child premaritally, and to differ from their spouses in ethnic identity. Compared to the married, the divorced were also less likely to have children and less likely to have considered themselves part of a religious group; even if they did belong to a religious group, they were less likely than the married to belong to the same one as their spouses. All of these factors can set the stage for marital misunderstandings, or at least may indicate that spouses lack sufficient common interests or experiences to handle the problems that can arise in marriage. The separated and divorced were also more likely to have been hospitalized for mental illness and to have made a suicide attempt. Their spouses were reported to be more likely than the married to have had

TABLE 3.3. Individual and Mean Risk Factor Scores and Scales:
Suburban Divorced and Married Samples

Risk factor items	% replying "yes"		Difference statistically significant?
	Divorced	Married	
Parental divorce by age 16 for subject	23.0	23.6	No
Parental occupations differed	73.7	75.7	No
Previous divorce for one or both spouses	30.1	20.0	Yes
Spouses' ethnic identities differed	29.0	16.1	Yes
Spouses' educational backgrounds differed	64.1	64.6	No
No religious denomination for one or both spouses	35.9	22.5	Yes
Denominational affiliation differed	49.7	26.6	Yes
Premarital conception	13.9	6.7	Yes
Married before age 20	23.4	28.7	No
No children of this union	43.1	27.3	Yes
Any psychological risk factors[a]	32.5	13.5	Yes

[a]Includes a "yes" reply to at least one of the following: suicide attempt, mental hospitalization, or problems with alcohol for respondent, or psychological problems of spouse mentioned as affecting the marriage.

health problems that affected the marriage, with many of these problems felt by the respondents to be psychological in origin.

The divorced not only scored higher than the married on 7 of the 11 characteristics examined, but they also had higher total risk scores when all of the factors were added together. Because the questions on parental divorce and ethnic identity were only asked of the divorced at the second interview when the sample was reduced in size, two scale scores each were computed for the divorced and married samples. Each of the indicators (e.g., a premarital pregnancy, any psychological risk factors, etc.) was given a score of 1. The total scores ranged from 0 to 9 for the shorter scale and from 0 to 11 for the longer scale. No respondents in either sample on either scale were without any risk factors for divorce, but the divorced had significantly higher mean scores on both the short risk factor scale (3.7 vs. 3.4 for the married; $t = 2.5$, $df = 384$, $p < .01$) and the long scale (4.1 vs. 3.7 for the married; $t = 2.8$, $df = 337$, $p < .005$).

Differences in Risk Factors by Race

Risk scores are not reported by gender here because the characteristics reported upon were those of the respondents and their spouses. There were, however, statistically significant differences by race, with whites in the divorced sample having higher mean risk factor scores than nonwhites. For whites, the mean risk score on the shorter scale was 3.7, as opposed to 3.3 for nonwhites ($t = 2.3$, $df = 207$, $p < .05$). On the longer scale, the mean risk score for whites was 4.3, compared to 3.5 for nonwhites ($t = 3.1$, $df = 159$, $p < .05$). There were no significant differences in risk scores by race for the married sample.

The fact that blacks (who constituted the bulk of the nonwhite sample here) are more likely to divorce than whites in the general population suggests one of several things about the risk factor scales. First, certain risk factors may be more important than others in producing differences in the likelihood of divorce by race. A second possibility is that although risk factors are correlated with the likelihood of divorce, divorce may be more determined by issues other than risk factors, such as economic issues. Third, the decision to divorce is a combination of such risk factors and other issues that have not been explored in this analysis. Research by Robert Hampton (1975) suggests a fourth possibility. Using data from the University of Michigan Panel Study of Economic Progress in 5,000 families, Hampton demonstrated that divorce rates for blacks were lower than those for whites when the effects of income, home ownership, and differences in family size were controlled for. These are all factors correlated with race, and when they were controlled for, blacks were 6% less likely than whites to separate or divorce. In the present suburban study, the sample was designed so that the subjects were similar to one another on almost all characteristics (a procedure similar to Hampton's statistical controls). As a result of such sampling controls, the nonwhite sample actually scored lower than the white one on the risk factors examined. Thus, in a study of divorce focused on working-class and middle-class suburban couples, nonwhites may have been less likely to divorce than whites.

Risk Scores for Marital Separations and Subjective Distress

If risk factors are cumulative in their effect, those with more risk factors may be expected to have more troubled marriages. Such troubles should be reflected in a greater likelihood of marital separations for the married, and, for the divorced, having separated prior to the separation associated with the divorce under study. Similarly, because those with higher risk scores as individuals and as couples have more incompatible statuses, which can create greater stress, higher risk scores should be associated with higher scores on psychological distress. This section explores these hypotheses with data on marital separations and subjective distress (feelings of depression and anxiety).

In the divorced sample, the respondents were asked, "Before the final separation, did you and your former husband/wife ever separate because of disagreements?" Married respondents were asked, "Have you and your husband/wife ever separated because of disagreements?" In both samples, those with higher risk factor scores were no more likely to have separated in the past than those with lower scores. Thus, having more risk factors did not create heightened discord that was manifested in marital separations. However, in both samples, high scores on the long risk factor scale were significantly associated with high subjective distress scores. The short risk factor scale was not associated with subjective distress for either the married or the divorced group.

To test the hypothesis that higher risk scores would be associated with higher distress, the risk scores were divided into low scores (scores of 3 or less) and high scores (scores of 4 or more). As anticipated, in the divorced sample, those with low scores on the long risk factor scale had a lower mean subjective distress score (1.8, as opposed to 2.7 for those with high risk factor scores; $t = 2.0$, $df = 158$, $p < .01$). Because some of the items in the long risk factor scale for the divorced were derived from data obtained at the second interview, subjective distress scores at the second interview, a year after the divorce was granted, were used. This means that the risk factors had a longer-term impact on adjustment. For the married, the mean subjective distress score for those with low risk factor scores were 1.6 and for those in the high-risk group was 2.4 ($t = 2.5$, $df = 176$, $p < .01$).

Summary of the Findings on Risk Factors

The data on risk factors support the view of the divorced as less traditional and conventional in their behaviors and as more psychologically troubled—factors that are considered part of the explanation of divorce as pathology. Even among individuals who lived in the same neighborhoods and were matched in such background characteristics as race, social class, and sex, those who divorced differed in some important ways from those who did not. The differences were more substantial than would be expected in a matched sample. From these data, however, it is not clear whether these differences were precipitants of the respondents' divorces or consequences of their failing marriages. Some factors, such as a premarital pregnancy, a previous divorce for either partner, and differences in ethnicity and religious denomination, were likely to be differences with which the couples started their relationships. Others, such as no children of the marital union and psychological problems for the respondent or spouse, may have been either factors that led to marital difficulties or decisions or reactions that resulted from marital discord. These data also illustrate the need for longitudinal studies of the married that are large enough in size and long enough in duration to be able to determine which factors in marriage are long-term irritants leading to divorce, as opposed to issues that become salient as a marriage begins to fail. The questions to be examined in the remainder of the book are these: How do characteristics such as those explored in this chapter affect the decision to divorce, and how do they affect people's ability to adjust to their divorces?

ATTITUDES ABOUT MARRIAGE AND DIVORCE: THE SUBURBAN DIVORCED AND MARRIED SAMPLES

The suburban divorced and married samples differed in risk factors that were associated with the decision to divorce. This section presents data indicating that the two groups also differed in their attitudes about marriage and divorce. These differences may have been the results of differences in exposure to the legal system, or they may represent different attitudes about the inviolability of marriage that enabled the divorced to consider dissolving their marital unions.

The married and divorced subjects in the suburban study were both told that the interviewer would "read some comments that people have made about marriage and divorce in general" (and for the divorced sample, "and about their reactions to their own divorces in particular"). Each subject was handed a response card with replies from 1 ("strongly disagree") to 5 ("strongly agree"), and was asked for his or her reactions to the statements.

Of the 10 statements displayed in Table 3.4, there were significant differences between the two groups on 6. Although both groups felt that "The main purpose of marriage is to make each partner happy," the married were significantly more likely to feel that "Couples are able to divorce far too easily today," that "Marriage is for life, even if the couple is unhappy," and that "Divorce is wrong except in the case

TABLE 3.4. Attitudes about Marriage and Divorce: Suburban Divorced and Married Samples

Attitudes about marriage and divorce[a]	Divorced		Married				
	Mean	SD	Mean	SD	t	df	p
The main purpose of marriage is to make each partner happy.	4.4	1.0	4.4	0.9	0.5	376	n.s.
Couples are able to get divorced far too easily today.	2.7	1.6	3.5	1.5	4.8	370	.001
Children are usually better off if their parents get divorced than if the parents stay together only for the children's sake.	4.1	1.2	3.3	1.5	4.9	263	.001
Marriage is for life, even if the couple is unhappy.	1.5	1.2	2.1	1.4	3.8	374	.001
Divorce is wrong except in the case of adultery.	1.5	1.1	2.1	1.4	4.6	373	.001
It is all right for a couple to decide to divorce if a marriage isn't really bad but is boring.	2.7	1.5	2.5	1.4	1.5	370	n.s.
It is all right for a couple to feel that if their marriage does not work out they can always get a divorce.	2.5	1.6	2.4	1.5	0.7	376	n.s.
The legal provisions for the division of property are fair.	2.9	1.6	2.5	1.2	2.3	272	.05
The legal provisions for alimony are fair.	2.7	1.5	2.4	1.2	1.4	289	n.s.
The legal provisions for child custody are fair.	3.5	1.4	3.0	1.2	2.8	221	.01

[a]A score of 1 indicates "strongly disagree" and a score of 5 indicates "strongly agree."

of adultery." The divorced were significantly more likely than the married to feel that "Children are usually better off if their parents get divorced than if the parents stay together only for the children's sake." These replies indicate more traditional, conservative attitudes about marriage and divorce among the married than among the divorced.

A number of subjects, especially among the married, said that they could not answer questions about the legal provisions in divorce because they just did not know enough about the subject; among those who did reply, however, the divorced respondents were significantly more likely than the married to feel that the legal provisions for the division of property were fair, as were those for child custody. There were no differences between the groups on the fairness of alimony provisions.

Differences by Race

Replies to these questions were examined by race and gender. There was only one difference by race for the divorced: Whites, with a mean score of 2.8, were significantly more likely than nonwhites, with a score of 2.2, to feel that "Couples are able to get divorced far too easily today" ($t = 2.7$, $df = 196$, $p < .001$).

Nonwhites in the married sample were significantly more likely to endorse the "happy partners" item, the "adultery as only basis for divorce" item, the "marriage . . . is boring" item, and the "if the marriage does not work out" item. The mean score for nonwhites on "happy partners" was 4.6 and for whites was 4.4 ($t = 2.0$, $df = 176$, $p < .05$). On "adultery as the only basis for divorce," the mean score for nonwhites was 2.6 and for whites was 2.0 ($t = 2.7$, $df = 173$, $p < .01$). For the "marriage . . . is boring" item, the mean score was 2.9 for nonwhites and 2.3 for whites ($t = 2.6$, $df = 174$, $p < .05$). For the "if the marriage does not work out" item, the mean score for nonwhites was 3.1 and for whites was 2.1 ($t = 4.0$, $df = 176$, $p < .001$). Because virtually all of the nonwhites in the sample were black, such attitudes may reflect the greater likelihood of direct or indirect experience with divorce in the black community. In such circumstances, even if divorce is not something a person wants for himself or herself, more reasons may become apparent and acceptable for marital breaks when divorce is more common. More generally, Norton and Moorman (1987) suggest this as a result of the increased numbers of divorces. Higher divorce rates produce a social climate in which divorce becomes more acceptable to others, who in turn divorce. The data from the divorced sample indicate that once people are separated, the differences in attitudes between whites and nonwhites decrease. In other words, if a person's attitudes are not already more open to a broader perspective on marriage and divorce, the person's own experience with divorce may change his or her attitudes.

Differences by Gender

There were a number of differences by gender in attitudes about marriage and divorce for both the married and divorced. Women in both samples generally took a more liberal attitude about divorce than did men. Among the divorced, women, with a mean of 4.5, scored significantly higher than men, with a mean of 4.3, on the "happy partners" item ($t = 2.2$, $df = 198$, $p < .05$). Women, with a mean score of 4.5, were also more likely than men, with a score of 3.6, to feel that "divorce is better for children" ($t = 4.2$, $df = 128$, $p < .001$). Women were also significantly more likely than men to feel that the laws about property, alimony, and child support were fair. For the item on property, the men's mean score was 2.6 and the women's score was 3.0 ($t = 3.0$, $df = 149$, $p < .01$); on the provisions for alimony, the mean score for men was 2.3 and for women was 3.2 ($t = -3.7$, $df = 145$, $p < .001$); and on custody, the mean score was 2.9 for men and 4.1 for women ($t = -4.9$, $df = 104$, $p < .001$). On the other hand, men, with a mean score of 1.7 compared to a score of 1.3 for women, were more likely to feel that "marriage is for life" ($t = 2.2$, $df = 198$, $p < .05$). Men, with a score of 1.7, also scored significantly more positively than women, with a score of 1.3, on the "adultery" item ($t = 2.18$, $df = 148$, $p < .05$). The generally more conservative stance that the men took may be related to the common finding that men are less likely to file for divorce than are women (Dixon & Weitzman, 1982; Goode, 1956). As a result, men may feel that divorce is imposed on them.

There were fewer significant differences by gender among the married; however, with a mean score of 3.6, women in this sample were more likely than men, with a score of 2.9, to feel that "divorce is better for children" ($t = 2.6$, $df = 133$, $p < .05$) and that the legal provisions for property division and child custody were fair. For the property question, the mean score for men was 2.8 and for women was 2.3 ($t = 2.3$, $df = 142$, $p < .05$); for the custody question, the mean score for men was 2.8 and for women was 3.4 ($t = -2.6$, $df = 115$, $p < .005$).

The married sample generally had a more conservative, traditional view of marriage, whereas the divorced respondents felt that the reasons for ending a marriage were somewhat more flexible. From these data collected at the time of filing for divorce, it is difficult to determine whether the divorced had more liberal attitudes about marriage and divorce before their marriages became troubled. The explanations advanced in explaining why risk factors make the divorced more prone to marital disruption may apply here as well. It is said that the unconventionality of the divorced, as reflected in their disregard for traditional ways of doing things, makes them feel that divorce is an option. On the other hand, the data from the nonwhite married respondents, who were likely to have had more exposure to divorce than many whites because of the high divorce rate in the black community, suggest that attitudes become less traditional as people accrue more experience with divorce. It is likely, then, that the majority of the divorced subjects at an earlier point may have resembled the married more closely in their attitudes. Data from Amato and Booth (1991b) also support this view. Using items drawn from this survey and additional ones, they found in a longitudinal study that the experience of divorce during the period of the study for the respondent, or earlier for his or her parents, led to more liberal attitudes toward divorce.

CONCLUSION

In this chapter, certain background characteristics for the divorce court-records-based samples have been examined. The samples were quite comparable in basic characteristics. The suburban divorced sample and the reconciled sample were similar in their distributions on sex, race, family social class, and the respondent's level of education. The divorced women in the county-wide marital transition study were comparable to those in the suburban divorced sample and the reconciled sample on social class and education, although there were differences on race between the marital transition sample and the women in the reconciliation study.

The suburban divorced sample has also been compared to the suburban married sample. The groups were similar in basic demographic characteristics; they did differ, however, on family income, age, number of children, and life cycle stage. Whites and nonwhites in the suburban divorced sample showed few differences. These findings, while highlighting some differences between these two groups and among the three court-records-based groups, provide greater confidence that any differences in findings among study groups that may be noted in the coming chapters are likely to be the results of the different marital statuses or of changes in attitudes and behaviors over time, not a result of the types of samples collected.

Even though the samples were successfully matched on basic background characteristics, those who divorced differed in other characteristics and behaviors from the married. Social and psychological characteristics implicated in previous studies as factors predisposing persons to divorce were also important in these samples. These included having previously been divorced, having a different ethnic identity from one's partner, belonging to no religious denomination (or, if belonging to one, having a different affiliation from one's partner), having conceived a child out of wedlock or having no children, and having one of several psychological problems. Not only did the divorced have higher scores on these individual items than the married; they also had higher scores when the items were summed. Higher scores were associated with heightened psychological distress as well. In light of the similarities in background of the two groups, the extent of the differences between the two groups was especially surprising. These data support the view that those who divorce have more characteristics or experiences that may predispose them to divorce. In addition, they marry partners with backgrounds dissimilar to themselves, who also are divorce-prone.

The divorced subjects also differed from the married subjects in having more liberal attitudes about the purpose of marriage and acceptable reasons for divorce. From these data, it is difficult to determine whether their liberal attitudes contributed to the divorce decisions or whether their experiences in going through divorce broadened their attitudes. Other longitudinal data suggest that the experience of divorce contributes to more liberal attitudes toward divorce. Chapter 4 traces some of the processes of estrangement that led to the decision to divorce.

NOTES

1. The Index of Social Position is based on the education and occupation of the marital partners. In the present research, it was modified from sole reliance on the husband's class position to take into account both the husband's and wife's positions. If the husband's social class position was higher than that of his wife, his status was used to define the family social class. If the wife's position was the higher of the two, then the family social class position was based on her status.

2. The occupational categories were as follows: (1) higher-level executives, proprietors of large concerns, major professionals; (2) business managers, proprietors of medium-sized businesses, lesser professionals; (3) administrative personnel, small independent businessmen, minor professionals; (4) clerical and sales workers, technicians, owners of little businesses; (5) skilled manual workers; (6) machine operators, semiskilled workers; and (7) unskilled employees.

3. In these samples, the main-line Protestants included American Baptists; American Lutherans; other Lutherans, denomination unspecified; the Disciples of Christ; the United Methodists; Presbyterians; other Protestants, denominations unspecified; Episcopalians; Christian Scientists; Unitarian Universalists; and members of the United Church of Christ.

4. Members of fundamentalist denominations in these samples included Southern Baptists; other unspecified Baptists; members of the African Methodist Episcopal and African Methodist Episcopal Zion churches; Missouri Synod Lutherans; Jehovah's Witnesses; and members of Holiness and Pentecostal groups and the Church of God.

CHAPTER 4

Estrangement:
The Emotional Divorce

*Old Steve was no big authority on relationships, but that morning in the
Century Plaza lobby, he left me with some words I never forgot.*
  *"Billy [a professional football player], I ain't too smart or I wouldn't
be trying to sell cork tile," he had said. "I know you play a tough sport.
You got them big, mean tackles comin' at you. But I'll tell you one thing
about life. You ain't took no lumps at all till you've tried marital discord."*

—Jenkins (1984, p. 45)

*A man whose wife was divorcing him shot her and then killed himself late
yesterday afternoon on a Regional Transit Authority bus, police said. . . .*
  *Detectives said Willie Montgomery had been served earlier this
week with a divorce action filed by his wife. . . .*
  *Mimi Williams [the woman's sister] said the Montgomerys had sepa-
rated about two years ago and contemplated divorce, but later reconciled.*

—The Plain Dealer (1987, p. B1)

The idea of ending a marriage by divorce does not generally leap
full-blown from the brows of the married, but rather develops as a
series of thoughts that grows in fits and starts into a catalogue of
slights, wrongs, and needs not met. Estrangement, or what Despert
(1962) and Bohannan (1970) have called "the emotional divorce," is
seen here as a series of stages during which at least one of the marital
partners begins to develop a feeling of alienation from the other and a
sense that the marriage is faltering, if not failing.

Reflecting upon their experiences, many divorced individuals report that this period of marital turmoil is the most distressing period of
the divorce process. The growing sense of estrangement may be
followed by efforts to repair the marriage or to handle the distress that
often accompanies the feeling of alienation. Some spouses are able to
make accommodations enabling them to continue to live together
amicably (or sometimes not so amicably); others may separate and
reconcile, only to find that things are worse or at least no better; others
proceed directly to file for divorce; still others see their marital relationships become more and more troubled; and, as the newspaper

story above details, a small number of relationships end in violent death.

This chapter explores this process of estrangement that precedes any formal steps to terminate a marriage. What are the factors that lead to alienation? Retrospective reports of the divorced, reconciled, and married respondents are used to describe the process of alienation. First, indicators of marital instability, including areas in which the divorced reported dissatisfication with their marriages, are explored; second, the timing of the decision to divorce is examined; and, third, some of the factors that may delay the divorce decision despite disappointment with the relationship are described. The data show not only the process through which those who decide to divorce go to reach their decision, but also an undercurrent of dissatisfaction with their marriages or partners among at least a minority of the married.

MARITAL STABILITY AND INSTABILITY

To explore the development of emotional distance between divorcing spouses, marital stability is treated here as a continuum. This differs from the traditional usage, in which, as Lewis and Spanier (1979) note, marital stability refers to outcome: Is a marriage intact or not? If not, has it been ended by the death of a spouse or by divorce, separation, desertion, or annulment? Although using stability as an outcome measure seems relatively straightforward, in practice it is more confusing. For example, in their review of literature on marital stability and marital quality, Lewis and Spanier (1979) state a central proposition of their theory as follows: "The greater the marital quality, the greater the marital stability" (p. 288). This statement suggests that stability, as in their usage of the term "quality," is part of a continuum from low to high; however, at another point in their discussion, they state that "Since *stability is an outcome variable*, the quality components of a marriage with low stability are considered to be the qualities at the time the relationship *terminated*" (p. 287; italics added).

It seems more useful to look at marriages as more and less stable, and then to look for indicators of the degree of their stability and satisfaction. To consider intact marriages as stable and those in which separation or divorce occur as unstable does not treat the dissolution of a marriage as a process, nor does it explore the extent to which decisions concerning marital continuity are exploratory, temporary, and often modified. By the same token, spouses who feel that their marriage is in trouble may go through a number of steps as they attempt to identify the problem and decide what to do about it. They recognize that the relationship is rocky and may need help to survive.

Instability, then, is better viewed as involving a number of different actions on the part of at least one spouse, whose conscious or unconscious intent is to assess the quality of the marital relationship and to prepare the spouse(s) for the possibility of ending the marriage. These include assessments of marital satisfaction, hesitancy about ending the marriage, and the formation of plans in case the relationship does end. Other actions include marital counseling; talking with family, friends, or a lawyer about a divorce; or actually filing for a divorce. Other work using this approach to marital instability includes that by Booth, Johnson, and Edwards (1983), Booth, Johnson, White, and Edwards (1985), and Booth and White (1980). With the high divorce rate, more and more people may be practicing "defensive marriage"— that is, hoping that their marriages will survive, but taking actions to defend and protect themselves against the possibility of dissolution. Prenuptial agreements setting out how assets will be divided in the event of a dissolution are examples of such defensive arrangements. Efforts to "hold back" and to protect oneself, although they may be realistic, may actually foster what one is hoping to avoid.

A relationship may be and remain unstable for a number of years, with one or both marital partners engaging in a number of these defensive actions without ever reaching a decision to terminate the marriage. Alternatively, a couple may move quite rapidly or slowly through the various stages to dissolution, sometimes even looping back to a period of greater satisfaction, only to restart the process later.

EMPIRICAL INDICATORS OF MARITAL INSTABILITY

Measuring marital dissatisfaction or unhappiness is difficult (Burr, 1973; Johnson, Booth, White, & Edwards, 1986; Lewis & Spanier, 1979), in part because of the widespread belief that marriage should be happy and that there is something wrong if one's own is not. It is embarrassing to admit to others that one's marriage is not all it should be. Defense mechanisms are also likely to come into play; that is, one denies difficulties about which one cannot "afford" to think. It reduces cognitive dissonance to consider one's relationship successful if it does not seem feasible or worth the emotional and social costs to end it. In the following sections, various indicators of dissatisfaction with marriage that were assessed in the Cleveland-area surveys are explored.

Role Expectations

Among the indicators of marital dissatisfaction used, divorced and married respondents in the longitudinal suburban survey were asked how well their spouses had met their expectations for various marital roles: "parent," "provider/homemaker," "sexual partner," "leisure-time companion," "someone to talk things over with," and "helpmate/partner." Replies were scored on a 5-point scale, with "very badly" equal to 1 and "very well" equal to 5. The divorced had significantly lower mean scores than the married on all of the marital roles (for all *t*-test results, $p < .0005$) and a wider range of scores, from a low of 2.2 for "someone to talk things over with" to a high of 3.5 for "sexual partner." Among the married all the mean scores were over 4, with the "parent" and "provider/homemaker" roles tied for the highest mean score (4.6). The next highest score for the married was 4.5 for the role of "sexual partner." For both the divorced and married, the areas in which expectations were least well met were "someone to talk things over with" (2.2 and 4.3, respectively), "leisure-time companion" (2.7 and 4.3), and "helpmate/partner" (2.7 and 4.4). This indicates both how difficult and problematic these roles can be in many "stable" marriages today, and, apparently, how important these roles are in either making or justifying the decision to divorce. The data support the long-standing thesis of Parsons and Bales (1955) and others (Goode, 1963; Riessman, 1990; Winch, 1971) that marriages today put enormous pressure on spouses to provide affectional support for each other—a function that is often more difficult to fulfill adequately than are instrumental marital tasks.

In this sample, as opposed to the reconciled sample (Kitson & Langlie, 1984), the marital expectation items did not produce a scale with adequate alpha reliability to permit the scores for the six items to be summed. As a result, the items are reported upon here individually. Although women in the divorced sample were significantly more disappointed in their husbands' role performance than vice versa (this was true of most roles; for *t*-test results, $p < .005$ or beyond), the ranking pattern for marital roles by gender was similar to that reported above. The roles for which expectations were least well met were "someone to talk things over with" (mean score of 2.0 for women and 2.5 for men), "helpmate/partner" (mean score of 2.4 for women and 3.0 for men), "parent" (mean score of 2.5 for women and 3.5 for men), and "leisure-time companion" (mean score of 2.5 for women and 3.0 for men). These data suggest that although women felt more strongly about the importance of these roles, both men and women were affected by them. There were no statistically significant differences by gender for the "provider/homemaker" and "sexual partner" roles. By race, there were no statistically significant differences for five of the six roles, but whites did have significantly lower mean scores for the "sexual partner" role than did nonwhites. Whites, with a mean score of 3.8, felt that their partners met their expectations less well than did nonwhites, whose mean score was 4.2 ($t = 1.9$, $df = 195$, $p < .05$).

As a second indicator of dissatisfaction, the divorced were asked, "Did your husband's/wife's behavior in any of these [marital roles] have any influence on the decision to divorce?" The married were asked, "Have any of these [marital roles] been a problem in your marriage?" Among the married, 70% said that none of the roles were a problem, and only 6.8% said that three or more were a problem. For the divorced, on the other hand, only 16.3%, said that none of these roles had influenced the decision to divorce, with 54% mentioning three or more problems. The roles that were the most influential in the divorce decision were, as above, "someone to talk things over with" (mentioned by 64.4%) and "leisure-time companion" (50.5%), followed by "helpmate/partner" (46.4%). Among the married, the most problematic areas were also "someone to talk things over with" (mentioned by 14.7%) and "leisure-time companion" (10.7%), followed by "sexual partner" (9.0%).

For the divorced, the role of "sexual partner" was less problematic than others; only 37.8% mentioned this, trailed only by "parent," mentioned by 30.3% as a problematic role. Either sexuality was seen as an instrumental activity, other roles were of much greater salience in the realm of marital problems, or respondents were less willing to indicate sexual dissatisfaction. Data from the reconciliation study support the instrumental view. When subjects in that study were asked which role expectations were best met by their partners, "provider/homemaker," with a mean of 3.8, and "sexual partner," with a mean of 3.5, received the highest scores (Kitson & Langlie, 1984).

Personal Growth

With the increasing emphasis on self-fulfillment and "doing your own thing," and with marriage seen as a place in which emotional needs will be met, individuals may also be dissatisfied if they see their partners or their marriages as a hindrance to personal growth. The divorced in the suburban sample were substantially and significantly more likely than the married to consider their marriages as alienating and as not promoting personal growth. Both groups were asked whether eight "reasons that have been given by people in describing their divorces" (or, for the married, "their marriages") were true for them. The statements included items such as "Our relationship was [is, for the married] boring; there were [are] no real 'lows' but no 'highs' either"; "Our relationship didn't [doesn't] let me and/or my spouse grow as a person"; and "When I saw [see] what other people my age were [are] doing with their lives, it made [makes] me realize that I've been missing something important." Other items (given in full in Appendix A) assessed not being ready for marital responsibilities, wanting the freedom of being single, work and friends' becoming more important than marriage, partners' interests growing apart, and the outside world's having more to offer than marriage. The questions were answered "yes" or "no."

On all eight items, the divorced were significantly more likely to answer "yes" than the married. The greatest difference between the divorced and the married was on the item "Our interests grew [have grown] further and further apart," to which 59.8% of the divorced agreed, versus only 6.2% of those in intact marriages ($\chi^2 = 119.6$, $df = 1$, $p < .001$). The divorced were more likely not only to answer positively on individual personal growth items, but also to agree with more than one item. A personal growth scale was computed by adding all the "yes" scores to the items. Only 8.6% of the divorced indicated that none of the statements characterized their marriage, as opposed to 70.7% of the married. With a mean score of 2.1 for the divorced and 0.6 for the married, the differences were highly significant ($t = 14.0$, $df = 285$, $p < .0005$). There were no significant differences in frequency of replies by gender or race among the divorced. This means that both men and women and whites and nonwhites facing a divorce were equally likely to experience a sense of alienation—a feeling that their relationships or partners did not accommodate their needs and desires, and that they were drifting away from their partners.

Role expectations for the spouse and the personal growth scale were significantly associated with each other. The higher the sense of alienation in the relationship, the lower the role expectation score, with the strongest associations between the personal growth scale and expectations for the spouse as "leisure-time companion" ($r = -.39$) and as "sexual partner" ($r = -.34$; for each, $p < .001$). These linkages again illustrate the importance of a sense of personal fulfillment in contemporary relationships.

Extramarital Sex

Although adultery has traditionally been regarded as a grounds for divorce, it may be either a cause or the result of marital estrangement.

For example, Bell, Turner, and Rosen (1975), Edwards and Booth (1976), and Glass and Wright (1977) found that extramarital sex was more likely when individuals were dissatisfied with their marriages. Furthermore, those who had been divorced were more likely to report having engaged in extramarital sex. Although the desire for other sexual partners would, for the most part, logically seem to be related to marital dissatisfaction, an individual's explaining it in these terms may also be a rationalization for socially unacceptable but desired behavior. Hunt and Hunt (1977) and Wiseman (1975) have suggested that some individuals use extramarital sexual relationships as a method of determining that they are still desirable, of building self-assurance, or of testing that alternatives to the current relationship will be available if this relationship ends. The suburban divorce data were examined to see how they fit these explanations.

At the second interview, the divorced respondents were asked whether their spouses had been involved with anyone else besides themselves during their marriages, and whether they themselves had had any extramarital involvements. Although this involvement was not specifically described as sexual, the lead-in to these questions concerned current involvement of the ex-spouse "with another woman/man"; this was followed with a query about whether the spouse was involved with this or any other person during the marriage. The context of the question and respondents' comments indicate that this question was treated as referring to sexual involvement.

Respondents reported more than twice as many affairs for their spouses as for themselves. Among those who answered "yes" or "no" (rather than "don't know") for their spouses ($n = 136$), more than half, or 52.9%, reported their spouses as having had at least one extramarital relationship. As for the respondents themselves, 21.7% ($n = 161$) reported at least one extramarital affair. This is probably an underestimate, since subjects in all types of research are less likely to report socially unacceptable behaviors for themselves than for others. In 14 couples, or 10.3% of the 136 cases with complete information, both the respondents and the spouses had had extramarital involvement.

The figures on involvements with others in the suburban longitudinal divorce survey were virtually identical to those in the countywide marital transition study. When separated and divorced women in the marital transition survey were interviewed shortly after filing for divorce, 20% ($n = 185$) said that they had been involved with another person during their marriages, and 50.3% said that their spouses had been so involved. Both sets of figures for the self in the Cleveland data are lower than those reported by Spanier and Thompson (1984) in their Centre County, Pennsylvania sample, which was partially drawn from court records. In that study, 38.5% of the male respondents ($n = 91$) and 37.8% of the female respondents ($n = 114$) said that they had engaged in "extramarital coitus," with 52.7% of the males reporting that their ex-wives had engaged in extramarital sex and 52.2% of the wives saying that their ex-husbands had been so involved.

It is difficult to determine whether the rates of extramarital involvement for the divorced in the suburban survey were higher or lower than those for the married. There was no good indicator of extramarital relationships among the married in the suburban sample. In a review of extramarital sexual behavior, Macklin (1987) cites the Kinsey reports' figures of 50% of American men (Kinsey, Pomeroy, & Martin, 1948) and 26% of women (Kinsey, Pomeroy, Martin, & Gebhard, 1953) as apparently the most reliable estimates of extramarital relationships, with the proviso that rates of extramarital sex for women aged 30 and under in 1975 were likely also to reach the 50% figure eventually (see Thompson, 1983, for similar conclusions). This suggests that the rates of extramarital sex reported in the Cleveland-area surveys are not particularly striking.

As noted above, extramarital sexual relations may be either a cause or a result of marital alienation, or the cause for one spouse and the result of other problems for the other spouse. If involvements are the result of problems in the individual or the marriage, they may be expected to have started earlier in the marriage. This view reflects the divorced respondents' reports of their own situation. To assess how long marital problems had existed, the divorced were asked, "It's hard, I know, to pinpoint this, but when would you say things started to go bad in your marriage?" The resulting figure was used to compute a percentage estimate of the proportion of a marriage that had been bad. The mean percentage of the marriage reported as bad was then compared with whether or not a subject had had any extramarital involvements. Extramaritally involved respondents reported a significantly greater percentage of their marriages as bad—a mean of 67.1%, as opposed to 56.8% for respondents who were not extramaritally involved ($t = 1.7$, $df = 148$, $p < .05$). The relationship between a spouse's reported extramarital relationships and the percentage of the marriage reported as bad was not statistically significant. This may have been a result of respondents' uncertainty about when their spouses became involved; of their lack of knowledge of such relationships; or of the use of a respondent's, not a spouse's, definition of when a relationship started to disintegrate. Given the large proportion of the marriages defined by the divorced as having been bad when affairs were started (two-thirds), these data suggest that at least for some individuals, extramarital relationships may have served as a "safety valve" or method of continuing a marriage that was in some ways unacceptable. Alternatively, with hindsight, an individual may "back-date" the time at which the marriage began to deteriorate.

Other data from the longitudinal suburban divorce study indicate that involvement with another man or woman may serve as a transition from a marriage, a way of testing desirability. Extramaritally involved subjects in this study were asked whether they were still seeing the persons with whom they were involved during their marriages. At the second interview, approximately a year after their divorce decrees were granted, the majority (61.8%) of these subjects said that they were no longer seeing the same persons. Among the remainder, three had married these persons, one respondent was engaged to the extramarital partner, and nine were still seeing these persons.

"Would You Marry the Same Person?"

Another indicator of marital dissatisfaction was the response to this question: "Knowing what you know now, if you could live your life again would you marry the same person, marry a different person, or not marry at all?" In some ways, the more interesting figure for the divorced is that 20.8% would marry the same person again, rather than that 58.5% would marry someone else and 20.8% would not marry at all ($n = 159$). Among the married, 5.6% stated that they would marry someone else, and another 8.4% reported that they would not marry at all. Thus, 14% of those currently married apparently felt that they had made a mistake ($n = 178$). Married subjects who reported at least one area of problematic role expectations in their marriages were significantly more likely to want to marry a different person (13.2% vs. 2.4% for those with no problems) or not to marry at all (15.1% vs. 5.6% of those with no problems; $(\chi^2 = 13.3, df = 2, p < .01; n = 124)$.

The misgivings of some of the married subjects were also reflected in replies to this question: "All in all, how happy has your marriage been for you?" Among the 135 married respondents who answered this question at their second interview, 5.8% reported that their marriages had been "very unhappy" or "somewhat unhappy," and another 10.4% responded "somewhat happy." These data, then, indicate an undercurrent of dissatisfaction among at least some of the married subjects.

Hesitancy to Divorce

Virtually all of the married and divorced respondents in the suburban study apparently engaged in a fairly continual assessment of the possible consequences of divorce, even if they had not actually moved to considering a divorce. The divorced at the second interview and the married respondents at the first interview were asked whether they ever thought of any of 10 reasons that might prevent or forestall a decision to divorce, such as "Getting divorced would mean a lower standard of living for me"; "I couldn't make enough money to support myself if I were divorced"; and "Because my parents' marriage wasn't very happy, I've probably tried harder in mine" (see Appendix A for the complete list of items). Almost all of the respondents in both samples mentioned having thought of at least one such negative consequence of the decision to divorce, with only 9% of the married ($n = 175$) and 6.3% of the divorced ($n = 155$) agreeing with none of these "yes" or "no" statements. These items suggest that even though divorce is more acceptable today as a solution to marital disharmony, individuals hesitate to end their relationships. They see divorce as entailing a number of social and personal costs.

The divorced mentioned significantly more reasons (a mean of 3.3) than did the married (a mean of 2.8; $t = 1.9$, $df = 328$, $p < .05$). There were, however, only three statistically significant differences in the frequency with which any of the individual reasons were mentioned in the two samples. The most frequently endorsed statement for both the married and the divorced was "I like the security of being married," with 68.7% of the divorced and 80.8% of the married agreeing with the item ($\chi^2 = 6.4$, $df = 1$, $p < .05$). The other items for which there were significant differences were "I think I expected too much from marriage" (43% of the divorced vs. 19.2% of the married; $\chi^2 = 21.7$, $df = 1$, $p < .001$) and "The alimony and child support payments my husband [I] can afford to pay aren't enough for me [my wife] to live on" (22% of the divorced vs. 9.8% of the married; $\chi^2 = 9.3$, $df = 1$, $p < .01$). It is striking that there were so few significant differences between the divorced and the married in the frequency with which individual hesitancy items were mentioned. These findings mean that thoughts about the possible impact of divorce were not uncommon among married persons who had little intention of divorcing. As a part of the continual evaluation of the viability of their marriages, apparently virtually all married persons contemplate the consequences of divorce.

Divorced women were significantly more likely to have thought of more consequences of divorce, with a mean of 3.7 versus 2.8 for men ($t = 2.7$, $df = 142$, $p < .005$). This is consistent with the data on differences in frequency of reported marital complaints by gender, to be presented in Chapter 5; women mentioned more complaints than men. There were, however, no significant differences by race in reasons for hesitating to divorce. Hesitancy to divorce and timing of the divorce were associated: The more reasons a person had for hesitating to divorce, the longer the period of time between suggesting a divorce and filing ($\tau_b = .14$, $p < .05$).

Reflecting the important role of economics and the performance of basic household tasks in marriage, respondents whose spouses met their marital role expectations as "provider/homemaker" well were significantly more likely to have mentioned a number of reasons for hesitating in their divorce decision ($r = .16$, $p < .05$). They were also significantly less likely to be hesitant about considering divorce if they felt that their spouses did not meet their expectations as "helpmate/partner" ($r = -.22$, $p < .01$). Thus, although issues of personal growth were important in evaluating marital quality, such concerns were assessed in the context of practical necessities.

Seeking Professional Help

Still another indicator of marital difficulties is turning to professionals for help with personal problems. As Kressel, Lopez-Morillas, Weinglass, and Deutsch (1978) have noted, there have been few estimates of the extent to which the divorcing seek therapeutic assistance. Although the problems for which such assistance is sought need not be psychological or involve the partner, there is generally an interpersonal component, with personal distress affecting the marital relationship and psychological distress correlated with seeking help or being willing to seek help (Gurin et al., 1960; Kessler, Brown, & Broman, 1981; Kulka, Veroff, & Douvan, 1979). Individuals may go for assistance for any number of reasons: problems with their children, work-related problems, depression, and so forth. In some cases, their problems may turn out to stem from the marital relationship or to be related to it. In a review of the literature on help seeking, Kressel (1985) reported that the separated and divorced were more likely than any other marital status group to have sought therapy.

Several indicators were used in the present research to assess the seeking of professional help. The first was the use of any professional help sources—physician; lawyer; psychiatrist or psychologist; clergyman, priest, or rabbi; marriage counselor; social worker; or other—in the past year. The second indicator was the use of mental health professionals in the past year, and the third was having sought help for "marital problems" previously.

The divorced at the first interview, or time of filing, were significantly more likely than the married to have turned to any of a number of professionals for help with problems (Table 4.1): 70.0% of the di-

TABLE 4.1. Sources of Professional Help Seen: Suburban Married and Divorced Samples

Source of professional help in year prior to interview	% reporting seeking help		
	Divorced, first interview ($n = 207$)	Divorced, third interview ($n = 132$)	Married, first interview ($n = 178$)
Any professional seen	70.0	36.4	47.8
Lawyer	51.2	18.2	16.3
Physician	18.4	6.8	31.5
Clergyman	17.9	6.8	7.9
Psychiatrist or psychologist	18.4	9.8	4.5
Marriage counselor	13.0	1.5	1.1
Social worker	6.8	6.8	3.4

Note. For the comparison of the distribution of professionals for the married and divorced at the first interview, $\chi^2 = 19.7$, $df = 1$, $p < .001$.

vorced respondents reported seeking such help in the year prior to the first interview, compared to 47.8% of the married. The divorced also saw significantly more professionals than the married—in fact, twice as many (a mean of 1.4 vs. 0.7 for the married; $t = 5.9$, $df = 382$, $p < .005$). It was not, however, specifically stated that the problems were marital when the respondents were asked whether help had been sought "during the past year" (the year prior to the divorce filing). The follow-up question for both groups about help for problems in earlier years of the marriage asked specifically about marital problems. At the second and the third interviews, the divorced were asked whether they had sought help from any of the professionals listed with "personal problems." (Unless otherwise noted, it is only the help seeking of the respondent that is being explored in this section. If he or she saw a therapist with a spouse, this is considered as help for the subject, but help sought solely by the spouse is not included unless specifically noted in the discussion.)

It seems reasonable to infer that much of this help was related to problems of the marriage, the decision to divorce, the divorce itself, or postdivorce adjustment, but this is not certain. The types of professionals used and changes in patterns of their usage across time support the assumption that divorce-associated problems were the primary causes of help seeking at the first interview. At the first interview, the divorced were significantly more likely than the married to have seen a lawyer ($\chi^2 = 51.2$, $df = 1$, $p < .001$), a clergyman ($\chi^2 = 8.4$, $df = 1$, $p < .01$), a psychiatrist or psychologist ($\chi^2 = 17.6$, $df = 1$, $p < .001$), or a marriage counselor ($\chi^2 = 19.5$, $df = 1$, $p < .001$) for help, whereas the married were more likely to have sought help from a physician for a personal problem ($\chi^2 = 8.9$, $df = 1$, $p < .01$). There were no significant differences between the groups in the proportion seeing social workers for help.

Although physicians and members of the clergy may provide advice and counsel, the most straightforward indicator of personal or interpersonal problems is a report of turning to a mental health worker (a psychiatrist or psychologist, a marriage counselor, or a social worker) for assistance. There was also a significant difference between the divorced and the married groups in seeking help from at least one such source at some point in their marriages, with 45.9% of the divorced turning to a mental health worker for help versus 12.4% of the married ($\chi^2 = 50.6$, $df = 1$, $p < .001$). Another 40.1% of the divorced reported having thought about seeking help for marital problems from some professional (mental health or other) even if they did not do so, as opposed to 12.0% of the married who reported this ($\chi^2 = 35.1$, $df = 1$, $p < .001$).

In further support of the supposition that help seeking for the divorced was related to the end of the marriage and the initial stages of the divorce process, help seeking for the divorced had decreased substantially by the third interview (2–3 years after the divorce), so that there were no longer any statistically significant differences between the married and divorced in any individual professionals seen except for physicians. The married continued to be more likely to have turned to physicians for help, with 31.5% reporting such help, as opposed to 6.8% of the divorce ($\chi^2 = 27.8$, $df = 1$, $p < .01$). In fact, by the time of the third interview, the married (as measured by help seeking at the first interview) were significantly more likely than the divorced to have sought help from a professional, with almost half having seen one versus somewhat over a third of the divorced ($\chi^2 = 4.0$, $df = 1$, $p < .05$).

The reason why the married were so much more likely than the divorced to turn to their physicians for help with personal problems is unclear. Among the possibilities are that the problems for which the married sought help may have involved their children, for whom they could obtain advice from their pediatricians. The divorced, however, might be expected to have had more behavioral problems with their children. It is also possible that the married individuals focused more on physical health problems than on psychological issues. Alternatively, a divorced individual might have felt embarrassed in talking about marital problems with the family physician, who might also have been treating the (ex-)spouse, or might have felt that a person is "supposed to" go to a mental health practitioner about divorce issues. Their physicians might also have referred them to other help sources; as a result, the respondents may not have remembered or considered this initial consultation and referral in their replies to the question. Finally, reduced finances may have made it more difficult for the divorced to seek help, from a physician or from any other professional; this would also account for their generally lower levels of help seeking compared to the married by the third interview. More data are needed on these points.

These data suggest that the divorced subjects were especially aware of personal or interpersonal difficulties and often made efforts to address them through the use of professional resources. It was not possible to determine whether the help seeking was due to psychological or social problems that in turn had an impact on the marriage, or whether it was a consequence of the wrangling, anger, and depression that are often present in a disintegrating relationship. The St. Louis, Missouri court-records-based study of divorce with a comparison sample of married subjects (discussed in Chapter 3) also sheds some light on this issue. In their study of psychopathology in marriage and divorce, psychiatrists Briscoe et al. (1973) found that 78% of the divorced women had diagnosable psychiatric illnesses, compared to 18% of the married women. Similarly, 68% of the divorced men and 34% of the married men were deemed to be clinically impaired. The figures from the suburban Cleveland study substantiate that there is more distress among the divorced than the married, as manifested by being significantly more likely to have sought professional help, to have turned to mental health workers for assistance, and to have thought about seeking help even if no help was actually sought. With the present data, the issue of psychological distress as a cause or an effect of the decision to divorce cannot be appropriately addressed; it needs to be examined in new research. The role of professional help sources as social supports is explored more fully in Chapter 9.

It is apparent from these community-based data, however, that many divorced persons do seek assistance from mental health workers and others in the period before they decide to divorce or during the divorce filing period. One of the criticisms leveled against Wallerstein and Blakeslee's (1989) book was the high level of therapy reported by the volunteer sample (Hetherington & Furstenberg, 1989). The suburban Cleveland data support the Wallerstein and Blakeslee finding in a sample based completely on divorce court records.

The Role of Therapy and Keeping Promises in Reconciliation

In the longitudinal suburban divorce study, no questions were asked about what (if any) impact therapy had on the decision to divorce, but data from the reconciled sample shed some light on this issue. With 50.4% of the reconciled seeking help from physicians, clergymen, psychiatrists or psychologists, marriage counselors, or social workers, there were no differences between the suburban divorced and the reconciled samples in the proportion of persons seeking help. However, with only 31.9% seeking help from a mental health worker (psychiatrist or psychologist, marriage counselor, or social worker), the reconciled were significantly less likely than the divorced to have sought this type of specialized help ($\chi^2 = 6.1$, $df = 1$, $p < .05$).

Whether an individual or couple sought professional help, key elements in reconciliation were making and (more importantly) keeping agreements about problem areas in the relationship. Those who had reconciled for at least a week were asked, "Before you and your husband/wife got back together [the divorce was withdrawn/dismissed], did you and he/she agree to make any changes in the way the two of you did things?" Respondents were then asked about nine areas of their relationships: work; raising the children; extramarital affairs; leisure time; alcohol, other drugs, or gambling; getting counseling; money management; gender roles (i.e., "what things you should do as a wife/husband and what your spouse should do as wife/husband"); and any other agreements that were made. Among the 119 who reconciled for at least a week, 85.7% made at least one agreement, with the average being 2.5 agreements. The most frequent of these agreements concerned gender roles (mentioned by 45.4%), use of leisure time (39.0%), and alcohol, other drug use, and gambling (29.4%).

The most important element, however, in a lasting reconciliation was not making agreements but keeping them. Seventy percent of the subjects reported that at least one of the agreements had been kept, and those who reported that the agreements had been kept were significantly more likely still to have been reconciled at the time of study (anywhere from 2 to 5½ years after filing). With dummy variables indicating separation or divorce (0) versus reconciliation (1) and agreements made and kept (0 for "no" and 1 for "yes"), making agreements was not significantly associated with having stayed reconciled ($r = -.07$), but keeping at least one of the agreements was significantly associated with continued reconciliation ($r = .27$, $p < .01$). This was true for seven of the nine individual problem areas as well; only two areas, raising the children and money management, were not significantly associated with permanent reconciliation. Therapy per se was significantly associated with making agreements for the reconciled ($r = .28$, $p < .01$), but it was not associated with keeping them. The folk saying "You can lead a horse to water, but you can't make it drink" comes to mind. Therapy may help to highlight issues or suggest steps for action, but unless a person or couple is able to make the commitment to change, the therapy may not be effective.

The importance of promises made and/or kept in reconciliation is reflected also in answers to the question "Why was the divorce withdrawn/dismissed?" The 119 subjects surveyed gave 203 answers to this question, with the most important reason being that changes or compromises had been made or promised (mentioned by 57.1% of the sample). Missing the home and children or realizing the sense of responsibility or investment that people had in their relationships was mentioned by 24.4%. Another 18.5% mentioned that their bluff had been called by the divorce action; the divorce action made them realize how much the relationship meant to them. Seventeen percent said that intervening events had made them change their minds. Thus, an inference from these reconciliation data is that in the longitudinal suburban divorce study, couples who divorced either did not make or were unable to keep the agreements that were made to attempt to repair the relationship.

Divorce Suggestion

At some point, dissatisfaction with aspects of the relationship becomes translated into suggesting a divorce as a solution to the marital problems. In the suburban divorce study, 24.2% ($n = 178$) of the currently married indicated that either they or their spouses had at one time or another suggested a divorce. The married were asked why the idea of divorce came up when it did. For the 43 who replied, 66 complaints, or an average of 1.5 complaints per person, were made. The same code was used to categorize these complaints as was used for the suburban divorced sample, although some codes were combined here. (The code is discussed more fully in Chapter 5; see also Appendix C.) The most frequent complaints were in the area of "financial and work-related problems," which were mentioned by 11 (25.6%) of the subjects. The next most frequent complaints, mentioned by 6 (14.0%, concerned "outside relationships," which included "extramarital sex" and "problems with in-laws and relatives." This was followed by three complaints, each mentioned by 5 respondents (11.6%); these were "lack of communication or understanding," "anger, jealousy, and violence," and "emotional/personality problems." As Chapter 5 indicates, these complaints were also among the reasons most frequently mentioned by the divorced for the breakup of their marriages. It is not clear what happened to change the situation so that the married couples remained together. The data from the reconciled suggest that the couples may have made some agreements to change behaviors that they were able to keep.

Both divorced men and women in the suburban study reported that wives were more likely than husbands to suggest the idea of a divorce first. Wives were twice as likely to have suggested a divorce as husbands were, with 62.8% of the women making the first suggestion, compared to 30.4% of the men; 6.8% of the suggestions were mutual ($n = 207$). Reports differed little by gender, with 60% of the men reporting that their wives first suggested a divorce and 65% of the wives saying that they themselves first suggested the divorce. Women were also more likely to suggest the divorce in the marital transition study, with 56.9% of the women reporting that they made the suggestion, compared to 28.1% who said that their spouses did; there was an increase in mutual suggestion to 14.9% ($n = 188$). Regardless of how the decision was made, study after study has now reported that women are more likely to suggest and to file for the divorce (Dixon & Weitzman, 1980; Goode, 1956; Gunter, 1977; Spanier & Thompson, 1984).

Previous Separations

The order in which steps occur on the way to divorce is not invariant, since couples choose different routes; however, Booth et al. (1985), in their predictive study of marital dissolution, found that divorce was more likely when attitudes and thoughts about ending the relationship were translated into actions. To separate from a spouse because of arguments or disagreements is one such fairly serious step. It suggests that there is so much disgust and anger with the partner that there is little energy left to try to work out the problems.

Separations in the Omnibus Marital Status Survey*

Data from the omnibus survey of marital status in Cuyahoga County, Ohio, indicate that about one in six couples reported having separated at some point in their marriages. (See also Bloom et al., 1977, for

*This section is adapted from "Marital Discord and Marital Separation: A County Survey" by G. C. Kitson, 1985, *Journal of Marriage and the Family, 47*, 693-700. Copyright 1985 by the National Council on Family Relations. Adapted by permission.

similar figures.) In this survey, a separation was defined as follows: "Did you ever separate for at least 48 hours because of arguments or disagreements and *then get back together again?*" (italics in the original). The minimum of a 2-day absence was used, to avoid the situation of a heated argument in which one spouse stormed out of the house only to return several hours later. A separation of at least 2 days was likely to mean that at least temporary alternative living arrangements had to be made.

Of the 166 separations that occurred among the 1,039 relationships reported upon, many ended in divorce (67.5%). However, a substantial number of the relationships (25.7%) continued at least until the time of the survey or else were ended by the death of one of the partners (6.8%). Thus a quarter to a third of separations occurred in continuing relationships, or at least relationships that continued until the time of the survey, as compared to two-thirds that were part of the divorce process. Over half (54.4%) of those who had separated in Cuyahoga County reported at least two separations, while 26.7% reported four or more separations. The total number of separations for the 166 persons reporting them was 456, for a mean of 2.7 and a median of 1.6. The mean length of separation for those who separated just once was 150 days, or 4.8 months; the median length of separation was 7.5 days. For those who had separated more than once, the mean length of the longest separation was 171 days (5.5 months), with the median being 30 days.

Separating from the spouse and suggesting a divorce were significantly associated. In this omnibus survey, 44.4% of those who had separated had suggested a divorce, as opposed to 5.1% of those who had not separated ($\chi^2 = 112.8$, $df = 1$, $p < .001$). In some ways, the more striking finding is that 55% of those who separated did *not* suggest a divorce. This means that separations fill other needs as well. Some separations apparently constitute a step on the way to a permanent separation or divorce, but others do not.

One possibility is that separations are less drastic actions than they appear, and instead constitute a "normal" part of generally satisfying marriages. Those who separated in the omnibus survey, however, had significantly higher rates of psychological distress and marital dissatisfaction than did those who had not separated; therefore, even though they are a normal part of marriage, they are associated with more distress. Second, some persons may remain in relationships in which separations occur because of psychological restraints (e.g., physical abuse) or structural restraints (e.g., low income or the presence of minor children). Although no data are available from this survey on the role of physical abuse in separations, other research supports such an interpretation (Hanks & Rosenbaum, 1977; Walker, 1979). In the Cuyahoga County omnibus survey, blacks, women, and those with low incomes and minor children were more likely to separate. When income and the presence of children were controlled for, the relationship between gender and separations became insignificant, suggesting that structural restraints did play a role for women. However, even with the addition of these control variables, blacks were still significantly more likely to separate than whites, so other explanations need exploring. A third possibility is that separations are used as dramatic gestures to force some action or reaction on the part of the spouse other than a decision to divorce. In this case, separations may serve as a conflict resolution technique—an effort to maintain a relationship, not a step in ending it. Threats and promises can be used as a method of attempting to resolve difficulties (Sprey, 1979).

Fourth, couples with low incomes who live in cramped quarters or who do not have occupations that provide an office to which to escape after arguments may use separations as a form of "time out" in order to cool off. In this case separations may be a way of continuing a relationship that, despite its problems, seems worth maintaining. Cohabitants who had previously divorced were subsequently more likely to separate, suggesting a fifth explanation: Some individuals who do not have other methods of coping with anger and hostility may resort to separations to handle their feelings. Such relationships, in which at least one of the partners is lacking in less dramatic communication skills, may be especially troubled. A sixth possibility is that some cohabitants may be more likely to report a history of separations because, having seen other relationships fail, they are quicker to decide that their partners are not keeping promises to change. Alternatively, some cohabitants and others may be unlucky or too dramatic in making their threats. Instead of responding with a promise to change, their partners accept the threat to end the relationship. Thus, separations may fill a number of different purposes.

Separations in the Longitudinal Suburban Study

Although separation may have occurred and divorce may have been contemplated, such actions were apparently not taken lightly and without efforts to work things out, because 44.1% of the 161 divorced respondents in the suburban study indicated at the second interview that they had separated prior to the separation that led to this divorce filing. Ten percent of those who had separated ($n = 68$) had separated five or more times, and the mean number of separations for the divorced was 2.3. In the 1985–1986 marital transition survey, 54.8%

($n = 188$) of the divorced had separated at least once prior to the separation associated with filing for the study divorce, with the mean number of separations being 2.1.

In the longitudinal suburban study, 9.6% of the married had separated from their spouses at least once. The married who reported separating from their spouses were significantly more likely than those who did not to have sought professional help with personal problems in earlier years of their marriage: 71% of those who separated sought help ($n = 17$), as opposed to 45.6% ($n = 160$) of those who had not separated ($\chi^2 = 4.8$, $df = 1$, $p < .05$).

Among the married couples who had separated, only 3 of the 17, or about a sixth, had separated two or more times. When the married subjects reported one or more areas in which marital role expectations were a problem in the marriage, they were significantly more likely to have separated at some point ($\chi^2 = 7.4$, $df = 1$, $p < .01$). Of those reporting one or more problem areas ($n = 53$), 18.9% reported a separation, compared to 5.7% of those with no problems in expectations ($n = 123$).

Fourteen percent of the divorced had filed for divorce previously in the suburban survey, whereas 2.3% of the married had done so. Similarly, 16.0% of the 188 women in the marital transition study reported a prior divorce filing. In still other indicators of the attempts couples made to keep their marriages going, 15.2% of the divorced in the suburban survey who were separated at the first interview reported that they had attempted to reconcile between the first and second interviews.

Continuum of Instability

These data illustrate that individuals go through a continuum of instability with various steps as they evaluate and re-evaluate their marriages. There is a substantial degree of similarity in the proportions of those in the 1974–1975 and 1985–1986 surveys who engaged in these behaviors. There are signs of marital instability and an exploration of alternatives before many couples decide to end their marriages. Couples generally do not move rapidly to the decision to divorce. Many persons weigh their options, seek professional help, and attempt trial separations before deciding to end their marriages. There are also apparently some couples who are unable to extricate themselves from neurotic interaction patterns and continue in relationships in which separations and reconciliations play a continuing part. It seems more useful to assess marriages in terms of such multiple indicators than in terms of a global marital satisfaction measure or a static concept of marriages as "stable" or "unstable."

Making Preparations to Divorce

Do hesitating about divorce and thinking of its social and economic consequences translate into making preparations for the divorce? At the third interview with the suburban divorced sample, the 133 respondents were asked to think back to before the divorce and indicate whether they had made any of eight preparations (e.g., "prepare for a career" or "build a nest egg") before the divorce. Of course, with hindsight, a subject might recall that there were more or fewer efforts at preparation than there really were. Nevertheless, these data are another indication of the deliberateness with which many people make the decision to divorce.

Only a quarter of the respondents indicated that they had made no preparations, with the mean number of preparations for the group being 2.1. The most commonly mentioned preparation was "learn about [my] legal rights in divorce" (mentioned by 40.2%); this was followed by "get counseling to help with the divorce decision" (34.1%), "get a job" (27.3%), "read about the experiences of other people who divorced" (24.4%), "learn about finances" (20.5%), "build a nest egg" (19.7%), "prepare for a career" (18.2%), and "learn to cook" (14.6%). The only statistically significant difference in preparations by gender was that women were more likely than men to report obtaining a job, with 41.7% of the 72 women reporting that they got a job, as opposed to 10.0% of the 60 men ($\chi^2 = 15.0$, $df = 1$, $p < .001$). There were no statistically significant differences in the total number of preparations for men or women. However, women were significantly more likely than men to make one of four financial or occupational preparations ("get a job," "build a nest egg," "learn about finances," or "prepare for a career"), with means, respectively, of 1.00 and 0.67 ($t = 1.7$, $df = 131$, $p < .05$).

These preparations were not simply normal changes or developmental steps that people made, but were divorce-related. A similar question was asked in the marital transition study; the divorced were significantly more likely than the widowed to make such preparations. In addition, widows with forewarning of their husbands' deaths were more likely to have made preparations than those without forewarning (Roach & Kitson, 1989).

In the suburban study, there was no association between the number of reasons why people hesitated to divorce and the making of financial or other preparations for the divorce. Once the situation became bad enough, caution was apparently tossed aside. The impact of these factors on the timing of the divorce decision is explored later in this chapter.

THE TIMING OF GETTING OUT

Some of the factors that individuals assessed in coming to the conclusion that there were problems in their relationships have been explored. But how bad does "bad" have to be before the decision is made to end the marriage? In this and the following sections, some of the social and individual or family characteristics that may speed up or delay the decision to divorce are examined.

Just how long does it take to disengage from the spouse? As noted above, the divorced in the suburban study were asked at the initial interview to indicate when "things started to go bad in your marriage." The mean length of time for which marriages were reported to have been bad was 4.1 years, with a median of 2.7 years and a range of less than 1 year to 29 years. The fact that virtually all respondents were able to answer the question in one way or another suggests that evaluations of marital quality are made fairly continually. One percent of the respondents indicated that things were bad even before the marriage began. For example, as one woman reported, "There was a prewedding pool party. He [the husband-to-be] embarrassed me by mentioning to everyone to look at my bust. He had no respect for me." Another 8.8% cited specific events as signs of deterioration of the relationship. For instance, one man said, "When our first son was born, she had difficulty with the pregnancy and bearing him." A woman described things as starting to go bad "Since I've been working at this job. Full-time employment started more arguments." Over 90% of the 205 subjects mentioned, at least retrospectively, a date when things started to go bad (e.g., "Four years ago, after three years of marriage," or "1968, I started to realize a lot of things"). Over 40% said that the relationship had started to deteriorate within the past 3 years, with 14.6% saying it had been bad for less than a year and 28.8% saying it had been bad for more than 1 but less than 3 years; for the remainder, however, the relationship had been declining for a longer period of time. Nineteen percent said that the relationship had been bad for more than 3 but less than 5 years, and an equal percentage said that it had been bad for more than 5 but less than 10 years. For 9.3%, the marriage had been bad for 10 or more years.

Based on the year each respondent reported that things started to deteriorate and the length of the marriage, an estimate was made of the proportion of each marriage that was bad. Slightly over half of the respondents (52.1%) retrospectively reported that over 50% of the marriage had been bad, with approximately two in five (38.9%) indicating that three-quarters to all the marriage had been bad ($n = 190$). For another 20.0%, a quarter or less of the marriage had been bad, while 27.9% reported that 26–50% of the marriage had been bad.

It was not simply that short marriages were immediately bad; some people apparently continued for long periods of time in relationships they considered unpleasant. This is illustrated by the mean length of time the marriage was felt to be bad, compared with the number of years respondents had been married. There was some inflation of the length of "badness" in this comparison, because length of a marriage in this study was defined as the number of years from the wedding until the couple's separation (or, if they had not separated, until the divorce filing), rather than the number of years from the wedding until the time of the interview. Length of badness was defined as the number of years reported from the date of the interview. Thus, marriages of less than 1 year were bad for 1.1 years. For marriages of more than 1 but less than 3 years, the mean period of badness was 1.8 years; for marriages of more than 3 but less than 5 years, it was 2.4 years; for those of more than 5 but less than 10 years, it was 4.4 years; and for those of 10 or more years, it was 8.1 years. These data indicate that a substantial number of individuals continued for relatively extended periods of time in relationships they deemed to be at least somewhat unsatisfactory.

As another indicator of the cautiousness and tentativeness of the divorce decision process, spouses generally separated before filing for divorce. Of the 183 respondents who were separated from their spouses at the time of the first interview, 64.5% had separated before filing for divorce. Twenty-eight percent had been separated at least 6 months before filing, whereas 36.6% had been separated less than 6 months. Presumably, this prefiling period was used to determine whether separation or divorce was the solution for a couple's marital problems. Another 26.8% separated from their spouses within 2 months of filing, and 8.7% did so 3 or more months after filing.

It is commonly held today that divorce has become so legally "easy" and so "ordinary" that many couples decide to divorce on a whim and rapidly terminate their marriages. The data presented above on the steps people take on the way to a divorce decision belie this perception. Those going through a divorce are quite aware of the difficulties involved and do not consider it so easy. The fact that those who have not experienced a divorce consider it an easy process, and therefore may not provide much assistance to the divorced, is a theme to which later chapters return.

CHARACTERISTICS OF TIMING OF THE DIVORCE

Speeding Up of the Divorce Process?

Even if some of the factors explored above are shown to have an impact on the time it takes to file for divorce, has the divorce process itself speeded up in the last several decades? Changes in the timing of the divorce process can be explored at least indirectly by comparing the time it took to obtain a divorce in the Cleveland suburban divorce sample of 1974-1975 and in the Cleveland marital transition sample of 1985-1986 to the time it took in William Goode's (1956) metropolitan Detroit sample of 1948. It should be kept in mind, however, that differences in the samples and the way in which questions were asked in the studies, rather than differences over time, could account for any changes observed. It will be recalled that in the Cleveland suburban study, all men and women who filed for divorce during selected months in certain suburbs were interviewed, regardless of their age or parenthood status; in the marital transition study, a sample of separated and divorced women were matched to widows by race, median income of census tract of residence, and age (approximately half of the subjects were under the age of 45 and half were over 45). By contrast, Goode only surveyed mothers aged 20 to 38. To reduce the potential impact of age, the Cleveland samples are reduced here to those women who were aged 38 or less. Goode's sample also differed from the Cleveland samples in its selection of women who had been divorced for varying lengths of time (2, 8, 14, and 26 months). He used this design to simulate a longitudinal perspective in a single interview study. Even with these differences, the two sets of data from Cleveland, collected approximately a decade apart, constitute a check on recent patterns in the timing of the divorce process.

Another difference between the studies is in the questions asked about the timing of the divorce. Goode asked his respondents, "How many months before *the filing of the suit* did **YOU YOURSELF** first seriously *consider* divorce?" and "Which of you first suggested the idea of a divorce?" (Goode, 1956, p. 358; italics and boldface type in the original). The questions asked in the Cleveland surveys differed somewhat, because some respondents in the pretest were unwilling to answer questions about the timing of the divorce based on when they themselves decided to divorce; they stated, "It's not *my* divorce—my wife [husband] wanted it." To get around this problem, respondents were first asked, "Thinking back, did you or your husband/wife first suggest the idea of divorce?" followed by "How long ago was that?" If divorce was suggested more than once, the first time it was mentioned was coded. The step of definitely deciding upon the divorce was not included. Any bias produced by the difference in question format would be in the direction of greater recency for the time period involved in the variable "serious consideration" versus "first suggestion." Therefore, the period of first suggestion to filing is treated as roughly comparable to Goode's periods of "serious consideration to decision" and "decision to filing."

With these differences in sampling and questions in mind, what (if any) differences were found in the timing of the divorce in these studies? In general, it took almost twice as long for people to move from first consideration to obtaining a divorce decree in Detroit in 1948 as it did in Cleveland in the mid-1970s. The median length of time in Detroit was 23.8 months with an estimated mean of 28.2 months, as opposed to a median of 11.0 months and a mean of 16.9 months in the Cleveland suburban sample (Table 4.2). In the Cleveland marital transition study, the median was 12.0 months and the mean 18.8 months. Even when the variation in the questions asked is taken into account, the difference in the length of the divorce process is unlikely to have resulted from a difference in the length of the prefiling period, at least in the 1948 and 1974–1975 data. Adding the median length of time from consideration to decision (4.6 months) and from decision to filing (3.2 months) would produce a median of 7.8 months for Goode's study (Table 4.3). There was less than a month's difference (0.8) between the Detroit median and the Cleveland suburban median of 7.0 months for suggestion to filing. The Cleveland marital transition study median of 11.5 months was longer than either of the others. More of these couples took a longer time to move from suggestion to filing, with close to half (48.5%) taking 13 months or longer, as opposed to 24.7% of the suburban divorced sample and 31% of the Detroit sample. It is unclear whether this is indicative of a trend toward the lengthening of the process or sample variation. These data need replication.

The more substantial difference between the samples was in the length of time between filing and obtaining the decree (Table 4.2). In the Detroit study, the median was 8.3 months (10% of the cases took 2 or more years), versus a median of 3.8 months in the Cleveland suburban sample and 4.0 months in the Cleveland marital transition sample. The differences are not simply due to differences in the length of the required legal period between filing and obtaining a decree, because Goode noted that the minimum waiting period was only 60 days in 1948. He did report, however, that few cases took so little

TABLE 4.2. Time from First Suggestion to Decree and Filing to Decree:
Metropolitan Detroit and Cleveland Suburban and Marital Transition Samples

Time (months)	Detroit (1948)[a]		Cleveland, suburban (1974–1975)[b]		Cleveland, marital transition (1985–1986)	
	Suggestion to decree	Filing to decree	Suggestion to decree	Filing to decree	Suggestion to decree	Filing to decree
0–5	6%	29%	21.5%	66.7%	13.6%	41.1%
6–11	15%	37%	30.8%	27.3%	31.8%	46.6%
12–23	30%	23%	30.8%	6.1%	25.8%	9.6%
24–35	23%	7%	3.1%	—	19.7%	2.7%
36 and over	27%	3%	13.8%	—	9.0%	—
Total	101%	99%	100%	100.1%	99.9%	100%
n	410	412	65	66	66	73
Median	23.8	8.3	11.0	4.0	12.0	5.8
Mean	28.2[c]	11.8[d]	16.9	4.6	18.8	7.0

[a]The data are from Goode (1956, pp. 137–138). Distribution of "suggestion to decree" and "filing to decree" collapsed for display. Based on when first gave serious consideration to divorce.
[b]Based on when divorce first suggested.
[c]Estimated mean with top category based on suburban divorce sample maximum of 110 months.
[d]Estimated mean with top category based on suburban divorced sample maximum of 84 months.

time to complete. In the Cleveland suburban and marital transition studies, almost two in five cases were settled within 2 months, and all were settled within less than 2 years. The differences between the Detroit and Cleveland data may have resulted in part from the greater responsiveness of the legal system and the decrease in societal reluctance to grant divorces and dissolutions by the time the 1970s Cleveland data were collected; both these factors were probably reflected in fewer legal hurdles before obtaining a decree.

Despite the differences in sampling and questions, it did take a shorter period of time to obtain a divorce in the mid-1970s and in the 1980s than it did in 1948. The differences, however, resulted not so much from a general speeding up of the personal decision process as from a shortening of the time it took to go through the legal process. Thus, couples still apparently do not decide to divorce lightly, and many take some time to reach this decision. In fact, there is some evidence from the most recent marital transition data of a lengthening of the decision process. This lengthening of the decision process may have contributed to the downturn in national divorce rates in the past decade. Once the decision to divorce is made and the legal system is entered, however, the actual granting of a decree now occurs fairly rapidly.

Demographic Differences in Timing of the Divorce

Goode (1956) found that varying amounts of delay in the divorce process were associated with race of the couple, steadiness of the husband's employment, duration of the marriage, number and ages of the children, and age of the respondent, but not with the husband's occupation or with income, religion, church attendance, or approval of the divorce decision by family and friends.

In the Cleveland suburban divorce data, there were no statistically significant associations between delays in the divorce process and the respondent's education, religion, church attendance, or family

TABLE 4.3. Time from Suggestion to Filing: Metropolitan Detroit and Cleveland Suburban and Marital Transition Samples

| Time (months) | Detroit (1949)[a] | | Cleveland, suburban (1974–1975) | Cleveland, marital transition (1985–1986) |
	Serious consideration to final decision	Final decision to filing	Suggestion to filing	Suggestion to filing
0–1	36%	31%	9.4%	7.6%
1–2	9%	18%	16.5%	7.6%
3–4	7%	12%	12.9%	19.7%
5–6	6%	13%	7.1%	7.6%
7–8	4%	3%	11.8%	3.0%
9–10	2%	2%	10.6%	3.0%
11–12	4%	10%	7.1%	3.0%
13–23	8%	5%	9.4%	19.7%
24 or more[b]	23%	5%	15.3%	28.8%
Total	99%	99%	100.1%	100.1%
n	423	423	85	165
Median	4.6	3.2	7.0	11.5
Mean	7.1	5.6	12.6	19.0

[a]The data are from Goode (1956, p. 138).
[b]Upper limit defined as 96 or more months.

social class. However, for respondents with longer marriages, respondents with children present, respondents with an increased number of children, and older respondents, the decision period was lengthened. This is indicated by the positive and significant Pearson's correlation coefficients between these variables and the length of time during which the marriage had been bad, the length of time between suggestion and filing, and the length of time between suggestion and obtaining the decree (Table 4.4). Those with lower incomes and older respondents were also more likely to have been separated for a longer time before obtaining their divorce decrees. Thus, people who were considering divorce did consider their responsibilities, such as children; their resources, such as income; their age; and the length of time they had been married in making the decision to terminate their relationships. These considerations did not necessarily prevent the divorce decision, but they did delay it.

Length of separation before obtaining the decree was also associated with race and premarital conception in the Cleveland suburban data. Nonwhites, virtually all of whom were black, took a longer period of time before obtaining the decree, as has been reported previously (Glick & Norton, 1971; Norton & Moorman, 1987). Part of this difference may have resulted from the fact that nonwhites had significantly lower incomes $(r = -.16)$. When a control was introduced for race, there was a significant association between income and length of separation before obtaining a decree, with those with low incomes taking longer $(r = .19)$.

As reported in Chapter 3, twice as many of the divorced respondents (13.9%) as of the married respondents (6.7%) had a premaritally conceived child (i.e., one whose birth date was less than 8 months from the date of the marriage). Premarital conception is thought to contribute to the likelihood of a marriage's ending in divorce, because it forces individuals to marry more rapidly than they had intended, perhaps without the educational or occupational training to provide a more economically stable marriage. Although nonwhites in the study were significantly more likely to have had a premaritally conceived child $(r = .25, p < .01)$, and were more likely to have experienced a longer period of separation, a control for race did not significantly reduce the relationship between premarital conception and length of separation before obtaining the decree. It may be that some spouses marry to give the child a name and separate fairly rapidly, but do not file for divorce immediately.

Although not as strong as the relationships with the demographic variables, there were also some statistically significant correlations between the timing variables, respondents' role expectations for their

TABLE 4.4. Pearson's Correlation Coefficients for Divorce Timing
Variables and Selected Demographic and Other Characteristics:
Suburban Divorced Sample

Characteristics	Divorce timing variables			
	Length of time marriage bad	Time between suggestion and filing	Time between suggestion and decree	Time between separation and decree
Income	.08	.04	.06	−.23**
Length of marriage	.18**	.35***	.42***	−.02
Age of respondent	.44***	.27**	.35***	.14*
Premarital conception	−.09	.01	.08	.36***
Presence of children	.29***	.22**	.22**	.11
Number of children	.47***	.33***	.38***	.04
Race	.04	.07	.09	.32***
Role expectations				
Parent	.11	−.14*	−.10	.01
Provider/homemaker	.17*	.09	.19**	.10
Sexual partner	−.17*	−.17*	−.18*	.19*
Leisure-time companion	−.14*	−.14	−.22*	.12
Someone to talk things over with	−.12	−.16*	−.18*	.08
Personal growth scale	.15*	.12	.13	−.10

*$p < .05$.
**$p < .01$.
***$p < .001$.

spouses, and the personal growth scale. When the partner was viewed
as fulfilling the "provider/homemaker" role well, the marriage was
reported to have been bad for a longer period of time, and there was a
longer period between the suggestion of divorce and the decree. Such
factors weighed heavily, then, in the decision to stay together. On the
other hand, when the more affectional aspects of the relationship were
viewed as not well met, there was a shorter waiting period. The roles
of "sexual partner," "leisure-time companion," and "someone to talk
things over with" were all negatively associated with the length of time
the marriage was bad, the time between suggestion and filing, and the
time between suggestion and decree. When the spouse was viewed as
fulfilling the "sexual partner" role well, the period between separation
and obtaining the decree was longer, as if the spouses were trying to

straighten out the other aspects of their relationship. Higher scores on the personal growth scale were also associated with a longer period of marital alienation, as indicated by a longer period for which the marriage had been bad and a longer time between suggesting the divorce and filing for it. There were no significant associations between the "helpmate/partner" role and any acceleration or delay in the divorce process. There were also no statistically significant associations between reasons for hesitating to divorce or divorce preparations and the timing variables.

These data on demographic and role expectation correlates of divorce timing illustrate that people assess a number of quite pragmatic matters in deciding whether and/or when to terminate their marriages. Despite the relatively greater frequency (and presumably, therefore, the greater acceptability) of divorce today, the length of the decision period is still affected by many of the same factors that Goode found over 40 years ago. The process seems to differ primarily in the speed with which cases are processed in the legal system once they are filed.

Gender Differences in the Timing of the Divorce?

Another area in which differences in divorce timing might be expected is that of gender. In other words, did a divorce move ahead more rapidly if the husband or the wife wanted the decree more? Since the end of World War II, there has been a substantial shift in gender role behavior in the United States—that is, in "appropriate" activities for men and women, and in the ways in which these roles and power relationships are acted out within the family. Reflecting upon these power relationships in the 1940s, Goode (1956) hypothesized that whereas wives were more likely to suggest and file for a divorce, husbands were actually more likely to be the first to want a divorce; they then consciously or unconsciously engaged in behaviors that forced their wives to suggest a divorce. Goode's data on the staging and timing of the divorce decision supported this interpretation. When the husband suggested the divorce, the median length of time from consideration to filing was 5.4 months, as opposed to 12.9 months when the wife suggested the divorce and 18.5 months when the suggestion was mutual. However, the social situation and relationships between the sexes in 1948 were different from those of today, so this finding may no longer hold true. Although Goode used reports from only one partner, the wife, to test his hypothesis, the best way to test it is with data from men and women in the same couples. But, since the hypothesis pertains to the relative status of men and women in the society, the next best way is to test it with data from male and female respondents, even if they are from different couples (as was true in the data reported upon here).

Although it was difficult in the present research to determine who initially wanted the divorce, one method involved using the length of time for which the marriage had been bad. When this was done, there were no statistically significant differences by gender in the percentage of the marriage that was reported to be bad. However, when the mean number of years the marriage had been bad was examined as compared to the percentage of "badness," men were significantly more likely than women to report that the marriage had been bad for a longer period of time. On the average, men said that their marriages had been bad for over 5.2 years, as opposed to 3.1 years for women ($t = 2.8$, $df = 185$, $p < .005$). This supports Goode's hypothesis that men are more likely to feel that the marriage has been bad for an extended period of time. How, then, does this become translated into the decision to divorce?

Goode (1956) suggested that men might play a more important role in the divorce process than women for several reasons. First, males were in the dominant position in the society and family, and therefore assumed the right to make major decisions. Second, their work required or allowed them to be away from home without as much question as was the case for women. They also generally had less interest in the home and were therefore more easily drawn into other activities. Furthermore, men had greater freedom to be away from the home for leisure-time activities as well as for work, because women assumed the bulk of household and child care activities. The husband, then, because of his greater power and freedom of movement, might engage (either consciously or unconsciously) in behaviors that would eventually force his wife beyond her limits of endurance and lead her into suggesting and filing for the divorce.

As described earlier in this chapter, wives in the suburban divorced sample were more likely to have first suggested the idea of a divorce. When the respondents were asked who insisted on the divorce, the proportions differed by gender, with more males than females reporting that the decision was mutual (20.4% vs. 11.5%, respectively). This may have been a face-saving device, or the males may have more aggressively pursued the goal they wanted all along once the issue had been broached.

In the Cleveland suburban data, there were no statistically significant differences in the mean length of the decision period by the partner who suggested the divorce or by gender of the respondent. When mutual suggesters were removed from the analysis and gender was treated as a dummy variable, there were still no significant differences. The relationships were not affected by controls for age, presence of children, or race; nor did the religion and church attendance of the suggester affect the relationship. So far, other than the finding that males reported that their marriages had been bad for a longer period of time than did females, the present data do not support Goode's hypothesis of greater male power in the divorce process. Next, data relating to Goode's other tests of his argument are explored.

Goode felt that because of the pressures of their positions and the expectations of their friends and family, higher-status husbands had a smaller range of socially acceptable behaviors that they could employ to force their wives into filing for divorce. As a result, he expected that the higher the husband's status, the greater the proportion of males who would suggest divorce and the greater the proportion of mutual suggestions. Although the differences by social class position of the husbands in the suburban data were in the direction hypothesized by Goode, they were, as he also found, *not* statistically significant, and are therefore not displayed. Higher-status males were not substantially more likely than their lower-status counterparts to suggest the divorce first or to make a mutual suggestion.

Goode (1956) went on to a further test of the husband's "greater choice and control in the strategy of divorce" (p. 147) by exploring the relative educational status of the two spouses. He felt that education might intensify the impact of the cultural differences in divorce power for the two sexes. In this test, he reasoned that when the education of the spouses differed, the proportion of wives who first suggested the divorce would be in conformity with the education of their spouses. Given their more limited range of socially acceptable behaviors, more highly educated husbands would be forced into suggesting the divorce first and into mutual suggestions. His data supported this interpretation, but the Cleveland suburban data did not: Although the proportions of husbands suggesting divorce and of mutual suggestions were higher at higher levels of education, the proportions did not steadily decrease with lower levels of education. An exception to the pattern was that when a woman "married down" (i.e., married a male with less education than she had), this action apparently increased his relative power, giving him greater power in the divorce process. In this case, 39.2% of the husbands suggested the divorce, the highest percentage doing so. Thus, these data, and those of Spanier and Thompson (1984) as well, do not support Goode's hypothesis of greater power for the male in the divorce decision.

CONCLUSION

This analysis of the process of estrangement leading to the divorce decision indicates that in the late 1940s and the mid-1970s, the median length of time for one or both marital partners to come to the decision to divorce was a little more than half a year. In the mid-1980s, it was closer to a full year. Despite the greater rapidity with which decrees were granted after the divorce was filed, the decision period itself was not much shorter than it was when William Goode collected data on the timing of the divorce decision over 40 years ago. In fact, there is some evidence that the decision period has been lengthening in recent years. Despite the growing feeling that couples divorce on a whim, these data suggest that individuals make a number of efforts to assess just how bad their relationships are and what can be done about them, including seeking counseling and trial separations before they decide to divorce. These data raise questions (which are addressed in the following chapters) about what it does to health status to live in a situation in which the relationship is not necessarily going well, but in which, for whatever reasons, the partners have not yet decided to end the marriage.

If the decision process is examined in terms of the rewards and costs of the exchange model of marriage and divorce, it can be seen that individuals contemplating divorce do attempt to weigh the negatives and positives of their marriages and the alternatives available. They assess costs such as the importance of a number of reasons for hesitancy in the divorce decision—the partners' ages, the length of the marriage, the responsibility for children, and the need to make preparations for living on one's own. They also assess marital rewards such as family income, the extent to which the spouse has lived up to expectations for marital roles, the personal growth and freedom the marriage has allowed, and the availability of alternative partners.

Although the women interviewed generally reported greater concerns about the consequences of the divorce, as indicated by more hesitancy and more financial and career preparations than the men, they also were more upset about how well their spouses met their marital role expectations. This was particularly true for the roles of "someone to talk things over with," "leisure-time companion," and "helpmate/partner." The importance of these roles reflects the increased importance of the affectional and supportive dimensions of the marital relationship, at least among suburban couples. As gender roles continue to change, these dimensions are also given more emphasis as the foundation for relationships. The data illustrate that the institutional power of husbands in manipulating their wives into filing seems to have lessened in the past quarter of a century. Husbands who are unhappy with their marriages are apparently less able today to force their wives into filing than was the case in the post-World War II period. By the same token, women seem to be less likely to feel that they have to stay in unacceptable relationships because they have few economic or social alternatives. As will be seen, being on one's own is not without its economic perils, but many women with more educational and employment experience apparently feel more competent to face these uncertainties today than was the case in the late 1940s.

CHAPTER 5

The Causes of Divorce

*[R]epresentative Pat Swindall, a freshman Republican from Georgia . . .
told the story of what he says was one of the last cases he encountered
before leaving his law practice to come to the House.*

His story went this way:

*"There was a lady that came to my office who wanted a divorce,
but before I talked with her about the divorce I decided that it might be
helpful if I found out if she had grounds for divorce."*

*"So I asked her if in fact she had grounds, and she looked at me and
said, "Yes, as a matter of fact, about an acre and a half."*

*"I looked at her and I said, 'Perhaps I am not communicating well. Let
me try again.' I then asked her if she had a grudge, and she looked and she
said, no, she did not have a grudge but she did have a double carport."*

*"I said, 'Let me try this one more time a little bit more to the point.' I
said, 'Does your husband beat you up in the morning?' She said, 'No.
Generally I get up earlier than he does.'*

*"At that point I began to recognize I was going to have to try a
different tack entirely, and I said, 'Ma'am, let me ask you, are you sure
you really want a divorce?"*

*"She said, 'No. Actually I don't want a divorce at all. It's my husband
who wants a divorce. He contends that we have difficulty communicating."*

—The New York Times (1985, p. A30)

The term "causes of divorce" has a number of meanings. First, there
are societal-level explanations—the kinds of broad social changes
(such as the shift from agrarian to industrial, urban, bureaucratic life)
that have been discussed in Chapter 1. A second meaning of the term
is the legal grounds for divorce—the situations society views as legally
acceptable reasons for ending marriage. The third meaning is correlates of divorce—social and psychological factors that have been
found by outside observers to be associated with a greater likelihood
of divorce. A fourth meaning is what those going through a divorce
themselves see as the causes of the breakdown of their marriage—their
self-described marital complaints. These four definitions of the term
"causes of divorce" do not necessarily coincide. This chapter examines
data on the legal, correlational, and marital complaints approaches to
the term "causes of divorce."

LEGAL CAUSES OF DIVORCE:
SHIFTS IN DIVORCE PRACTICE

As noted in Chapter 2, until May 1974 Ohio had a fault-based system of divorce, in which a plaintiff claiming innocence of any wrongdoing sued his or her partner, the defendant, for divorce on the basis of at least 1 of 10 legally admissible grounds, or reasons for ending a marriage. Like virtually all the other states in the mid-1970s, Ohio shifted to a less restrictive approach to divorce. In May 1974, a "no-fault" provision was added, in which a couple could be divorced without any other grounds than that they had not cohabited for 2 years. On September 23, 1974, a third category was added: "dissolution of marriage." Under this provision, the guilt or innocence of the marital partners does not have to be proven. As in the breaking of a civil contract, the spouses agree to the dissolution of their marriage and make arrangements for the division of property, custody of and visitation for the children, alimony, and child support. They then sign a separation agreement, which becomes final in 30 days, at which point the marriage is "dissolved." States have adopted different terminologies for fault-based and no-fault divorces, but the basic distinction is that between the use of legal grounds to dissolve a marriage and a no-fault dissolution in which both partners agree to end the relationship.

By design, 3 of the 4 months sampled in the suburban divorce study fell into the period after dissolution of marriage was added. Even with the addition of the no-fault and dissolution provisions, about two-thirds of the cases filed in the suburban divorce study used at least 1 of the 10 legally admissible grounds. Approximately a quarter used the provision of dissolution of marriage, with 6% using the provision of living apart. To some extent, this may have been the result of slowness on the part of lawyers in shifting to the newer grounds. This pattern still continued at the end of the decade. Combining 1978 and 1979 Ohio court data, Sterin and Davis with McGraw (1981) reported that only 23.3% of the cases in Cuyahoga County were filed as dissolutions. This was lower than the proportion of dissolutions for the state as a whole, which in the comparable period of 1978 totaled 48.5%. In 1985–1986, in the county-wide marital transition survey, the number was substantially greater: 66.3% of the filings were dissolutions. Thus, with increased exposure to the no-fault provisions, lawyers in the mid-1980s finally began to use the provision of dissolution more frequently.

For the 67.8% ($N = 572$) of the fault-based divorce cases in the total suburban sample eligible for study, only 5 of the 10 legally acceptable grounds for divorce in Ohio were used, and only 2 ("gross neglect of duty" and "extreme cruelty") were mentioned frequently.

Of the 681 grounds mentioned, or a mean of 1.8 for the 388 fault-based divorces, "gross neglect of duty" was mentioned by 19 out of every 20 plaintiffs (96.4%), and "extreme cruelty" by almost three-quarters of all the subjects (72.4%). These grounds were trailed by those mentioned by only a handful of individuals: "willful absence of the defendant for one year" (5.2%), "adultery" (1.5%), and "habitual drunkeness" (0.3%). (The grounds do not total 100% because of multiple mentions.) None of the remaining legal grounds were used: "bigamy," "impotence," "fraudulent contract," "imprisonment," and "procurement of a divorce in another state by virtue of which the party who procured it is released from the obligations of the marriage, while such obligations remain binding on the other party." With the majority of those using legal grounds mentioning just two, these data illustrate that the grounds used in fault-based divorces are often used in such a way as to produce the equivalent of uncontested divorces. As law professor Herma Hill Kay (1970) noted in commenting upon the fact that 95% of California divorces in 1966 were granted on the grounds of "extreme cruelty," "The California situation thus illustrates the wide gulf that exists between theory and practice in the divorce area" (p. 227).

The almost complete unanimity of legal grounds used in filing for divorce prevents their use for any meaningful analysis of factors that actually produced breaks in relationships. Divorced respondents were aware of this difference between their legal escape route and their marital situation, as one male respondent in the suburban study said in response to the question "What caused your marriage to break up?":

> "That all depends on what you mean. By the book, mental cruelty. Nothing really, we just didn't get along. Nothing specific. Basically, I was so wrapped up in school and work, going to college full-time and working full-time. She felt no need to be married with the type of life we were leading. Communicating was very difficult because of so little time together."

CORRELATES OF DIVORCE*

A second meaning of the term "causes of divorce" is correlates of divorce—social and psychological risk factors that have been found by researchers to be associated with greater likelihood of divorce. Many

*Portions of this and the following section are adapted from "Marital Complaints, Demographic Characteristics, and Symptoms of Mental Distress in Divorce" by G. C. Kitson and M. B. Sussman, 1982, *Journal of Marriage and the Family*, 44, 87–101. Copyright 1982 by the National Council on Family Relations. Adapted by permission.

of these factors have been reviewed in Chapter 3; this chapter explores whether or how these factors are associated with marital complaints. As the data presented in Chapter 3 indicate, such correlates may serve as predictors of the increased likelihood of divorce, but they do not in and of themselves foster an understanding of why couples divorce. What is it about low income or lack of education that increases the likelihood of divorce? Hypotheses have been advanced about the mechanisms through which such correlates or risk factors lead to divorce. However, these have rarely been tested, in part because studies of divorce correlates have often been by-products of research on other topics, in which the perceptions of those going through a divorce have not been explored. Instead, the demographic characteristics of those who divorced have been examined, and comparisons have been made between the characteristics of the married and divorced.

Each method of exploring the cause of divorce produces a different perspective on the issue. For example, as noted earlier, several studies have reported that premarital pregnancy is associated with divorce. Although, as reported in Chapter 3, significantly more of the divorced than of the married respondents in the suburban study were premaritally pregnant, only 1% of the divorced respondents specifically mentioned premarital pregnancy as a cause of their divorces, as noted below. Some of the factors related to premarital pregnancy—immaturity, financial and employment problems, marrying too young—were mentioned; however, no factor occurred in the factor analysis of marital complaints that reflected this cluster of items regarding premarital pregnancy. The event itself either was not central to the thinking of the respondents or was an issue that some were unwilling to discuss. It may also be difficult for a parent to fault the timing of his or her child's arrival when the child, regardless of when he or she was conceived, is cherished. This raises questions about a number of other variables that have been found to be correlated with the decision to divorce. It is not clear what these variables are measuring and what their meaning is for the person experiencing the divorce. If there is a relationship between risk factors and marital complaints, then certain types of risk factors should be associated with certain types of marital complaints.

MARITAL COMPLAINTS: THE PERSPECTIVE
OF DIVORCED PERSONS

This leads to the final meaning of the term "causes of divorce"—the issues that the marital partners themselves view as the reasons for the divorce. Few studies have examined the causes of divorce as perceived by the divorcing participants. In his 1948 study, William Goode (1956) found that the types of marital complaints divorced women made varied by social class, length of marriage, and rural versus urban origin. Levinger (1966) corroborated the presence of social class differences in a study of the marital complaints that divorcing couples with minor children gave to marriage counselors during court-required predivorce interviews. He found that lower-class respondents were more likely to mention failure to perform instrumental family tasks because of inadequate financial resources, excessive drinking, or physical abuse. In the middle class, the problems mentioned focused less on tasks and more on affective relationships (e.g., complaints of lack of love, infidelity, and excessive demands). Levinger also found that women made more complaints than men and were more likely to complain of "mental cruelty." Men, while also mentioning lack of love and neglect, were more likely to complain about in-law problems or sexual incompatibility. The relationships between marital complaints and such factors are examined here to see whether they are correlated as Levinger found.

Variables Correlated with Marital Complaints

In 1948, when Goode gathered his data, the refined U.S. divorce rate was 11.2 per 1,000 married females; by contrast, the rate was 19.3 in 1974, when the suburban divorce research reported upon here was begun (U.S. Bureau of the Census, 1975, 1976). As the frequency of divorce increased, divorce laws were revised to reflect changing social attitudes about gender roles, marriage, and divorce. As a result, the kinds of complaints people made to "explain" the breakup of their marriages should differ from those made in earlier years. With the acknowledgment that any difference found in complaints may be due partly to sampling variations, interviewing bias, or other causes, the suburban divorce data are compared to Goode's 1948 findings in order to explore any differences in types or frequency of complaints. Marital complaints from the 1985–1986 marital transition survey are also examined, to see how these complaints compare to those made in 1974–1975. The differences in complaints between the two periods are likely to be slight. In addition, differences in demographic characteristics on the "instrumental" versus "expressive" dimension of complaints are likely to be found. The types of complaints made are also likely to be related to people's place in the life cycle and social structure.

Relatively little research has examined differences or similarities in marital complaints by race. When race is discussed, it is generally in terms of the greater likelihood of divorce among blacks as compared to whites. Economic factors, such as income, unemployment, and underemployment, have been implicated in a number of studies as factors accounting for the high divorce rate among blacks (Bishop, 1980; Cherlin, 1981; Crain & Weisman, 1972), so it may well be that complaints related to economic issues are more common among blacks.

Another issue is the relationship between the perceived causes of the divorce and its consequences for the respondent's mental health status. As discussed earlier, numerous studies have shown that the divorced have higher rates of physical and mental health disturbance than the married. The reasons for these differences are less clear (for reviews of explanations, see Bachrach, 1975; Bloom et al., 1978; Kitson et al., 1985; Kitson & Raschke, 1981; Segraves, 1982; Somers, 1979). With two out of three divorced persons remarrying (Norton, 1991), cross-sectional surveys of marital and health status may in part be reporting the heightened distress of the recently separated and divorced, rather than long-term effects. Distress may also vary among the divorced according to the reasons for the marital breakup. Relatively little is known about the relationship between the reasons for the breakup and the health consequences for the divorcing person. Robert Weiss (1975) has suggested that as people struggle to make sense of the breakup of their marriages, they fashion their marital complaints into "accounts"—"a history of the marital failure, a story of what their spouse did and what they did and what happened in consequence" (p. 14). The level of emotional turmoil is likely to be high and to produce symptoms of distress until individuals are able to develop their accounts. Some reduction in distress should ensue as explanations are formulated.

Rasmussen and Ferraro (1979) argue that the major causes of divorce are a couple's long-standing marital problems, which become the justification for the failure of the relationship when one or the other partner wants out of the marriage. If Rasmussen and Ferraro are correct, complaints should have little impact on adjustment. Individuals will have lived with the problems for years and presumably will have adapted with greater or lesser ease. However, if complaints reflect unpleasant conditions in a disintegrating relationship or constitute "the straw that broke the camel's back," thus precipitating the break, they may have differential impact on mental health, depending on the complaint. For example, Robert Winch (1971) hypothesized that the more frustrating the interaction with the marital partner, the greater the relief a spouse would feel at the end of the relationship. The consequence of this should be less disturbance in health. In the postdivorce period, the health of the former marital partners may actually improve over what it was during the later stages of a frustrating marriage.

Both Winch (1971) and Weiss (1975) suggest that a partner who feels "responsible" for ending a marriage because he or she is no longer able to bear the spouse's failings (e.g., alcoholism or mental illness) will feel guilty and remorseful about the decision. These feelings in turn may manifest themselves in symptoms of health disturbance. According to Weiss (1975), the complaint with probably the most devastating impact on the individual's sense of self-worth is discovering that the spouse has been unfaithful. Other types of marital complaints may produce neither gratification nor frustration but simply indifference, signaling the accumulated debris of the ending marriage. Such complaints may show little relationship to health status.

Do people's perceptions of the reasons for their divorces remain the same or change over time? There has been little discussion in the literature of changes in marital complaints as time passes from separation. It is possible, however, that the reasons people originally gave for their divorces will change as tempers cool and the partners have time to reflect on the reasons for the marital breakdown. In fact, as part of separation and divorce therapy, marriage counselors work to rephrase the decision to divorce into an issue of joint responsibility rather than the result of "his" or "her" problems (Kaslow, 1981). Thus, some changes in perceptions of the reasons and responsibility for the breakup may be expected as time passes from the decision to divorce.

The hypotheses to be explored in the remainder of this chapter may be summarized as follows. First, divorcing men and women should make different types of marital complaints about the reasons for the failure of their marriages. Second, complaints should vary by race, with nonwhites more likely to make complaints about economic issues. Third, changes in social attitudes and conditions suggest that the types of marital complaints made in the 1970s should differ from those made in the 1940s, whereas complaints made in the 1980s are likely to be similar to those in the 1970s. Fourth, marital complaints should be associated with demographic characteristics, such as social class, education, income, number of years married, age, parental divorce, and premarital pregnancy. Fifth, the types of marital complaints individuals mention should have differing impact on their mental health, both at first and across time. Marital complaints that reflect uncertainty about the reasons for the breakup or center on failings of the other partner should be more strongly associated with mental health distress or illness contacts. Complaints identified as irritants or frustrations should be associated with an increased sense of well-being and fewer symptoms of health disturbance. Finally, the question of whether persons going through a divorce continue to report the same marital complaints all through the divorce process, or whether with reflection and hindsight their perceptions begin to change, is explored; the latter should be the case.

The Marital Complaint Measures

The question used to develop the measure of marital complaints for the suburban study was "What caused your marriage to break up?" All replies were coded using two different methods. First, the code developed by Goode (1956, pp. 113–123) in his study of Detroit women's adjustment to divorce was used. In this code, each complaint is coded as present or absent. There are 12 descriptive categories and a 13th called "miscellaneous." Goode's "miscellaneous" category was divided into its component parts, and another category "other complaints not mentioned in the Goode code" was added, making a total of 17 complaint categories.

As a result of the difficulty in using Goode's approach to code all the complaints mentioned in the 1970s, a second code was developed in which space was allocated for mention of as many as 10 complaints per individual (only one respondent, as it turned out, made this many complaints). Replies were summed to produce frequencies of mention for each of the complaints. For each of the codes, complaints were coded 0 if not mentioned and 1 if mentioned. (See Appendix C for the marital complaints code used for the Cleveland suburban divorce study and the marital transition study.)

Replies to all questions in the survey were coded twice by two coders, and any differences between the codes were reconciled. The intercoder reliability was 91% for the Goode code and 84% for the Cleveland code. Reliability for the second code was lower because coders made finer distinctions. The way in which the two codes were used is illustrated by the reply of a woman enrolled in a graduate program:

> "Well . . . (*respondent lights cigarette*), that question would take about 3 years to answer. We got married very young, both of us. We had known each other since the ninth grade. We got each other through school and into a stable employment situation. We both got to feeling that we were missing out on experiencing other things, not only with the opposite sex, although this was a factor. We felt we were inhibiting each other in certain ways. In particular, there is the fact that I am challenging the traditional wife role by going on

to get a degree. Even though he was supportive of me, it was a threat to him. We both used to do the cooking, and then when I started to school, I would be too tired to cook. The structure of our relationship had to change, and he wasn't willing to change. I don't feel this is a tragic event, I feel this is a move ahead."

This statement was coded as including three complaints from the Goode code and four from the Cleveland code. The three used from the Goode code were "personality," "authority," and "value conflict." "Personality" is coded as a complaint when comments reflect the respondent's "belief that the fundamental problems was one of personality, including comments such as 'He was emotionally immature.' 'Neither of us were ready to get married—our personalities clashed.' 'Change in my husband's attitude and personality after being overseas in the war'" (Goode, 1956, p. 123). "Authority" is defined as follows: "[T]he wives were not allowed to run things in their own way or to make decisions as they chose, and instead had to cater to their husbands' wishes" (Goode, 1956, p. 121). The third code used was "value conflict," defined as follows: The spouse "may have had a strong interest in the home, but different views of what was right, good, beautiful, etc." from those of his or her partner (Goode, 1956, p. 121).

According to the Cleveland marital complaint code, which was expanded to capture contemporary marital issues and problems, four complaints were noted for the graduate student: "too young at time of marriage," including a feeling that the couple was not ready for marriage and had missed out on things; "conflict within the individual," including a desire for freedom, independence, and a life of one's own (this complaint category also included complaints concerning women's liberation, desires to be single again, unhappiness with the marital role, a sense of being stifled by the marriage, and boredom in the relationship); "joint conflict over roles," including disagreements over appropriate roles for husbands and wives, gender role conflict, authoritarianism, controlling and manipulative behavior, and being judgmental or too paternal or maternal; and "inflexible; stubborn," including an unwillingness to accept change.

Table 5.1 displays the frequency distribution of marital complaints from the Goode code and the distribution of replies by gender. The most frequently mentioned complaints in the suburban sample according to the Goode code were "personality," "home life" (meaning lack of interest in the home, children, or marital partner), "values," "other complaints" (not covered in the Goode code), and "authority." Complaints in Goode's "miscellaneous" category were mentioned by 20.2% of the respondents in the suburban study, as opposed to 12% in Goode's.

TABLE 5.1. Percentages, Rankings, and Kendall's Tau$_b$'s for the Goode
Marital Complaint Code by Gender: Suburban Cleveland Sample

| Goode marital complaint categories | Mentions of the complaint by gender | | | | τ_b (1 = male, 2 = female) |
| | Female | | Male | | |
	%	(Rank)	%	(Rank)	
Personality	57.0	(1)	45.5	(2)	.12*
Home life	41.6	(2)	42.0	(3)	−.01
Values	41.1	(3)	41.0	(4)	.01
Authority	31.8	(5)	21.0	(6)	.13*
Other complaints	37.4	(4)	46.5	(1)	−.09
Drinking	22.4	(6)	7.0	(9)	.22***
Complex[a]	19.6	(7)	6.0	(10)	.20**
Miscellaneous	19.0	(8)	22.0	(5)	—
Sex problems	11.2		5.0		.11*
Extramarital sex, wife	1.9		10.9		−.19**
Felonies	3.7		1.0		.01
Physical defects	0.9		3.0		−.07
Forced marriage	0.9		2.0		−.04
Nonsupport[b]	16.8	(9)	4.0	(12)	.21***
Extramarital sex, husband	15.9	(10)	3.0	(10)	.22**
Consumption[c]	15.9	(10)	7.9	(8)	.12*
Relatives	8.4	(12)	16.8	(7)	−.13*
Desertion	4.7	(13)	4.0	(11)	.02
(n)	(107)		(101)		(208)
(Mean number of complaints	(3.21)		(2.55)		

[a]"Complex" includes "running around" or "other women/men" (but not a specific
person), or two of the following complaints: "staying away," "drinking," "gambling,"
"out with the boys/girls."
[b]"Nonsupport" includes the complaint that the spouse was not an adequate provider for
the needs of the family, did not work, or did not bring home his or her paycheck.
[c]"Consumption" includes complaints concerning the management of money, either
because the spouse "threw money around," was wasteful, or gambled.
  *$p < .05$.
  **$p < .01$.
  ***$p < .001$.

Factor Analysis of Complaints

The responses for the marital complaint code developed for the
Cleveland suburban study were factor-analyzed to determine whether
commonly occurring patterns of marital complaints would emerge.
Just as there are demographic correlates of divorce, it was expected
that there would be identifiable patterns in marital complaints across

marriages. An orthogonal solution with an equimax rotation was used, because it produced the most parsimonious set of factors while minimizing their overlap. Because of its large size, the correlation matrix is not displayed. Relatively few of the correlations were over .20, indicating that the relationships between the complaints were not very strong. The 1985–1986 data were also factor-analyzed with similar results. These findings indicate that although certain kinds of complaints are quite common, couples produce their own idiosyncratic mixes of complaints. Bloom, Niles, and Tatcher (1985), in a convenience sample of newly separated persons, also found that marital complaints were quite individual and uncorrelated. As a result, it is difficult to develop profiles of complaints.

The seven strongest factors in the suburban study—all with eigenvalues larger than 1.9—were used in the analysis. These factors accounted for 28% of the total variance (Table 5.2). Only those items with coefficients of .25 or higher were used in constructing the factors. Each factor has been named for its strongest coefficient or for a common set of problems running through it. Although these factors do not necessarily represent frequent patterns of marital complaints within the sample, they are statistically significant sets of complaints highly related to the decision to file for divorce. Perhaps the most interesting of these is Factor 3, Physical and Psychological Abuse. The items in this cluster ("disagreements over friends," "disapproval of type of spouse's employment," and "actual physical abuse") reflect many of the conditions described in the literature on family violence (Walker, 1979).

The most frequently mentioned complaints according to the Cleveland code were "lack of communication or understanding" and "joint conflict over roles" (Table 5.3). (Only the more frequently mentioned of the 31 complaints are displayed, but the complaints are rank-ordered on the basis of the full distribution.) This is followed by "not sure what happened" with an attempted explanation. This code was developed because such uncertain statements seemed to come up often. The replies of two male respondents illustrate this phenomenon:

"I don't know. (*Pause*) It was strange. She said I wasn't paying her enough attention. I was in the Army; I'd come home, eat; I was tired and go to bed. She had insomnia and might be up all night while I slept. In the morning. I'd get up and go to work while she was asleep. It's a mystery to me."

"That's a good question. I really don't know. A lot of it was my discontent with the situation. [Query: What situation?] She was

TABLE 5.2. Factor Score Coefficients for Marital Complaint Factors:
The Cleveland Marital Complaint Code

Items in factors	Factor score coefficients[a]
Factor 1: Conflicts over the Children	
Disagreements over child rearing and discipline	.299
Jealousy or dislike of child(ren)	*.645*
Concern over effect of discord on the child(ren)	.071
Factor 2: Sexual Problems Due to Health	
Using spouse; demanding	.170
Drugs (cocaine, marijuana, heroin, etc.)	.153
Sexual problems due to health	*.736*
Factor 3: Physical and Psychological Abuse	
Disapproval of type of spouse's employment	.306
Actual physical abuse	.197
Disagreements over friends	*.607*
Factor 4: Gambling and Criminal Activities	
Gambling	.282
Other, anger, jealousy	.179
Criminal activities	*.561*
Factor 5: Generalized Discontent	
Sexual problems due to health	.231
Other, finances, work	*.446*
Other, anger, jealousy	.208
Disagreements over having child(ren)	.213
Disagreements over friends	.188
Factor 6: Financial and Employment Problems	
Sexual incompatibility	.189
Financially irresponsible	*.267*
Disagreements over money	.103
Not a good provider	.210
Unemployment; sporadic employment	*.271*
Health problems	.166
Actual physical abuse	.106
Factor 7: Internal Gender Role Conflict	
Conflict within the individual	*.546*
Other, outside relationships	.228
Disapproval of type of spouse's employment	.153

[a]Scores used to compute each factor are italicized.

TABLE 5.3. Percentages, Rankings, and Kendall's Tau$_b$'s for Associations between the Cleveland Marital Complaint Code and Gender: Suburban Divorced Sample

Cleveland marital complaint categories	Mention of the complaint by gender[a]				τ_b
	Male		Female		
	%	(Rank)	%	(Rank)	
Lack of communication or understanding	26.5	(1)	31.8	(1)	.06
Joint conflict over roles	20.6	(2)	16.8	(7)	−.05
Not sure what happened (with attempted explanation)	17.6	(3)	1.9	(28)	−.27***
Different backgrounds; incompatible	17.6	(3)	16.8	(7)	−.01
Change in interests or values	16.7	(5)	18.7	(6)	−.03
Problems with in-laws and relatives	13.7	(6)	7.5	(18)	−.10
Factor 7: Internal Gender Role Conflict	13.7	(6)	9.3	(16)	−.07
Too young at time of marriage	12.7	(8)	12.1	(11)	−.01
Overcommitment to work	12.7	(8)	3.7	(24)	−.16**
Not enough social life together	12.7	(8)	12.1	(11)	−.01
No sense of family	12.7	(8)	15.0	(9)	.03
Jealousy	10.8	(12)	7.5	(18)	−.06
Extramarital sex	10.8	(12)	20.6	(4)	.13*
Untrustworthy; immature	9.8	(14)	21.5	(2)	.16**
Other, personality	8.8	(15)	8.4	(17)	−.01
Arguing all the time	7.8	(16)	12.1	(11)	.07
Disagreements over money	7.8	(16)	7.5	(18)	−.01
Out with the boys/girls	7.8	(16)	19.6	(5)	.17**
Alcohol	7.8	(19)	21.5	(2)	.21***
Factor 6: Financial and Employment Problems	6.9	(19)	15.0	(9)	.13*
Inflexible; stubborn	6.9	(19)	12.1	(14)	.09
Emotional/personality problems	4.9	(22)	12.1	(14)	.13*
External events	4.9	(22)	0.9	(31)	−.12*
Desertion	3.9	(24)	3.7	(25)	.00
General neglect of household duties	3.9	(24)	5.6	(21)	.04
Self-centered	3.9	(24)	2.8	(27)	−.03
Factor 3: Physical and Psychological Abuse	3.9	(24)	5.6	(21)	.10
Factor 1: Conflicts over the Children	2.9	(28)	1.9	(28)	−.03
Threatened physical abuse	2.0	(29)	5.6	(21)	.09
Premarital pregnancy	2.0	(29)	0.9	(31)	−.04

[a]Gender is treated as a dummy variable with male = 0 and female = 1.
*$p < .05$.
**$p < .01$.
***$p < .001$.

really cold and unfeeling. I like the out-of-doors and activities. She didn't. I don't know the woman after 5 years of marriage; I don't understand the woman any more. She's like a total stranger. I don't even know what she wants, really!"

Other frequently mentioned complaints were "different backgrounds; incompatible" "change in interests or values," "problems with in-laws and relatives," and complaints included in Factor 7, Internal Gender Role Conflict. These data indicate that the distribution and types of marital complaints mentioned by respondents in the suburban sample did differ from those in the earlier Goode study; however, this observation can be more accurately assessed by examining the women in the suburban sample, who were the most nearly comparable to Goode's subjects.

Differences in Complaints across Decades

As discussed in Chapter 4, Goode's (1956) metropolitan Detroit sample was composed of mothers aged 20 to 38 who had been divorced from 2 to 26 months. It is not possible to compare the two samples on the time dimension, and it should be recognized that the time factor may have had an impact on the reporting of complaints. The sample also had a lower proportion of blacks than did the Cleveland suburban sample. With these sample differences in mind, women in the two studies who were mothers aged 38 and under are compared.

In order to make the Cleveland suburban data more nearly comparable to the Detroit data demographically, the sample was weighted on education. Since the late 1940s, the level of education has risen in the United States. For example, in 1947 the median number of years of schooling completed for females was 9.3; in 1975 the figure was 12.3, and in 1985 it was 12.6 (U.S. Bureau of the Census, 1975, 1976, 1985). Therefore, the Cleveland data were weighted so that the educational breakdown was the same as that used in the Detroit data. For example, 19% of the Cleveland suburban mothers aged 38 and under were college graduates, and only 14% had not completed high school. In Goode's sample, 2% were college graduates and 61% had not graduated from high school. In the suburban sample, those who were not high school graduates were overweighted to represent 61% of the total, and so forth.

Table 5.4 displays three distributions and rankings of marital complaints. The first set of columns gives the unweighted marital com-

TABLE 5.4. Responses to the Goode Marital Complaint Code for Mothers Aged 38 and Under: The Unweighted and Weighted Cleveland Suburban Sample and the Detroit Sample

Goode marital complaint categories	Cleveland mothers (unweighted sample, 1974–1975)			Cleveland mothers (weighted sample, 1974–1975)[a]			Detroit mothers (1948)[b]		
	% responses	% respondents	(Rank)	% responses	% respondents	(Rank)	% responses	% respondents	(Rank)
Personality	17	58	(1)	17	53	(1)	11	29	(5)
Home life	13	44	(2)	14	44	(2)	9	25	(6)
Values	13	44	(2)	10	30	(4)	8	21	(7)
Authority	9	32	(4)	11	33	(3)	12	32	(2)
Other complaints	13	32	(4)	15	28	(5)	—	—	—
Drinking	7	23	(6)	7	24	(6)	12	30	(4)
Complex	6	21	(7)	7	21	(8)	12	31	(3)
Nonsupport	6	16	(8)	2	5	(12)	13	33	(1)
Extramarital sex, husband	4	14	(9)	7	22	(7)	6	16	(9)
Consumption	4	14	(9)	2	6	(11)	8	20	(8)
Miscellaneous	3	13	(11)	4	14	(9)	4	12	(10)
Sex problems		9		1	4			—c	
Felonies	—c	2		1	2			—c	
Forced marriage	—c	2		2	8			—c	
Relatives	3	9	(12)	3	9	(10)	2	4	(12)
Desertion	2	5	(13)	1	2	(13)	3	8	(11)
Total	99			100			100		
(n)		(57)			(57)			(425)	
(Total number of complaints)	(191)			(175)			(1,100)		
(Mean number of complaints)	(3.35)			(3.07)			(2.61)		

[a] Weighted by Detroit sample values on education.
[b] Replies to "Would you state, in your own words, what was the main cause of your divorce?" The data are from Goode (1956, p. 123).
[c] < 1% of responses.

plaint distribution and complaint rankings for Cleveland women who were mothers aged 38 or less; the second set of columns gives these data for the same group weighted by the 1948 educational values; and the third set of columns gives Goode's Detroit data.

There are some small differences in the ranking of complaints for the unweighted and weighted Cleveland suburban data. The major difference, however, is that between these data and Goode's. Even for the weighted Cleveland suburban data, the distribution and types of complaints women mentioned in 1974 and 1975 were very different from those mentioned in 1948. For example, "nonsupport" ranked 1st as a complaint in 1948 and 12th in 1974–1975. "Personality" and "home life" were the most frequent complaints for the Cleveland mothers and were ranked 5th and 6th, respectively, by those in Detroit.

The marital complaints mentioned most frequently in 1948 might be considered more "serious" "nonsupport," "authority," the complex of activities involved in being "out with the boys/girls," and "drinking"). In the Cleveland data, complaints concerning affective/emotional aspects of marriage were more frequent ("personality," "home life," "authority," "values"), followed by "other complaints" not even mentioned by the Detroit respondents. One possibility is that marriages were more unhappy, marital situations more desperate, and economic deprivation more of an issue before couples decided to divorce in 1948. If so, this may have made adjustment to divorce more difficult as well. On the other hand, the differences in samples may account for these variations in ranking. Greater emphasis should be placed on value and opportunity changes over the 25-year period—an increasing concern that marriages should be emotionally and sexually satisfying, and an increasing belief in the need for a mentally healthy environment for the procreation and rearing of children. Thurnher, Fenn, Melichar, and Chiriboga (1983) also found a shift in the type of complaints made in a court-records-based sample in the San Francisco/Oakland, California area in the 1970s, compared to Goode and Levinger's earlier studies.

General Differences in Complaints by Gender

The hypothesis that the types of complaints mentioned by men and women in the Cleveland suburban divorce study would differ was supported for both the Goode and the Cleveland marital complaint codes, although the differences were less striking with the Cleveland code (Tables 5.1 and 5.3). Furthermore, when the Goode code was used, women made significantly more complaints than men—a mean of 3.2 versus 2.5 ($t = 2.0$, $df = 206$, $p < .025$). The differences were not statistically significant when the Cleveland code was used; women made 3.4 complaints versus 3.0 for men.

Although it is a less powerful technique than Pearson's correlation coefficient, Kendall's tau$_b$ is used here to describe the relationships between complaints and subject characteristics, because this statistic makes fewer assumptions about the nature of the distribution of the data. Women were significantly more likely than men to make complaints about "personality," "authority," "drinking," the "being out with the boys" complex, "sex problems," "nonsupport," "extramarital sex, husband," and "consumption" (money management) when the Goode code was used (Table 5.1). Men were significantly more likely to mention "extramarital sex, wife" and "relatives." Although complaint frequency did differ somewhat, there was relatively little difference in the rankings by gender for the first five complaints. If Goode's "miscellaneous" category is combined with "uncodable complaints" (complaints that could not be coded according to Goode's categories), 47% of the females and 59% of the males mentioned complaints that were mentioned either infrequently or not at all by women in the 1948 Detroit study.

With the Cleveland marital complaint code, there was more variation in the rankings by gender than with the Goode code (Table 5.3). For example, the second most frequent complaint for men was "joint conflict over roles," disagreements over appropriate gender roles for men and women. This complaint was ranked eighth for women. For women, the second most frequent complaint was a tie between "alcohol" and the spouse's being "untrustworthy; immature."

When responses concerning "joint conflict over roles" and Factor 7, Internal Gender Role Conflict, were combined, 34.3% of the men and 26.1% of the women made such complaints. This type of complaint is illustrated by the following comments. A woman married for 18 years noted:

> "We owned two stores, and I had to work 7 days a week. I'm a very independent person. He wanted me to cater to him. I couldn't do the things I wanted to do as a person."

A man employed as an engineer noted:

> "About a year before all of this [the divorce filing], she got a job as a waitress. She had done well, being promoted and complimented by customers, fellow employees, and superiors. She found herself too confined as a housewife and found me no longer personally of interest. She wanted to make new relationships."

And, finally, a man noted:

> "I didn't want to break up. She has never understood the world. She was longing for this freedom. She married too soon without ever being free. I couldn't impress upon this woman about the need to do household chores, mind the kids, and so forth. That world out there that she wants is a jungle!"

The high frequency with which these complaints were mentioned suggests that married couples were struggling with issues involving the desire for personal growth and the development and allocation of roles within the family. These conflicts, in turn, created dissension when spouses could not reconcile their differing expectations and desires.

The third most frequent reply for men was "not sure what happened"—a statement that, as noted earlier, was followed by an attempted explanation. In Weiss's terms, those who express such uncertainty may be people who are still developing and rehearsing their "accounts" of the marital breakup. As indicated in Chapter 4, women, more often than men, first mentioned the idea of the divorce and then filed. Consequently, they probably devoted more time to developing their accounts. This interpretation is inferred from the ranking of the response "not sure what happened": For women, it ranked 28th out of 31 complaints.

Among those relationships for which there were statistically significant differences, men were more likely than women to be unsure about what caused the breakup of their marriages. They were more likely to mention "overcommitment to work," "problems with in-laws and relatives," and "external events" (e.g., a death in the family, a job change, or a third party or thing—"It's his/her/its fault; fate") as reasons for the breakup. Women were significantly more likely to complain of "extramarital sex," "untrustworthy, immature," "out with the boys," "alcohol," Financial and Employment Problems (Factor 6), and "emotional/personality problems."

The differences by gender when the Cleveland code was used were not as striking as those found when the Goode code was used, those reported by Levinger (1966), or those found by Thurnher et al. (1983). Nevertheless, the hypothesis regarding gender differences in types of complaints was supported. One possible explanation for the few differences by gender found when the Cleveland code was used is that both the Goode and Levinger complaint codes were based on women's perceptions of complaints. Goode studied *only* women's perceptions of marital complaints. Levinger, on the other hand, analyzed records concerning child custody decisions in which the focus was upon the fitness of the parent (usually the mother) to care for the children. The Cleveland suburban divorce study examined both males' and females' perceptions and feelings.

Another possible explanation is that attitudes about marriage and divorce and women's roles outside the family changed between 1948 and the mid-1970s. Men and women may have evaluated their marriages more similarly than they did in 1948 or 1965. Brown (1976) has corroborated this interpretation by also reporting relatively small sex differences in marital complaints. The types of complaints reported by Granvold, Pedler, and Schellie (1979) and Kelly (1982) in their convenience sample studies are similar to those found here. In a sample based partly on court records and partly on convenience, Riessman (1990) also describes similarities in the types of complaints made, but gender-linked differences in the way those complaints are described. The apparent decrease in gender differences in types of marital complaints may reflect greater freedom and means in the 1970s and 1980s to move in and out of marriage, particularly to leave an unbearable marriage—an option not readily available to women in the past.

An earlier report (Kitson et al., 1985) reviewed the five most common marital complaints in nine studies of divorce, all but two of which had been conducted in the United States, and found striking similarities in causes. Eight of the nine studies mentioned extramarital sex as a cause of the breakup, with the majority of other complaints focused on interpersonal issues such as lack of communication, love, or family life and conflicts over roles. Examining data on divorce in more traditional societies, which was drawn from the Standard Cross-Cultural Sample (Murdock & White, 1969), Betzig (1989) found extramarital sex to be the most common marital complaint, trailed by an instrumental complaint of inadequate economic support.

Placing Blame For the Divorce

Despite the likelihood that each partner contributed to the disintegration of a marriage, respondents were more likely to blame their partners than themselves for the breakup. In 7% of the cases the respondent took most of the blame; in 71% the spouse was viewed as mostly to blame; and in 21% the respondent stated that both parties contributed to the failure of the marriage ($n = 205$). Men were more likely to blame themselves for the breakup than were women: 14 men

(14.1%) gave replies that reflected self-blame, compared to 1 woman (0.1%). Women were more likely than men to blame their spouses (83.8% vs. 57.6%). Men were more likely than women to give replies in which the blame was shared (28.3% vs. 15.2%). Prudence Brown (1976) found a similar pattern in her study of couples who went to the Wayne County (Detroit, Michigan) Circuit Court Marital Counseling Service, but Thurnher et al. (1983) found blame more evenly divided by gender.

By the third interview with the suburban sample, there was a substantial shift in the attribution of the cause of the divorce to a feeling that it was the fault of both parties, rather than only the spouse's fault. Although by the third interview only 7.0% of the respondents felt that they were to blame, just over half (51.2%) considered the breakup mutually caused, in contrast to 41.9% who felt it was the spouse's fault. Of those who were coded as considering the divorce the spouse's fault at the first interview ($n = 92$), 52.2% still felt this way, whereas 45.7% now felt it was mutually caused and 2.2% felt it was their own fault. Among those who considered the divorce mutually caused at the first interview ($n = 29$), 75.9% still did, whereas 10.3% assigned the blame only to themselves and another 13.8% to their spouses.

Types of Complaints by Race

Because of the economic focus of much research on racial differences in divorce, it was anticipated that blacks, who comprised the vast majority of the nonwhite population in the Cleveland suburban divorce study, would mention more concerns about economic issues than would whites. This was not the case; there were no significant associations between race and marital complaints reflecting economic concerns.

Only a few complaints in the suburban study differed by race. With race coded 0 for whites and 1 for nonwhites, whites were significantly more likely than nonwhites to mention the following complaints: "change in interests or values" ($\tau_b = -.13$, $p < .05$); "alcohol" ($\tau_b = -.12$, $p < 05$); and "other, personality;" ($\tau_b = -.15$, $p < .05$). Nonwhites were significantly more likely than whites to mention "other, lack of investment" in the family; ($\tau_b = .16$, $p < .01$) and Physical and Psychological Abuse, Factor 3; ($\tau_b = .17$, $p < .01$) as issues in the breakup.

Like the issue of premarital pregnancy—which, as noted above, was rarely mentioned by those who were divorcing as a reason for the end of their marriages—economic problems may not seem to be *"the issue"* forcing a breakup. Economic hardship may constitute a backdrop against which family members play out their daily lives; it may increase the importance of other concerns, highlight shortcomings of the spouse, and lead to arguments and disagreements. Still, this does not mean that economic problems will be seen as a principle reason for the marital breakup.

Marital Complaints in the Marital Transition Study, 1985–1986

Marital complaints made in the late 1940s differed from those made in the mid-1970s, as the comparisons of data from Detroit and Cleveland have shown. But what, if any, differences are there in complaints made by two groups of women surveyed approximately 10 years apart in the same metropolitan area? The 1985–1986 county-wide marital transition sample was asked the same marital complaint question as were the respondents in the suburban study: "What caused your marriage to break up?" As indicated in Appendix C, some categories were added for marital complaints in this sample that were not part of the code for the suburban sample; for the most part, however, the complaint categories were similar. In addition, for comparability, the marital transition data were coded according to the seven factors identified in the initial study.[1] Men in the suburban study were dropped from this analysis.

Although the complaints displayed in Table 5.5 varied somewhat in their rankings, 9 of the 10 most frequently mentioned complaints in 1974–1975 were also in the top 10 in 1985–1986. The only one of the most frequently mentioned complaints in the suburban divorce sample that did not rank so highly in the marital transition sample was "joint conflict over roles," which was the 7th most common complaint in the mid-1970s but the 21st in the mid-1980s. Similarly, Factor 5, Generalized Discontent, a potpourri of complaints about money, work, sexual problems, and disagreements over having children and over friends, was ranked 7th in the marital transition sample but 28th in the suburban sample.

As indicated by the complaint "joint conflict over roles," one area in which complaints decreased quite substantially between the mid-1970s and mid-1980s was that of conflicts within and between individuals over roles. In the mid-1970s, when replies to Factor 7, Internal Gender Role Conflict (9.3%), and "joint conflict over roles" (16.8%) were combined, a little over a quarter (26.1%) of women mentioned such complaints. In the mid-1980s, only about one in seven women (13.8%) mentioned either Factor 7 (7.4%) or "joint conflict over roles" (6.4%). It is not known how men ranked these complaints in the 1980s, but it would seem, at least from the women's perspective, that the

TABLE 5.5. Percentages and Rankings for Marital Complaints by Women in the Suburban Divorce Study (1974-1975) and the County-Wide Marital Transition Study (1985-1986)

Cleveland marital complaint categories	% respondents, 1974-1975 ($n = 107$)	(Rank)	% respondents, 1985-1986 ($n = 188$)	(Rank)
Lack of communication or understanding	31.8	(1)	33.0	(1)
Alcohol	21.5	(2)	22.3	(4)
Untrustworthy; immature	21.5	(2)	12.8	(9)
Extramarital sex	20.6	(4)	33.0	(1)
Out with the boys/girls	19.6	(5)	14.9	(6)
Change in interests or values	18.7	(6)	22.9	(3)
Different backgrounds; incompatible	16.8	(7)	11.2	(10)
Joint conflict over roles	16.8	(7)	6.4	(21)
No sense of family	15.0	(9)	13.3	(7)
Factor 5: Generalized Discontent	1.9	(28)	13.3	(7)
Factor 6: Financial and Employment Problems	15.0	(9)	19.7	(5)

struggles couples experienced over appropriate roles for men and women in the 1970s had abated somewhat by the 1980s. Attitudes and behavior about what men and women should do at home and at work would seem to have shifted during this period, so that such issues apparently became less salient as a reason for seeking a divorce, at least for women. The next step is to look at demographic correlates of marital complaints.

Demographic Differences in Complaints

The types of marital complaints mentioned in the suburban study were analyzed by demographic characteristics. Complaints were divided into two categories: "instrumental" (task-oriented) and "expressive" (affectional/emotional) complaints. Instrumental complaints were those detailing behaviors that made it difficult to perform the basic economic, child-rearing, and household tasks required to maintain a minimal level of functioning in a marriage.[2] It was hypothesized that respondents with less education, lower social class position, fewer years of marriage, and lower incomes would be more likely to make instrumental marital complaints.

For instrumental complaints, 34 of the 57 relationships for which any associations were found were in the predicted direction (in 4 cases no association was found, with $\tau_b > .005$). Only the 8 complaints for which statistically significant relationships occurred are displayed in Table 5.6. As expected, education was associated with complaints about the former spouse's being "out with the boys/girls" and with Physical and Psychological Abuse (Factor 3); those with less education were more likely to make these complaints. Those who were lower in social status were more likely to mention "threatened physical abuse" or "actual physical abuse," "out with the boys/girls," and Conflicts over the Children (Factor 1). Income was correlated with complaints of "out with the boys/girls," "general neglect of household duties," Gambling and Criminal Activities (Factor 4), and Financial and Employment Problems (Factor 6); those with less money were more likely to make these complaints. Although the majority of the relationships were in the predicted direction, in no case were those who had been married for a shorter period of time significantly more likely to mention instrumental complaints. Finally, in contradiction to the hypothesis, those who were higher in social class status were more likely to mention being "too young at time of marriage."

Expressive complaints were those that detailed difficulties in communication, lack of companionship, and feelings of lack of care and regard from the spouse.[3] Of the 63 associations with the expressive complaints, 36 were in the predicted direction. Two of the statistically significant ones, as expected, were that more respondents with higher levels of education mentioned "change in interests or values" and Internal Gender Role Conflict (Factor 7). Those with lower levels of education were less likely to mention "no sense of family" and Sexual Problems Due to Health (Factor 2). Respondents with higher social class status were more likely to complain of "lack of communication or understanding," "changes in interests or values," "different backgrounds; incompatible," and "overcommitment to work." Those who had been married longer were more likely to mention "changes in interests or values" and "no sense of family," whereas those who had been married for shorter periods of time were more likely to mention "problems with in-laws and relatives" and Sexual Problems Due to Health (Factor 2). Respondents who reported higher incomes were also more likely to mention "overcommitment to work" and "self-centered" as spousal complaints.

Although there were associations between types of marital complaints and demographic variables, the complaints in the suburban

TABLE 5.6. Kendall Tau$_b$'s for Associations between the Cleveland Marital Complaint Code and Demographic Characteristics: Suburban Divorced Sample

Cleveland marital complaint categories	Demographic characteristics			
	Respondents' level of education (1 = graduate degree or professional)	Social class (I-V)	Number of years married	Income last year
Instrumental complaints				
Too young at time of marriage	−.07	−.12*	−.05	−.07
Threatened physical abuse	.10	.16**	−.05	−.07
Out with the boys/girls	.13*	.14*	−.09	−.16**
General neglect of household duties	—^{a}	.03	—^{a}	−.11*
Factor 3: Physical and psychological abuse	.13*	.12	.01	—^{a}
Factor 4: Gambling and Criminal Activities	.06	.02	−.03	−.11*
Factor 1: Conflicts over the Children	.07	.12*	−.07	−.01
Factor 6: Financial and Employment Problems	−.04	−.07	−.09	−.17***
Expressive complaints				
Lack of communication or understanding	−.09	−.16**	.03	.08
Change in interests or values	−.19***	−.17**	.10*	.08
Different backgrounds; incompatible	−.08	−.12*	−.02	.08
Overcommitment to work	−.10	−.19**	.08	.26***
Self-centered	.01	−.04	.04	.12*
No sense of family	.17**	.07	.13*	.02
Problems with in-laws and relatives	−.10	−.06	−.11*	−.02
Factor 2: Sexual Problems Due to Health	.14*	.04	−.13*	.07
Factor 7: Internal Gender Role Conflict	−.13*	−.02	−.10	.03

^{a}Correlation > .0051.
*p < .05.
**p < .01.
***p < .001.

Cleveland study were less strongly associated with these characteristics than the complaints examined in previous research. The sign test (Loether & McTavish, 1974) was used to determine whether the observed proportions of relationships in the predicted directions were simply chance occurrences. The z statistic for the proportions of complaints predicting either instrumental (.596) or expressive (.571) orientations was not statistically significant when a one-tailed test was used. This indicates that in the sample of suburban residents there were no striking differences in types of complaints by the demographic characteristics of the subjects. This may be another reflection, along with the reduced gender differences in types of complaints, of a general societal shift—in this case, a shift to standards for evaluating marriages that are not so closely tied to demographic considerations.

Age at Marriage, Premarital Pregnancy, Parental Loss

Among other factors reported as "causes" of divorce, age, as expected, was associated to some extent with complaints related to immaturity and lack of opportunity to explore options before marriage. Those who were younger were significantly more likely to mention "too young at time of marriage" as a marital complaint (Table 5.7). However, with a correlation of $-.17$ this was not a particularly strong association, suggesting that the link between marital breakup and respondents' age at marriage was not foremost in their minds. Younger subjects were also more likely to report as complaints "out with the boys/girls," "extramarital sex," and Internal Gender Role Conflict (Factor 7). None of the significant associations between age and the complaints was related to money—one of the issues that analysts suggest is a problem in young marriages. It does appear, however, that some younger persons may have less commitment to the marriage, as illustrated by the types of complaints mentioned above. Older subjects were more likely to mention "alcohol" as a problem, to feel that there was "no sense of family," and to report Conflicts over the Children (Factor 1) and Internal Gender Role Conflict (Factor 7). More marital complaints were significantly associated with age than with length of a marriage, as indicated in Table 5.6, despite the fact that these two variables were understandably associated with older persons' being likely to be married longer.

Premarital pregnancy was significantly, but weakly, associated with a *complaint* of "premarital pregnancy" and was negatively associated with "lack of communication or understanding." Thus, the fact of a premarital pregnancy did not seem to be directly linked in the respondents' minds with the end of their marriages.

TABLE 5.7. Kendall's Tau_b's for the Associations between Marital Complaints and Year of Birth, Premarital Pregnancy, and Childhood Loss of Parents: Suburban Divorced Sample

Cleveland marital complaint categories	Background characteristics						
	Respondent's age	Premarital pregnancy[a]	Respondent's parents divorced	Respondent's father died	Either spouse's parents divorced	Either spouse's father died	Either spouse's mother died
Too young at time of marriage	-.17**	.11	.02	-.08	.04	.01	.02
Lack of communication or understanding	-.10*	-.19*	.11	—	.04	.03	-.14*
Jealousy	-.04	-.11	.10	.18*	.08	.08	.18*
Premarital pregnancy	.06	.15*	-.05	-.03	-.07	-.04	-.03
Alcohol	.12*	-.10	-.02	.03	.05	.03	-.07
Inflexible; stubborn	.02	—	.05	.03	.06	-.04	.13*
Disagreements over money	-.03	-.02	.03	.30***	.12	.16*	-.06
Out with the boys/girls	-.14**	.04	.10	-.09	.16*	-.07	—
General neglect of household duties	.04	-.03	.13*	-.04	.15*	-.06	-.04
No sense of family	.12*	.06	.01	.01	.02	—	.01
Extramarital sex	-.02	.07	-.01	—	-.04	-.07	.17*
Factor 1: Conflicts over the Children	.16**	—	.16*	.15*	.18*	.04	-.04*
Factor 2: Sexual Problems due to Health	-.07	—	-.03	-.02	.16*	-.02	-.02
Factor 7: Internal Gender Role Conflict	.16**	-.11	.02	-.08	.13	-.12	.02

[a]Based only on couples with children ($n = 118$).
* $p < .05$.
** $p < .01$.
*** $p < .001$.

136

The death of a parent or a parental divorce has been thought to influence children's relationships with and expectations about others. The explanations for this include deficits in life resulting from the reduced economic circumstances that many single-parent families experience; lack of role models; parental personal instability passed on to the offspring; and lack of parental supervision, leading to riskier marital choices and less competent marital role performance. In this sample, the variables used to examine this issue included death of the respondent's father, divorce of the respondent's parents, death of either marital partner's father or mother, and divorce in either set of parents. In all cases, the variables were coded for losses before age 11, the age period at which the influence is felt to be greatest (Dohrenwend & Dohrenwend, 1981). (So few of the respondents' mothers had died before the respondents were aged 11 that this variable was not analyzed separately.)

When their own parents had divorced, respondents were more likely than those without a parental divorce to mention marital complaints of "out with the boys/girls," "general neglect of household duties," and Conflicts over the Children (Factor 1). These complaints suggest that their expectations for spouses and marriage may have been quite high, with perhaps more desire for togetherness, higher expectations for role performance, and a desire for special care to be taken of the children. Alternatively, they may have consciously or subconsciously picked spouses with problems in these areas because of what they had previously seen in their parents' marriages.

Death of the respondent's father or of either spouse's mother or father was associated with a complaint of "jealousy." Given the method of coding, it is not possible to determine whether the spouse made this complaint about the respondent or the respondent made it about the spouse. In either case, however, it suggests that one or the other partner wanted more support and attention from the other and felt slighted, or, alternatively, may have been more outgoing and seeking of such attention from others, thereby eliciting this complaint from the spouse. "Disagreements over money" were associated with the subject's father's having died and less strongly associated with either spouse's father's having died; this latter association probably resulted in part from the strong relationship of this variable with the death of the respondent's father.

Among the parental loss variables, the greatest number of marital complaint associations occurred with the death of either spouse's mother. When this occurred, respondents were more likely to report marital complaints of "jealousy," Conflicts over the Children (Factor 1), "inflexible; stubborn," and "extramarital sex." They were also less likely to report "lack of communication or understanding" as a problem. When examined *ex post facto*, such complaints are associated with a sense of insecurity in relationships, a seeking out of approval and sexual reassurance, and concern about how one's own children are treated—all of which may have resulted from the respondents' own prior experiences. These analyses suggest the utility for other investigators of attempting more fully to understand the meaning of such frequently mentioned divorce "causes" as age, parental loss, and premarital pregnancy.

Frequency of Expressive, Instrumental, and "Serious" Complaints

As part of determining whether marital complaints were associated with demographic characteristics, complaints in the suburban divorce study were also combined into categories of "expressive" (affectional/emotional) and "instrumental" (task-oriented), as noted above. In addition, a third category was created, that of "serious" complaints. "Serious" complaints are those that have traditionally been considered especially important reasons for divorce, such as extramarital sexual relations, drinking and other drug use, gambling, threatened or actual physical abuse, emotional or personality problems, desertion, or criminal activities. (There is some overlap in these complaints with those in the other two categories.) Virtually all of the respondents (88.6%) mentioned at least one expressive complaint. Fewer respondents mentioned instrumental complaints (57.4%), and fewer still mentioned serious complaints (31.1%). The mean number of expressive complaints mentioned was 1.8, compared to 0.8 for instrumental complaints and 0.4 for serious complaints. The data thus highlight the importance of affection, emotional regard, and companionship as especially noteworthy issues in contemporary marriages that fail.

Risk Factors for Divorce and Marital Complaints

In Chapter 3, risk factors for divorce have been discussed. The question to be addressed here is whether these risk factors are associated with certain types of marital complaints. Risk factors are characteristics that are believed to increase the likelihood of divorce. Are they then associated with specific types of marital complaints that are indicative of such structural, social, and psychological differences between the partners? The answer is yes; although the number of significant differences was again small, the ones that were found supported the predicted association with the risk factors. Those with higher scores on both the short and long risk factor scales (which included parental divorce and differences in ethnic identity—items only asked about at the second interview, $n = 161$) were more likely, as expected, to report "different backgrounds; incompatible" (τ_b for short form $= .10$, τ_b for long form $= .13$, p's $< .05$); Sexual Problems Due to Health (Factor 2; τ_b's for both forms $= .12$, p's $< .05$); and "untrustworthy; immature" (τ_b for short form $= .16$, $p < .01$; τ_b for long form $= .14$, $p < .05$). These types of marital issues or complaints illuminate issues that the demographic risk factors are said to be measuring.

Those with lower risk factor scores on the short risk factor scale were less likely to report complaints of "jealousy" $\tau_b = -.16$, $p < .01$). The longer risk factor scale was associated with complaints of being "too young at time of marriage" ($\tau_b = .13$, $p < .05$) and "general neglect of household duties" ($\tau_b = .14$, $p < .05$). Finally, both the short and long scales were associated with instrumental complaints about the spouse (respective τ_b's $= .12$ and $.25$, p's $< .05$). Those who made instrumental complaints about the spouse were more likely to have a number of risk factors predisposing the couple to divorce. Thus, the risk factor scales highlighted instrumental issues in marriages that failed. Expressive issues were not identified by these measures; this suggests that risk factors, or demographic correlates, may decrease in importance as factors associated with failed marriages if couples continue to focus on affectional issues in their relationships.

Marital Complaints and Mental Status

Is mental and physical health disturbance more likely to be associated with certain kinds of marital complaints? It was hypothesized that responses of bewilderment about the cause of the breakup, complaints concerning perceived failings of the spouse, or experiences that reflected badly upon the respondent would be associated with distress. There is some support for this hypothesis in the suburban divorce data.

Table 5.8 displays the significant relationships between marital complaints and the four adjustment variables of subjective distress, attachment, self-esteem, and the illness contacts index. Complaints that previous research has highlighted as being particularly distressing in divorce produced significant associations. Higher scores on subjective distress, the measure of depression and anxiety, were associated with these complaints: "untrustworthy; immature," "extramarital sex" and Sexual Problems Due to Health (Factor 2). In addition, when complaints were combined, both "serious" complaints and "stable" complaints (those that continued to be mentioned with similar fre-

TABLE 5.8. Kendall's Tau$_b$'s for Associations between the Cleveland Marital Complaint Code and Subjective Distress, Attachment, and Self-Esteem: Suburban Divorced Sample

Cleveland marital complaint categories	Adjustment variables			
	Subjective distress	Attachment	Self-esteem	Illness contacts
Different backgrounds; incompatible	.04	−.11*	.04	−.02
Desertion	.05	.07	.15**	.04
Untrustworthy; immature	.11*	.00	.06	.06
Emotional/personality problems	.02	.01	−.05	.11*
General neglect of household duties	.00	−.10*	−.04	−.01
Joint conflict over roles	−.05	−.06	−.04	−.11*
Extramarital sex	.13*	.13*	.11*	.03
Factor 2: Sexual Problems Due to Health	.14*	.13*	−.05	.07
Factor 6: Financial and Employment Problems	−.09	−.13*	−.04	.02
Factor 7: Internal Gender Role Conflict	−.08	−.05	−.13*	−.01
Serious complaints	.11*	.06	.01	.07
Stable complaints	.09*	−.05	.02	−.02

*$p < .05$.
**$p < .01$.

quency at the beginning and end of the study) were associated with greater psychological distress.

Higher attachment scores were associated with complaints of "extramarital sex" and Sexual Problems Due to Health (Factor 2). These findings suggest that respondents still cared strongly for their partners, but were torn by the seriousness of the complaints. High self-esteem scores (which indicated *lower* self-esteem) were associated with complaints of "desertion" and "extramarital sex." Although causality in these relationships cannot be determined, it seems likely that such marital complaints may make individuals feel especially unloved, regretful, or distressed about the end of their marriages; these feelings, in turn, are likely to affect self-esteem. The distress, confusion, and anger created by a spouse's infidelity are illustrated by the comments of several respondents. One college-educated father of three noted:

"My wife was running around with another guy from work. Prior to that, she was showing less and less interest in our objectives. I was going to college, and she got interested in bridge and astrology, and she lost interest in the children and home."

A woman noted:

"Another woman, a younger woman. We were in business. When you are in business and it's prosperous—the other woman sought prestige and older men just eat that up. I have my pride. Everyone knew about it. I contributed a lot to the marriage, and I was not going to be humiliated by another woman."

Another man lamented:

"I can't tell you what caused it. I caught my wife with another man. Why she was with another man, I can't know. I caught her more than once. He used to drop her off in front of the house. She came home one day, packed up her clothes, and left."

A housewife with a junior high school education explained:

"He was working with this girl and started going around with her, and that's when I filed for a divorce. There wasn't anything else. Things were usually pretty much all right for us."

Contrary to expectation, none of the associations between the mental health measures and the complaint "not sure what happened" were statistically significant. It was thought that the lack of a coherent "account" of the marital failure would be more distressing, but this turned out not to be the case.

The hypothesis that complaints focusing on areas of marital frustration or irritation would be associated with a sense of relief did find some support. Respondents who mentioned "lack of communication or understanding" as a complaint had lower scores on the attachment scale, meaning that they were less likely to be attached to their (ex-)-spouses. Respondents who mentioned "general neglect of household duties" and Financial and Employment Problems (Factor 6) also had lower attachment scores. Similarly, higher self-esteem scores (again, indicating *low* self-esteem) were associated with a complaint of Internal Gender Role Conflict (Factor 7). Presumably, self-esteem was enhanced through reducing the conflict over gender roles by ending the relationship; alternatively, those who were unwilling to accept a situation in which their needs were unmet may have had a stronger sense of self.

The Illness Contacts Index was only associated with two complaints. "Emotional/personality problems" were associated with more illness contacts, whereas "joint conflict over roles" was related to fewer contacts. Emotional problems of the spouse were likely to be long-term issues that had—and even after separation still could have— a wearing effect on the respondent's health. On the other hand, with the partner gone, conflicts over gender roles could become a much less pressing issue.

These findings indicate that although a number of marital complaints were associated with symptoms of mental health disturbance, the likelihood of distress was not the same for all kinds of complaints. Complaints reflecting irritation with the ex-spouse or the relationship were actually associated with a sense of relief. Complaints reflecting negatively upon the respondent's self-esteem and those producing feelings of guilt or uncertainty about ending the marriage were correlated with symptoms of distress. Contrary to expectation, uncertainty about why the marriage ended was not associated with greater distress.

Marital Complaints and Mental Health Help

The demonstration of a relationship between some types of marital complaints and psychological distress supports a view of divorce as a disturbing event for many who experience it. But, although it seems logical to suppose that different kinds of marital complaints are more or less likely to *produce* psychological distress among the divorced, it is important to keep in mind that psychological distress may itself be a *cause* of the divorce (see, e.g., Blumenthal, 1967; Briscoe et al., 1973). If so, people who are psychologically upset may make complaints that differ from those of people who are not. To test this possibility, the relationship between mental health help and marital complaints was examined.

Seeking help from a mental health worker (a psychiatrist or psychologist, a marriage counselor, or a social worker), either in the past year or earlier in the marriage, was associated with making certain kinds of complaints about the spouse's psychological makeup. It was as if a cousnelor helped form, validated, or reinforced a subject's views of the marital situation. When help was sought from a mental health worker, the divorced were significantly more likely to mention psychological issues as marital complaints. These included "untrustworthy; immature" ($\tau_b = 12$, $p < .05$); "emotional/personality problems" ($\tau_b = .11$, $p < .05$); or "other, personality" problems ($\tau_b = .12$, $p < .05$).

Although those who sought therapy were more likely to frame their concerns about their spouses in psychological terms, there were no other differences between the groups in terms of complaints. Therapy, then, may have helped to define the source of the breakdown as the spouse's problem.

Changes in Marital Complaints over Time

Do people's perceptions of what caused the failure of their marriages stay the same, or do they change over time? To address this issue, respondents at the third interview in the suburban divorce study (2-3 years after the divorce) were asked, "Looking back over your marriage, what would you now say caused your marriage to break up?" Table 5.9 displays the most frequently mentioned complaints by whether they were discussed only at the first (time of filing) interview, at both the first and the third interviews, or only at the third interview.

Approximately 4 years after separation from the spouse, some types of complaints decreased in salience. Complaints that were mentioned initially, but did not continue to be mentioned, were probably factors associated with the turmoil surrounding the disintegration of the marriage, and therefore were not necessarily primary complaints or "causes" of the breakup. Attention is focused here on complaints for which 50% or more of all the mentions occurred at the first interview. The complaint that was most commonly mentioned at the first interview but not subsequently was "arguing all the time," with 78.3% of its mentions occurring initially. This was followed by "inflexible; stubborn" (77.8% of its mentions at the first interview), "out with the boys/girls" (71.4%), "overcommitment to work" (61.9%), "not enough social life together" (66.7%), and "joint conflict over roles" (67.5%). With hindsight, all of these complaints can be thought of, to some extent, as the result of the process of disintegration. When spouses are not getting along well, avoidance is one method of handling the situation. This may include working long hours, going out with others, and having little interest in spending leisure time together. By the same token, arguing and stubbornness may be factors associated with the wrangling that occurs as a relationship is breaking up.

The next set of complaints mentioned only at the first interview by more than 50% of those mentioning them constitute a mixed bag, with some issues that move toward more substantive matters; some of these were also themes that recurred at the third interview. They included Financial and Employment Problems (Factor 6), Internal

TABLE 5.9. Percentage Distribution and Rank of Frequent Marital
Complaints at the First and Third Interviews: Suburban Divorced Sample

	% mentioning marital complaints ($n = 133$)			
Cleveland marital complaint categories	Only at first interview	First and third interview	Only at third interview	Total number mentioning complaint
Lack of communication or understanding	37.1	37.1	25.8	62
Change in interests or values	32.6	28.2	39.1	46
Different backgrounds; incompatible	31.7	26.8	41.5	41
Joint conflict over roles	67.5	15.0	17.5	40
Untrustworthy; immature	51.4	28.6	20.0	35
Extramarital sex	34.4	34.4	31.3	32
Factor 7: Internal Gender Role Conflict	54.2	12.5	33.3	24
Arguing all the time	78.3	—	21.7	23
Too young at time of marriage	45.4	36.4	18.2	22
Factor 6: Financial and Employment Problems	54.5	13.6	31.8	22
Alcohol	42.9	42.9	14.3	21
Emotional/personality problems	42.9	23.8	33.3	21
Overcommitment to work	61.9	9.5	28.6	21
Out with the boys/girls	71.4	4.8	23.8	21
Not enough social life together	66.7	9.5	23.8	21
Inflexible; stubborn	77.8	5.6	16.7	18
Problems with in-laws and relatives	41.2	35.3	23.5	17
Disagreements over money	53.3	6.7	40.0	15
Jealousy	53.3	20.0	26.7	15
Other, personality	66.7	6.7	26.7	15

Gender Role Conflict (Factor 7), "disagreements over money," "jeal-ousy," and "untrustworthy; immature."

With time to reflect upon reasons for the breakdown of their marriages, respondents mentioned certain kinds of complaints with greater frequency. Some of these, among the most frequently men-tioned complaints at the first interview (see Table 5.3), became even more commonly mentioned. Among these was "different back-grounds; incompatible," mentioned by 41.5% of the subjects for the first time at the third interview. This was followed by "change in interests or values," "emotional/personality problems," Internal Gender Role Conflict (Factor 7), Financial and Employment Problems (Factor 6), and "extramarital sex." To some extent, these complaints may have stemmed from a greater realization of just how different the partners were or had become during the marriage, as well as from an acknowledgment of problems and issues that were harder to face earlier in the divorce process.

In addition to complaints that increased or decreased in importance over time, other complaints were mentioned as problems in the marriage at the first interview and were still seen as such at the third interview. The most prominent of these was "alcohol," with 42.0% of those who mentioned it initially still doing so at the third interview. Other such complaints included "lack of communication or understanding," "too young at time of marriage," "problems with in-laws and relatives," and "extramarital sex."

As indicated in Table 5.8, relatively few individual complaints were significantly associated with psychological distress initially. Did this pattern hold across time? To address this issue, the relationship between marital complaints made at the first interview and subjective distress at the third interview was examined; in addition, complaints made at the third interview were examined in connection with distress at that interview. Only one complaint that was significantly associated with distress initially, "extramarital sex" was still associated with distress at the third ($\tau_b = .15$, $p < .05$). To have the marital bonds of sexual intimacy and trust broken continued to gnaw at, and produced long-term distress for, some of the subjects. The only other associations between complaints made at the first interview and distress at the third reflected a sense of relief. Distress was significantly lower for those who at the first interview mentioned "other problems with the children" ($\tau_b = -.19$, $p < .01$) and "joint conflict over roles" ($\tau_b = -.17$, $p < .05$). These concerns apparently no longer grated to such an extent with the spouse gone.

At the third interview, several complaints not previously significantly associated with distress became so. When "overcommitment to work" ($\tau_b = .13$, $p < .05$) and "general neglect of household duties" ($\tau_b = .17$, $p < .05$) were reported as complaints, respondents were more distressed. That these complaints continued to be associated with distress suggests that some subjects might still have preferred to be with their spouses if only the partner had not been over- or under-performing in certain role areas. Those at the third interview who reported "disagreements over money" as a complaint were less likely to be distressed at that interview ($\tau_b = -.14$, $p < .05$), presumably, again, because this was no longer an irritant over which the couples haggled.

CONCLUSION

The data presented above suggest that each of the three meanings of the term "causes of divorce" explored in this chapter—the legal grounds used, the risk factors for divorce, and the divorced person's perception of the reasons for the marital breakup—produces only a partial picture of what happens when marriages end. The least complete information is produced by use of the legal grounds for divorce. Only 2 from Ohio's list of 10 grounds for fault-based divorce were used with any frequency in the Cleveland-area suburban divorces studied: "gross neglect of duty" and "extreme cruelty."

The types of marital complaints made in the late 1940s and the mid-1970s differed, but there was much less variation in the types of complaints made in the 1970s and the 1980s. Furthermore, men and women differed somewhat in the types of complaints made. There were few differences by race in complaints, with little support for the proposition that economic issues would be of greater importance for nonwhites than for whites.

The data do illustrate that marital complaints were not randomly distributed in the suburban divorced population studied. Demographic characteristics such as gender, social class, length of marriage, income, education, and age, and experiences such as childhood parental loss and premarital pregnancy, did contribute to respondents' perceptions of the reasons for their marital breakups. Such factors were not necessarily conscious in the subjects' minds, but were represented by statistically significant correlations between marital complaints and these factors. The number of significant associations was, however, fairly small. These data do suggest that there is utility in continuing to explore the role of risk factors singly and jointly, in measures that may be able to predict the likelihood that a divorce will occur.

As for the impact of marital complaints on adjustment, there were some associations between marital complaints and indicators of psychological status. Complaints that reflected upon the respondents' self-esteem or produced guilt about ending the marriage, such as complaints of extramarital sexual relations or other serious complaints, were associated with heightened distress and lowered self-esteem. Other complaints, however, which reflected irritants that a person was presumably glad to have removed, were associated with fewer adjustment difficulties.

The analysis indicates that early in the divorce process, the "accounts" or perceptions of those going through the experience may be used to explain away behavior or rationalize the end of marriage, rather than to get at the root of the reasons for the breakup. With time, some of the complaints that seem to be correlates of the breakup process itself, not necessarily causes of the divorce, fall away. On the other hand, some complaints, such as the use of alcohol and physical abuse, appear to be long-standing concerns and have an impact on the respondent's health status. The divorced person's perception of and experiences in the marriage are important in understanding the impact of the end of the relationship upon his or her health functioning. In the next chapter, the impact of the divorce process on health status is explored.

NOTES

1. It was hypothesized that the types of complaints made should vary by demographic characteristics. Given this hypothesis, another possible explanation for any differences in marital complaints between the mid-1970s and the mid-1980s might be the use of age as a stratifier in the later sample. As a result, to determine whether the fact that the marital transition sample was evenly split between women aged 44 and under and those aged 45 to 62 could have affected the results, the suburban divorce sample was split into these two age groups and cross-tabulated with the marital complaints code. Only seven marital complaints differed significantly by age group, the same number as were significant when age was treated as a continuous variable, as in Table 5.7. Four of the complaints in the two age distributions were the same: "emotional needs not met," a complaint more common among the young; "other, lack of investment" (in the family) and "extramarital sex," more frequent complaints of older women; and Financial and Employment Problems (Factor 6), a group of complaints more common among the young. With the exception of "extramarital sex," the complaints that differed by age were not among the most frequent complaints. These findings suggest that the method of sampling used in the county-wide marital transition study did not substantially affect these results.

2. Instrumental complaints included the following: "too young at time of marriage," "disagreements over money," "desertion," "alcohol," "threatened physical abuse," "premarital pregnancy," "other problems with children," "out with the boys/girls, "general neglect of household duties," "joint conflict over roles," "other, role conflicts," Factor 3, Physical and Psychological Abuse;

Factor 4, Gambling and Criminal Activities; Factor 1, Conflict over the Children; Factor 5, Generalized Discontent; and Factor 6, Financial and Employment Problems.

3. Expressive complaints included the following: "lack of communication or understanding," "change in interests or values," "overcommitment to work," "jealousy," "untrustworthy; immature," "inflexible, stubborn," "self-centered." "other, personality," "not enough social life together," "no sense of family," "other, lack of investment" (in the family), "extramarital sex," "problems with in-laws and relatives," "not sure what happened," Factor 2, Sexual Problems Due to Health, and Factor 7, Internal Gender Role Conflict.

C H A P T E R 6

The Impact of Divorce on Emotional Adjustment

[Comedian/songwriter Kip Addotta] refers to his ex-wife as "Plaintiff."
Romance gone rotten, he says, is bad for the soul but good for business: "I
get to write songs like I'm So Miserable Without You, It's Just Like Having
You Around.*"*

—Callan (1986, p. 61)

W‍hat happens to the psychological and physical health of men and women who divorce? What kinds of feelings do they experience? How do those feelings change over time? Despite increasingly clear evidence of the personal turmoil and psychological toll that divorce often takes on spouses going through the end of a marriage and on their children, research on divorce has spent more effort on defining who divorces than it has on what happens to them after the divorce. Although psychological distress in divorce is often discussed, there are few descriptions of the proportions of the divorced population who experience such symptoms, or of the ways in which such symptoms change across time.

In this chapter, cross-sectional and longitudinal data on adjustment to divorce are described for the suburban divorced and married samples. Psychological symptom data in the county-wide marital transition study are also examined. Other issues to be explored include changes in psychological and physical health across time, delineation of the periods in the divorce process that the divorced perceive as most distressing, and a description of differences in adjustment by race and gender. Finally, the effect on adjustment of other life events occurring simultaneously with or subsequent to the divorce is described.

ADJUSTMENT AND PHYSICAL ILLNESS SCORES FOR THE DIVORCED AND MARRIED

Although the primary focus of this chapter is on psychological adjustment and the factors that make it easier or harder for the divorced to cope with the changes they face, marital disruption is associated not only

149

with psychological distress, but also with higher rates of physical illness and mortality from natural and violent causes (Gove, 1973; Shoenborn & Marano, 1988; Smith et al., 1988; Trovato & Lauris, 1989; Verbrugge, 1979). This section, therefore, discusses both psychological and physical health scores for the divorced and married in the suburban sample. The indicators of distress include the measures assessing adjustment (subjective distress, attachment, self-esteem, and illness contacts) as well as a measure of psychosomatic symptoms. The divorced and married were asked about nine psychosomatic conditions: "asthma," "allergies," "headaches," "backaches," "indigestion," "nervous stomach," "irregularity," "trouble with menstrual periods" (for women), and "pain in chest." According to what is known about adjustment to divorce, the divorced respondents should have more symptoms of psychological and physical distress than would the married. The number of divorced cases at the first interview has been reduced to 178, the number for whom there is a married match. This provides a more stringent test of the similarities and differences between the two groups.

Symptoms of Physical and Psychological Distress at the Time of Filing

As expected, at the first interview (conducted at the time of filing for divorce), the divorced exhibited significantly more symptoms of physical and psychological distress than the married. This was, on the average, a year after separation for the divorced, with the median being 5 months. Their mean subjective distress scores (3.4) were higher than those of the married (2.3), meaning that they had more symptoms of anxiety and depression ($t = 3.8$, $df = 348$, $p < .005$). The divorced also had more problems in terms of self-concept, as indicated by their higher mean scores on the self-esteem measure (18.2 vs. 16.9 for the married; $t = 1.9$, $df = 348$, $p < .05$). Their physical health was poorer as reflected by their higher mean illness contacts scores (3.4 vs. 2.0 for the married; $t = 5.3$, $df = 348$, $p < .005$). Finally, they reported more psychosomatic complaints (a mean of 2.1 vs. 1.7 for the married; $t = 2.4$, $df = 348$, $p < .01$).

The extent of turmoil that some of the separated and divorced subjects were experiencing compared to the married subjects is illustrated by scores on individual items of the subjective distress scale. For the five items with the highest frequency of reply, the divorced had significantly higher scores than the married on four. The divorced reported "worrying a lot" (43.6% vs. 25.8%; $\chi^2 = 11.8$, $df = 1$, $p < .001$), "anxiety" (31.4% vs. 20.3%; $\chi^2 = 5.5$, $df = 1$, $p < .001$); "trouble sleeping" (25.6% vs. 16.3%; $\chi^2 = 4.6$, $df = 1$, $p < .05$); "sadness or depression" often or most of the time (18.0% vs. 4.5%; $\chi^2 = 15.8$, $df = 1$, $p < .001$); and "poor appetite" (14.0% vs. 5.1%; $\chi^2 = 8.0$, $df = 1$, $p < .01$). There were no significant differences in "irritability," with 34.5% of the divorced reporting it, as opposed to 29.2% of the married.

The findings support the view that early in the divorce process the separated and divorced were having emotional difficulties that were presumably related to the changes brought about by the decision to end their marriages and file for divorce. But, even with these data, the same issue discussed earlier arises: Does the marital turmoil preceding the decision to divorce and the divorce process itself lead to these higher scores, or do the social and psychological characteristics of the divorced make them more prone to disturbance, and therefore distinguish them from their married neighbors?

Marital Turmoil and Indecision as Stressors

Several additional pieces of information support the conclusion that whatever other characteristics distinguish the married and divorced, marital turmoil and distress constitute significant stressors that are associated with health disturbance. First, as an indication of the toll that marital unhappiness takes on health status, the quarter of the married sample who reported that they and their spouses had seriously discussed filing for divorce, and those of the married who had actually separated at some point from their spouses, had significantly higher scores on subjective distress and psychosomatic complaints than those who did not. The mean level of subjective distress for those who had ever suggested divorce was 3.1 versus 1.7 for those who had not, F $(1, 176) = 11.6$, $p < .001$. The mean number of psychosomatic complaints for those who had suggested divorce was 2.6 and for those who had not was 2.0, F $(1,176) = 5.0$, $p < .05$. Married respondents who had previously separated from their spouses also had significantly higher subjective distress scores (3.2 vs. 1.9 for those who had not), F $(1, 175) = 5.1$, $p < .05$. There were no major differences in their self-esteem and illness contacts scores. (For more on the relationship between marital separation, reconciliation, and health status, see Kitson & Langlie, 1984.)

Retrospective Reports of Changes in Feelings and Behaviors

The restrospective self-reports of the divorced clearly support a crisis interpretation—that is, the view that the turmoil surrounding the breakup of the marriage increases distress. When the divorced subjects in the longitudinal suburban study were asked to reflect on their experiences, they recalled that the divorce process during its early stages had a number of dislocating effects, but that these decreased with time.

The divorced were asked at the second (or first postdivorce) interview about 14 different feelings or behaviors that might have affected them at some point in the divorce process: "before the decision to divorce," "at the time of the decision," "at the final separation," "when first filing for divorce," "at the final divorce decree," "now," or "never." Here, the focus is on the 8 of these 14 feelings or behaviors that were most commonly mentioned as problems.

Virtually every respondent (93.8%; $n = 161$), reported at least one of the problem areas, with the average being 4.8. They were most likely to report "feeling low or down" (85.4%). This was followed by "loneliness" (84.9%), "trouble working efficiently" (81.0%), "drinking more" (76.5%), "smoking more" (76.1%), "poor health" (75.5%), "trouble sleeping" (69.0%), and "weight change" (41.6%). Although two in seven mentioned at least one of the periods as the most distressing, the most frequently mentioned period was "before the decision to divorce"— the period of indecision and ambivalence about what course of action to take—which 51% mentioned as the most distressing. Women were more likely than men to mention this period: 58.5% of the women picked it, as opposed to 41.5% of the men ($\chi^2 = 14.3$, df $1 = 1$, $p < .05$). This was, however, the only significant time period difference by gender. For both groups, the number of troubles and the percentage reporting them decreased from that period of indecision. The periods with the second and third highest ratings were "at the time of the decision," mentioned by 42.4%, and "at the final separation," mentioned by 40.8%. For most of the divorced subjects, these two periods represented the period before the first of the three interviews with them.

For four of the eight problem areas, women were significantly more likely than men to report being troubled by various symptoms. Eighty-seven percent reported "poor health" at some point in the divorce process, compared to 61.6% of the men ($\chi^2 = 14.6$, $df = 1$, $p < .001$). Women also more often reported "trouble sleeping" (76.1% vs. 60.0%; $\chi^2 = 4.7$, $df = 1$, $p < .05$); "trouble working efficiently" (90.8% vs. 69.0%; $\chi^2 = 12.1$, $df = 1$, $p < .001$); and "feeling low or down" (94.3% vs. 74.3%; $\chi^2 = 12.3$, $df = 1$, $p < .001$). Although the gender differences were not statistically significant for the other four areas, in every one of the eight problem areas the women had higher scores than the men.

These data illustrate the dislocating impact of divorce in a number of areas of individuals' lives; indicate either that women were more affected by these than men or that women were more willing to acknowledge their distress; and support the findings from other retrospective research concerning initially high levels of divorce distress that decrease with time (Albrecht et al., 1983; Chester, 1971; Chiriboga & Cutler, 1977; Goode, 1956; Jacobson, 1983).

CHANGES IN HEALTH AND PSYCHOLOGICAL STATUS FOR THE DIVORCED ACROSS TIME

In this examination of changes in health status scores for the suburban divorced sample over time, the number of cases has been reduced to 133, the number remaining in the study at the conclusion. In this way, changes in scores are reported for the same set of people across time. This provides some assurance that reductions or increases in scores are not results of the differing composition of the samples.

On all of the adjustment and physical health measures, the initially high scores for the divorced went down substantially and significantly between the first and second interviews (Table 6.1). This interview took place an average of 2 years after separation, with the median being 18 months. The divorced had less subjective distress, improved self-esteem, decreased attachment, fewer illness contacts, and fewer reported psychosomatic complaints at the second interview. Their subjective distress and illness contact scores remained elevated by comparison with those of the married respondents reported above, but their self-esteem scores and psychosomatic complaint scores were no longer significantly different from the married scores (for subjective distress, $t = 1.8$, $df = 239$, $p < .05$; for illness contacts, $t = 2.4$, $df = 239$, $p < .01$). These data support the view that divorce in its early stages represents a crisis during which individuals experience difficulties in adjustment.

By the third interview, the scores for the divorced decreased still more, so that comparisons for only one of the common indicators for the divorced and married, subjective distress, was statistically significant ($t = 1.9$, $df = 247$, $p < .05$). By this measure, the divorced continued to be more anxious and depressed than the married as long as 4 years after separation from their spouses. Although the other scores for the divorced at the third interview did not increase enough to result in statistically significant differences from the scores for the married, two went up enough that the divorced had significantly higher scores on the illness contacts measure and psychosomatic complaints at the

TABLE 6.1. Mean Health and Psychological Status Indicator Scores at Three Time Periods: Suburban Divorced Sample

Health and psychological status indicators	Interview 1 (time of filing for divorce; $n = 129$)	Interview 2 (year after decree granted; $n = 124$)	Interview 3 (2–3 years after divorce; $n = 133$)
Subjective distress[a]	3.0	1.7	2.3
Attachment[b]	9.7	7.7	6.4
Self-esteem[c]	18.2	16.5	15.9
Illness contacts index[d]	3.4	2.5	2.6
Psychosomatic complaints[e]	2.3	1.7	1.9

[a]Scores ranged from 0 to 24 (higher scores indicated higher distress).
[b]Scores ranged from 4 to 20 (higher scores indicated higher attachment).
[c]Scores ranged from 10 to 50 (higher scores indicated *lower* self-esteem).
[d]Scores ranged from 0 to 15 (higher scores indicated more illness).
[e]Number of complaints (of a possible 9).

end of the study than at their second interview (for illness contacts, $t = -2.1$, $df = 123$, $p < .05$; for psychosomatic complaints, $t = -1.7$, $df = 123$, $p < .05$).

Although these data indicate that the suburban divorced sample had higher mean scores on the various indicators of health and psychological status than did the married, they do not indicate what proportions of the samples were experiencing symptoms initially and across time. A relationship can be statistically significant without necessarily affecting very many people. The data in Table 6.2 address this issue. The range of scores was divided, where possible, into four categories: no symptoms or indicators of the behavior or attitude, and low, moderate, and high symptom scores. The table shows that the distress experienced was substantively important, not simply a statistical relationship involving extreme cases. For example, only about one-sixth of the divorced, as opposed to one-quarter of the married, were without any symptoms of subjective distress at the first interview. Although symptom levels went down with time, the divorced continued to have higher levels of distress across all three of the interviews than did the married.

At the first (or time-of-filing) interview, virtually all of the separated and divorced had some continuing attachment to their (ex-)spouses, with close to a quarter having high scores on the measure. There are no comparison scores for the married on the attachment measure. At the second interview, a year after the divorce decree was

TABLE 6.2. Indicators of Adjustment for the Suburban Divorced Sample at Three Interviews and the Suburban Married Sample: Frequencies and Mean Scores

Adjustment indicators	Divorced			Married
	Interview 1	Interview 2	Interview 3	
Subjective distress				
No symptoms	14.4%	28.8%	22.6%	26.4%
1–4 symptoms	55.2%	53.7%	60.9%	59.6%
5–9 symptoms	26.4%	14.4%	14.3%	12.4%
10–14 symptoms	4.0%	3.1%	2.3%	1.7%
Total	100.0%	100.0%	100.1%	100.1%
(*n*)	(201)	(160)	(133)	(178)
(Mean)	(3.4)	(2.4)	(2.6)	(2.0)
(*SD*)	(3.0)	(2.8)	(2.6)	(2.3)
Attachment				
None (score of 4)	15.3%	35.6%	41.3%	—
Low (scores of 5–9)	43.1%	36.9%	42.1%	—
Moderate (scores of 10–14)	18.3%	22.5%	12.7%	—
High (scores of 15–20)	23.3%	5.0%	4.0%	—
Total	100.0%	100.0%	100.1%	—
(*n*)	(202)	(160)	(126)	—
(Mean)	(9.8)	(7.4)	(6.5)	—
(*SD*)	(5.0)	(3.7)	(3.3)	—
Self-esteem				
High (scores of 10–18)	57.2%	70.1%	69.0%	71.6%
Moderate (scores of 19–28)	35.6%	26.6%	27.9%	23.7%
Low (scores of 29–45)	7.2%	3.2%	3.1%	4.7%
Total	100.1%	99.9%	100.0%	100.0%
(n)	(194)	(154)	(129)	(169)
(Mean)	(18.2)	(16.4)	(16.0)	(16.9)
(*SD*)	(6.7)	(5.8)	(5.4)	(5.7)
Illness contacts index				
None	10.9%	38.5%	31.6%	12.9%
Low (scores of 1–5)	69.1%	54.0%	57.1%	74.7%
Moderate (scores of 6–10)	15.4%	6.9%	9.0%	11.8%
High (scores of 11–15)	4.5%	0.6%	2.3%	0.6%
Total	99.9%	100.0%	100.0%	100.0%
(*n*)	(201)	(161)	(133)	(178)
(Mean)	(3.2)	(1.7)	(2.3)	(1.0)
(*SD*)	(3.2)	(2.3)	(2.8)	(0.5)

granted, only 5% of the respondents had high attachment scores, whereas those who exhibited no attachment doubled from approximately one in seven to two in seven. At the third interview, the number of persons with high scores remained about the same, with a decrease in the number with moderate attachment and an increase in the number of respondents reporting low attachment. Nevertheless, 2–3 years after the divorce was granted, or about 4 years after separation, 6 out of 10 of the divorced still reported some lingering signs of attachment. Thus, although strong feelings of attachment decreased fairly rapidly, they did not completely disappear during the study period.

The proportion of the divorced sample with low self-esteem was not very high; even at the first interview, it was only 7.2%. By the second interview, a year after the divorce decree was granted, the number of persons with high self-esteem scores increased quite rapidly, with the scores for the divorced and married becoming similar and remaining that way.

From the time of the first interview, at which only 1 in 10 divorced persons had no indicators and 1 in 5 had moderate or high scores on the illness contacts index, the situation had changed quite substantially by the second interview. The divorced were more than three times as likely not to have any indicators (no illnesses and no health care contacts) as were the married, and quite unlikely to have moderate or high scores. By the third interview, more of the divorced were reporting problems, but they were still substantially more likely than the married to report no illness contacts or days lost to illness. Part of this shift may have been a result of the costs of health care: As Chapter 8 discusses in more detail, the incomes of many of the divorced respondents decreased significantly, and they may have felt that they could not afford to stay home in bed when ill.

These findings illustrate that substantial numbers of the divorced compared to the married were impaired by symptoms and feelings that appeared to be related to or affected by the turmoil of breaking up their marriages. The adjustment difficulties being experienced were not simply statistically significant but substantively unimportant phenomena. Many of these people going through divorce were wrenched by the continuing pulls of attachment toward their (ex-)spouses; suffered from a variety of physical ailments; and were buffeted by doubts, challenges, and uncertainties that manifested themselves in depression, anxiety, sleeplessness, and (in some cases) severe doubts about self-worth.

Although the data in Table 6.2 illustrate the proportions of persons affected adversely in various ways by divorce, they also produce a somewhat misleading picture. It was not simply that the divorced improved in adjustment in a straightforward progression; instead, some people became better adjusted, others made no changes, and still others actually experienced *more* symptoms of disruption in their functioning as time passed from the divorce filing. In Table 6.3, changes in scores between the first and second, second and third, and first and third interviews are displayed. If a person's score on an adjustment variable moved in the direction of more symptoms (say, from 2 to 3 or from 4 to 7 symptoms from one interview to the next), that person is included in the "worse" category; if a person's score

TABLE 6.3. Changes in Scores between Interviews for the Suburban Divorced Sample

Adjustment indicators	% change in scores between:		
	Interviews 1 and 2	Interviews 2 and 3	Interviews 1 and 3
Subjective distress			
Worse	24.0	34.1	27.1
No change	22.1	29.3	18.6
Improved	53.9	36.6	54.3
Total	100.0	100.0	100.0
(*n*)	(154)	(123)	(129)
Attachment			
Worse	19.5	19.7	13.1
No change	19.5	31.6	19.2
Improved	61.0	48.7	67.7
Total	100.0	100.0	100.0
(*n*)	(154)	(117)	(130)
Self-esteem			
Worse	35.6	40.4	25.0
No change	8.2	13.2	8.9
Improved	56.2	46.5	66.1
Total	100.0	100.1	100.0
(*n*)	(146)	(114)	(124)
Illness contacts index			
Worse	17.4	41.9	27.9
No change	23.2	33.9	20.2
Improved	59.4	24.2	51.9
Total	100.0	100.0	100.0
(*n*)	(155)	(124)	(129)

decreased, he or she is included in the "improved" group; a person whose scores were the same at two interviews (or who showed no symptoms at two interviews) is included in the "no change" category.

On all four of the adjustment indicators displayed, at least half of the respondents improved in their functioning between the first and second or the first and third interviews, with the greatest improvement occurring in attachment. At the same time, however, from about a sixth to a third of the individuals experienced *more* symptoms between the first and second interview. Self-esteem was the dimension most affected, followed by subjective distress, attachment, and the illness contacts index. About a seventh to a quarter of the subjects had more signs of adjustment difficulty at the third interview than they did at the first interview, but the majority either remained the same or improved.

The point at which a number of subjects experienced added troubles was between the second and third interviews: Disturbances in functioning occurred *after* the acute crisis of the period of separation and divorce filing, and persisted even 2–3 years after the divorce was granted. Such increases in difficulties were most common on the illness contacts index, followed by self-esteem, subjective distress, and, finally, attachment. Many of these differences, as discussed above, were not large enough to be statistically significant, but they were undoubtedly bewildering and discouraging to those experiencing them. As will be discussed below, this distress may not have been associated with the divorce itself, but with other life events that the divorced were experiencing. Whatever its cause, the course of post-divorce adjustment was not a smooth one for many persons. Although they experienced an overall improvement in symptomatology, some lagged behind, and others experienced renewed or increased symptoms as time passed.

POSITIVE AND NEGATIVE AFFECT: CROSS-SECTIONAL AND LONGITUDINAL DATA

The less statistically reliable but longitudinal data for the Positive and Negative Affect subscale scores for both the suburban married and divorced samples provide an additional perspective on the issue of adjustment. As reported in Chapter 2, these short psychological well-being measures were administered to the divorced and married in the suburban study at all interviews, and also to the divorced in the marital transition study. These scales have lower alpha reliability scores than the other adjustment measures being used, as Chapter 2 notes, but they serve as a check on the possibility of introducing errors by using cross-sectional adjustment data for the married in comparison to the longitudinal data for the divorced. The scores for the married were virtually the same on these subscales at the first and second interviews. This was interpreted as support for comparing the married subjects' cross-sectional subjective distress, self-esteem, and illness contacts scores to the longitudinal divorce scores. Here, this assumption is examined.

Cross-Sectional Comparisons

The suburban divorced sample has significantly higher mean scores (1.8) than the married (1.1) on the Negative Affect subscale at the first interview; that is, they had a lower sense of psychological well-being ($t = 4.6$, $df = 242$, $p < .005$). For the divorced, the Negative Affect scores decreased across the three interviews, indicating an increase in psychological well-being as time passed: At the second interview their mean score was 1.4, and at the third it was 1.1. Furthermore, unlike the longer measure of anxiety and depression (the subjective distress index), the Negative Affect subscale showed virtually no difference in scores for the married and divorced groups at the end of the study. Although mean scores for the divorced increased somewhat on the Positive Affect measure at the second (4.0) and third (3.8) interviews, there were no statistically significant differences between the married and the divorced on the Positive Affect measure at either set of these interviews. As measured by their scores on the Positive and Negative Affect subscales, the divorced at the end of the study were similar to the married in their sense of psychological well-being. Thus, these short five-item subscales indicated that after an initial period of distress, the scores of the divorced became like or returned to scores like those of the married. The longer (22-item) subjective distress measure still indicated significantly higher scores for the divorced than for the married at the end of the study. The differences between the two measures resulted from the greater number of items in the subjective distress measure, which increased the amount of variance in replies.

Was Divorce Less Distressing in the 1980s?

The psychological well-being scores for the divorced in the county-wide 1985-1986 marital transition study address the issue of changes in psychological health status scores over time. It is possible, as divorce became even more frequent in the late 1970s and 1980s, that going through a divorce became less distressing than in earlier years. The marital transition data do not support this view, however: The Negative Affect scores of women in the suburban divorce study at the first interview in 1974–1975 and divorced women in the marital transition survey in 1985–1986 were virtually identical (a mean score of 2.0 for divorced women in the marital transition sample and 1.7 for women in the suburban sample—not a statistically significant difference). Thus, on the dimension of negative affect, going through a divorce seems to have had the same distressing impact on well-being in the 1970s and 1980s. Women in the marital transition sample did, however, have significantly higher scores on the Positive Affect subscale than did those in the suburban sample (a mean score of 3.8, compared to a mean of 3.4 for the suburban sample; $t = 2.4$, $df = 289$, $p < .05$). The meaning of this finding is unclear, given the negative feelings both groups of women experienced and other findings. For example, when the marital transition sample and the 1974–1975 suburban married sample were compared, there were no significant differences in Positive Affect scores, but there were differences in Negative Affect scores. With a mean Negative Affect score of 2.0, the divorced women in the marital transition sample were significantly more distressed than the suburban married group, with a mean score of 1.0 ($t = 7.8$, $df = 264$, $p < .001$).

LEVELS OF PSYCHOLOGICAL IMPAIRMENT

Although the heightened psychological symptoms of the divorced have often been discussed in the literature, including the greater likelihood that separated and divorced persons will seek outpatient therapy or be hospitalized for a psychiatric disorder (Bebbington, 1987; Bloom et al., 1978; Rushing, 1979; Somers, 1979), there have been few attempts to illustrate how many of the divorced in a community-based sample are significantly impaired in their functioning. The items used in the subjective distress index for the suburban divorced and married samples were drawn from a longer scale that included some items that seemed less relevant for a community-based sample and were therefore dropped (Spitzer et al., 1970). This decision meant, however, that there were no norms for determining what proportion of the sample was likely to be significantly impaired.

In the marital transition study, a scale was used that allowed some estimates to be made. This was the 20-item Zung Self-Rating Depression Scale, which assesses affective, cognitive, behavioral, and psychological symptoms of depression (Zung, 1965). The 4-point scale has these response categories: "none or a little of the time," "some of the time," "a good part of the time," or "most or all of the time." Some of the items are reverse-scored to avoid response biases. Examples of items include the following: "I feel down-hearted, blue, and sad"; "Morning is when I feel best"; "I have trouble sleeping through the night"; "I feel that others would be better off if I were dead"; and "I feel hopeful about the future." Scores of 60 and above are indicative of significant impairment (Dye, 1982). Almost three-quarters of the marital transition sample (73.1%) had no or minimal depression (scores of 0–49), with 14% having moderate to severe symptoms of depression (scores of 60 and over) and the remaining 12.9% of the sample having mild to moderate symptoms (scores of 50–59). These data suggest that although substantial numbers of the respondents exhibited signs of distress, a relatively small number of persons (fewer than one in six) were experiencing severe distress. At least some of the people surveyed were undeniably experiencing depressed affect, but the data indicate that the majority of individuals were still able to function fairly adequately.

TAKING STOCK

What do these findings tell us about adjustment to divorce? First, the divorce process in its early stages is associated with adjustment difficulties, as reflected in a heightening of physical and psychological symptoms. Second, this increase in symptoms is substantive, not simply statistical; substantial numbers of individuals in these studies experienced distress. Third, although adjustment difficulties generally decreased with the passage of time, some divorced persons experienced increased symptoms as time passed. Fourth, despite the increasing numbers of persons experiencing divorce, the event is still a difficult one for people to handle; there were no significant differences in Negative Affect subscale scores of the divorced samples interviewed in the 1970s and the 1980s. Breaking up a once (perhaps still) important relationship continues to create distress. Finally, the baseline adjustment level for the divorced is still unclear. By the indicators of physical and psychological adjustment, the level of distress for the divorced went down within approximately 18 months of separation, or a year after the divorce was granted, to become comparable to that of the married. But, even 4 years after separation, the divorced had somewhat higher scores than the married on subjective distress. On the other hand, less reliable but longitudinal measures (the Positive and

Negative Affect subscales) for both the suburban married and divorced samples indicated no differences between the two groups at the 4-year interview.

From these data, it can be concluded that by the end of the study, at best, there were no differences in psychological and physical adjustment for the married and divorced groups; at worst, the divorced still were having somewhat more difficulty. In either case, the strong impression is that although the early stages of the divorce process constitute a substantial blow to physical and psychological health status, most individuals bounce back with time.

AGE AND ADJUSTMENT

Researchers have hypothesized that divorce in longer marriages at older ages creates more problems in adjustment (Hagestad & Smyer, 1982; Hennon, 1983; Lloyd & Zick, 1986). Such divorces, it is thought, create greater strain because they are so unexpected and out of the ordinary, in view of the fact that divorce generally occurs in the earlier years of marriage. Results from several recent studies have called this hypothesis into question, however. Data from both the marital transition study (Roach & Kitson, 1989) and a national stratified probability sample (Gove & Shin, 1989) have shown that age is inversely correlated with difficulties in adjustment to divorce: Younger persons, not older ones, have greater difficulty in coping. It may be that divorces occurring early in a marriage are as "off-time," to use Neugarten's (1979) phrase, as deaths at a young age (Kitson, 1991b). Virtually no one marries intending to divorce. Thus, to have marital hopes and plans dashed can be devastating. Generally, in longer-term marriages, there are some long-standing signs or indications of growing estrangement in the couple. As a result, although the timing of the actual breakup may be surprising, the presence of marital problems per se may be less so.

The relationship between age and psychological distress was examined in the suburban divorce data as well. It will be recalled from Chapter 3 that only a quarter of the suburban divorced sample was aged 40 or older and that only 22 persons, or 10.6%, were aged 50 or older. This meant that the distribution of cases was truncated for the exploration of age effects; as a result, the data were explored in several different ways. First, Pearson's correlation coefficients were computed. This technique showed that age was not significantly correlated with any of the psychological and physical adjustment variables for the total sample or for the sample broken down by gender. With one exception, analysis of variance also showed no significant differences for the total sample or by gender when age was collapsed into categories as follows: (1) 34 and under, 35 to 49, and 50 and over; (2) 29 and under, 30 to 39, and 40 and over; (3) 39 and under and 40 and over; (4) 44 and under and 45 and over. The one exception was that age was associated with the illness contacts index: Those who were 40 and over had significantly higher scores on this index than those 39 or under (a mean score of 5.3 vs. 3.5 for the younger group), F (1,199) = 4.00, $p < .05$. Illness scores generally do increase with age; in fact, such scores are often aged-standardized. Thus, the finding that illness levels among the divorced varied by age does not constitute strong support for the increasing impact of divorce by age. These data showing little or no effect of age on adjustment, and the recent Roach and Kitson (1989) and Gove and Shin (1989) data showing an inverse relationship between age and adjustment, call the hypothesis of greater distress in divorce at older ages into question. Among the few studies that have examined this issue previously, several have used samples that included only middle-aged and older subjects (Deckert & Langlier, 1978; Hagestad & Smyer, 1982), and have assumed as a matter of fact that such divorces should be difficult. Chiriboga's (1982) research used a sample with a limited number of older persons and found increased effects with age. This issue needs further examination in studies with sufficient numbers of older and younger subjects to allow exploration of a variety of social, economic, and psychological dimensions of adjustment.

CONTROLLING FOR PROBLEMS IN MEASURING ADJUSTMENT

Although longitudinal data have many advantages, particularly in assessing an event such as divorce that involves change, they also present difficulties. Among these is that when changes over time are examined, a few individuals with high scores may disproportionately influence the comparisons being made. Taking account of initial adjustment scores in analyses involving the later interviews makes it possible to determine which individuals actually improved the most. This can be done by statistically controlling for the earlier values through the use of difference, or change, scores as displayed in Table 6.3 above. This section examines the longitudinal adjustment data by gender and race, with and without controls for the adjustment scores at the beginning of the study.

Gender Differences in Adjustment

Although the scores for the divorced of both sexes were significantly higher than those of their married counterparts at the first interview, there were no statistically significant differences by gender for the divorced on two of the five indices, self-esteem and attachment (Table 6.4). Divorced women, however, were significantly more likely than divorced men to have high mean scores on subjective distress, the illness contacts index, and psychosomatic complaints. These effects were confirmed using multivariate analysis of variance (MANOVA), F (5, 186) = 7.0, $p < .001$.

Among the married, women scored higher on the same three indicators as their divorced counterparts: subjective distress, illness contacts, and psychosomatic complaints. However, when the effects of all four of these adjustment measures were taken into account in a MANOVA, only two of these differences remained statistically significant: subjective distress and psychosomatic complaints, F (4, 161) = 6.7, $p < .001$. This means that although illness contacts were significantly associated with gender, the correlations of this variable with the other dependent variables were such that when the adjustment measures were examined simultaneously, the effect of gender on physical illness was accounted for by its association with the other adjustment measures.

Given the high scores for the married women, this suggests that once the initial period of crisis in the divorce had passed, the baseline scores for divorced women might be higher than those of divorced men. If so, gender, not marital status, may be the major contributor to differences in physical and psychological health. This is an issue to be explored in greater detail in the chapters to come.

At the second interview, divorced women's scores continued to be higher than the men's on subjective distress and psychosomatic complaints. At the third interview, their scores were significantly higher than men's on the illness contacts index and on psychosomatic complaints. However, when the adjustment measures were examined simultaneously using difference scores (the scores at the second interview minus those at the first interview, and those at the third interview minus those at the second interview), there were no statistically significant differences by gender. The scores by gender decreased substantially and did not increase at the end of the study at a differential rate. Furthermore, there were no statistically significant differences by gender between the scores at the first and third interviews. When the initial scores were controlled for, gender did not account for the differences in the final scores. The effect of gender, if any, occurred

TABLE 6.4. Gender Differences in Mean Adjustment Scores for the Suburban Divorced Sample at Three Interviews and for the Married Sample

Indicators of psychological and physical distress	Divorced												Married			
	Interview 1 (df = 199)				Interview 2 (df = 159)				Interview 3 (df = 131)				(df = 176)			
	Males (n =98)	Females (n =103)	t	p	Males (n =73)	Females (n =88)	t	p	Males (n =61)	Females (n =72)	t	p	Males (n =83)	Females (n =29)	t	p
Psychological distress																
Subjective distress	3.0	3.8	−1.9	.05	1.9	2.8	−2.0	.05	2.6	2.6	0.01	n.s.	1.3	2.6	−3.9	.005
Self-esteem	18.4	18.0	0.4	n.s.	16.4	16.4	0.0	n.s.	16.0	16.1	−0.1	n.s.	16.5	17.2	−0.7	n.s.
Attachment	10.2	9.4	1.1	n.s.	7.3	7.5	−0.3	n.s.	6.5	6.6	−0.2	n.s.	—	—	—	—
Physical distress																
Illness contacts index	2.7	3.8	−2.6	.005	1.4	2.0	−1.5	.05	1.8	2.6	−1.7	n.s.	2.0	2.7	−2.1	.05
Psychosomatic complaints	1.6	2.0	−5.2	.005	1.1	2.1	−3.8	.005	1.8	2.6	−1.7	.05	1.7	2.5	−3.2	.005

primarily in the initial problems of adjustment and did not affect long-term adjustment.

Race Differences in Adjustment

There were no differences in adjustment scores by race for the married at the first interview when the scores were examined independently or jointly (Table 6.5). Divorced nonwhites, however, had significantly lower scores on two of the four indices when they were examined individually: subjective distress and attachment. When the scores were examined jointly, there were significant differences on these two measures and on psychosomatic complaints, F (5,186) = 4.6, p < .001. Thus, nonwhites seemed to have less difficulty adjusting than did whites.

At the second and third interviews, nonwhites continued to fare better emotionally than whites. Nonwhites had significantly lower subjective distress and attachment scores and higher self-esteem scores, as indicated by their lower scores on the measure. At the third interview, nonwhites continued to have lower subjective distress and higher self-esteem scores, but the differences on attachment were no longer significant. When the difference scores were examined between the first and second interviews and then the second and third interviews, there were no differences by race. However, when the difference scores for the adjustment measures were examined at the end of the study while controlling for those at the beginning, the two groups did differ, F (5, 111) = 2.3, p < .05. Whites had higher attachment and psychosomatic complaint scores than nonwhites even when controls were introduced for their original scores.

What might account for these racial differences? One possibility tested for is that because nonwhite respondents took a longer time to separate and file for divorce, as shown in Chapter 4, differences in length of the period of adjustment accounted for the differences. However, none of the associations between race and the health indices was reduced significantly by controlling for the length of time the marriage was bad before the divorce, the length of time between separation and filing for divorce, or the length of separation.

Another possible explanation is that because divorce is more frequent among urban blacks than whites, there may be less stigma attached to being divorced among blacks, who constituted the vast majority of the nonwhite group being studied. Under these circumstances, divorce may be viewed as a regrettable necessity, but an event that is a fairly acceptable (and perhaps even an expected) part of the life course. As a result, marital disruption may be less distressing than it

TABLE 6.5. Racial Differences in Mean Adjustment Scores for the Suburban Divorced Sample at Three Interviews and for the Married Sample

Indicators of psychological and physical distress	Divorced												Married			
	Interview 1				Interview 2				Interview 3							
	White (n=149)	Nonwhite (n=52)	t (df=199)	p	White (n=123)	Nonwhite (n=38)	t (df=159)	p	White (n=104)	Nonwhite (n=29)	t (df=131)	p	White (n=131)	Nonwhite (n=47)	t (df=176)	p
Psychological distress																
Subjective distress	3.8	2.1	4.2	.005	2.6	1.6	2.0	.05	2.9	1.6	2.4	.01	1.9	2.4	1.2	n.s.
Self-esteem	18.4	17.7	0.4	n.s.	16.8	14.9	1.7	.05	16.5	14.3	1.9	.05	16.7	17.5	-0.8	n.s.
Attachment	10.4	8.0	3.4	.01	7.8	6.4	2.0	.05	6.5	6.7	-0.4	n.s.	—	—	—	—
Physical distress																
Illness contacts index	3.2	3.3	-0.01	n.s.	1.7	1.8	-0.4	n.s.	2.2	2.5	-0.5	n.s.	2.2	2.8	-1.6	.05
Psychosomatic complaints	1.6	2.9	5.2	.005	1.7	1.8	-0.4	n.s.	2.2	2.5	-0.5	n.s.	2.0	2.4	-1.0	n.s.

167

is for whites, for whom it is a relatively less frequent event and may thus be more stigmatized. For example, in a community sample that assessed the amount of adjustment required by different life events, black subjects rated divorce as a less stressful event than did whites (Dohrenwend et al., 1978). This interpretation is explored further in Chapter 10. Other explanations for white and nonwhite differences in adjustment are examined in Chapter 11.

THE IMPACT OF OTHER LIFE EVENTS ON THE DIVORCED*

As another method of examining the disruptive potential of divorce, all of the suburban divorced and married subjects were asked whether any of 55 "common experiences . . . happened to you or to members of your family during the past year." Based on the work of Myers, Lindenthal, Pepper, and Ostrander (1972), queries were made about life events. Both positive events (e.g., "promotion") and negative (e.g., "out of work over a month"), and those involving losses (e.g., "death of a loved one") and gains (e.g., "birth of a child"), were included. (See Appendix A for the complete list of events.) Here, events that happened to the respondents or to the respondents and other members of their families are examined.

Life events need not simply be negative or involve losses to require change or adaptation that may adversely influence health status (Holmes & Rahe, 1987). Furthermore, not all events have the same impact; some events require more change or adaptation than others do (Dohrenwend et al., 1978; Ross & Mirowsky, 1979). For this reason, weighted life events scores based on judges' ratings as to the amount of readjustment an event is likely to require are often used to gauge the relative impact of these stressors. For example, a divorce is rated as requiring more adjustment than a significant increase in income. Here, the ratings developed by Dohrenwend et al. (1978) on the basis of a community sample's replies are used.

If divorce is a stressor with multiple impacts on a variety of areas of a person's life, different profiles of events for the divorced and married should be expected. Dohrenwend et al. (1978) have suggested that clusters of related events may be associated with certain kinds of major disruptions in a person's life, such as divorce. In other words, one event may be the source or "cause" of other events (Hill, 1958). For

---

*Some of the data in this section were originally presented in somewhat different form in Speagle and Kitson (1982).

example, moves at the time of a divorce may be the result of the change in marital status, either because one spouse must find a new dwelling or because both must move to smaller quarters because of reduced income. In the suburban divorced study, if these changes were temporary and related to the dislocations brought on by the divorce, the event profiles of the divorced and married groups should become more nearly similar by the third interview.

Frequency of Events

Table 6.6 displays the 15 most common events for the divorced at the first and third interviews, with comparisons to those for the married. The types of events are mixed, with some indicating positive changes, and others reflecting reversals. The divorced initially reported "change in number of family get-togethers"; more disagreements with family, friends, and neighbors; more moves; and more employment changes. This was the period during which the majority

TABLE 6.6. Frequent Life Events for the Suburban Divorced Sample at First and Third Interviews and for the Married Sample

	% reporting		
Life event	Divorced: Interview 1 ($n = 201$)	Divorced: Interview 3 ($n = 133$)	Married ($n = 177$)
Go on vacation	35.8	45.1	45.2
Change in number of family get-togethers	29.4	20.3	15.3
Major improvement in finances	22.4	40.6	24.3
Trouble with in-laws	22.4	9.0	10.2
Financial status worse	21.9	5.3	7.3
Serious disagreement with others	14.4	3.8	5.6
Changes at work	12.9	16.5	9.0
Promotion	12.9	15.0	7.9
Death of a pet	11.4	6.8	7.9
Major house remodeling	10.9	12.0	16.9
Move to same type of neighborhood	10.4	8.3	4.0
Change to same type of job	10.0	11.3	5.1
Out of work over a month	10.0	7.5	1.7
Temporarily laid off	9.5	1.7	4.0
Significant work success	8.5	11.3	5.0

separated and filed for divorce. By the end of the study, 2–3 years after divorce, the frequencies for such events had for the most part shifted toward those of the married.

Initially, the divorced not only experienced significantly more events than the married, as indicated by their total mean life events scores (3.3 vs. 2.4 for the married; $t = 3.9$, $df = 340$, $p < .001$, but also reported events that required more adjustment, as reflected in their higher total mean weighted scores (1.1 vs. 0.8 for the married; $t = 4.3$, $df = 340$, $p < .001$). Since, by definition, all of the divorced experienced a divorce and the married did not, the divorce itself and its associated legal activities were not included in the list of events. As a result, the higher life event frequencies for the divorced actually were underestimates of the events these subjects experienced. There were also significant differences in the mean number of negative events for the divorced (1.5 vs. 0.6 for the married; $t = 5.6$, $df = 340$, $p < .001$); in the judged severity of the negative events affecting the divorced (a mean of 0.6 vs. 0.2 for the married; $t = 6.2$, $df = 340$, $p < .001$); and in the amount of adjustment required for their weighted score for positive events (a mean of 1.1 vs. 0.4 for the married; $t = 8.6$, $df = 340$, $p < .001$). However, the total number of positive events did not differ significantly. Scores on events defined as exits or entrances (others leaving or entering the household) also did not differ for the two groups.

These data illustrate that much of the change initially engendered by divorce involves other unpleasant experiences, including other losses. During its early stages, those going through a divorce experienced more negative and positive events than a comparison group of married persons. The next section examines whether these events did indeed cluster differently for the divorced and the married. If so, these differences in event profiles are likely to have resulted from the impact of the divorce.

Life Events Associated with Divorce

To determine whether there were differences in the event profiles for the two groups, an oblique factor analysis was conducted on the life events data for the divorced and married at the first interview and for the divorced at the third interview. This type of factor analysis looks for correlations among variables; it does not necessarily indicate the most frequent events, but rather those that "stick together" and represent significant clusters of activities. Because the first factor would be the most likely to reflect any differences between the two groups, only the factor score coefficients for it are displayed in Table 6.7. Several

TABLE 6.7. Life Events Factor Score Coefficients for the Suburban Divorced Sample at First and Third Interviews and for the Married Sample

	Factor score coefficient		
Life event	Divorced: Interview 1 ($n = 201$)	Divorced: Interview 3 ($n = 133$)	Married ($n = 177$)
In detention or jail	.887	—	—
Fired from a job	—	.724	.895
Loss of driver's license	.821	—	—
Arrested	.773	—	.723
Entered the armed forces	.686	—	—
Court appearance (not for divorce)	.501	—	.442
Lawsuit or legal action	.341	—	.313
Out of work over a month	—	.673	.619
Temporarily laid off	—	—	.457
Serious disagreement with others	—	—	.459
Trouble with boss	—	—	.437
Significant work success	—	—	.412
Promotion	—	—	.395
Trouble with in-laws	—	.634	—
Changes at work	—	.398	—
Big work reorganization	—	.313	—
Return to work	—	—	.353
(% of variance)	(13.7%)	(12.1%)	(20.8%)
(Eigenvalue)	(3.6)	(2.9)	(4.2)

things are illustrated by this table. First, the patterns of events, as expected, were different for the two groups at the first interview. The events for the married occurred primarily in the domain of work activities. For the divorced at the first interview, there were no such job-related events with factor score coefficients over .30 (the cutoff for inclusion of events in the factors). Although the married reported some entanglements with the police and legal systems, the separated and divorced reported more such activities. These legal activities were in addition to those related directly to the divorce.

By the time of the third interview, the factor structure for the events the divorced were experiencing was closer to that of the married. Involvements with the legal system had dropped out, and three of the four events in the first factor were now work-related activities.

"Trouble with in-laws" also entered this mix of items, presumably either a continuing problem associated with the divorce or a problem with new in-laws. A second point about the items in Table 6.7 is that virtually all the events included for the divorced were negative or loss-related. Positive events required adjustment, but they did not cluster together in the manner of certain kinds of negative events for the divorced. Troubles seemed to come together, positive events one at a time.

Changes in Life Events by the Third Interview

As shown above, by the third interview the mix of events for the divorced had shifted from what they were at the first interview. Nevertheless, the mean number or weighting of events for the divorced did not change. They reported as many life events as at the beginning of the study (a mean of 3.3). By the end of the study, the events reported by the divorced were significantly less likely to be negative (a mean of 0.3 vs. 0.5 at the first interview; $t = -3.0$, $df = 133$, $p < .01$) and more likely to be positive (a mean of 1.7 vs. 1.3 at the first interview; $t = 3.1$, $df = 133$, $p < .01$). Other researchers have suggested that the frequency and severity of life events are important correlates of health disturbance in both the short and the long run (Dohrenwend & Dohrenwend, 1981; Elliott & Eisdorfer, 1982). If so, even 4 years after separating from their spouses, the divorced were at increased risk. The next issue to be explored is whether the event-filled nature of the divorced subjects' lives contributed to their difficulties in adjustment.

Life Events and Adjustment

Both the cross-sectional and the longitudinal data indicate that those among the divorced who reported experiencing more life events also had more problems in adjustment, as indicated by their Pearson's zero-order correlation coefficients. At the first interview, an increased number of illness contacts was associated with more total life events ($r = .18$, $p < .01$), with a higher weighted total life events score ($r = .24$, $p < .001$), and with more negative life events ($r = .27$, $p < .001$). Attachment was negatively associated with positive life events ($r = -.17$, $p < .05$); in other words, those who were more attached were less likely to report positive life events. Subjective distress, self-esteem, and psychosomatic complaints at the first interview were not associated with the life events scores.

On the other hand, at the third interview, subjective distress was associated with the total number of life events ($r = .18$, $p < .05$), with the total weighted life events score ($r = .19$, $p < .05$), and with negative life events ($r = .21$, $p < .05$) experienced in the year prior to this final interview. Illness contacts continued to be associated with the total weighted life events score ($r = .19$, $p < .05$) and with the weighted score for negative life events ($r = .19$, $p < .05$). Psychosomatic complaints were also associated with negative events ($r = .20$, $p < .05$). There were no significant associations with attachment or self-esteem.

With data from just one time period, it is hard to sort out the cause and effect of these relationships. Do those experiencing problems in adjusting to divorce have more difficulty coping with the tasks and responsibilities of daily life? Or does experiencing more life events make it more difficult to adjust both to them and to divorce-related events? The longitudinal data indicate that experiencing more life events at the first interview was associated with more difficulties in adjustment at the second interview but not at the third. Those with higher weighted and total life events scores at the first interview had higher subjective distress scores at the second interview, after the decree was granted (respectively, $r = .20$, $p < .01$, and $r = .18$, $p < .05$). Those with higher illness contacts scores were also higher on both total life events ($r = .17$, $p < .05$) and the weighted total score ($r = .20$, $p < .05$). Negative events at the first interview were also associated with higher scores at the second interview on subjective distress ($r = .24$, $p < .01$) and on illness contacts ($r = .20$, $p < .01$). This suggests that the effect of life events on health status can be long-lived. The life events scores themselves were correlated: Those with higher total weighted and positive scores at the first interview also had higher life events scores on these measures at the third interview, with correlations, respectively, of .27 ($p < .01$) and .25 ($p < .01$). There was, however, no association across time between the two negative events scores.

One event that can be particularly distressing is moving. Often the family house is sold and the profits are split between the partners, requiring both partners to move. In a divorce, it is more commonly the husband who moves out of the family home, leaving it to his wife and children. However, the wife may find that she cannot afford to keep up the rent or mortgage payments on her salary alone, or the house must be sold as part of the property settlement, so she too may have to move.

At the third interview, everyone in the suburban study was asked how many times they had moved since January 1974, 4–5 years earlier. With an average of 1.5 moves, the divorced were three times as likely to have moved as the married, who reported an average of 0.5 moves.

Although 41.7% of the women did not move, compared to only 27.9% of the men who reported no moves, when women moved they were significantly more likely than men to have moved multiple times. Women who changed residences moved an average of 2.7 times versus an average of 2.0 times for men ($t = 2.0$, $df = 131$, $p < .05$). With an average of 1.7 moves, whites were significantly more likely to have moved than nonwhites, who made an average of 0.7 moves ($t = 2.9$, $df = 131$, $p < .001$).

Moving was associated with greater distress. Among the 30 divorced subjects who moved three or more times, or on the average once every 1½ years during the study period, their rates of subjective distress were significantly higher (3.7 symptoms vs. 2.4 symptoms for those who moved two times or less; $t = -2.2$, $df = 131$, $p < .05$). These moves occurred in the context of other losses, such as coping with the changes brought about by the absence of the spouse, economic difficulties, and changes in friendship patterns. The move itself may have occasioned starting children in new schools, learning about the location of new shops and new routes to work, and developing new helping resources such as neighbors and babysitters. It is in this way that life events can continue to pile up as situations continue to change after a divorce.

With these data, one possible source of the continuing difficulties in adjustment for the divorced has been identified: The high number of life events that the divorced experienced during the initial stages of marital dissolution remained elevated as much as 4 years later. This suggests, first, that divorce is not simply one event, but an event that leaves in its wake a series of other events. McCubbin and Patterson (1983) have noted a similar phenomenon in studying the families of war prisoners. After passing through the initial period of crisis at the time of such major, stressful life events, there may then be a "pileup" of other associated events that themselves trigger additional adjustment difficulties. These stretch out and complicate the period of adjustment. (For other divorce research taking this perspective, see Buehler, Hogan, Robinson, & Levy, 1985–1986; Chiriboga et al., 1991; Tschann, Johnston, & Wallerstein, 1989.) A second point is that the adjustment difficulties produced by life events may not show up immediately, but may surface at some later time. Third, the divorced compared to the married experienced not only more life events but also more *negative* life events, both initially and several years after the divorce. This supports the hypothesis that even for those who choose to end their marriages, marital separation and divorce involve not just change but a series of losses. Loss seems to have an especially severe impact on health status (Parkes, 1972; Simos, 1979).

CONCLUSION

These longitudinal and retrospective data on difficulties in adjustment and heightened levels of life events for the divorced show conclusively that the initial stages of the divorce process produce disturbance in a number of areas of individuals' lives, and that this distress decreases as they move further from the period of indecision about whether to divorce. Women and whites have greater difficulty adjusting than do men and nonwhites. What is left uncertain is the baseline postcrisis level of adjustment for the divorced. Is it eventually the same as that of the married? Do those who choose to divorce suffer, as some propose, from social and psychological pathologies that perpetually distinguish them from the married? Alternatively, is the process of marital breakdown and recovery so severe that individuals do not fully recover from it or take substantially longer than anticipated to do so?

The fact that other studies have also found long-term distress for the divorced suggests that these issues need to be explored more fully. For example, Wallerstein and Kelly (1980) went back to reinterview the divorced families in their study for a third time 4–5 years after separation, because the rates of disturbance still seemed high at the second interview, approximately 18 months after separation. Wallerstein and Blakeslee (1989) and Wallerstein (1991) found high levels of distress for some subjects at a 10-year and a 15-year follow-up, respectively. Bloom, Hodges, et al. (1985) added a 4-year follow-up to their study of the impact of marital separation on adjustment to continue to assess the impact of an intervention program, because distress seemed surprisingly high at the 30-month evaluation. Individuals in the intervention group continued to improve in their functioning 4 years after separation. Hetherington et al. (1976) used a somewhat different time frame—2 months, 1 year, and 2 years *after* the divorce was granted. They found the highest distress among their sample of parents of nursery-school-age children 1 year after divorce. In a 6-year follow-up when the study children were aged 10, Hetherington (1987) found that the men had better general life satisfaction than the women. Women who were not remarried were more lonely and depressed and felt less in control of their lives than women in the nondivorced and remarried control groups.

These data and those of other researchers provide some support for the presence of longer-term distress in divorce after an initial decline. But what does this mean? In a sense, the situation is not unlike that of the glass half filled with water: Is it half empty or half full? Are the divorced substantially more distressed than the married or marginally different? It depends on one's perspective. If the aim is to demonstrate that those who divorce are different from those who do not, then perhaps the continued differences should be emphasized. If the focus is on how individuals reintegrate after what appears to be (at least for some) a substantial, pervasive psychological, social, and even physical blow precipitated by the marital rupture, then the similarity between the two groups at the end of the present study is striking. Furthermore, one potential reason for the elevated scores of the divorced has been identified: Breaking up a marriage entails a number of changes, and such changes themselves can produce other disruptions and long-term difficulties in adjustment. These changes appear to contribute to the continued, heightened distress of the divorced.

CHAPTER 7

Children in Divorce: Parents' Perceptions of the Impact of Divorce on Their Children

Marriages don't last anymore. When I meet a man, the first question I ask myself is, "Is this the man I want my children to spend their weekends with?"

—Comedienne Rita Rudner, quoted in *The Plain Dealer* (1988, p. 3)

In Chapter 6, men and women's emotional responses to their divorces have been explored. Many are adversely affected, at least in the short run. What impact does the divorce decision have on their children? Research on children and divorce reports that children are also affected, but do parents see this? This chapter reports on parents' perceptions of how the divorce affected their children. The types of problems parents see in their children are explored, and the question of whether divorced parents report more changes in their children than parents in intact families is examined. On the basis of what is known about divorce adjustment for parents and children, more reports of problems should be expected in the divorced families. Also described are the characteristics of divorced parents who do and do not see positive and negative divorce-related changes in their children.

Currently, approximately 2% of U.S. children under age 18 experience a divorce in their families in a given year (Glick, 1988). It is estimated that before they reach the age of 18, 40% of U.S. children will spend part of their childhoods in homes in which a divorce has occurred (Glick, 1988). As Hernandez (1988) reports, others project even higher proportions of children likely to experience the disruption of their parents' marriages, with estimates as high as 70% of white children and 90% of black children. What does the divorce experience mean for the development of children in both the short and long run? How do parents see their children as responding?

177

THE IMPACT OF DIVORCE ON CHILDREN
The Basis of Concern

The health and well-being of children whose parents have divorced are of concern to society ·for several reasons. First, children are innocent bystanders who cannot protect their own physical and psychological interests. Therefore, their rights should be protected for them when events, such as divorce, occur that may threaten their well-being (Goldstein, Freud, & Solnit, 1973). In recent years, much of this concern has focused on the need (1) to identify whether children of divorce are likely to be at risk for psychiatric disturbance, either immediately after the divorce or later as adults; and (2) to determine which children as adults are most likely to divorce, thereby possibly repeating the cycle for their own children.

A second basis for this concern for the well-being of children is not simply humanitarian. If the majority of parents, and more especially children, who have experienced divorce are impaired in their functioning (as some fear), and divorce continues at high rates, this could have serious consequences for the future of the society. From the perspective of the society, the function of the family is to produce and socialize the members of the next generation, so that they in turn will (1) continue to perform the work of the society; (2) marry and produce the next generation, and (3) nurture and socialize these newly produced members to continue the cycle. If events such as divorce reduce the supply of appropriately socialized young adults, this could seriously affect the future well-being of the society. As has been noted earlier, those who as children experienced the divorce of their parents are somewhat more likely to divorce themselves as adults. In addition, some limited research suggests that children whose parents divorce are less likely to obtain the kind and amount of education they would have if the parents had continued to live together (Cooney, 1988; Wallerstein & Corbin, 1986; Wallerstein & Huntington, 1983). Unless educational arrangements are written into the divorce agreement, the responsibility for child support ends at age 18. Many mothers, who generally become the custodial parents, have lower incomes than their former spouses, making it difficult for them to finance the education of their children on their own. Thus, at a time when the world market is becoming increasingly competitive for the United States, more children who as adults might have been able to obtain the education or training to find positions commensurate with their abilities may not be able to do so because of limited economic resources. The issues that divorce raises for the well-being of children therefore run the gamut from the immediate social and psychological well-being of the children to long-term consequences for the society.

Problems in Assessment

Studies of the impact of divorce on children are dogged by the same problems that have made it hard to assess the quality of the results of studies of divorce adjustment in adults (Blechman, 1982; Demo & Acock, 1988; Emery, 1988; Krantz, 1988; Kurdek, 1989; Zaslow, 1988, 1989). Convenience samples are often used; such samples are likely to have special characteristics or concerns that may make their members different from the general divorced population (Wallerstein & Kelly, 1980) or even from the general married population (Hetherington et al., 1976; Hetherington, Cox, & Cox, 1978). Studies may be based on clinical populations, with no clear notion of the community-wide distribution of the characteristics being assessed (Kalter, 1977). Results may be hampered by the small number of children being assessed (Hess & Camara, 1979); the lack of nondivorced comparison groups; reductions in sample size when children are examined by age (Wallerstein & Kelly, 1980); and analysis of data from several children in the same family (Furstenberg, Nord, Peterson, & Zill, 1983). This last factor "double-counts" the adjustment of some children, because the level of adjustment among family members is likely to be correlated, as Kalter, Kloner, Schreier, and Okla (1989) have reported. Finally, some studies have only examined children in a limited age range (Hetherington et al., 1978). Given developmental differences in children's responses to divorce by age, it is important to avoid overgeneralizing from these data.

A further problem in studies of children's reactions to the divorce of their parents is that the norm against which they are assessed is the nuclear, and therefore two-parent, family. Thus, regardless of the character of the family relationships, two parents are always assumed to be better than one. Therefore, any one-parent family is *ipso facto* deviant. Furthermore, as Herzog and Sudia (1970) noted in their landmark review, many early studies that reported poor adjustment for children in single-parent homes did not distinguish among the reasons for parental absence: death, divorce, war service, or jail. Children's responses are likely to vary, depending on the reasons for their fathers' absence. Although researchers are becoming increasingly aware of these problems, many conclusions about the impact of divorce on children are based on such data.

Even when population-based sampling is used, studies may be hampered by reliance on the reports of parents and/or teachers about the children's reactions, rather than on direct assessment of the children's reactions (Fulton, 1979). This is likely to produce particular problems, as noted later in this chapter, because parents may under- or overreport changes in their children. Only a relatively few studies have directly assessed the whole family unit: the mother, the children, and sometimes the father (Forehand & McCombs, 1988; Forgatch, Patterson, & Skinner, 1988; Furstenberg et al., 1983; Guidubaldi & Perry, 1985; Hetherington et al., 1976; Kurdek, 1987; Wallerstein & Blakeslee, 1989; Wallerstein & Kelly, 1980).

Children's Reactions to Divorce: Findings in the Literature

The literature on children and divorce is quite clear in suggesting that most children, like their parents, find the breakup of their families distressing. Depending on a child's age, sex, temperament, and circumstances, the distress may be short- or long-term. Among the responses to the divorce of their parents that children commonly display are grief, anxiety, guilt, and depression; shame, anger, and resentment; poor school performance; physical illness; and attention-seeking, aggressive, acting-out, or antisocial behavior (Cherlin et al., 1991; Derdeyn, 1977; Emery, 1988; Forgatch et al., 1988; Hetherington, 1989; Hetherington et al., 1976; Hetherington, Stanley-Hogan, & Anderson, 1989; Kalter, 1990; Kelly, 1988; Krantz, 1988; Kurdek, 1989; Mauldon, 1990; Wallerstein, 1991; Wallerstein & Blakeslee, 1989; Wallerstein & Kelly, 1980). These symptoms may be subtle or may represent quite dramatic shifts in a child's personality and behavior, and they may be immediate or delayed. Some more recent reports indicate that in the long run, the negative effects of parental divorce on children may be less severe than was previously thought (Hetherington, 1989; Kalter, 1990; Kurdek, 1981). It is also important to keep in mind, however, that even a "temporary" period of disturbance of 1 or 2 years may represent a quarter, a third, or half of a child's life if he or she was 3 to 8 years of age at the time of the divorce.

Because of these potential problems, some reliable method of locating children who need assistance in handling their feelings about and adjusting to the divorce of their parents is required. It is reasonable to assume that parents are the persons in a child's life who are best able to assess how the child is coping with the changes a divorce brings. It has been demonstrated in Chapter 6 that the divorce process does produce at least temporary disturbance in functioning for almost all adults. Although this may affect their judgment somewhat, parents nonetheless remain the most knowledgeable sources of information about their own children. They are the observers with the most experience in assessing their children's normal behavior, likes and dislikes, daily habits, and responses to crises. Although the distress of divorce may well lead to distortion in parents' reports of their children's responses, it is plausible to argue that parents are or can be far better informants than teachers, ministers, physicians, relatives, or friends of the family, who may be less emotionally involved in the divorce but who know the children less well. Furthermore, when teachers or others pinpoint difficulties, parents are the ones who must be convinced that help is needed.

Because data on children themselves were not gathered in the present research, it is not possible to compare parents' perceptions of their children's responses to divorce with direct measures of those responses for each child. However, other research has demonstrated not only that children of divorce show more changes in affect and behavior than comparable children from intact homes (Hetherington et al., 1978), but also that a substantial proportion of these children show continuing disturbances in behavior and affect (Hodges, 1986; Jacobson, 1978a, 1978b, 1978c; Kalter, 1977,1990; Kelly & Wallerstein, 1976; Wallerstein, 1991; Wallerstein & Blakeslee, 1989; Wallerstein & Kelly, 1974, 1975, 1976). It is safe to assume on the basis of what is known that, like their parents, many children are affected by the divorce in its early stages. The numbers who are affected in the long run are somewhat more questionable; many adults recover, but children may be more vulnerable developmentally, and some may have long-term difficulties. (See Amato & Booth, 1991a, for psychological, social, and marital difficulties reported by adult respondents whose parents had divorced in the subjects' childhood.)

THE QUESTIONS ASKED
ABOUT THE CHILDREN'S BEHAVIOR

Because the focus of the longitudinal suburban study was on the adjustment of adults to divorce, relatively few questions were asked about the children's adjustment, and none were asked of the children directly. In this section, only divorced and married parents with children aged 18 and under are examined.

At the first interview, divorced respondents with children were asked, "How did your child(ren) react to the decision to divorce?" At both the first and third interviews, they were asked, "Have you noticed any differences in your child(ren)'s behavior from what it was before the decision was made to divorce?" These included seven areas of affect and behavior, ranging from "happiness" to "getting into trouble" (see Appendix A for the items).

Parents in the married sample were asked about the same affects and behavior, but these questions were introduced as follows: "Have you noticed any difference in your child(ren)'s behavior in the past few months?" This introduction was somewhat different from that of the divorced. Replies were coded in the same way as for the divorced; nevertheless, one explanation for any differences in replies between the two samples may be this introduction. (The results, however, suggest that this is unlikely.)

In reply to all of these questions, when parents made any comments—including "I don't know what she thinks about this" or "I don't see any change"—these comments were coded. For many of the analyses reported below, replies were collapsed into "negative reactions" (behaviorally or emotionally worse; upset; physical symptoms; or ambivalence, some negative and some positive reactions); "positive reactions" (behaviorally or emotionally improved); and "no change" (no difference, no effect, no change; no discussion of children's feelings; don't know their reactions). The replies were coded for the youngest or only child, the oldest child, and the children as a group. This was done because the youngest and oldest children define the limits of the life cycle stage currently occupied by a family, and the concern in this research was more with the impact of the family structure on adjustment than with its impact on the children per se. The code for the children as a group was added because parents sometimes said "They are doing better" or "They are doing worse," without mentioning specific children.

FINDINGS AT THE FIRST INTERVIEW
(TIME OF FILING)

Parents' Perceptions of Children's Responses to Divorce

Not surprisingly, parents indicated that when their children were told about the decision to divorce, the most common reaction was a negative one. But only 36.6% reported such reactions for a youngest or only child, whereas 59.4% reported this for an oldest child. In light of clinical reports that even very young children are likely to have some negative reaction to the divorce of their parents, it is noteworthy that the next most common reply was that a child was "too young" to react or that they "did not know" what the child's response was, with 33.8% of those reporting on a youngest or only child giving these replies and 9.4% of those reporting on an oldest child. Twelve percent of the parents reporting on a youngest or only child and 9.4% reporting on an oldest child said that the child responded positively. Open approval (acceptance, a positive response, or other behavioral or emotional approval) was reported by 9.9% of those with a youngest or only child and 18.8% with an oldest child. For 7.0% of the parents reporting on a youngest child and 3.1% with an oldest child, the child had not been told, his or her response was ambivalent, or there was no discussion of the child's feelings. These data suggest that more efforts may be needed to educate parents that even very young children may be at least temporarily adversely affected by divorce, and that the parents should be on the lookout for the often subtle signs of such possible disturbance.

Table 7.1 displays the frequencies of parents' replies for a youngest or only child and an oldest child for each of the areas of feelings and behavior about which parents were asked. The number of replies is fairly small, so to some extent it is misleading to use percentages, especially for the behaviors of the small number of older children. For example, a reply of 50% may entail reports on two of four children. Nevertheless, the figures illustrate some trends.

For youngest children, the most common reply was "no change." The replies for the divorced and the married parents were not substantially different, despite the likelihood, based on what is known about responses to divorce, that the divorced parents' children were likely to be experiencing a substantial amount of distress. The areas in which both youngest and oldest children were reported to be experiencing the most distress were "happiness," "school work," "general behavior," and "health." The most striking finding, however, is that parents involved in divorces reported so few changes for youngest or only children: From over half to over 90% reported no differences or changes in the individual categories of behavior or affect. With oldest children, the parents were more likely to see some changes, and more commonly these changes were negative. Kurdek and Siesky (1978), in a study of parents drawn from the organization Parents Without Partners, also reported relatively few child-centered problems considered to be "moderate" or "severe" concerns.

Because the number of mentions of changes was low, the replies for the youngest or only child, the oldest child, and the children as a group were combined into two dummy variables; at least one mention of negative changes and at least one mention of positive changes for any of the children, with each type of change coded 1 and no mentions coded 0. Multiple mentions were not included, both because some

TABLE 7.1. Suburban Divorced and Married Parents' Perceptions of Changes in Their Youngest or Only and Oldest Children

Parents' perceptions of changes in affect and behavior	Happiness		Getting along with friends		Getting along with family		School work		Health		General behavior		Getting into trouble	
	Divorced	Married	Divorced	Married	Divorced	Married	Divorced	Married	Divorced	Married	Divorced	Married	Divorced	Married
Youngest or only child														
Negative changes	28.3%	15.6%	5.1%	7.6%	10.8%	17.9%	22.6%	10.5%	15.2%	24.1%	29.2%	22.6%	5.4%	3.6%
Positive changes	17.4%	40.6%	5.1%	34.6%	2.7%	32.1%	22.6%	63.2%	13.0%	6.9%	14.6%	22.6%	—	—
No changes	54.3%	43.8%	89.7%	59.7%	86.5%	50.0%	54.8%	26.3%	71.7%	69.0%	56.3%	54.8%	94.6%	96.4%
Total	100.0%	100.0%	99.9%	99.9%	100.0%	100.0%	100.0%	100.0%	99.9%	100.0%	100.1%	100.0%	100.0%	100.0%
(n)	(46)	(32)	(39)	(26)	(37)	(28)	(31)	(19)	(46)	(29)	(48)	(31)	(37)	(28)
Oldest child														
Negative changes	60.0%	42.9%	16.7%	44.4%	—	66.7%	20.0%	35.7%	40.0%	33.3%	22.2%	45.5%	6.7%	45.5%
Positive changes	26.7%	50.0%	33.3%	44.4%	50.0%	33.3%	46.7%	64.3%	40.0%	33.3%	11.1%	54.5%	—	—
No changes	13.3%	7.1%	50.0%	11.1%	50.0%	—	33.3%	—	20.0%	33.3%	66.7%	—	93.3%	54.5%
Total	100.0%	100.0%	100.0%	99.9%	100.0%	100.0%	100.0%	100.0%	100.0%	99.9%	100.0%	100.0%	100.0%	100.0%
(n)	(15)	(14)	(6)	(9)	(2)	(9)	(15)	(14)	(5)	(3)	(9)	(11)	(15)	(11)

families had more children and because some more talkative parents mentioned more positive and negative changes than did others, thereby skewing the distribution. The codes reported upon were designed to indicate the presence of any changes. With a mean score of 0.3 for both sets of parents, the divorced parents were no more likely than the married to mention negative changes; with a mean of 0.8 versus 0.3 for the married, the divorced were significantly more likely to mention positive changes ($t = 16.9$, $df = 229$, $p < .001$). Among the married, 31.5% of the parents ($n = 108$) mentioned at least one negative change in their children, whereas 29.3% of the divorced parents ($n = 123$) mentioned any negative changes. A third (33.3%) of the married parents mentioned a positive change, as opposed to 78.0% of the divorced.

Possible Reasons for Parents' Not Reporting Changes

How might these findings be explained? Among the possibilities are the following: The children were able to hide their distress; they had less distress than other children experiencing divorce; their parents were so engrossed in their own adjustment problems that they could not see their children's problems; or the parents were using denial because it was too difficult to cope with the children's problems produced by the decision to divorce.

A study of nursery school children whose parents were divorcing provides some clues to explain these findings (McDermott, 1968). In this study, many mothers reported that their children did not even ask about their fathers' absence. Because of a child's dependence upon the remaining parent, and guilt and confusion about the divorce, he or she may feel that if the mother stopped loving the father she could equally as easily stop loving the child. Thus, by not asking about the divorce, the child may feel that he or she is avoiding giving the mother any cause to be angry and to withdraw affection. Another process feeding into the picture of parental lack of awareness is that a common response of children, particularly young ones, when faced with an unsettling event is denial. This may lead parents to the conclusion that such children are unaffected by the divorce. It is likely, therefore, that some parents do not report divorce-related changes in their children because the children themselves carefully avoid all references to or discussion of the divorce, and parents, for their own reasons, are reluctant to raise the issue.

Almost all parents feel some guilt about the breakup of their marriages; they feel especially guilty in regard to the consequences of their decision for the well-being of their children. As a result, they may deny their role in producing a child's unhappiness or may be unwilling to allow a child to express his or her feelings about the divorce. Parents and children may therefore collude with each other to avoid discussing the divorce or feelings about it. Children may not want to upset their parents, and vice versa.

In a study reporting on both parents' perceptions of the impact of the divorce on their children, Wallerstein and Kelly (1977) noted that a parent's role in the divorce proceedings colored his or her awareness. The parent who initiated the divorce saw the children as little affected by the divorce, whereas the parent who did not want the divorce and who felt "injured and abandoned" saw the children as disturbed by the event. Therefore, such differences between parents may be expected according to their role in instigating the divorce.

Yet another reason why some parents may avoid discussing the divorce with their children, and thereby learning how they are reacting, is that the parents feel uncertain about their ability to handle the children by themselves (McDermott, 1970). As reported in Chapter 6, self-esteem and self-confidence are often affected by divorce. Divorced parents with a low sense of competence or self-esteem may be unable to admit that their children have been affected by the divorce, since to admit this might force the parent to recognize his or her own feelings of incompetence in coping with divorce-related changes.

For many parents, the period following physical separation is so upsetting that they are emotionally unavailable to their children. This unavailability may produce a "moratorium" on parenting. This would suggest—if data have been gathered from both parent and child—that parents who are themselves distressed should have distressed children. However, when parents are used as the observers for both themselves and their children, clinical data suggest that the parents' distress may obscure their ability to see the effects that divorce is having on the children (Wallerstein & Kelly, 1976). This is the opposite of what Goode (1956) found in his survey of divorcing mothers. Whereas the majority of the mothers surveyed here did not find their children harder to handle at any point during the divorce process, Goode found that when a mother's "distress" or "trauma" score went up (indicating inability to sleep, more smoking, etc.), she was more likely to report that a child had been difficult to handle at some time during the divorce process. It would seem, however, that difficulty in handling the children is different from awareness of changes in affect or behavior. If a child is depressed, and perhaps quieter than normal as a result, he or she may be easy to handle but nevertheless may be reacting strongly to the divorce. Therefore, parents who are more emotionally disturbed by the divorce may be less likely to report changes in their children's behavior than those parents who have fewer symptoms of distress may be.

Children's ages may also make a difference in parents' perception of changes, with parents of young children being less likely to see changes. Small children are often less verbal and less aggressive in expressing their feelings than older children (Kalter, 1990), and their responses may therefore be less noticeable to their parents. Some parents also mistakenly think that preschoolers are "too little" to understand or to be upset by the turmoil of the divorce and the loss of one of their parents. Parents of preschoolers seem to have a particularly difficult time telling their children about the divorce and noting changes in their children that are related to the divorce. In McDermott's (1968) study of nursery school children, the school personnel noticed changes in the children before the parents informed the school about the divorce. In many cases, it was only after inquiring about changes in a child that a teacher would learn about the divorce from the parents.

Correlates of Perceived Changes in the Children

This section addresses the issue, as reviewed above, of whether there is a pattern to whether divorced parents are more versus less likely to see changes in their children at the time of filing. The first of the variables to be examined is stage of the family life cycle, to determine whether the divorced parents in this study saw differences by the age of the children. The second is a set of three indicators of the parents' adjustment: subjective distress, attachment, and self-esteem. The third group of variables is demographic characteristics (number of minor children, race, gender, social class, and income) that may have influenced the likelihood of parents' reporting changes in the children. Finally, indicators of the parents' feelings about the divorce are examined. These include who suggested the divorce (coded only for the respondent or the spouse—those few cases in which the suggestion was mutual have been dropped in this analysis); scales assessing reluctance to divorce and relief mingled with guilt about the divorce; and an item assessing anger with the spouse.

Reluctance to divorce and feeling pressured to divorce were assessed by these four items: "I'm going ahead with the divorce only because it's what my (ex-)husband/wife wants"; "I feel as if I've been dumped"; "Perhaps with all things considered, we should have tried longer"; and "I feel as if this is all a horrible mistake." These items were scored from 1, "not at all my feelings," to 5, "very much my feelings." Scores ranged from 4 to 20 with an alpha reliability of .80. Relief tinged with guilt about the divorce was assessed with the following four items: "This has been coming for a long time, and I'm glad we've finally made the break"; "It isn't an easy decision to divorce your husband/wife, but basically I'm relieved"; "Although this is the right decision, I know it's hurt my (ex-)husband/wife very badly"; and "I feel a little guilty about the divorce, but it was the right decision for us." These items were scored on the same 5-point scale described above; scores again ranged from 4 to 20, with an alpha reliability in this case of .64. Anger at the spouse was assessed by one item, "I'm angry at my husband/wife," which was again scored from 1 to 5 as above.

The primary finding in regard to family life cycle stage was that significantly more negative changes were reported by parents of younger children than by those of older ones. Parents with children in the primary grades reported the highest frequency of negative changes (46.2%), followed by those with preschoolers (25.0%), those with teenagers (20.0%), and those with at least one teenager and younger children (15.8%; $\chi^2 = 8.4$, $df = 3$, $p < .05$).

There were no differences in perceptions of changes by race or gender of the parent, by the number of children living at home, by income in the last year of the marriage, or by anticipated income in the coming year. There were differences by social class position, with working-class or lower-class parents (Hollingshead [1957] Classes IV and V) significantly more likely to report positive changes in the children ($\chi^2 = 6.6$, $df = 2$, $p < .05$). Forty-two percent of these parents reported positive changes, compared to 28.6% of those in the highest-status groups (Classes I and II) or those in the middle class (Class III).

There were no significant differences for the associations between reports of positive or negative changes and who suggested the divorce, subjective distress, or attachment. Self-esteem was associated with reports of positive changes in the children ($r = -.21$, $p < .05$): Those with low-esteem were less likely to report positive changes. Although relief at the decision to divorce and anger were not associated with changes, reluctance to divorce was associated with both reported negative changes ($r = .20$, $p < .05$) and positive changes ($r = .21$, $p < .05$). That is, those who were more reluctant reported both more negative and more positive changes in their children.

FINDINGS AT THE THIRD INTERVIEW

Perceived Changes in Children

At the third interview (4 years after separating), when parents were asked again about their children's response to the divorce, two additional questions were asked: "Do you think the divorce has changed your ex-spouse's relationship with the child(ren)?" and "Do you think the divorce has changed your own relationship with the child(ren)?" In each case, if changes had occurred, the respondent was asked how the relationship had changed.

One of the problems in assessing the impact of divorce on children is disentangling the impact of this event from normal developmental changes. To address this issue more directly, the parents were also queried, "Do you think the children have (child has) changed in any ways as a result of the divorce?" As with the affect and behavior questions asked at the first interview, relatively few parents mentioned changes or divorce-specific changes, so composite scales of negative and positive changes were constructed.

Respondents reported positive changes in their own relationships with their children (18.9%; $n = 74$) and negative changes for their ex-spouses' relationships (24.3%). Only a few (5.4%) saw any positive changes in their ex-spouses' relationships with the children, whereas some saw negative changes in their own relationships (13.5%). By far the most frequently mentioned positive change in the respondents' relationships was being "emotionally closer" to the children. This was trailed by "increased respect, regard, or appreciation"; "more contact or time to spend" with the children; and the children's being "less hostile or angry." The most frequently mentioned negative relationship change for both the respondents' and the ex-spouses' relationships was having "less contact or time to spend" with the children. Other negative changes were feeling "less close," "less support and guidance," "less respect," and "more anger."

Only six parents, or 8.1% of those with minor children, felt that the divorce had had a negative impact on their children. The concerns mentioned included that the children were "less thoughtful and considerate" and "less close" to the respondents. Among the positive changes mentioned by approximately one in five of the parents were that the children were "more thoughtful and considerate," "less tense," and "happy with and encouraging of [the parents'] dating." Given the kinds of divorce-related changes in children that have been described by other researchers, these comments have a certain hollowness and self-centeredness. The changes are almost exclusively seen from the parents' perspective, not the children's. In fairness, the focus of the entire survey was on the respondents' reactions to divorce, but these comments suggest that the parents may have had some difficulty in taking the children's perspective.

In response to the affect and behavior questions that were also asked at the first interview, 20.3% of the parents at the third interview saw positive changes in "happiness," "general behavior," "school work," and so forth, and another 16.2% saw negative changes. There were no significant Pearson's correlations among these different measures of parents' perceptions of their children's response to the divorce. The reports of positive and negative behavior and affect from the first and third interviews were also not significantly correlated with one another. The mean number of negative changes at the first and third interview was 0.2, but the same people did not report problems at the two interviews. The Pearson's correlation between the two periods was −.07. Similarly, the correlation between the positive changes in affect and behavior at the two interviews was .12. At the third interview (2–3 years after the divorce was granted), when it might be expected that if children had initially been adversely affected by the divorce they would have been doing better, parents did not report an increase in positive changes. In fact, at the first interview the mean number of positive changes reported was 0.7 and at the second it was 0.2, so that significantly fewer changes were reported upon at the later date ($t = 10.9$, $df = 74$, $p < .001$).

These negative results mean one of several things. First, perceptions of changes in the children's relationships with the respondents or ex-spouses, perceptions of divorce-related changes in the children, and perceptions of changes in affect and behavior may be tapping completely different dimensions with no overlap. This seems improbable, because changes in one area of a child's life are likely to affect other domains. A second and more likely explanation is that what parents are able to report is a limited part of what is happening to their children. In fact, the events they are reporting upon may be, to some extent, almost random. In most research in the social sciences, earlier scores on the same scales are correlated with later scores, but here they were not.

Correlates of Perceived Changes in Children

Table 7.2 displays the variables that were significantly associated with parents' perceptions at the third interview of their children's responses. Men saw more negative changes in their relationships with their children, whereas women saw more positive changes. For men, much of this change was probably related to the reduced contact they had with their children as the noncustodial parents. Respondents with more children saw more positive changes in the children that were attributed to the divorce, and also reported positive changes in the children's relationship with the respondents. These children may have been pitching in and helping with tasks, recognizing the parents'

TABLE 7.2. Pearson's Correlations between Demographic Variables and Perceived Changes in Children: Suburban Divorced Parents at Third Interview

Demographic variables	Positive changes in behavior	Positive divorce-related changes	Negative changes in relationship with respondent	Positive changes in relationship with respondent	Negative changes in relationship with spouse
Gender	.11	.23	−.28**	.29**	.13
Number of children	.22	.28*	−.08	.41**	.14
Who suggested divorce	−.11	−.23	.02	−.23	−.29*
Income	−.04	−.08	.28**	−.15	−.12
Social class	−.26*	.01	−.27*	.01	.01

*$p < .05$.
**$p < .01$.

burden. Those of higher social class reported fewer positive changes and more negative changes in their relationships; such parents may have been fairly strict in their demands upon the children, producing more potential conflict.

When a respondent first suggested the divorce, he or she saw fewer negative changes in the children's relationship with the ex-spouse. With more income, respondents reported more negative changes in their relationships with the children. There were no significant associations between the parents' perceptions of the children and race, subjective distress, attachment, self-esteem, reluctance to divorce, relief at the decision to divorce, or anger.

In these parental self-report data, relatively few developmental or specifically divorce-related effects were apparent for children. Using self-report measures for parents and for adolescents aged 11–15 in a longitudinal study, Forehand and McCombs (1988) reported that children's behavioral changes followed their mothers' distress; that is, the mothers' reaction to the divorce affected their children's response at the second interview. In a test of this model with the present data, only two measures of the parental emotional response at the time of filing were associated with any of the reports of the children's behavior at the third interview. Low self-esteem was strongly associated with reported positive changes in a child's relationship with the other parent ($r = .45$, $p < .001$), and feeling relieved at the decision to divorce was associated with perceived negative changes in a child's relationship with the ex-spouse ($r = .25$, $p < .05$). These data, then, indicate little support for associations between a parent's emotional response and a child's behavior, either cross-sectionally or longitudinally.

CHANGES IN PARENTAL AWARENESS OVER TIME?

The data presented in this chapter indicate that from the parents' perspective, the divorce and its sequelae had little positive or negative impact on their children. Most parents saw few changes in their children. As Fulton (1979) and Kurdek and Siesky (1978) also reported, relatively few factors were correlated with parents' perceptions of problems. When the parents felt the children had been influenced, the divorce was more often seen as having a positive than as having a negative impact.

How can these data be reconciled with the substantial body of literature indicating that most children do experience distress in the short run at the breakup of their parents' marriages, and that some experience long-term difficulties? The key seems to be that these suburban parents in general were not especially aware of changes in their children, as is also illustrated by the relatively few comments the married parents made.

It is also possible that parents in the 1970s were less aware of the potential impact of divorce on children than parents are today. A number of books, television shows, and magazine and newspaper articles concerning the impact of divorce on children have appeared since then. To explore the possibility that parents have become more aware of the potential impact of divorce on children, the frequencies of open-ended replies mentioning divorce-related concerns about the children were tallied for a similar question asked in the 1974–1975 and 1985–1986 surveys. In the suburban divorce survey, respondents were asked, "What have been the most difficult kinds of adjustments for you to make since the decision to divorce?" In the later county-wide marital transition survey, they were asked, "What have been the most difficult kinds of adjustments for you to make since the divorce was filed/granted?" Replies are only reported for women with children aged 18 or younger.

In the suburban divorce survey, only 9.0% ($n = 67$) of the mothers reported concerns about the children, compared to 28.6% ($n = 84$) who mentioned such concerns a decade later. In two surveys a decade apart whose focus was almost exclusively on adult adjustment to divorce, these data suggest the possibility of a growing awareness of the impact of divorce on children. Even so, fewer than 3 in 10 mothers of minor children mentioned such concerns in the 1980s. These data suggest the need for continued educational efforts about the potential impact of divorce on children.

At the same time that parents may not be aware of changes, they do not knowingly want to do things that will hurt their children. As a result, it may be too painful and threatening for them to admit to themselves or others that the decision to divorce, which seems the best course of action, may be a decision that could adversely affect their children. It is also protective of the parents' own sense of efficacy to deny any changes. As reported above, those parents with low self-esteem were the ones more likely to notice changes in the children. Finally, the parents' own level of distress at the time of filing for the divorce may have blinded them to their children's concerns.

CONCLUSION

This research has focused on children aged 18 and under. Researchers have recently begun to look at the impact of divorce on families in which the parents divorced when the children were in late adolescence or adulthood (Cooney, Smyer, Hagestad, & Klock, 1986; Lang & Pett, 1989). They are also exploring what happens to family relationships in adulthood when divorce occurred in earlier years. Adult children report being pulled to take sides and feeling guilty or angry as they try to figure out how to care for their parents as they age (Cooney & Uhlenberg, 1990). This is especially true for care of a noncustodial parent who maintained minimal financial or emotional contact in earlier years. Issues such as these need further exploration, because the impact of divorce does not stop with the decree or even the end of child support.

The data presented here illustrate the need for more detailed examination of the impact of divorce on children. This includes use of standardized measures collected from parents and their children, and, where possible, from teachers and others familiar with the children. These analyses indicate that parents do not see the decision to divorce or the postdivorce changes that occur as having much impact on their children. It is difficult to reconcile these findings with those from the Cleveland-area surveys showing heightened distress for the parents, and those of other researchers reporting heightened distress for children whose parents divorce.

C H A P T E R 8

The Economic Divorce

Destitituion is just a divorce away.
—Rossi (1986, p. 13)

LOS ANGELES—Joanna Carson received only a fraction of the money she sought from her estranged husband, Johnny Carson, but her attorneys say she's satisfied with the $35,000 a month she'll collect until her divorce from the Tonight Show *host is settled.*

Maxwell Greenburg and Arthur Crowley, Mrs. Carson's lawyers, called the temporary support agreement announced Wednesday a victory "for the rights of women to control their own destiny."

Mrs. Carson's attorneys had asked for $220,000 a month in temporary support after outlining her expenditures over the past 10 years.

Among other things, they said she needed almost $5,000 a month for household help, $1,400 for groceries, $10,000 for upkeep of two New York City apartments, and $5,000 for department store bills.

—St. Petersburg Times (1984, p. 3A)

The image many people have of the divorced, particularly of divorced women, is a scaled-down version of Joanna Carson's situation—women lolling around at home eating bonbons while their ex-husbands slave to support them in the style to which they have grown accustomed. In reality, the data on the economics of divorce more clearly reflect a picture of economic hardship, especially for women, with men suffering less or no financial difficulty (Arendell, 1986; Espenshade, 1979; Garfinkel & McLanahan, 1986; Hoffman & Duncan, 1988; Morgan, 1991; Riessman, 1990; Sidel, 1986; Weitzman, 1985).

Dissolving a marriage in any jurisdiction requires dissolving an economic unit—a process described by Bohannan (1970, 1985) as "the economic divorce." The primary focus of this chapter is on the economic circumstances of the suburban divorced sample compared to those of the married sample, with some comparisons between the suburban divorced and marital transition samples.

This chapter was initially written by William M. Holmes and subsequently revised by Gay C. Kitson.

FACTS AND FIGURES

Although Ohio is not a community property state, state laws often define a married couple as a single economic unit, particularly in community property states (Bohannan, 1970; Freed & Foster, 1983; Wilson, 1982). In many suburban communities, like those reported upon here, both the husband and wife work either to maintain a middle-class standard of living (Moore & Sawhill, 1976) or simply to make ends meet (Hill, 1983). Even with income from two wage earners, families may experience significant economic stress (Aldous, 1969a; Galligan & Bahr, 1978; Garbarino, 1976; Hampton, 1979; Hill, 1983). The wife's contribution to the family's income is often substantially less than that of her husband (Ehrenreich & Piven, 1984; Masnick & Bane, 1980; Weiss, 1984; Weitzman, 1985). As a result, in a divorce the wife may find her income substantially reduced.

Even when child support or alimony payments are ordered and paid in a divorce, they do not generally maintain the former level of income of the married couple. For example, in 1985, 74.0% of the 4.4 million women with a child under the age of 21 who were due child support payments actually received them. Of these, 2.1 million, or 48.2%, received the full amount due. The mean amount of child support actually received per family due it was $2,215, compared to a mean of $2,495 that was supposed to be paid. In that year, of the 19.2 million ever-divorced or currently separated women, 14.6% reported being awarded alimony. Of the 840,000 payments due, only 73.3% received some alimony in 1985, with an average payment of $3,976 (U.S. Bureau of the Census, 1987b). Lack of payment or partial payment increases the economic and psychological pressures on the custodial parent; it creates such concerns and doubts as "How can I make ends meet?" "Will the payments come eventually?" "How much can I rely on these payments as part of my income?" "How dare he treat me and our children this way?"

The result of these payment problems and women's often lower levels of occupational preparation is that a significant percentage of divorced persons who have custody of children (generally women) are living below or near the poverty line. Poverty rates for mother-only families have been higher than those for other groups (two-parent families, the disabled, and the aged) for somewhat over 15 years. Among whites the population of mother-only families grew substantially from the 1950s to the 1970s, with marital disruption accounting for 45% of the growth in the 1950s and 1960s and about 57% of the growth in the 1970s. Never-married mothers account for small proportions of this increase (Garfinkel & McLanahan, 1986). Among black mother-headed households, the relative importance of divorce declined while the importance of never-married mothers increased. In the 1950s, 45% of the increase in black mother-headed households was due to formerly married mothers. The figure dropped to 30% in the 1960s and only 3% in the 1970s. At the same time, the proportion of never-married mothers increased from 9% in the 1950s to 20% in the 1960s and 23% in the 1970s (Garfinkel & McLanahan, 1986).

Curiously, although those below the poverty level are less frequently awarded child support than those above the poverty line (Cassetty, 1978), the majority of low-income mothers who are due support receive at least some of it, whereas those of higher economic status are less likely to receive what is due them. These differences are decreasing, however. In 1981, 60% of poor mothers received some payments, compared to 44% of mothers above the poverty line (computed from U.S. Bureau of the Census, 1983; see also Cassetty, 1978); in 1985, 65.7% of women with incomes below the poverty level received payments, compared to 62.1% with incomes above that level (U.S. Bureau of the Census, 1987b).

Why have those in a better position to pay child support been less likely to make the payments owed? Explanations for nonpayment of support are many, including the view that income does not stretch to cover the expenses of two households, but this is true for low- and high-income families alike; indeed, the economic pressures are greater for low-income families, since they have less discretionary income. Divorced men's income generally does not decrease as much as women's, if it decreases at all. In fact, men's income may go up as the men advance in their careers (Espenshade, 1979; Sterin et al., 1981; Wallerstein & Kelly, 1980; Weitzman, 1985). Since the avenues for advancement are generally greater for those with higher-paying jobs, the reason for lower compliance with support orders is unclear. There may also be more pressure to pay and more monitoring of payments for low-income families because of eligibility requirements for welfare programs. Others report that financial payments may not be made because of continuing conflict between the spouses or because of the psychological problems of one or both spouses; these issues make people unable to separate their own concerns from the needs of their ex-spouses and children (Wallerstein & Huntington, 1983; Wallerstein & Kelly, 1980). Some men only continue support and noncustodial visitation until they remarry (Furstenberg et al., 1983). But why such issues apparently affect middle- and high-income families more than they do low-income families is still unclear.

The impact of nonpayment of child support is more than simply economic. Visits between the noncustodial parent and his or her children are related to the payment of child support; lack of payments or fewer payments are associated with less contact (Furstenberg et al., 1983). Children cope better with the divorce of their parents when they are able to maintain contact with the noncustodial parent (Ahrons, 1981; Wallerstein & Kelly, 1980).

The economic disruption of divorce is considerable, especially for the dependent person in the marital relationship—and this is more often the wife than the husband (Arendell, 1986; Espenshade, 1979; Kreisberg, 1970; Weitzman, 1985). As one investigator has put it, "Poverty has become more the norm than the exception after divorce" (Kircheimer, 1980, p. 21). Over half of the families in the Aid to Families with Dependent Children program are there because of circumstances surrounding a divorce or separation (Kircheimer, 1980). Half of all female-headed families in the United States lived in poverty in 1978 (U.S. Bureau of the Census, 1980). This proportion had increased to 60% by 1984 (Sidel, 1986). The income of a single custodial parent is rarely enough to meet the expenses of the modern family (Aldous, 1969b; Carter & Glick, 1970; Cutright, 1971; Hannon, Tuma, & Groenfeld, 1977; Weitzman, 1985). If divorce occurs in households in which there was previously a single male breadwinner, a substantial drop in income will occur almost automatically for the female. Because wives generally have lower-status jobs than their husbands, the drop in income for women is more substantial than it is for those men who lose their wives' contribution, even if the women are employed (Weiss, 1984).

THEORETICAL APPROACHES TO THE ECONOMICS OF DIVORCE

It has been argued that economic problems constitute the most important issue in the decision to divorce (Becker, 1974; Hannon et al., 1977) and in the consequences of the breakup (Becker, 1973). This viewpoint, referred to as the "political economy" perspective, maintains that couples divorce when it is to their economic advantage. It assumes that the value of the economic contribution of each spouse to a stable marriage is approximately the same, even though these contributions are not always monetary. If the actual or potential economic contribution of a spouse should change, then the one who makes the greater contribution will want out of the marriage so that he or she can form a marriage with a new partner who is able to make an equal contribution. If the material costs of leaving the marriage are too great, however, the more economically advantaged partner may instead try to help the spouse improve his or her economic contribution. A corollary of this perspective is that spouses who make smaller economic contributions to their marriages will have less power to force an equitable settlement and will receive less from it than their partners. Such economic determinism downplays the importance of nonmaterial considerations in interpersonal relationships, such as love, caring, intimacy, nurturance, and procreation.

An alternative approach, the "exchange theory" of divorce, implies that staying married or getting divorced is influenced by more than the economic contributions of marital partners. Love, companionship, understanding, a sense of being needed, and other noneconomic contributions to marriage also have an effect (Kitson, Holmes, & Sussman, 1983; Levinger, 1976; Nye, 1979). The subjective evaluation of a person's contribution or gain may be far more important than the economic value of that contribution or gain. According to this viewpoint, the person who can recognize the greater economic gain from a divorce may not want to divorce or may even maximize economic rewards of the settlement for the partner, because his or her subjective evaluation of the spouse remains high. Thus, the attitudes of a divorced person toward his or her ex-spouse may be more important in influencing the economic outcome of the divorce than purely economic considerations may be. For example, motives of revenge or compassion may lead a person to press for a settlement contrary to that dictated by purely economic interests. This view asserts that marriage and divorce cannot be reduced purely to "the cold economic facts" (Goode, 1974, p. S27). Economic factors do, however, play a role in addition to other influences. The relative explanatory power of the political economy perspective versus the exchange perspective is an issue to which this chapter returns at several points.

ECONOMIC CONTRASTS BETWEEN THE MARRIED AND DIVORCED SAMPLES

As indicated in Chapter 3, the suburban divorced and married samples did not differ in level of education of the respondents' fathers or in level of education, occupation, and social class of the respondents. In the suburban study, then, the socioeconomic origins of the divorced as compared to the married sample did not contribute to the likelihood of divorce. This approach to sampling, in which an effort is made to match the subjects on background characteristics (so that, ideally, the only major difference between the two groups will be their marital status), differs from that of cross-sectional studies; in the latter, the divorced are generally found to be of lower socioeconomic status than the married, although even these differences are smaller than they were in earlier historical periods (Norton & Glick, 1979).

Despite the samples' comparability in background, the economic situation of the divorced in the suburban study did differ from that of the married, both during the last year of marriage and after filing for divorce. As will be described below this was reflected in income, employment status, and the number of sources of income reported. Differences were further magnified by race, gender, and the presence of minor children in the household. These indicators consistently showed the divorced to be in a more difficult economic position than the married. The economic status of many of the subjects after the divorce was filed was substantially different from their predivorce status and from that of the comparison married families. Thus divorce played a role in determining economic status, even though the married and divorced samples were initially similar in background characteristics.

Differences in Income

At the first interview, all subjects were asked about "the total income for your family for the last year of your marriage (before taxes)." The choices ranged from "under $1,000" to "$30,000 or over." Grouped means were computed.[1] With the samples reduced to the 161 matched divorced and married families at the first interview, income for the last year of marriage for the divorced sample was approximately $1,600 less than that of the married respondents, with a mean of $17,189 for the divorced and $18,810 for the married ($t = 1.8$, $df = 160$, $p < .05$). It is difficult to determine how much of this was a "real" difference between the two groups in before-divorce income; how much was due to differences in the length of separation; how much was determined by whether the divorce was granted by the time of the first interview; and how much was based on the definition of "family" that the subjects used. For example, some of the divorced subjects were separated from their spouses for long periods of time before the divorce was filed. For these people, family income in the last year of marriage, then, may have been income several years earlier. Despite the wording of the question, still others may have already begun to consider "family" those currently living in the household, which might not have included the person who was soon to be or was already the ex-spouse. Alternatively, and probably correctly, the divorced sample may actually have had less income than the married.

Even with difficulties in interpretation of the data from the last year of marriage, the gap increased between the divorced and married in terms of income expected by the respondents for the coming year. When respondents were asked, "What do you think your income is likely to be in the coming year?", the divorced were expecting a mean of $11,771 versus $19,987 for the married—a difference of over $8,200 ($t = 9.0$, $df = 154$, $p < .001$). The actual mean income of $13,287 for the divorced sample at the second interview, a year after the divorce was granted, was higher than the estimate. Nevertheless, the actual income for the divorced was still $6,700 lower than that anticipated for the married, which may also have been an underestimate of actual income. Inflation exacerbated the problem. The loss of income for the divorced meant a greater loss in purchasing power than that experienced by the married couples because of the greater impact of inflation on the budgets of poorer families. Basic necessities constitute a higher percentage of expenses for the poor. They have less discretion about not buying goods or buying more cheaply, because they are already not buying as much and buying cheaper goods.

Despite these early differences in income for the divorced and the married, the differences were substantially reduced by the third interview. For the divorced, income increased from a mean of $13,287 at the second interview, or 1 year after the decree, to $19,227 at the third interview, 2-3 years after the divorce was final. This, in all likelihood, did not entirely eliminate the income differences between the two groups. Income for the married was likely to have gone up in the interim as well, but they were not asked about income in their follow-up telephone interviews. Nevertheless, the gap appears to have been reduced; in any event, many of the divorced experienced significant improvements in income. These improvements were, however, generally related to remarriage. The 28.9% who were remarried at the third interview had somewhat over 40% more income than those who remained single (a mean of $26,662 vs. $15,152). Single persons constituted 61.7% of the sample at the third interview. Cohabitants, who comprised 9.3% of the sample, had an income in between ($23,125). Thus, those who did not remarry were, for the most part, more economically distressed than those who remarried or cohabited.

Before an improvement in income for everyone by the third interview, most of the divorced suffered a decline in income in the year after filing for divorce. Men, women, nonwhites, whites, and those with and without minor children in the home—virtually all had less income at the second interview than at the first interview, measured here as income in the last year of marriage (Table 8.1). This drop was greater for women (down 37.4%), for those with children present in the home (a decrease of 28.9%), and for whites (down 24.3%) than for those without children in the household (down 15.3%), nonwhites

TABLE 8.1. Mean Income by Race, Gender, and Presence of Children in Respondent's Household for the Suburban Divorced at All Three Interviews

Race, gender, and presence of children	Interview 1					Interview 2					Interview 3				
	n	Mean income[a]	t	df	p	n	Mean income	t	df	p	n	Mean income	t	df	p
Race															
White	144	$17,257	1.3	191	n.s.	118	$13,072	−0.5	153	n.s.	101	$19,480	0.5	126	n.s.
Nonwhite	49	$15,306				37	$13,973				27	$18,278			
Gender															
Male	96	$17,552	1.2	191	n.s.	68	$17,493	5.6	153	.005	58	$23,940	5.1	126	.005
Female	97	$15,979				87	$10,000				70	$15,321			
Presence of children															
No children present	118	$17,042	0.5	191	n.s.	90	$14,433	1.9	152	.05	71	$20,747	1.9	126	.05
Children present	75	$16,320				64	$11,609				57	$17,333			
Race and presence of children															
White															
No children present	92	$17,190	−0.1	142	n.s.	70	$14,336	1.9	115	.05	59	$21,364	2.1	99	.05
Children present	52	$17,375				47	$11,096				42	$16,833			
Nonwhite															
No children present	26	$16,519	0.9	47	n.s.	20	$14,775	0.6	35	n.s.	12	$17,708	−0.3	25	n.s.
Children present	23	$13,935				17	$13,029				15	$18,733			
Gender and presence of children															
Male															
No children present	77	$17,610	0.1	94	n.s.	53	$16,943	−0.9	65	n.s.	43	$23,163	−1.0	56	n.s.
Children present	19	$17,316				14	$19,571				15	$26,167			
Female															
No children present	41	$15,976	0.0	95	n.s.	37	$10,838	1.0	85	n.s.	28	$17,036	1.4	68	n.s.
Children present	56	$15,982				50	$9,380				42	$14,179			

[a]Income reported at Interview 1 was income for the last year of marriage.

(down 8.8%), and men (down 0.3%). These figures on declines in income are closer to Hoffman and Duncan's (1988) estimate of a one-third decline than to Weitzman's (1985) estimate of a 73% decline.

Not everyone's income subsequently improved at an equal rate. Nonwhites and men had smaller income increases than did women or white respondents. Between the second and third interviews, income for nonwhites increased by 23.6%, compared to an increase of 32.9% for whites; women's income increased by 34.7%, compared to an increase of 27.1% for men. In this suburban sample, there were no significant differences by race in mean income at any of the interviews. The differences in income for men and women were significant at the second and third interviews, with men having higher incomes.

Women with children made the least improvement in actual income. The mean income of $9,380 for this group at 1 year after the decree was granted was less than for all other groups, but fairly close to the 1978 median income of $8,580 for families headed by women (U.S. Bureau of the Census, 1980). Many of the women in the suburban study had separated from their husbands in the year prior to the divorce. Thus, their initial financial stress was severe. Temporary assistance would have helped until they were able to get back on their feet economically. Even by 2–3 years after the divorce was granted, however, the income of women in general, and of women with children present in particular, did not quite reach the level of income in the last year of marriage. Women without children made the most improvement in income, from a mean income of $10,838 the year after the divorce decree was received to $17,036 at the third interview—an increase in income of 36.4%, compared to an increase of 33.8% for women with children present. Nevertheless, those without children living with them had significantly higher incomes at the second and third interviews. When the presence-of-children data were broken down by race, whites without children present continued to have significantly higher incomes. This was not true for nonwhites, however; there were no significant differences among nonwhites. Whites with children present had the lowest incomes, but these differences did not hold by gender. There were no significant differences in income by the presence of children for men and women.

In the 1985–1986 county-wide marital transition data, there were also significant differences in income by race in the last year of marriage. White women reported average incomes of $28,215 in their last year of marriage, compared to $22,655 for nonwhites ($t = 1.8$, $df = 178$, $p < .05$). Similarly, although the income anticipated for the coming year went down substantially for both groups, white women continued to have significantly higher incomes—an expected mean of $16,258, compared to $12,155 for nonwhites ($t = 2.0$, $df = 180$, $p < .05$).

The marital transition study used somewhat different income codes than did the suburban study, so both groups were recoded to match each other in order to illustrate differences in income levels between the 1970s and 1980s.[2] This recoding procedure increased income slightly for the suburban sample and reduced income for the marital transition sample somewhat. For example, the mean income for the suburban divorce sample in the last year of marriage without the recoding procedure was $16,762 and with it was $16,912; for the marital transition sample, the figures were $27,319 and $26,333, respectively. Because only women were interviewed in the marital transition survey, the income figures reported for the suburban divorced sample are only for women in the comparisons that follow.

Given inflation and the passage of time, as might be expected, the marital transition sample had a higher mean income in the last year of marriage and in expected income in the coming year than did the suburban sample. In order to compare the two groups more directly, income was translated into constant dollars. Constant dollars are based on the Consumer Price Index for all U.S. urban consumers, with 1982–1984 indexed at 100. Because income was reported for a 2-year period for both samples, the monthly index figures for 1974 and 1975 and for 1985 and 1986 were averaged.

In constant dollars, divorced women in the marital transition sample actually lost economic ground compared to the suburban sample. Mean income in constant dollars in the last year of marriage ($24,252) and income expected in the coming year ($14,420) were lower for the 1985–1986 marital transition sample than they were for the suburban sample (respectively, $29,891 and $15,516). Thus, the economic situation of families and especially of divorced women did not improve in the intervening decade. (On this point, see also McLanahan & Booth, 1989.)

Changes in Credit

People who divorce are faced not just with a reduction in income; many are also faced with less flexibility in terms of credit, which further reduces their financial options. In the county-wide marital transition study, the 187 divorcees who replied to questions about their credit situation indicated various problems. For example, 17.1% were denied credit when they sought to establish it in their own names; 4.3% reported that their credit was canceled; 7.0% indicated that the limit on their credit cards had been lowered; and 18.7% were pushed for speedy collection of joint debts. Because there were no men in this study, no data are available on credit for men, but it is likely that they experience fewer problems.

Employment Differences

The employment status of the separated/divorced and the married in the suburban study differed, especially for women. At the first interview, 69.4% of the divorced sample were employed full-time or had a full-time job plus a part-time job; this contrasted with 57.3% for the married. These percentages for employment are slightly higher than the 54.4% reported by the U.S. Bureau of the Census (1980) for married families, as a result of the inclusion of those having second jobs in addition to full-time work. In the Cleveland suburban study, compared to the married, the separated/divorced were less often employed only in part-time work (5.8% vs. 10.1% for the married); were more likely to be unemployed but looking for work (7.8% vs. 0.6%); and were less likely to be solely homemakers (10.2% vs. 24.2%).

At every interview, divorced women who were looking for work reported greater difficulty than men in finding full-time work. For example, 80.8% of the men were employed full-time at the first interview, compared to 58.9% of the women. In parallel with the drop in income noted at the second interview, full-time employment fell to 70.0% for the men and 56.8% for the women. By the third interview, however, full-time employment increased again to 85.2% for men and 81.6% for women. The comparable 1979 figure for men in the U.S. labor force was 95%, and that for women in the labor force was 91% (U.S. Bureau of the Census, 1980).

Nonwhites were also more likely to be unemployed and looking for work than were whites. At the first interview, 17.3% of nonwhites and 10.5% of whites were unemployed. The divorced were unemployed as often as the married. The same was true for working at a full-time job plus a part-time job. These findings indicate that in the early stages of divorce employment changes occur, especially for women. Homemakers are forced into the labor market and may have difficulty in finding jobs. Women who already had part-time jobs at the time of the divorce did not have as much difficulty in finding full-time jobs as those who were unemployed or who were homemakers. Once a homemaker entered the labor force, she was reluctant to leave it upon remarriage. By the third interview, only three women were full-time homemakers. Concerns about a career, having an independent source of income so as to be less dependent in a new marriage or in case the new relationship fails, paying the continuing expenses of child rearing, and possibly offsetting the loss of the ex-spouse's alimony and child support payments are some of the reasons the women may have had for not leaving their jobs and returning to the full-time homemaker role upon remarriage.

Sources of Income

The divorced also had significantly fewer sources of income than the married. At the first interview (i.e., at the time of filing for the divorce), the average number of income sources for the divorced sample was 1.6, as opposed to 2.1 for the married ($t = 5.2$, $df = 376$, $p < .0005$). Among the divorced, 10% of the subjects, all women, reported no current source of income. These women were presumably living on savings or loans, or residing with other people. All of the married sample reported at least one source of income, with many having two sources (commonly, the respondent's and the spouse's jobs). The fact that the married families more often had two wage earners was one of the reasons why they had more income than the divorced. However, by the third interview (2–3 years after the divorce was final), the average number of income sources reported by the divorced (1.9) was not much different from that initially reported by the married (2.1). At this point, about a third of the divorced had remarried or were cohabiting. These changes in number of income sources parallel the reduction in the income gap between the two groups, reported above.

The married and divorced samples also differed in the sources of their income. At the first interview, 80.7% of the separated or divorced respondents received money from their own jobs, compared to 66.9% of the married. However, when respondents married to employed spouses were taken into consideration, 83% of the married families had income from a job of the husband or wife—a figure similar to that for the divorced. Employment of spouses contributed income to the family in 70.2% of the married families, as compared to 9.1% of the divorced (in these cases, the respondents had not yet separated from an employed spouse who was still living at home at the first interview and contributing to the income of the family). At the initial interview, some of the separated or divorced also obtained contributions from the spouse who had moved out of the home "for general expenses" (11.1%), but this decreased to 2.2% by the third interview. Only 15.5% of the sample initially reported receiving temporary or permanent child support payments; this was 35% of those having custody of the children (all women except for one man). Thus, two out of three of the divorced respondents with children did not report receiving child support from their spouses at the first interview, but such payments increased later, with 19.5% reporting such payments at the second interview and 23.5% at the third. Respondents were not asked about alimony at the first interview, when so many were still awaiting their decrees.

Because of diminished support or no support from departing spouses, divorced subjects had to rely on family, friends, or welfare more often as a source of income than did the married. One in six of the divorced received financial help from their families (16.6%), compared to 1 in 13 (7.3%) of the married. The divorced were six times more likely than the married to receive money from friends (6.6% vs. 1.1%), and five times more likely to obtain help from the public welfare system (5.5% vs. 1.1%). In addition, the married were more than two and a half times as likely as the divorced to have other sources of income, such as investments.

The pattern of income sources changed for the divorced across time. As noted, contributions from the ex-spouse decreased between the first and third interviews. Contributions from friends also decreased (the proportion of respondents reporting these declined from 6.6% to 3.8%). Use of savings increased from the first (22.6%) to the third interview (31.1%, a figure comparable to that for the married at 30.9%), as did employment of children, which increased by 167% (from three families to eight; this was, however, still a small minority of families). The increased use of savings reflected either greater pressure to dip into reserves or, more likely, the increased ability to save as available income increased. The amount of help from families or from welfare agencies remained about the same at the third interview as at the beginning of the study. Support from a spouse or partner in the home also increased (from 9.1% to 25.0%); this resulted mainly from cohabitation or remarriage.

Property Settlement

More economic contrasts can be found in the property settlements of the divorced. Nationally, a property settlement was granted to 35.6% of the estimated 16.5 million ever-divorced women in 1986, as compared to 42% of the 14.2 million ever-divorced women in 1982 (U.S. Bureau of the Census, 1983, 1987b). An inequitable property settlement can contribute to the economic difficulties of divorced persons. To encourage equitable settlements, students of family law commonly advocate that property should be allocated according to the net needs of a spouse (Bohannan, 1970; Wilson, 1982). The reasoning behind this approach is that women have the greater net need, because they have custody of the children, lack prior work experience, or lack appropriate education. Although this equity criterion may affect the provision of alimony and child support, it is not applied much to the division of property. Women tend to receive less property in settlements than men, partly as a result of discriminatory laws (Oldham, 1981; Wilson, 1982) and misperceptions of these laws (Weitzman, 1985).

Revenge and self-abnegation also figure in many property settlements (Bohannan, 1970). Some spouses attempt to take every bit of property as a way of punishing their ex-spouses. Others refuse an equitable share in order to avoid accepting anything from their former partners. Consequently, even though the law and public policy usually call for an equitable division of property, the result is frequently inequitable. Except in the case of home ownership, women in the suburban study often obtained less property than men.

Men and women differed in how the property division was decided upon and who received the home, business, or miscellaneous property. The divorced subjects were asked at the second interview, a year after receiving their decrees, "How did you arrive at the division of property? Did you and your ex-husband/ex-wife work it out yourselves; did the lawyer(s) work it out; or was it decided in court?" Over half of the sample reported using mutual discussion (53.2%), lawyers (25.3%), and court hearings (7.6%), with the remainder using a mixture of methods. Men reported relying mostly on mutual discussion (62.2% vs. 23.3% of the women), whereas women more often relied upon the advice of a lawyer (53.3% vs. 21.6% of the men). Twenty-three percent of the women, compared to 16.2% of the men, used a combination of discussion with their spouses, advice from lawyers, and/or court decisions to reach a property settlement. It may be that men see themselves as having more control of the property division process than they actually do.

In the majority of the cases (69.2%), women received most or all of the interest in the home, compared to 42.5% of the men. Men virtually always obtained the family business (if any) and a larger share of the miscellaneous property, such as rental units or a second home. One hundred percent of the women reported receiving less than a one-third interest in miscellaneous property, whereas only 45.5% of men reported this. An approximately equal division was reported for 27.3% of the men, and more than a two-thirds interest for the remaining 27.3%. Despite women's greater reported reliance on legal counsel, the property settlement they received did not markedly improve compared to men's unless a home was the only form of property held. Alternatively, their settlements could have been worse without legal counsel.

Although the net needs of women (exclusive of children) will more nearly equal those of men as the sexes become more nearly equal, until that time a closer look is needed at property settlements and ways in which the property other than the house can be used to balance net needs. This is particularly true since the net needs of custodial parents do (and will in the future) still exceed those of noncustodial parents. Given that women generally maintain custody of children and have less earning power, a strictly equal division of property will tend to favor a noncustodial father and fail to address the needs of a custodial mother. Child support alone does not redress this inequity.

At the second interview, the divorced were asked how satisfied they were with the divorce settlement in general and with the division of property. Replies were scored from 1 ("very dissatisfied") to 5 ("very satisfied"). There were no significant differences by gender in satisfaction with the settlement in general or the property division in particular. Respondents differed by race in their satisfaction with the divorce settlement and property division: The mean score for whites on satisfaction with the settlement was 3.5, as opposed to 4.1 for nonwhites ($t = 2.3$, $df = 158$, $p < .05$), while whites' satisfaction with the property division was 4.0 and nonwhites' was 4.6 ($t = 2.3$, $df = 152$, $p < .05$). These differences occurred despite the fact that nonwhites received less in the settlements than did whites. This was especially true for women; nonwhite women were less likely to be awarded the house, furniture, or bank account than white women. In part, this finding may reflect the relative net worth of blacks (who constituted the preponderance of the nonwhite group in this sample) and whites. In 1984, data from a Current Population Report indicated that the median net worth of the typical black household was $3,397—less than a tenth that of white households, with a median of $39,135 (*The Plain Dealer*, 1986). It may be that minority-group women's relief at ending their unsatisfactory relationships was so great that settlement issues were of less concern, especially when there was less property available over which to fight. This issue needs further exploration.

Alimony

Alimony has its origins in the obligation of a husband to support a wife because she assumed an economically dependent role in the marriage, caring for the household and nurturing the children. It was assumed that after divorce few such women would be able to support themselves because of their limited involvement in work outside the home (Weitzman & Dixon, 1980). Another basis for alimony has been its use as a punishment for a husband who has mistreated his wife and its denial as a punishment for a wife who has been "immoral" (Freed & Foster, 1983; Weitzman & Dixon, 1980). Both of these reasons have less currency and are used less often today. However, the inability of a spouse to support himself or herself, or a grievous fault on the part of the partner, is still an occasional basis for awarding alimony (Oster, 1987). Today, alimony is generally restricted to a fixed period to allow the recipient time to become self-sufficient—a use referred to as "rehabilitative maintenance" (Freed & Foster, 1983).

At the second interview in the Cleveland suburban study, the subjects were specifically asked about the court order for alimony. In a little over a quarter of the cases (28.0%), alimony had been awarded to the wives; no husbands received alimony. Comparable national figures were as follows: 14.3% of female-headed families were awarded alimony in 1978, 14.9% in 1981, and 14.6% in 1985 (U.S. Bureau of the Census, 1983, 1987b). Thus, women in this study were more likely to be receiving alimony than was true nationally.

In the suburban study, the alimony payments awarded in the mid-1970s ranged from $25 to over $1,000 a month, with the mean payment awarded totaling $330.44. This was somewhat lower than the actual amount, because the six women awarded $1,000 or more were treated as having been awarded $998 a month. Another eight women were awarded a cash settlement, with the amounts awarded varying from $600 to over $100,000. Of the 37 women still receiving (or supposed to be receiving) alimony at the second interview, approximately three-quarters (73.0%) reported receiving the payments regularly; six women (16.2%) had received no alimony payments at all, and four women (10.8%) received their payments irregularly. The actual amount of money received averaged $227.62, with no women receiving $998 or more a month.

In this study, the divorced who did receive alimony found that within a short time payments ceased or were legally terminated. By the third interview, 22.2% of the women were still legally due alimony. Nearly half of those still receiving alimony had an increase in the amount paid between the second and third interviews. About two-thirds of those due payments were receiving them, whereas 31.1% were simply not being paid; no payments were reported as occurring irregularly.

The higher alimony rates in the Cleveland suburban study are confirmed by a second set of data. In the 1985–1986 marital transition study, 28.7% ($n = 174$) of the women reported being awarded alimony payments, with 3.4% of these payments being temporary because the divorce was not yet final at the time of the interview. Another 4.5% of the women reported being awarded other assets, including having the ownership of their family homes put in their own names. The average amount of alimony awarded in 1985–1986 was $610.21, but this included payments for four subjects who were awarded alimony of over $1,000 a month, with one person awarded $2,850 and another $4,400. When these four cases were treated as receiving $998 a month, as they were in the suburban divorce data, the average payment awarded to the subjects in 1985–1986 was $461.53. As opposed to what was awarded, the actual payments received per month averaged $544.59 (or $418.92 when the four highest awards were treated as $998). Eight of the 38 women awarded alimony, or 21.0%, were not receiving any of it.

Translating the alimony figures for the suburban divorce and marital transition data into constant dollars revealed that the level of payments awarded in the 1980s did not keep pace with inflation. When $998 was used as the top amount of alimony awarded in both groups, the mean suburban award of $330.44 translated into $640.85 in constant dollars in the late 1970s, whereas the 1985–1986 mean figure of $461.53 translated into $425.03 in constant dollars. Thus, on the average, metropolitan Cleveland women in the 1980s were awarded a lower constant-dollar amount in alimony than they were a decade earlier.

Special mention should be made of the relationship between alimony and self-esteem. Stereotypes of this relationship abound. Both the suburban divorce and the county-wide marital transition research, as well as the research of Weitzman and Dixon (1980) and Sidel (1986), clearly refute the belief that many divorcees live off their alimony in idle luxury. In addition, the occupational status of women who received alimony improved: Those who received alimony had a greater increase in their occupational status than those who did not. Alimony does apparently provide a cushion that allows women to obtain additional training or to take a lower-paying job that has more potential for longer-term occupational improvement. This supports the view that alimony can help a divorced person who is unemployed or underemployed to improve his or her occupational status. More attention needs to be paid to providing a larger proportion of divorced women with alimony or other financial supports that will assist them in making this transition.

Child Support

The obligation to support one's own children is, of course, the reason for child support. It is based in statutory and case law on the doctrine of parental responsibility for the "best interests of the child" (Freed &

Foster, 1983; Goldstein et al., 1973). The biological tie is unchanged by the divorce. Even though common residence ends with the divorce, and even if the social tie between parent and child is severed, the obligation to support one's offspring remains. Inability to pay child support is the only reason accepted for nonpayment.

In this study, 15.5% of the subjects at the first interview reported receiving temporary or permanent child support payments. At the second interview, when the respondents were specifically asked about child support, 42.3% reported that child support had been awarded. In only one case was a woman paying child support to her husband. The modal payment per child was $100 per month; payments ranged from $40 to $300, with the mean being $113.31. For the 63 respondents who were awarded support, at the second interview 82.5% reported that it was paid as ordered, whereas 3.2% reported that the payments were irregular and 14.3% said that payments were never made. At the third interview, 35.3% of the 130 persons who replied to this question should have been receiving or paying child support, and 84.7% were actually doing so. Two-thirds of the subjects reported no change in the amount of child support. However, there was a tendency for payments previously made weekly to be paid monthly and for those who had not been paying to start paying. On the other hand, approximately a quarter of the subjects (28.7%) received less support at the third interview than at the second. As a result, a substantial percentage of the divorced were under greater economic stress than they had been previously, because the reduction in child support occurred simultaneously with the complete loss of alimony.

In the 1985–1986 marital transition survey, 57 women reported being awarded temporary or permanent child support payments. The payments ranged from $6 to over $997 per child, with an average of $236.17. Of the 54 reporting on payment schedules, 36 (66.1%) reported receiving the payments due them in whole or in part. A sixth (16.7%) had not received any payments. Translation of the mean child support payments in the 1974–1975 and 1985–1986 studies into constant dollars again revealed that the level of payments did not keep up with inflation. The mean suburban child support payment of $113.31 per child translated into $219.75 in constant dollars. For the marital transition sample a decade later, the mean payment of $236.17 translated into $217.51 in constant dollars. Thus, despite increasing concerns about the adequacy of support for children in divorce, no real improvement in the amounts of payments awarded occurred during this decade in the Cleveland area.

The problems with child support payments are exacerbated by the length of time to be covered by such awards if children were young at the time of the divorce. For example, a child of 5 is due payments until he or she is 18, a 13-year period. A fixed award decreases in value as time passes. In the marital transition survey, the respondents were asked whether any arrangements had been made for cost-of-living adjustment in child support payments; 85.0% indicated that no such arrangements were made. Provisions for cost-of-living adjustments should become a standard part of child support payment schedules.

A further child support issue is the problem that children in divorced families may face in obtaining funds for post-secondary school education or training. A custodial mother's income may continue to be limited, and a noncustodial father's legal responsibility ends when his child is aged 18 unless the divorce agreement stipulates otherwise. In the suburban divorce study at the second interview, 42.4% of the 85 respondents with children indicated that educational provisions had been made. The major provision, mentioned by half of the 36 who had made arrangements, was that the noncustodial parent would pay the total amount. Other arrangements included sharing costs and a rather vague "if something is necessary, arrangements will be made." In the marital transition survey, more than two-thirds (68%) of the 60 women replying indicated that no arrangements had been made; 16.7% mentioned arrangements for college education, 8.3% said that arrangements had been made for special classes, and 10.0% indicated that arrangements had been made without specifying what they were. Thus, children of divorce can be affected adversely in monetary terms, not only in the short run, but also in their longer-term life chances.

As Wallerstein and Huntington (1983) and Wallerstein and Corbin (1986) have dramatically illustrated, even when parents in high-income areas such as Marin County, California have the funds and make arrangements for education, the children may be shortchanged in the type of school they are allowed to attend (children may be attending state schools instead of the private schools they might have expected to attend if their families had remained together). In addition, the parents may not follow through on the educational agreements made and may not actually make the payments. Such issues have long-term implications not only for the children involved, but also for the society in the provision of education and training for the next generation.

At the second interview, the suburban divorced sample was asked how satisfied they were with the court order for child support on a scale from 1 ("very dissatisfied") to 5 ("very satisfied"). The mean score was 3.7 for the 71 persons involved, with 62.0% "very satisfied" or "satisfied" (scores of 4 or 5) versus 23.9% who were "very dissatisfied" or "dissatisfied" (scores of 1 or 2); the remainder were ambivalent or neutral. Thus the majority of subjects were generally satisfied with the court order for child support.

Feminization of Poverty

The comparison of the divorced respondents with the married ones in the suburban study reveals that significant economic losses occurred as an initial consequence of divorce. The economic hardship for most of these persons, especially for custodial parents (who were generally mothers), was considerable. Although economic resources gradually improved after the divorce, the average increase did not place the divorced at parity with the married families. Furthermore, comparisons of economic data collected in the mid-1970s and mid-1980s data suggest that the situation for women in the 1980s was actually relatively worse than in the earlier period.

These findings show that among the divorced, women had greater economic losses than men, and nonwhites had greater losses than whites. For many women, this led to existences at poverty or near poverty. Divorce contributes to the "feminization of poverty"—the increasing tendency for the poor to be composed of female-headed households (Brandwein et al., 1974; Ehrenreich & Piven, 1984; Garfinkel & McLanahan, 1986; Masnick & Bane, 1980; McLanahan & Booth, 1989; Moynihan, 1985; Sidel, 1986). By 1984, 61% of all poor adults were women (Moynihan, 1985). More than half of the children in female-headed households were living in poverty (54.0%), compared with one-eighth (12.5%) of the children of all other families. According to projections of the National Advisory Council on Economic Opportunity, if the increase in poverty in female-headed households continues at the rate it did between 1967 and 1978, then poor families in America will be comprised solely of female-headed households and their children by the year 2000 (Ehrenreich & Piven, 1984). The divorced with children face a significantly bleaker situation than do married persons with children.

ECONOMIC ADAPTATIONS

The data discussed up to this point indicate that many of the divorced in this study, especially women, had economic difficulties associated with the disruption of their marriages and the establishment of new lives. Many, in fact, were faced with significant economic deprivation—at least relative, if not absolute deprivation—as well as a gap between resources and the demands made upon them. In this section, adaptations the divorced respondents made to ease these financial stresses are described.

"Economic adaptations" are financial changes made by the divorced in anticipation of or in response to the divorce. As Moen, Kain, and Elder (1983) note, "Adaptive strategies are the mechanisms families use to regain control over desired outcomes in the face of economic change" (pp. 218-219). To make these adaptations, some individuals changed their employment status, others their occupations, and still others their sources of income.

Economic changes may occur prior to filing for a divorce, as well as after it. Those adaptations that occurred prior to filing are called "economic preparations" here; those that occurred after the filing are called "postdivorce responses."

Economic Preparations

As noted in Chapter 4, as part of the estrangement process and in anticipation of the decision to divorce, many of the divorced retrospectively reported making preparations or seeking information. Among these preparations were entering the labor force, building a nest egg, and obtaining career training.

The use of such preparations differed by gender and race. Females were much more likely to have sought a job than were males, primarily because many women were previously full-time homemakers. As was reported above, some women who had worked part-time shifted to full-time work in preparation for the divorce. Nonwhites were more likely than whites to have prepared for a career (34.5% vs. 13.5%), in part because more whites already had career training. As noted earlier in this chapter, nonwhites also had higher rates of unemployment at the initial interview. When income and employment were controlled for by race, racial differences in the likelihood of making preparations disappeared. Apparent gender and race differences in preparations for divorce can be attributed to differing economic situations. Many of those who had less education and career training to begin with used the educational system as a way of preparing for the economic consequences of divorce—a finding similar to that of Houseknecht and Spanier (1980).

Obtaining training, seeking a job, and building a nest egg had no immediate impact on income. Those who became employed actually had less income than those who did not become employed. However, this is the result of the fact that poorer respondents obtained a job in anticipation of divorce, and (presumably) started their work in entry-level positions. When prior income was controlled for, getting a job in advance of the divorce had no direct impact on income after the divorce.

Economic preparations mainly increased income by furthering occupational advancement—a factor associated with greater income at the third interview. This supports the findings of Sidel (1986) and Hill (1983) that occupational upgrading is a major source of income improvement for American families. Occupational improvement varied by gender, with 26.4% of the women and 8.2% of the men improving their occupational status between the first and third interviews. Because the men studied tended to start with higher occupational statuses, women undoubtedly felt greater pressure to upgrade their occupations. Men may have already had an occupation providing an acceptable wage, especially since the men may have increased their per capita income by "divesting" themselves of their wives and children.

Making preparations did not immediately influence subsequent employment. Those who got a job in advance were as likely as others to have full-time employment at both the second and third interviews. The pressure for a divorced person (especially a woman) to be employed is apparently so great that even without advance preparation, persons out of the labor force must enter it, and those who are in it must try to improve their employment situation.

Postdivorce Responses

In response to the financial problems reported above, many of the divorced subjects were forced to change their economic circumstances after their divorces became final. The most common adaptations chosen were additional education, changes in occupation, changes in employment status, increases in the number of hours worked, and changes in the number of sources of income. Still others were the use of savings, receipt of alimony and child support payments, or changes in subjective satisfaction with the standard of living. Some of these responses have been described earlier in this chapter. In this section, these changes are elaborated upon and their consequences discussed.

Increases in Educational Status

As part of their efforts at self-improvement and advancement, by the third interview two out of every five of the divorced women (39.4%) had obtained additional education, as opposed to about one in six

(16.9%) of the men ($\chi^2 = 9.2$, $df = 1$, $p < .01$). All of this course work for the 28 women reporting it was in degree programs: About a third were enrolled in graduate or professional training, and about 40% had either graduated from college or were taking college courses without yet having graduated. The remainder were taking technical courses (e.g., typing, computer keypunching, or beauty/cosmetology courses), and one person had completed her high school equivalency requirements.

Although the women's level of education was generally lower than that of their husbands at the time of the divorce, there were no significant differences in the amount of education received during the marriage, with 34.0% of the men and 27.5% of the women obtaining additional education during the marriage. Thus, divorce itself seems to have been a spur to further educational activity for the women.

Changes in Occupational Status and Employment

By a year after the divorce was granted, more than twice as many divorced respondents had improved their occupational status as had suffered a setback, with 16.7% experiencing a decrease and 35.4% an increase in status. The remaining 47.9% reported a stable occupational status. For the one in six whose occupational status decreased, the decline most often occurred when skilled manual workers took a lower-status job. These lower-status jobs were so diverse that they do not permit generalizations about the types of jobs taken. Upward mobility was primarily the result of shifting from being a student, having a clerical job, or being a machine operator to becoming the head of a small business, a member of a minor profession, or (to a lesser extent) a business manager. The largest change was from the status of being a student to that of becoming the owner or manager of a small business or becoming a minor professional (e.g., an artist, assistant manager, child care worker, dental hygienist, insurance agent, reporter, sales representative, travel agent, or realtor).

These data indicate that education is very important to improving the occupational status of the divorced. For more than one-third of the subjects, occupational status eventually improved after filing for divorce. In fact, by the third interview, a number of the divorced had improved their occupational status sufficiently through promotion or better jobs to increase their social class position. This was three times as common for women as for men, with 26.4% of the women experiencing such an increase in social class position as compared to 8.2% of the men.

As reported earlier in this chapter, homemakers were the group most likely to change their employment status, and they tended to become full-time workers. Respondents who were employed tended to take on a part-time second job. Even with these adaptations, the greater reliance of the divorced upon themselves as single wage earners still left them more vulnerable to economic distress if they became ill, injured, or unemployed, especially because employee benefits are generally limited at best for those in low-paying jobs.

Changes in the Number of Sources of Income

The divorced had fewer income sources than the married at the first interview, but a substantial percentage increased the number of their income sources over the course of the study. In fact, 57% of the divorced increased their income sources between the first and second interviews. Part of this increase was the result of alimony or child support, but at least half of the increase cannot be attributed to these divorce-related sources. Aside from alimony and child support, one person in three still had an increase in sources of income. This most often was a result of income from a new spouse or from adding a part-time job to a full-time one. In contrast, one person in eight, or 12.5%, had a reduction in the number of sources of income; most often this resulted from the termination of alimony payments. These people were not able to replace alimony with an alternative source of income, and they suffered a constriction in the resources available to them. The remaining 30.5% reported no changes in the number of income sources.

Some of the divorced responded to the economic pressures by increasing the number of hours they worked. For example, one-half of the respondents worked longer hours by the second interview than they did at the first. No one worked fewer hours. Respondents who worked longer hours did so largely by acquiring a part-time second job or changing occupations to those that required more supervisory and administrative time. They did not add significant overtime to their current jobs.

Changes in Satisfaction with Standard of Living

Changing one's subjective perception of economic circumstances is an alternative to changing the objective conditions (Moen et al., 1983). Some of the divorced altered their subjective satisfaction with their standard of living as an alternative or complement to changing their objective economic conditions. On a scale scored from 1 ("very dissatisfied") to 5 ("very satisfied"), respondents were asked at the second interview how satisfied they were with their standard of living before filing for divorce and currently—"that is, the kind of house, clothes, car, (if children: opportunities for the children,) and so on." The mean score for the period of the marriage was 3.5 and for 1 year after divorce was 3.6, indicating that the divorce per se did not change satisfaction levels. One-third had no change in satisfaction with their standard of living between the period before the divorce was filed and a year after the decree was granted. Slightly more reported increased than decreased satisfaction (36.3% vs. 30.3%). Given that one person in six was dissatisfied with his or her standard of living both before the divorce and at the second interview, this slight change was primarily the result of a slight increase in satisfaction on the part of individuals who felt neutral about their standard of living during their marriages.

The mean satisfaction score at the third interview, 3.8, was a little higher than it was earlier. The major predictor of increased satisfaction with the standard of living at the third interview was the level of satisfaction recalled as existing before the divorce. Those who were highly satisfied before the divorce were likely to have a decline in their satisfaction. Those who recalled being dissatisfied before the divorce became more satisfied after the divorce. Satisfaction with the standard of living was greatly influenced by actual income: Divorced persons with incomes over $10,000 were nearly four times as likely to feel good about their standard of living as those with incomes less than $10,000. Actual income did not, however, affect negative feelings about an individual's standard of living. Approximately 11% of those with incomes over $10,000 were dissatisfied with their standard of living, compared with 10% of those with incomes under $10,000.

Remarriage and Economic Improvement

Remarriage is, among other things, another possible response to the economic situation of the divorced. Are people with greater economic resources more likely to remarry than than those with fewer resources? If employment and higher income encourage remarriage, this would support the political economy view. If those with less income and poorer employment are more likely to remarry, this contradicts that view. According to Becker (1973, 1974), the poor do not become divorced to marry the rich because the rich will not have them. Wealthy persons divorce because they reject spouses who do not pull their economic weight in the relationship.

Table 8.2 displays relationships between marital status at the third interview and employment and income at the first interview. If re-

TABLE 8.2. Employment, Income, and Marital Status:
Suburban Divorced Sample

Employment status and mean income	Marital status at third interview				
	Single (n = 74)	Remarried[a] (n = 36)	Cohabiting[b] (n = 11)	Total	n (121)
Employment status at first interview					
Full-time or more	59.8%	32.4%	7.8%	100.0%	102
Part-time	57.1%	42.9%	0.0%	100.0%	7
Unemployed	66.7%	11.1%	22.2%	100.0%	9
Homemaker	81.8%	9.1%	9.1%	100.0%	11
Mean income expected in next year as reported at first interview					
Men	$15,355	$21,296	$10,883	$17,110	59
Women	$8,512	$7,107	$7,000	$8,070	62
Total	$11,378	$15,778	$9,090	$12,479	121
Mean income at second interview					
Men	$15,120	$23,405	$16,250	$18,690	50
Women	$10,208	$7,071	$6,750	$9,257	68
Total	$11,890	$16,871	$10,550	$13,254	118

[a]"Remarried" includes those who married after divorce and then separated from or divorced the new partner.
[b]"Cohabiting" includes those who cohabited between the second and third interview but were not cohabiting or remarried at the third interview.

sources predict remarriage, then those with more resources at the first interview, as measured by income and employment, should be remarried at the third interview. The findings show that full-time employment status at the first interview did not encourage remarriage. In fact, although the numbers involved are small, more of those who were initially working part-time were remarried by the third interview. Higher anticipated income in the year to come at the first interview did encourage remarriage by the third interview for men but not for women. These patterns continued when actual mean income at the second interview (not the income anticipated at this point) was used: Men with higher incomes were more likely to be remarried. These data suggest that higher income for men may encourage reaffiliation— an issue to be discussed more fully in Chapter 10. Women who anticipated more income at the first interview were less likely to have remarried by the third interview. Similar findings also occurred at the second interview for women: Those with lower incomes at the second interview were more likely to have remarried or to be cohabiting at the third interview. These findings are contrary to the political economy view. Even if the marriages that occurred were all marriages of economic necessity, this would not support the political economy model. A basic assumption of political economists is that the poor are economically unattractive as marital partners; thus, the poor should have greater difficulty in finding partners with whom to marry and should be less likely to remarry. The fact that this is not what was observed challenges political economy theories of marriage and divorce.

CONCLUSION

The divorced often underwent significant economic troubles associated with their divorces; this was especially true for women. Furthermore, although many of the divorced improved their economic circumstances by 2–3 years after the divorce, some continued to have problems at that point. At the end of the study, women and nonwhites continued to have lower average incomes than did men and whites. Data comparing mean income levels in constant dollars for the data collected in the 1970s and 1980s showed that divorced women actually lost economic ground in terms of their average income, average alimony payment, and average child support payment received. Even in the mid-1980s, relatively few women reported the inclusion of cost-of-living clauses in their schedules of support payments or agreements about paying for the children's education. Many women and children had economic difficulties, affecting both their current situation and the future prospects of the children. The view that economic self-interest is not the driving mechanism of marriage and divorce is bolstered by the finding that remarriage was more likely to precede income improvement than to follow it; this is not consistent with the assumptions of Becker's (1973, 1974) theory.

From the present data, economic improvement appears to be associated with job changes and with altered perceptions of one's situation. As an economic support, assistance in occupational improvement also appears to be important. Alimony, although infrequently awarded, helped women improve their occupational status. Given that alimony helped women to become economically productive and did not create a life of "idle luxury" for them, its wider use in the early years of divorce could reduce the burden of these families on others later.

Other economic support includes help from family and friends or the use of savings; this support, however, tends to be of limited duration. Furthermore, alimony and child support decline or disappear with time. Although for most of the subjects in the study, the initial economic trauma of the divorce was reduced by improved financial circumstances later on, this was not always the case. For some (principally those with custody of children, an extremely important population in divorce), the economic problems resulting from divorce continued several years afterwards. If positive economic adaptations to divorce are to be encouraged, ways must be found to improve people's employment situations, especially those of custodial parents.

NOTES

1. To close the open-ended "$30,000 or over" income category and to provide greater variability for higher incomes, the midpoint for this category in grouped mean calculations for the suburban divorced and married samples was defined at $40,000. The midpoint for the "under $1,000" category was $500.

2. Income in the marital transition study was coded as follows: under $5,000; $5,000 to $9,999; $10,000 to $14,999; $15,000 to $19,999; $20,000 to $24,999; $25,000 to $29,999; $30,000 to $34,999; $35,000 to $49,999; and $50,000 or over. To make comparisons possible, the two samples were recoded to the following midpoint values: $2,500; $7,500; $12,500; $17,500; $22,500; $27,500; $32,500; and $40,000.

Social Support in Divorce

Self-help is the best help.
—Aesop (1965, p. 114)

*"Home is the place where, when you have to go there,
They have to take you in."*
—Frost (1914/1963, p. 28)

The quotations above illustrate two approaches to what to do in the face of difficulties—be self-reliant, or turn to others (especially members of one's family, who are supposedly obliged to help). In the potential trauma and disruption of a divorce, it may not be realistic to expect divorced persons to solve every problem and bear every burden themselves. They may indeed need help—and not just from their families—as they face the challenges and opportunities of the old roles and problems they retain and the new ones they acquire. Support from others can be of assistance; ironically, however, as the data below indicate, help from others (even family members) may not really be of assistance and can in fact make things worse.

This chapter poses and answers a series of questions about social support: From whom do the divorced receive help? What kind of support do the divorced receive, and does it differ from that received by the married? Does the nature of support change over time? Does the provision of support affect adjustment to divorce, and, if so, which types of support are most effective in reducing distress? Finally, why is it that support can be of help in some situations and not in others?

DEFINITION OF SOCIAL SUPPORT

"Social support" is help that people receive in performing the activities required or permitted by their social roles. Support springs from the bonds and obligations of relationships with family, friends, and ac-

This chapter was initially written by William M. Holmes and subsequently revised by Gay C. Kitson.

quaintances (at work, at school, and in organizations), as well as from contacts with helping professionals (Lin, Simeone, Ensel, & Kuo, 1979). Social support provides meaningful attachments to others, integration in a network of shared relationships, opportunity for nurturing others and being nurtured by them, reassurance of an individual's worth through performance of valued social roles, a sense of reliable alliance with kin, and access to guidance in times of stress (Cobb, 1976; Wan, 1982). The nature of help can range from informal encouragement by family and friends to payment for professional services or provision of services or money by governmental or voluntary agencies.

Social support has been shown to aid people in adjusting to stressful life events (Berkman & Syme, 1979; Cassel, 1976; LaRocca, House, & French, 1980; Lin et al., 1979; Myers et al., 1972; Nuckolls, Cassel, & Kaplan, 1972; Schlesinger, 1978; Williams, Ware, & Donald, 1981). Other researchers, however, report that support is associated with heightened distress (Greene & Feld, 1989; Milardo, 1987; Wilcox, 1981). The means by which social supports affect physiological and psychological distress are unclear (Berkman & Syme, 1979). It is clear that loss of or changes in possessions, position, or relationships with others can disrupt accustomed ways of thinking, perceptions of the self, the performance of tasks, and interactions with others (Parkes, 1971). In such situations, a person's assumptions need to be examined and retested, and habits need to be modified. Supportive persons may reduce the feeling of being in a strange, ambiguous, or unexpected situation. Support brings assurance that although some of a person's life has been modified, much of it remains the same. This continuity helps people to re-establish their equilibrium and routines more rapidly (Parkes, 1972). Support at the time of stressful events may also reduce anxiety and the number of otherwise unmet needs (Kaplan, Cassel, & Gore, 1977). Primary groups such as families or friendship networks may provide support for an individual by taking over or assisting in the performance of instrumental tasks, by providing a setting for expressing emotions and testing coping strategies, and by maintaining continuity in other aspects of a person's life (Litwak, 1985). Relationships thus serve to buffer or mediate some of the stress-producing aspects of life changes (Dean & Lin, 1977). They do so, in part, by providing feedback or evidence from others that actions are leading to the desired outcome in the new situation and by providing opportunities to express pent-up emotions during conditions of uncertainty and indecision (Cassel, 1976).

Although in every society the extended family is the major source of help, comfort, and assistance to members who are in need (Shanas

& Sussman, 1981; Sussman & Burchinal, 1962a, 1962b), not everyone in the family benefits from these supports, nor does every member participate in the system of exchange and reciprocity that binds the family together and helps its members to overcome their problems. Even so, most people are members of such a network for at least part of their lives. Friendship networks, interest groups, and human service agencies may partially substitute for or supplement help from the family if it alone cannot provide enough or appropriate support. This is more likely when the family cannot adequately respond, such as situations in which the performance of formerly routinized tasks is thrown into disarray, patterns of exchange and reciprocity are disrupted, or family members do not have the skills needed to provide appropriate assistance. Help from outside sources is particularly useful when the family and alternative sources of help have similar structures (Litwak, 1985).

The availability of supports depends in part on a person's position in a network of persons willing and able to provide support (McLanahan, Wedemeyer, & Adelberg, 1981). The larger the kinship and friendship network, the more people there are who can be called upon for help when it is needed. Members of primary groups are not always able or willing to help, however. A divorce upsets the pattern of exchange in a family and kin network. Family members may not approve of the decision to divorce. There may be strained relationships with in-laws. Some friends become defined as "his" or "hers," thereby further cutting potential support (Miller, 1970). In situations such as divorce, the source and type of support available to a person may be more problematic, and help may be needed from outside one's circle of family and friends. It is also the case that the help offered may not actually be helpful. "Help" may include bad advice, actions that restrict a person's options, or advice that leads to anger and frustration ("I'm telling you this for your own good," "What you need to do is . . .").

Variables Assessing Support

In the present research, the major independent variables assessing social support were respondents' reports that during the past year they had received any of the following types of help: "financial support" (money, gifts, food, or housing); "service support" (babysitting, errands, invitations to social events); or "information, guidance, or counseling" (someone to talk with, moral support, and/or counseling). For each type of help, the measure was scored 0 if no help was received, and 1 if help was received from any of the following sources: spouse's family, respondent's family, friends or coworkers, and children. With the answers to these questions, it is also possible to examine patterns of support—that is, whether respondents received combinations of help (e.g., financial and service support, service support and information) from each of the sources. These measures indicate what kind of help was given and by whom, but do not indicate the quantity or quality of help received. Other support measures are described in greater detail in later sections of the chapter as they are introduced.

Complexity of Support

Although research has shown that social supports help people adjust to crises, there are many different types and sources of support. No single act universally qualifies as a social support. Receiving one type of support from one source may be unrelated to receiving another type of support from another source. The same support given to different people may not have the same consequences. Because of this complexity, most of the findings reported in this chapter are effects of individual types of supports, rather than a single summary index.

This problem is illustrated by examining the internal consistency (alpha reliability) of a set of commonly used measures of social support (see, e.g., Wilcox, 1981). The support items asked about at the first interview in the suburban divorce survey were factor-analyzed using a principal-factor solution and a varimax rotation. The factor score coefficients in Table 9.1 indicate that if the items were added together, the resulting scale would have a modest to poor alpha reliability for the total sample. When weights derived from the factor analysis were applied to the measures, a more reliable scale resulted, as indicated by the higher theta reliability coefficients. However, it would be difficult to understand the meaning of the scale, since one support item might be weighted three times as heavily as another, a second two times as much, and so forth, and only the total scale score would be displayed. It is for this reason that support is examined in terms of individual items in this chapter.

SOURCES AND TYPES OF SOCIAL SUPPORT

This section examines the sources and types of help the suburban divorced sample received, and compares this support to that received by the married sample. As the discussion above illustrates, support comes from informal and formal sources, and both types of support are examined here. Changes in patterns of support over time are also explored.

TABLE 9.1. Factor Score Coefficients and Alpha and Theta Reliability for Sources of Social Support for Divorced Sample

Sources of social support	Factor score coefficients
Help from ex-spouse's family	.127
Help from own family	.610
Help from friends/coworkers	.267
Help from children	−.015
Read or discuss divorce	−.145
How often see ex-spouse's parents/grandparents	.025
How often see ex-spouse's siblings	.045
How often see ex-spouse's other relatives	−.016
How often see own parents/grandparents	−.014
How often see own siblings	.028
How often see own other relatives	.013
Number of confidants	.172
How often attend church/temple	−.086
Receiving any professional help	.013
Help with role responsibilities	−.026
Alpha reliability	.47
Theta reliability	.63

Informal Sources of Help

Who Helped?

For the divorced at the first interview, but not the married, the most likely source of help was their own families. Of the divorced respondents, 63.4% reported receiving some help from their own families in the year prior to the interview, compared to 57.4% of the married; this difference was not statistically significant. Thus, even though Chapter 6 has shown that the divorced respondents had substantially higher rates of psychological and physical distress than the married, and it is thought that help is more likely to be forthcoming at a time of crisis, they were not substantially more likely to receive help from the source that would most typically be expected to offer it. With 58.7% of the friends and coworkers of the divorced giving help, compared to 61.4% for the married, there were also no significant differences between the samples in help received from this source. This result was obtained despite the fact that, on the average, the divorced reported having significantly more friends than the married with whom they could "occasionally talk over confidential matters" (a mean of 2.9 vs. 1.9; $t = 4.6$, $df = 375$, $p < .001$).

There were significant differences between the divorced and married in the provision of support by an (ex-)spouse's family and a respondent's children, with the married receiving more help than the divorced in each case. Of the divorced, 36.6% received help from their ex-spouses' families, compared to 51.4% of the married who received help from their in-laws ($\chi^2 = 8.4$, $df = 1$, $p < .01$). It is not known whether the level of support from the spouses' families before the divorce was filed was as high as it was among the married. There is some evidence, such as reports of problems with in-laws as a marital complaint (Chapter 5) and less knowledge of the socioeconomic background of in-laws (Chapter 3), to suggest that contacts may have been few; therefore, help may have also been infrequent. Even so, it appears that in divorce, familial support rapidly shifts to blood relatives.

Among the divorced, 19.8% of the children provided assistance to their parents, as opposed to 29.7% among the married ($\chi^2 = 5.1$, $df = 1$, $p < .05$). It is unlikely that the divorced subjects' children were simply not providing help; rather, as indicated in Chapter 3, the children of the married were older on the average than those of the divorced, and were therefore more able to provide help. The net result, however, was that at the very time the divorced were likely to be in need of support, they had one less source on which to depend in their support network.

By the time of the third interview (2–3 years after the divorce, or 4 years after the separation), help from both the respondents' and the ex-spouses' families had decreased significantly. At the third interview, 53.8% (a mean of 0.5) of the respondents' families were giving help, down from 63.4% (a mean of 0.6) at the first interview ($t = 6.7$, $df = 129$, $p < .001$). For the ex-spouses' families, 12.8% (a mean of 0.1) were giving help at the third interview, compared to 36.6% (a mean of 0.4) at the first interview ($t = 6.7$, $df = 129$, $p < .001$). Help from the respondents' children increased from 19.8%, or a mean of 0.2, to 29.6%, a mean of 0.3, presumably as the children became a little older and better able to provide more assistance ($t = 2.5$, $df = 121$, $p < .01$). Friends and coworkers were as likely to be providing help at the end of the study (58.0%) as they were at the beginning (58.7%), after offering even higher levels of help at the second interview, 1 year after-divorce (64.0%).

Types of Support Received

Table 9.2 displays the proportion of respondents receiving no help and those receiving any help with financial matters, services, or information, and combinations of more than one type of help. Changes in patterns of support for the divorced are indicated by the contrasts between replies at the first interview, when the divorce was filed, and at the third interview, approximately 2–3 years later. For purposes of comparison, the replies of the married at their first interview are also shown.

Financial help (in the form of money, gifts, food, or housing) was the most common type of support received by the divorced at the first interview and also by the married, with a respondent's family being the major source of this help. Information, guidance, or counseling (talking things over, learning new skills, and moral support) was the next most common type of help, with friends somewhat more likely to provide this help than family members for both the married and

TABLE 9.2. Proportion Reporting Social Support by Type and Provider: Divorced and Married Respondents

Study group and provider of support	No support	% reporting			
		Any support			
		Financial	Service	Information, etc.	More than one type
Divorced, first interview (n = 202)					
Respondent's family	36.6	44.6	31.2	36.1	33.6
Ex-spouse's family	63.4	19.8	16.3	20.3	12.9
Friends/coworkers	41.3	15.9	30.8	44.3	25.4
Respondent's children	80.2	6.4	5.0	13.4	4.0
Divorced, third interview (n = 133)					
Respondent's family	46.2	32.6	28.0	32.6	32.9
Ex-spouse's family	87.2	6.8	6.0	3.8	2.3
Friends/coworkers	42.0	13.0	26.7	48.9	26.7
Respondent's children	70.4	8.0	10.4	19.2	8.0
Married, first interview (n = 177)					
Respondent's family	42.6	36.9	30.7	33.0	29.0
Spouse's family	48.6	31.6	28.2	23.7	22.6
Friends/coworkers	38.6	13.1	39.2	43.2	27.3
Respondent's children	70.3	10.3	20.6	13.1	12.6

Note. Sum of row percentages exceeds 100% because of multiple types of support received.

divorced. The divorced were somewhat less likely than the married to receive services (babysitting, being driven places, help with errands, invitations to social events, and dates) from friends at either the first or third interview. It may be that the divorced were less able to reciprocate these services, and therefore the exchange process broke down. With family, on the other hand, the calculus of exchange may have been longer-term, with the expectation that help might be provided for one member at one point and repaid at a later time, because "the family" should continue through time with less expectation of immediate payback or exchange. Such behavior has been called "prescriptive altruism" (Fortes, 1969; see also Bloch, 1973). For the divorced, multiple types of help were more likely from a respondent's family at both the first and third interviews. Among the married, the differences among groups in the provision of multiple supports were less striking.

These analyses indicate that both initially and across time, the divorced had somewhat less support available to them than the married. Declining support for the divorced over time may have been the result of many factors. Fragmentation of bonds with the ex-spouse's relatives may have been one of these factors; Anspach (1976), Colletta (1979), and Spicer and Hampe (1975) also describe a reduction in interaction with kin of the ex-spouse. As discussed in Chapter 8, economic circumstances for the divorced tended to improve somewhat with time. Moreover, some subjects remarried, and others routinized ways of coping to replace ad hoc support; as a result of these changes, less help may have been needed. Disapproval of the divorce may have alienated some potential sources of support. Finally, although it is possible to mobilize support for a short period of time, it is harder to sustain support over a longer period of time. The attention of potential helpers may have been taken up by other (to them) more pressing, immediate issues, and by the needs and desires of the helpers to get back to their own lives. It is also likely that people may not have realized the extent of disruption and continuing difficulty experienced by the divorced. This diminution of support was more true for the respondents' families than for friends. In addition, the divorced may have felt freer to communicate their continuing concerns and problems to their friends than to their parents and other kin.

Help with Role Responsibilities

One way in which support may provide assistance is through offering help with role responsibilities—that is, the tasks of daily living that have to be performed (e.g., caring for children, feeding and clothing oneself and others, maintaining a relatively clean home, and managing contacts with outside agencies and organizations). This section explores how the divorced managed these tasks of daily living. The divorced respondents were asked at all three interviews, and the married were asked at the first interview, who had "full, major, or equal, responsibility" for 21 different groups of household tasks (see Appendix A for the full list).

Typically, among the divorced, the respondents had full responsibility for performing these activities. The period in which the respondents were most likely to bear this responsibility alone was after separation or divorce, but before remarriage or establishment of a new relationship; for most people, this interlude occurred at the time of the second interview. For this reason, the replies of the divorced at the second interview were compared to those of the married at the first interview. A substantially higher proportion of the divorced than of the married had full responsibility for all 21 daily activities. For 17 of the 21 tasks, over 50% of the divorced subjects reported that they had full responsibility for each of them. In no case did as much as 35% of the married sample report full responsibility for any task.

The five roles for which the approximately 160 divorced respondents were most likely to have sole responsibility at the second interview were "handling financial affairs" (76.4% vs. 29.8% of the married), "dealing with the authorities" (such as the police, government officials, and inspectors, if such contacts were necessary; 72.0% vs. 29.9%); "dealing with the church or YMCA/YWCA" (71.2% vs. 21.9%); "washing and taking care of the car" (69.4% vs. 29.1%); and "maintaining social activities" (e.g., inviting people over, making arrangements to go out; 68.4% vs. 18.6%). These data underscore the fact that people whose marriages end must struggle with an increased burden of responsibility for maintaining a social support system.

In addition to the much smaller proportion of married subjects who reported full responsibility for activities, the ranking of role responsibilities was different, with only one overlap with the divorced in the top five activities—"dealing with the authorities." The distribution of full responsibilities for tasks for the married was also more in line with traditional gender role expectations. The first-ranked activity was "doing laundry" (34.3%), followed by "cooking" (32.6%), "dealing with the school" (31.7%), "painting and repair work around the house" (31.2%), and "handling financial affairs" (29.8%).

In addition to the code for whether the respondent had full responsibility for a task or set of tasks, a second code was developed that detailed who, if anyone at all, helped with the tasks. As reported above, the most common pattern for the performance of household tasks was that the divorced person had sole responsibility. As would be expected, married respondents had help from a spouse or shared responsibility more often than the divorced. These variations are illustrated by the help patterns reported for three roles: "helping the children with homework," "disciplining the children," and "painting and repair work around the house." Replies for the first and third interviews for the divorced and for the first interview for the married are discussed, because data from the third interview illustrate patterns of role responsibilities 2–3 years after the divorce, when patterns had presumably become more stable.

Of the married respondents with school-age children, 76.2% reported that they shared the responsibility of "helping the children with homework" with their spouses. This was the case for only 18.8% of the divorced at the first interview, a time at which some spouses were still living at home. Being solely responsible for this activity was true for only 15.5% of the married, whereas 58.0% of the divorced respondents had this as their sole responsibility at the first interview. In other initial help patterns, older children helped their younger siblings with school work, either alone (15.9%) or with the respondent (2.9%). This help pattern was not reported for the married.

By the third interview, the responsibility for "helping the children with homework" was shared by only 9.6% of the former partners. Sole responsibility for the task was carried by 48.1% of the divorced respondents. At the third interview, a new spouse helped with the children's homework in 13.4% of the divorce study families, with 9.6% helping with homework and 3.8% solely responsible for it. At this final postdivorce interview, in 7.6% of the cases a relative helped with homework, or the respondent and one of his or her children helped another child (7.7%), or siblings helped one another (3.8%).

Responsibility for "disciplining the children" was shared between the parents in 89.8% of the married group, but in only 37.1% of the divorced group at the first interview. The respondent or the spouse had sole responsibility for discipline in only 10.2% of the married families (8.3% of the respondents, 1.9% of the spouses), but among the divorced one or the other spouse had sole responsibility in 57.7% of the cases (56.7% of the respondents and 1.0% of the ex-spouses). Furthermore, among the divorced, sharing the responsibility for discipline between the respondent and ex-spouse declined from 37.1% at the first interview to only 6.2% at the third interview. The main source of help with discipline came with remarriage, with 21.5% of respondents saying they shared discipline with their new spouses. To a lesser extent, help also came from relatives (10.8%) or the person the subject was dating (4.6%). The respondent's children also helped with disciplining their siblings (2.1% at the first interview and 4.6% at the third interview);

this was true for only one married family. Thus, children took on more tasks involving supervision of their siblings homework and discipline in the divorced than in the married families.

One set of tasks for which it might be expected that responsibilities would be less likely to be shared is "painting and repair work around the house," because these have traditionally been male tasks. At the first interview, home repairs were the sole responsibility of the respondent or of the spouse in 51.2% of the married families (31.2% of the respondents and 20.0% of the spouses) and 65.6% of the divorced families (61.1% for the respondents and 4.5% of the ex-spouses). In one out of three of the married families, this task was shared between the spouses, in contrast to 7.0% of the divorced. For the divorced, help with home repairs changed across time. At first, the most likely source of help other than the ex-spouse was hired help; either the hired help worked alone, or the respondent did some tasks and paid for assistance with the rest (10.1%). This was followed by relatives (9.6%). The person helping was usually a male relative, working either alone or with the respondent. By the third interview, the use of hired help had declined, but 9.9% of the divorced sample continued to report that relatives lent a hand. For 16.2% of the subjects, a new spouse was reported to be sharing or to have taken over repair work. With these changes, the percentage of respondents solely responsible for repairs decreased to 47.7%.

These data on role responsibilities illustrate that the divorced had substantial responsibility for many time-consuming tasks. In general, they had less help from others than the married; as a result, they turned to a variety of people for assistance. Help therefore was fragmented. The children of the divorced respondents shouldered responsibility for their siblings to a greater degree than was true among the married, forcing these "parental children" to grow up faster than they might have otherwise. Compared to the reports of shared help with household repairs, the data on child care activities illustrate that some activities brought into a subsequent marriage continue to be the sole responsibility of one spouse. The new spouse may be unwilling, unable, or not permitted by the spouse or (perhaps more especially) his or her children to share responsibility for these activities.

Formal Sources of Help

This section explores the role of formal sources of assistance—that is, individuals, activities, agencies, and organizations making organized, institutionalized efforts to provide support to those in need. In some cases, the provision of help itself constitutes the support, as in economic assistance; in other instances, the relationship between the helper and client and the insights achieved through that interaction provides assistance, as in psychotherapy or supportive counseling. Sometimes the boundary between formal and informal help is fuzzier, as is the case with the contribution of participation in certain organizations and activities. The focus of the organization, such as a religious denomination, may provide solace; or participation in the activities of the organization may provide meaning and support in and of themselves or through meeting new people, at which point the informal aspects of support are likely to come back into play.

Welfare Organizations

One source of assistance that is often reported to be important among the divorced was little used in this study—welfare agencies. This is in part a result of the focus in this study on subjects who lived in working- and middle-class communities. In any event, these data indicate that relatively few became so depleted of resources as to have to turn to such agencies for assistance. Only 5.5% of the divorced and 1.1% of the married were receiving help from Aid to Families with Dependent Children or other public assistance programs at the first interview. As noted in Chapter 8, this proportion did not change much across the period of the study.

Professional Help with Personal Problems

Professionals were the major source of formal help provided to the divorced. As discussed in Chapter 4, the suburban divorced respondents at the initial interview were significantly more likely than the married to have turned to any of a number of professionals (physicians; lawyers, psychiatrists or psychologists; members of the clergy, including priests, rabbis, and other religious leaders, marriage counselors; or social workers) for help with problems. To review these findings briefly, lawyers were the group most likely to have been consulted by the divorced in the year prior to the divorce. The next most likely sources of help for the divorced were psychiatrists/psychologists, physicians, and members of the clergy. Among the married, the leading source of professional assistance was physicians, followed by lawyers and clergy.

In the marital transition study, the divorced women were also asked whether they or their spouses turned to any of the professionals listed above. These women were significantly less likely than their women counterparts in the suburban study to have turned to any of the professionals listed for help. Seventy percent of the suburban divorced sample had seen some professional, compared to 51.1% of the marital transition sample ($\chi^2 = 20.1$, $df = 1$, $p < .001$). Much of this decrease could be attributed to significantly less reported contact with lawyers. Only 18.3% of the marital transition sample reported having sought help from a lawyer in the year prior to the divorce, compared to 60.7% of the suburban sample ($\chi^2 = 54.2$, $df = 1$, $p < .001$). The decrease was not accounted for by the ex-husbands' having been the ones to have sought legal advice. The reasons for this finding are unclear. Those in the marital transition sample were also significantly less likely to have sought help from physicians, with 13.0% reporting this versus 24.3% of the suburban sample ($\chi^2 = 6.2$, $df = 1$, $p < .05$). The percentages seeking help from clergy, psychiatrists/psychologists, marriage counselors, or social workers were quite similar. The proportions seeking help from any mental health worker (psychiatrist/ psychologist, marriage counselor, or social worker) were also comparable: 36.4% of the suburban divorced women sought such help, as opposed to 28.7% of the marital transition sample. Thus, the suburban divorced sample sought more professional help than the married, particularly from lawyers and physicians. There were, however, no significant differences between the two divorced samples in seeking help from mental health workers.

Differences in Whom the Divorced Turned to for Help

Members of informal support networks tend to be channels to formal systems (Litwak, 1985; Suchman, 1965). Variations in the use of informal supports should foster understanding of which professionals the divorced person will use. Having informal support at the first interview (help from family, friends, or children, and leisure-time activity) was cross-tabulated with seeking help from the professionals discussed above. Having informal support was generally associated with seeking help from professionals. The causal order of these associations is not known, but it can be inferred from what is known about social support.

Physicians were more often a source of support when the divorced reported having a number of friends with whom to talk over confidential matters: 46% of those reporting any confidants reported turning to their physicians for help, whereas only 10.5% of those without confidants did so ($\chi^2 = 8.8$, $df = 1$, $p < .01$). The respondents' race, education, income, and amount of life stress as measured by life events were not related to seeing a physician for help.

Going to a minister, priest, or rabbi was significantly more likely when respondents reported that they also had received help from their own families: 25% of those who received help from their families sought help from a member of the clergy, versus 12.5% of those who received no help from their families ($\chi^2 = 4.5$, $df = 1$, $p < .05$). Not surprisingly, seeing the clergy also varied by whether a person reported belonging to a religious denomination, with 25.3% of those so affiliated and 3.5% of those not affiliated seeking help. Roman Catholics accounted for most of this type of help seeking. Half of the 45 persons who sought help from clergy were Catholics; this constituted 37.8% of the 45 Catholics in the study. Thus, as indicated in Chapter 3, although there were no differences in the proportions of the married and divorced samples seeking divorce by religious denomination, Catholics who were contemplating or who had experienced a divorce were more likely than those of other denominations to seek help from their priests.

Psychiatrists or psychologists, marriage counselors, and social workers were seen under similar circumstances. However, respondents sought help from them not simply because of the divorce but because of the accumulation of other life events as well, many of which, as seen in Chapter 6, may themselves have been precipitated by the divorce. None of the 15 respondents who reported no stressful life events (other than the divorce) in the prior year had consulted a therapist, whereas those who reported at least some other stressful life events were more likely to have sought such help.

Religious Institutions and Activities

Religion may provide support to individuals in a number of ways. As indicated above, members of the clergy may provide direct assistance through counseling. Membership in a church or synagogue and attendance at its services can provide emotional solace, while interactions with other members may also provide support and a feeling of being a valued person. On the other hand, a number of religions have had, and some still do have, restrictions about the participation of divorced persons in rituals of the denomination, such as the ability to take communion or the sacraments; some also limit the ability of divorced persons to remarry and remain in good standing as members of their denominations. Thus, the end of the marriage could produce the need for religious support and comfort, or it could produce a desire to withdraw from contacts for fear of disapproval or as a result of a feeling of personal failure in meeting denominational standards.

As seen in Chapter 3, the divorced were less likely than the married to belong to religious denominations or to attend church or synagogue services; they were also more likely to report little or no influence of religious beliefs on daily life, as well as to report a religious affiliation different from that of their marital partner. It seems likely that these characteristics were long-standing and not simply the result of changes at the time of the divorce, but these questions were asked at the time of the divorce filing. At the least, this makes it difficult to interpret differences in church attendance and the influence of religion between the married and divorced as results of changes brought about by the divorce and reactions to it.

Answers to another question, however, suggest that some of the divorcing subjects did turn to religion for support, whereas others apparently withdrew at the time of the marital breakdown. At the first interview, the suburban divorced respondents were asked, "During this period of the divorce, would you say you are attending church/ temple more or less frequently or about the same as before?" The married were asked about changes in their attendance "during the past few months." Among the divorced, 23.4% ($n = 128$) reported that they were attending services more often, compared to 10.3% ($n = 146$) of the married; 53.1% of the divorced said their attendance was the same, as opposed to 76.7% of the married; and 23.4% of the divorced said they were attending less often, compared to 13.0% of the married ($\chi^2 = 17.2, df = 2, p < .001$). Thus, the divorce apparently influenced attendance both positively and negatively.

At the second and third interviews, more of the divorced subjects reported increases in their church attendance as compared to the married at the first interview, with 19.5% of the divorced reporting increased attendance at the second interview ($n = 158$) and 24.7% ($n = 89$) at the third. At the second but not the third interview, more of the divorced than the married reported less attendance, with 20.7% reporting this at the second interview and 14.6% at the third interview. The proportions of the divorced who reported attending church at least monthly were quite similar across the three interviews (respectively, 41.5%, 40.7%, and 41.8%). Thus, as with other types of support, some divorced persons apparently turned to their religious denominations for solace and support, whereas others did not. There was an apparent increase in attendance in the early stages of the divorce. Overall, however, by the end of the study, the married (as assessed at the first interview) still had higher attendance rates than the divorced.

Leisure-Time Activities

Another way of coping with loneliness and life changes is to fill leisure time with activities. Some of these activities occur in organized settings, and others do not. Such activities may lead to meeting new friends, and thus may further aid adjustment. At the first interview, all of the respondents were asked whether they engaged in a list of 21 leisure-time activities. These ranged from "reading" and "watching TV, listening to records/radio" to "attending concerts" and "social drinking in bars" (see Appendix A for the full list). Ninety-two percent of the married and 85.6% of the divorced reported some leisure-time activity. The married, however, reported participating in significantly more of such activities than the divorced, both initially and across time. At the first interview, the married reported a mean of 11.2 activities, compared to 8.6 for the divorced ($t = 2.4$, $df = 173$, $p < .01$). Over the period of the study, the divorced became more active in leisure-time activities, with an increase to an average of 9.6 activities at the second interview and 10.2 activities at the third.

It is unclear why the divorced participated in fewer activities than the married. It is possible, however, that the psychological and financial dislocations of the end of the marriage and the early period of the divorce, combined with their increased responsibilities for tasks of daily living, gave them less time, energy, and money for involvement in activities.

Although the activities most frequently mentioned by the married and divorced initially and across time were "watching TV, listening to records/radio" (mentioned at the first interview, respectively, by 92.1% and 85.6%) and "visiting with friends" (82.0% and 76.7%), the divorced were more likely than the married to engage in some activities by the time of the third interview. These included "going dancing" (respectively, 45.1% and 29.8%); "taking part in sports" (57.9% vs. 47.8%); "social drinking in bars" (36.1% vs. 23.0%); "self-improvement activities" (e.g., school, aerobics, and other exercise; 48.1% vs. 30.3%); "going for drives in car" (50.4% vs. 34.9%); and "reading" (79.0% vs. 70.8%). The activities the divorced chose seemed more self-absorbed than those of the married. At both the beginning and the end of the study, they engaged in less volunteer work (13.6% at the first interview, compared to 21.9% of the married), belonged to fewer organizations (39.1% vs. 48.3%), entertained less often at home (63.2% vs. 76.4%), and visited relatives less often (69.3% vs. 80.9%) than did the married.

In another sign of improved finances, more of the divorced reported traveling and taking vacations as time went on (59.4% at the third interview vs. 40.6% at the first). However, even at the final interview fewer of the divorced reported travel and vacations than the married (70.2% at the first interview).

Few of the divorced attended meetings of groups for the divorced, such as Parents Without Partners. Over the course of the study, some individuals reported attending such meetings and then stopping. At the first and second interviews, 5.9% participated in such groups; at the third interview, 6.9% participated. However, for the most part, those attending at the third interview did not include those who participated at the first interview. By the third interview 5.3% reported dropping this activity, and an additional 2.0% did so at the second interview. By the end of the study, a total of 13 subjects had participated in groups for the divorced.

Although divorced subjects at the first interview in the marital transition study only reported on participation in groups for the divorced an average of 5 months after separation, instead of over a several-year period as in the longitudinal suburban study, a similarly small percentage of divorced subjects reported involvement in groups for the divorced (6.4%). Robert S. Weiss (1973) has noted that the number of persons involved in Parents Without Partners is not large, given the size of the divorced population. Women participate more often than men, with those who remain in the organization often developing the same-sex support group, although they are still interested in developing relationships with members of the opposite sex. Bohannan (1985) maintains that although the number of divorce support groups has grown in the past 20 years, general-purpose support groups such as Parents Without Partners have been supplanted by special-interest groups organized around common interests and activities, such as religious denominations, tennis, skiing, or playing bridge.

What Would Aid Adjustment?

At the second interview, the suburban divorced sample was asked, "Since the divorce suit was filed, is there a particular person who has been especially helpful to you in adjusting to the divorce?" Somewhat over a third of the 161 respondents (35.4%) indicated that no one had been especially helpful. Another 22.4% of the sample mentioned a relative, and an equal percentage mentioned a friend. Next in importance was a person the respondent was dating, followed by 3.1% who mentioned a coworker and 2.5% who mentioned professional help (replies did not total 100% because of multiple mentions). Next, the respondent was asked how the person or persons mentioned had been helpful. Among the 94 respondents who gave explanations, by far the most frequent response, mentioned by 92.6%, was that the respondent was able to talk freely to this person and that he or she was able to understand. The second most frequent response, mentioned in 18.1% of the instances, was that the person helped to "resocialize" the respondent by encouraging involvement in activities that helped the respondent to forget the ex-spouse and become independent. Task-based or instrumental help was mentioned infrequently; help with children was mentioned in 7.4% of the replies, financial help in 6.4%, and help with household tasks in 2.1%.

The suburban divorced respondents were also asked at the second interview about programs or other types of assistance that might have helped them. Over three-quarters (78.0%) said that there were no programs that would have helped. Among the remaining 33 respondents, the most helpful potential resources, mentioned by 39.4%, were professional guidance or family services. The second type of potential help, mentioned by 33.3%, was a support group for divorced persons. This was apparently distinct from a group such as Parents Without Partners; it would seem to be more like widow-to-widow support groups, in which widows help other widows to cope with their loss (Silverman, 1981). The remaining replies included mentions of financial assistance, help with tasks, and a religious or spiritual program.

In addition, the divorced were asked at the second interview what kinds of services would help them in the future. A little over half of the respondents had ideas of what could help ($n = 80$). The most frequent reply was financial assistance, mentioned by 33.8%; a mixed bag of services was the next most frequent mention (31.3%), followed by 17.5% who mentioned professional guidance or family services.

A decade later, the divorced in the county-wide marital transition survey were also asked at the second interview about "special programs or assistance that would have made things easier for you or would help you now." The replies were similar to those in the suburban study. A little over a third (36.2%) mentioned things that had helped them or would help others. The most commonly reported need for the 30 who talked about what was lacking was divorce support groups, mentioned by 33.4%. Some wanted the group to be age-specific (6.7%) or issue-specific (6.7%). Another 10.0% mentioned groups for children—either for the children alone (3.3%) or for children and a parent (6.7%). By contrast, 31.6% ($n = 38$) mentioned that a support group had helped them.

These data suggest that in the metropolitan Cleveland area, at least, there appears to be a need for more support groups. The groups available now are generally groups such as Parents Without Partners; special-interest activity groups (skiing, bicycling, etc.); time-limited educational support groups for the separated, similar to the program described by Robert Weiss (1975); or primarily social, often religion-based groups. Many people apparently feel a need for help that could best be provided by other divorced persons.

Gender and Race Differences in Support

Gender

The focus above has been on patterns of support. These patterns, however, may also vary by gender and race. In general, when there were differences between men and women in the suburban divorce study in the utilization of help sources, women were more likely to have sought help or to have been offered it than were men (Table 9.3). Men did not receive more help than women from any source of support available to them. This finding supports that of other studies, which report women as being more likely to seek help when it is needed and available (Gurin et al., 1960; Kessler et al., 1981; Veroff, Kulka, & Douvan, 1981). Women were significantly more likely than men to have obtained support from their families, from their friends and coworkers, from their children, from any of a number of professionals combined, and from lawyers in particular. Women reported having at least some responsibility for significantly more daily tasks than did men. There were no differences by gender in the provision of support by ex-spouses' families; in the mean number of leisure-time activities reported; in changes in church attendance; or in the use of clergymen, physicians, psychiatrists/psychologists, marriage counselors, or social workers individually, or mental health workers as a combined category.

Race

There were no significant differences by race in the provision of support by ex-spouses' or respondents' families or by respondents' children. Whites received significantly more help from friends and coworkers than did nonwhites. Whites and nonwhites did not differ in the mean number of household responsibilities for which they were responsible. With two exceptions, there were no differences by race in the proportions receiving help from any professionals as a group, or from different types of professionals. Whites were, however, more likely than nonwhites to have sought help from the clergy. In addition, when mental health practitioners were combined, whites were more likely to have sought help from at least one of them than were nonwhites. There were also no differences by race in changes in church attendance. Nonwhites were, however, significantly more likely to be involved in leisure-time activities than were whites.

Summary

This section has examined the patterns of support the suburban divorced sample reported at the beginning of the study and across time. Despite the fact that the divorced had higher levels of distress than the married, as demonstrated in Chapter 6, they did not receive more help than the married from family and friends. In fact, at a time of presum-

TABLE 9.3. Social Supports at Time the Divorce Was Filed by Gender and Race

Type of support	Gender				Race			
	Male (n = 102)	Female (n = 107)	χ^{2a} $(t)^b$	p	Male (n = 153)	Female (n = 56)	χ^{2a} $(t)^b$	p
% receiving any help from (ex-)spouse's family	39.4	34.0	0.6	n.s.	36.2	37.7	0.0	n.s.
% receiving any help from respondent's family	50.5	75.7	13.8	.001	65.1	58.5	0.7	n.s.
% receiving any help from friends/coworkers	44.4	71.8	18.0	.001	63.1	46.2	4.6	.05
% receiving any help from respondent's children	12.1	27.2	15.9	.001	20.8	17.0	0.4	n.s.
Mean number of responsibilities	13.4	15.5	(−4.0)	.001	14.4	14.6	(−0.3)	n.s.
% receiving any help from professionals[c]	59.0	80.4	11.1	.001	68.0	58.9	1.5	n.s.
% receiving any help from clergy	18.0	24.3	1.2	n.s.	21.1	9.1	3.9	.05
% receiving any help from physician	18.0	29.0	3.5	n.s.	17.8	20.0	0.1	n.s.
% receiving any help from lawyer	49.0	61.7	14.2	.001	52.0	49.1	0.1	n.s.
% receiving any help from psychiatrist/psychologist	21.2	28.0	1.4	n.s.	20.5	12.7	1.2	n.s.
% receiving any help from marriage counselor	15.0	12.1	0.4	n.s.	15.1	7.3	2.2	n.s.
% receiving any help from social worker	7.0	11.2	1.7	n.s.	7.9	3.6	0.6	n.s.
% receiving any help from therapists[d]	24.5	36.4	3.0	n.s.	35.3	17.9	5.1	.05
% reporting change in church attendance	42.6	50.7	0.8	n.s.	26.2	39.6	2.7	n.s.
Mean number of leisure activities	8.7	8.4	(0.5)	n.s.	8.2	9.4	(−1.9)	.05

[a]Degrees of freedom for $\chi^2 = 1$.
[b]Degrees of freedom for $t = 207$.
[c]Clergyman, physician, lawyer, psychiatrist or psychologist, marriage counselor, or social worker.
[d]Psychiatrist or psychologist, marriage counselor, or social worker.

241

ably increased need, they received less support—in part because their ex-spouses' families were less likely to give them help, and in part because their children were generally younger than those of the married and therefore less able to give them help. In other indicators of possible sources of comfort and support, the divorced were more likely than the married to have sought help with personal problems from professionals, less likely to have been involved in leisure-time activities, more likely to have made changes in their attendance at religious services near the time of the divorce, and much more likely to have full responsibility for daily tasks than were the married. Women generally received more help than did men, whereas there were relatively few differences by race in the provision of support.

SUPPORT AND ADJUSTMENT

In this section, the role that support plays in adjustment to divorce is explored. What becomes apparent here is that some supports facilitate adjustment and others do not. Not every source or type of support is helpful; sometimes "help" from others can make the situation worse. Moreover, factors that help adjustment in one area may hinder it in others.

Because of the number of support and adjustment measures, the focus in this section is upon the relationship between supports and subjective distress—the feelings of anxiety and depression that the divorced subjects reported. In addition, the associations of the support measures with the subjective distress measure were more numerous and stronger than those with the other adjustment measures (attachment, self-esteem, and illness contacts).

The association between support provided at the time the divorce was filed (the first interview) and adjustment 2–3 years after the decree was granted (the third interview) was generally stronger than that between support and adjustment at either the first or second interview. As a result, the focus of the analyses that follow is on the relationship between support provided at the first interview and subjective distress at the third. An additional advantage of using data collected at different time periods is that the causal influence of support can be ascertained. The strength of these relationships suggests that support may make the most difference in aiding adjustment when it is received fairly early in the divorce process. Relationships are explored between subjective distress and the following: receiving help from the respondent's family; receiving help from professionals; receiving help with selected role responsibilities; and attending church.

Subjective Distress and Help from the Respondent's Family

As indicated by analysis of variance, receiving some types of help was associated with less distress than having received no help, F (7, 120) = 3.2, $p < .01$). Mean subjective distress scores were lowest for those who received services (e.g., babysitting, being driven places, invitations to events, etc.) (1.7), followed by those who received financial support combined with services (1.7) and by those receiving information and guidance alone (2.1). Receiving no help was less distressing (3.1) than receiving information and guidance in combination with services (3.3) or in combination with financial help (5.7). It would seem that the string attached to the services or money was advice that may have been unsolicited or that a person may not have liked to hear.

Although the findings are more unstable because of the small number of cases in some categories and are therefore not displayed, the results of the analyses for help from friends and coworkers, children, and the ex-spouse's relatives were similar to those for receiving help from the respondent's family, when it was possible to compare the findings. Receiving services was related to lower mean distress scores. Thus, the divorced appear to have benefited most from direct action (services) without potentially judgmental commentary (information and guidance).

It can be argued that the effects of patterns of social support at the first interview on subjective distress at the third interview were artifacts of prior levels of distress. Did receiving financial help and advice from one's family, for example, actually impair mental well-being? Could it be that those who were more psychologically distressed sought or received support from their families in such a way that advice was proffered along with the services? Initial levels of support that were associated with distress at the third interview continued to be associated with it after the effects of distress at the first interview were controlled for; therefore, they are not displayed here. Thus, the effects of these patterns of support were not artifacts of the prior level of distress. The supports had a real effect in increasing or decreasing subsequent emotional well-being. At the same time, however, controlling for the effects of subjective distress at the first interview made an independent contribution to the analysis, reducing the magnitude of the effects of support on distress. This means, as Chapter 11 demonstrates in more detail, that the initial level of distress had an influence on later distress in addition to the effect of the supports. Those who were worse off initially tended to be the ones who were worse off later, but their distress was reduced by some patterns of support.

Subjective Distress and Help from Therapists

In general, those who sought help with their personal problems from professionals had higher distress scores than those who did not, both initially and across time. The Pearson's correlation between subjective distress at the first interview and having sought help from therapists (psychiatrists or psychologists, marriage counselors, or social workers) in the last year of marriage was .22 $(p < .01)$. At the third interview, those in the suburban study who had sought help from therapists in the year preceding the interview also had higher levels of subjective distress $(r = .28, p < .001)$. Similar findings have also been reported for widows and divorcees in the marital transition survey (Kitson & Zyzanski, 1987). Presumably, distress led to the seeking of help, but it is also possible that discussing emotionally charged issues may have increased an individual's level of discomfort.

There were also differences in the amount of distress subjects experienced, depending on whether they obtained individual or conjoint therapy—that is, whether the husband and wife were seen alone or together in a joint session with the therapist. To determine the patterns of seeing psychiatrists/psychologists, marriage counselors, and social workers, each respondent was asked at the first interview whether he or she had seen a professional alone (individual therapy), whether both spouses had seen a professional together (conjoint therapy), whether each spouse had seen a professional separately (concurrent therapy), whether the spouses had seen a professional alone and together (concurrent and conjoint), or whether neither had seen a professional at all. With a mean subjective distress score of 1.5, a divorced person who saw a psychiatrist or psychologist conjointly with his or her ex-spouse in the year prior to the divorce was much less upset by the third interview than a respondent from any other group, $F (4, 128) = 2.7, p < .05$. The next least upset group consisted of those who did not see a psychiatrist or psychologist at all (2.4). These two groups were the only ones whose subjective distress scores were lower than the overall group mean distress score of 2.6. With a mean of 5.7 and only three cases, the most upset group during the third interview consisted of those in which the respondent and the ex-spouse had seen a psychiatrist or psychologist separately in the year before the divorce. When either respondent or the ex-spouse saw a therapist alone, the mean distress levels were, respectively, 3.7 and 3.1. (The level of distress reported upon when the ex-spouse had sought therapy was that of the respondent.) The contrast between the levels of distress of those who had conjoint therapy and those who sought individual therapy is striking. Even though the number of cases is small, it appears that the situation in which both partners were so distressed as to need professional help, but were unwilling or unable to work on their problems together, produced the most difficulty. Going together to a therapist appears to have produced much better results than going separately.

There were not enough cases in all of the categories of types of therapy to do a similar analysis for social workers and marriage counselors individually. However, when psychiatrists/psychologists, marriage counselors, and social workers were grouped together as therapists, a similar pattern occurred for having sought help in the earlier years of the marriage, F (3,129) = 4.5, $p < .01$. When no help was sought, the mean subjective distress score was 2.2. If the spouses went together to a therapist, the mean was 2.4; if the respondent and spouse went separately, the mean was 3.4; and if the respondent went alone, it was 4.9. Thus, seeing a therapist together with the spouse in earlier years of the marriage made more of a positive difference in adjustment after the divorce occurred than having seen a therapist alone.

There are several explanations for these findings. First, spouses who are willing to work together to try to strengthen or perhaps to save their marriages before the decision to divorce, or who are able to work out details of the divorce jointly after the decision is made, are individuals who are willing to attempt to communicate with each other. They are also, presumably, more willing to see their problems as relational rather than simply as "his" or "hers." Although individual divorce counseling has been found to be more effective than conjoint therapy (Beck, 1976; Cookerly, 1976), more recent research has found that conjoint therapy is more effective in helping both married couples and the divorced (Goldenberg & Goldenberg, 1985; Piercy & Sprenkle, 1990; Ro-Tack, Wellisch, & Schoolar, 1977).

Literature on family therapy also supports an interpretation of lower distress when clients see a therapist together. If problems stem from interactions between family members rather than from individual psychopathology, addressing these issues may be facilitated when people use the behavioral-systems perspective of family therapy, rather than a more intrapsychic perspective common with individual therapy (Goldenberg & Goldenberg, 1985; Ro-Tack et al., 1977; S. J. Schultz, 1984; Weiss, 1981). If this explanation is correct, then these findings also challenge the psychopathological model of divorce and support the view that it is a relational crisis.

For the most part, the respondents who had sought therapy with their spouses had no special characteristics distinguishing them from those who had not. In most respects they resembled the other divorced persons. They were no less angry at their spouses, nor was there more mutual blaming. They did, however, tend to have more education (23.9% of those with a college degree went to a therapist together, as opposed to none of those with less than a high school education). Whites were also more likely to see a therapist together (16.6% vs. 3.8% of the nonwhites), but this was partly a result of greater amounts of education among white subjects. More educated persons are said to be more introspective (Gurin et al., 1960), and this may also have played a role. None of the reported causes of divorce was related to the type of therapy chosen. Thus, those with less difficult problems were not more likely to seek conjoint help.

Subjective Distress, Role Responsibilities, and Church Attendance

There were no significant associations between role responsibilities and subjective distress. Role responsibilities were examined in several ways. These included the total number of tasks for which respondents had responsibility, individual items, and changes in responsibilities between the first and the third interview. Thus, the degree of subjective distress individuals were experiencing at the end of the study was not affected by the responsibilities they bore.

Attending church also provided solace for the divorced, as indicated by lower subjective distress scores. Those who attended church or synagogue more than once a month had significantly lower subjective distress scores ($r = -.24$, $p < .01$).

These findings indicate that some types of support can help individuals adjust to divorce, and that other types may slow adjustment, if not actually hinder it. It is not simply that the more distressed sought help. Support does help. This still leaves unanswered the question of why support helps.

WHY ARE SUPPORTS HELPFUL?

Why social supports have a positive or negative effect has not been well understood. Among the explanations are that supports facilitate the performance of instrumental tasks, provide emotional solace and guidance, and maintain continuity by reducing the amount of change a person experiences. Each of these explanations implies different relationships between social supports and adjustment.

The instrumental explanation implies that anything that improves task performance will promote adjustment. From this viewpoint, money and donated services should have equal effects, and it should not matter much from whom the support is received. This clearly does not agree with the present findings. Services were generally more helpful than financial support; moreover, financial assistance and advice together were less helpful than either offered alone. These findings do not support a purely instrumental explanation for the effects of social supports.

The explanation that supports provide emotional solace and guidance does not closely agree with the findings, either. Information and guidance alone had a neutral effect; financial support and information/guidance generally had a negative effect. In fact, seeing a therapist with one's spouse was the only instance in which solace or guidance seemed to have a consistently positive effect.

The effects of continuity and change on adjustment have also been examined. The lack of any association between the measures of role responsibility or of changes in responsibilities and lowered distress precludes change reduction or continuity in role responsibility as a link between social supports and adjustment.

Thus, none of these three explanations about why assistance from others affected adjustment has been supported in these findings, largely because no type or source had a significant additive effect on adjustment. The effects were usually conditional and dependent on the joint combination of source and type of support. Receiving certain types of support from the wrong source was worse than receiving no aid at all. These interactive effects require a different explanation of social supports.

When patterns of support that were beneficial or harmful are reviewed, it appears that harmful patterns were those that led to the potential for conflict between the giver and receiver of support. In contrast, helpful patterns tended to promote the social solidarity of the groups in which individuals were a part. For example, receiving both financial help and advice from relatives tended to create problems in adjustment, whereas receiving services without financial help or advice did not create such problems. Perhaps when both financial help and advice were proffered, recipients may have felt more beholden to follow the advice because they needed the material assistance, and may have been irritated or angered as a result. Indeed, receiving services was generally more beneficial to adjustment than receiving either financial help or information and guidance. Services, by their very nature, require social exchange between parties and can lead to a greater sense of social solidarity and an enhanced structure of shared meaning. Certain types of support from some sources do not help adjustment (and may hurt) when the supports lead to conflict or fail to promote social solidarity between the source of support and its recipient. This conclusion is supported by the finding of McLanahan et al. (1981) that social supports promote social integration, and by that of Wilcox (1981) that help from a source of conflict does not promote adjustment.

CONCLUSION

The availability of social support was highly variable for the subjects in the suburban divorce study. Many had only minimal support. At the time the divorce was filed, the divorced were no more likely than the married to have received help from their own families or from friends or coworkers, much less likely to have received help from their spouses' relatives, and less likely to have received help from their children. However, the divorced were demonstrated to have been experiencing substantially more distress than the married, and as a result may well have needed more assistance.

Support was often not available because marital disruption apparently fragmented support networks, resulting in less support being available when an increase in support may have been needed, especially from an ex-spouse's family. Support was most often obtained from a respondent's own family, when family members were available. There was a reduction in the amount of support from the family over time. Support from a subject's children and from friends and coworkers remained stable, and in fact even increased over time for children. These findings mean that those who failed to adjust to their divorces within the first few years were faced with diminishing help from their already reduced support network. It was important for the divorced to establish a stable way of meeting their problems fairly quickly, rather than relying on ad hoc procedures, so that the subsequent reduction in support would not further disrupt their situation. Building a stable network of mutually helpful people was central to enhancing adjustment across time. Adding new social ties (whether through new friends, coworkers, or a new spouse) may have also compensated for reduced help from earlier sources.

Social support did in some instances reduce subjective distress— the feelings of anxiety and depression that the divorced were experiencing. Others who obtained support sometimes found that more problems were created than solved by receiving that support. Help from family members had both positive and negative effects. In general, services were more helpful in reducing distress than was either financial assistance or information and guidance. Obtaining financial support and advice from the same source seemed to pose particular problems for adjustment. If the divorced have to receive financial help, it may be better for them if they are not given advice along with the financial help.

When a divorcing couple saw a therapist together, this generally enhanced subsequent mental health adjustment; when they saw therapists separately, this was associated with less improvement in mental health later. It appears that counseling for the divorcing may be more beneficial if it is conjoint therapy rather than individual treatment. More research is needed on this important point.

Why should seeing a therapist together be so much more beneficial than seeing one separately? The answer may be related to the greater education of those who saw therapists together. An alternative answer is that a therapist who is seeing both a husband and a wife may have a more realistic picture of each spouse and his or her actions than does a therapist who must rely upon the one-sided reports of an upset (ex-)spouse. The enhanced ability of the therapist to test the reality of the patients' or clients' statements is likely to be to the patients' benefit. The behavioral-systems perspective of conjoint therapy may also help overcome resistance to treatment more easily than an individually oriented perspective (Weiss, 1981). If this is correct, it should support the view that divorce is more often a problem of transitional crisis than of individual psychopathology.

Another possibility is that those who go to therapists together may believe they have a mutual interest in dealing with their problems. If they share a belief that they must work together in adjusting to their situation, then working together toward a common end may help their adjustment. This view is explicitly part of the "therapeutic alliance" strategy of family therapy (Davatz, 1981) and supports the view of divorce as a transitional crisis. Most importantly, however, (ex-)-spouses in conjoint therapy are individuals willing to attempt to communicate with each other about problems in the relationship, rather than "his" or "her" problems.

The findings do not provide much support for traditional explanations of why supports affect adjustment. Purely instrumental assistance did not help greatly. Supports that promoted divorced persons' sense of social solidarity and their feeling of shared meaning with others did benefit subsequent adjustment. Supports, especially services, that did not involve the potential for conflict or loss of self-esteem and that promoted a feeling of being an active member of a social network appeared to be the most beneficial. This finding is consistent with

Litwak's (1985) view that the greatest benefit results when primary groups and helping organizations share functions in a complementary fashion. As Chapter 10 discusses, rebuilding a social network is a central issue with which the divorced are faced. Positive supports provided by the rebuilt network should also help adjustment to divorce.

Life after Divorce: The Alternatives

Long divorced, we have, rightly or wrongly, never become unmarried. Often I have felt through the years that our lives might have been better if we had stuck out the difficult years of our marriage, but I do not know if she would agree with that. We never venture into the realm of what might have been. I refer to her in conversation as my wife, never my ex-wife, and there is not a day in which she does not occupy my thoughts for some period of time. We communicate regularly and mail each other clippings we cut out of newspapers, and I no longer resent, as I once did, addressing her as Mrs. E. Griffin Dunne rather than as Mrs. Dominick Dunne.

—Dunne (1987, p. 2)

Dear Ann Landers:

My brother, John, was married at 20 and divorced at 21. My wife and I do not believe in divorce. It is against our religion.

John visited our children every weekend. They loved him dearly and he was devoted to them. When he was 36, John met a not-quite-divorced woman and they began to carry on. Strangely enough, mother liked the woman and welcomed her into the family. My wife and I decided we could not expose our children to such immoral behavior and banned him from our home. (To this day my wife blames our son's divorce on the example set by John.)

Six months ago mother died. John and his wife were at the funeral. I went over to him, feeling that at such a time two brothers should comfort one another. He turned to me and said, "It's too late. Mother was the only reason to forgive you and she is gone. My wife and I will comfort each other. I hope your principles will comfort you."

I know I did the right thing but I can't sleep at night. I thought it was my mother's death. Now I'm not so sure. I feel depressed and isolated. My wife is impatient with me.

Any Name But My Own

Dear Any Name:

It's the guilt over your brother that is keeping you awake nights. The decision to keep him from your children was a bad one. Get counseling and talk it out. I hope John forgives you and your myopic, stiff-necked wife.

—Landers (1984, p. 7-F)

A woman without a man is like a fish without a bicycle.

—Gloria Steinem, quoted in Adams (1989, p. 222)

251

What happens *after* a divorce occurs? As noted in previous chapters, more is known about who divorces and why than about what happens to them after their marriages have been dissolved. The data presented in Chapter 6 indicate that for many divorce produces a major upheaval in physical and psychological health, but one that generally improves with time. For others, as illustrated by the Dominick Dunne quotation above, the process of social and psychological disengagement may never be entirely complete. Still other divorced persons may be (or may feel they are) treated differently by others because of their change in marital status, as the letter to Ann Landers poignantly describes. At the same time, the divorced themselves may struggle with the issue of whether they want to invest in another relationship.

How, then, do the divorced go about this process of restructuring their lives? The steps individuals take in the postdivorce period and the feelings they experience as they are restructuring their lives constitute the focus of this chapter. As discussed in Chapter 2, few studies have followed a group of the divorced far enough into the postdivorce period to describe their new lifestyles, regardless of whether they have remained single or remarried.

Among the issues to be explored in this chapter are the following: With hindsight, how do the divorced view their experiences? Do divorced people feel that they are treated differently by others because of their divorces? What do they see as the easier and harder parts of the divorce? To what extent do divorced spouses still keep in contact with each other? What do the divorced think about the legal process they have experienced? Finally, it is often assumed that the "natural" state for adult men and women (especially women) is to be partnered by a person of the opposite sex, if not married. To what extent are members of the opposite sex a part of postdivorce activities and hopes? Is it possible to predict which people will remarry rapidly and which will not? Does adjustment differ for the remarried, cohabiting, or engaged and for those who remain single?

DIVORCE AS DEVIANCE: FEELING STIGMATIZED

Do divorced persons feel that they are treated differently, and often less well, by others because of their divorces? If so, just how common are these experiences? Curiously, although stigma has been mentioned by many researchers as an issue faced by the divorced, it has generally been dismissed in the same breath as having diminished in importance in recent years. As a result, there are few data on feelings of stigmatization among the divorced. Surveys that have asked about the morality of divorce and attitudes about separation and divorce indicate more liberal attitudes about these issues in the 1970s and 1980s than in the 1950s and 1960s (McRae, 1978; Thornton, 1985). On the other hand, Gerstel (1987) found in open-ended interviews with divorced persons that many felt that others treated them less well because of their divorced status and that they were excluded from social activities. In a small convenience sample of custody arrangements, Luepnitz (1982) found that almost all the women in her study reported some form of discrimination or loss of status because of being divorced parents, compared to a third of the men.

Findings from Open-Ended Questions Regarding Stigmatization

Direct Experience of Stigma

In the suburban divorced sample, a number of the divorced did indeed feel stigmatized. At the second interview, when they were asked, "Have you been in a social situation in which you felt someone thought less of you when he or she found out that you were divorced?", over one-fourth (26.7%; $n = 161$) indicated that this had happened to them. This percentage is hardly different from what William Goode (1956) found when he asked the same question in the late 1940s in Detroit, Michigan; 30% of the 425 women he surveyed felt that they had been discriminated against by others. Given what seem to be substantial shifts in attitudes about divorce since the late 1940s, the similarity in replies is startling.

When the respondents were asked to illustrate how others treated them after learning about the divorce, the most common response, mentioned by 72.7% of the 33 who reported this, was that they were made to feel "less respectable," "dishonest," or "stigmatized." The next most frequent reply, mentioned by 21.2%, was "religious or moral disapproval," followed by 6.1% who reported that others made "snide comments."

Fearing Others' Reactions to the Divorce

Another dimension of feeling stigmatized is reluctance to discuss the divorce with others for fear of their negative reactions. At the first interview, the divorced were asked, "Was there anyone you hesitated to tell about the plan to divorce?" Close to half (47% of the 198 respondents who answered the question) indicated that there was at least one person they hesitated to tell about their divorce plans. Such reluctance to discuss the divorce illustrates that the experience is somehow viewed negatively. (In this section, percentages do not total 100% because up to two replies were coded for each question.)

There were no differences in reluctance by gender. The divorced were the most reluctant to tell their parents or "the family" in general. Fifty-two percent mentioned hesitancy in telling family members, followed by 27.2% who said they hesitated to tell "everyone" or "most people"; 18.1% who indicated reluctance to tell the spouse's family; and 8.5% who mentioned coworkers ($n = 94$).

When asked why they hesitated, 30.4% said that they felt others would disapprove or that they feared a negative reaction. Other common replies included feeling embarrassed, stigmatized, or a failure, or dreading hearing "I told you so" (mentioned by 29.3%); wanting to spare the feelings of others because "they would worry" (27.1%); and a feeling that the matter was private and therefore "nobody else's business" (21.7%). Virtually all of these replies indicate a fear of negative reactions from others concerning the decision to divorce. Whether these are the "real" reactions of others or projections of divorced persons' own feelings of failure, they do indicate the currency of stigmatizing attitudes.

Family Attitudes about the Divorce

When asked, "Did anyone in your family or your husband's/wife's family encourage you either to stay married or get divorced from your husband/wife?", 54.7% indicated that someone either encouraged or discouraged their plans. Not surprisingly, family members were the most likely to express an opinion. Sixty-eight percent of the respondents who received input from others indicated that it came from their own families, whereas 52.2% mentioned their spouses' families. There were no differences by gender in the frequency with which comments were received; men were as likely as women to receive advise, counsel, support, or disapproval. Thus, the feeling that others might "butt in" was well founded. In 67.2% of the 100 instances in which others offered opinions about the divorce decision, the commenters were reported to approve of the decision in general, or because they disliked the spouse or his or her behavior, or because they disliked the respondent. Slightly less often (63.6% of the reported instances), commenters disapproved of the decision in general because they liked the spouse, felt that the divorce was an embarrassment, or felt that the respondent would be stigmatized by others.

When asked at the second interview, "In general, would you say that the members of your family disapprove of the divorce, are neutral, approve, or just do not care?", 53.4% indicated family approval; 28.8% reported neutrality; 12.3% reported disapproval; 4.1% felt that their families just did not care; and 1.4% indicated that they did not know their families' reaction ($n = 144$). As for the spouses' families, 28.3% of the respondents indicated disapproval; 18.4% reported neutrality; 22.4% reported approval; 6.6% felt that the spouses' families did not care; and 24.3% did not know. There were no statistically significant differences by race in rates of family disapproval. Although the concordance was not extremely high, when a respondent reported that his or her family disapproved, he or she also tended to report that the spouse's family disapproved (Table 10.1). The same held true for those who were neutral or approving. Whether these reports reflect the reality of the situation or the respondent's perceptions of it, they suggest a context in which those going through divorce see ending a marriage voluntarily as negatively valued.

The issue of approval is not simply a curious sidelight to the

TABLE 10.1. Reported Reactions to the Divorce by Respondent's and Ex-Spouse's Families, and Help from Respondent's Family at the Second Interview: Suburban Divorced Sample

	Reaction of respondent's own family		
	Disapprove	Neutral	Approve
Reported reaction of ex-spouse's family[a]			
Disapprove	45.5%	32.3%	42.0%
Neutral	36.4%	51.6%	12.0%
Approve	18.2%	16.1%	46.0%
Total	100.1%	100.0%	100.0%
(n)	(11)	(31)	(50)
Receiving any help from own family[b]			
No help	44.4%	40.5%	20.5%
Any help	55.6%	59.5%	79.5%
Total	100.0%	100.0%	100.0%
(n)	(18)	(42)	(78)

[a]$\chi^2 = 19.6$, $df = 4$, $p < .001$.
[b]$\chi^2 = 15.4$, $df = 2$, $p < .001$.

process of divorce. The reaction of the respondent's family was associated with the reported provision of support by the family: When the family was felt to disapprove, respondents reported less help.

The respondents' families were significantly less likely to approve of the decision to divorce when the divorced couple's income was high in the last year of marriage. When the couple's income was under $10,000, 77.4% of the families were reported to approve of the decision to divorce. When income was between $10,000 and $19,999, 55.6% approved, and when it was $20,000 or more, 40.0% approved ($\chi^2 = 19.4$, $df = 4$, $p < .001$). Thus, a divorced couple's resources apparently entered into a family's perception of the appropriateness of a divorce. The reasons for the divorce also entered into a family's reaction to the divorce decision. As seen in Chapter 5, more "serious" marital complaints, such as alcoholism, physical abuse, and criminal activities, were more common among lower-income families; when such complaints were mentioned, respondents reported their families as being more likely to approve of the divorce decision. However, neither the combined variable of "instrumental" complaints nor that of "stable" complaints (see Chapter 5) was associated with family approval. When the more frequent complaints were looked at individually, the only one associated with family approval was "change in interests or values." There was no relationship between type of complaint or any of the more frequent complaints and the spouse's family's attitude about the divorce.

All of these findings, of course, reflect only the divorced persons' perspective. From these data, there is no way of knowing whether the respondents' and spouses' families actually responded similarly; whether they did or not, however, the respondents perceived their reactions in this manner. Such data may be better indicators of the respondents' own fears and sense of failure concerning the breakup of the marriage than they are of their relatives' actual reactions. It is not known whether families who disapproved did indeed help less or whether subjects who were themselves embarrassed about the breakup avoided their families, imputing their own reactions to others. There is little research in which a divorced person's network has been interviewed to determine the congruity in friends' and relatives' views of the divorce; such a study would be useful. In any case, the data from the suburban study indicate that negative attitudes about divorce are still surprisingly common. The locus of these negative attitudes is not clear. Others may treat a divorced person differently, or he or she (rightly or wrongly) may perceive such treatment from others. Nevertheless, both explanations indicate the importance of not "failing" at marriage. In the late 20th century in the United States, there is still antipathy to divorce.

Findings from a Scale for a Sense of Stigmatization

This section identifies some of the explanations that have been advanced to account for the feeling on the part of the divorced that others either disapprove of the decision to divorce or treat them differently because of their divorced status. It also tests these explanations against the present data. Changes over time in the sense of being stigmatized are likewise examined.

Possible Bases of Stigmatization

One possibility to account for the perceived negative attitudes of others is that becoming divorced involves shifting to a less desirable marital status. This is especially true for women, whose status has traditionally been derived from that of their husbands. Although a fairly strong undercurrent of social disapproval to divorce has been identified, the antipathy to divorce was said to be even greater in earlier generations. Under such circumstances, older women, in particular, may be expected to feel more sense of stigma associated with being divorced. Those who do not want the divorce or whose families disapprove of the decision may also feel more poorly treated. Another possible foundation for a sense of stigma, as discussed in Chapter 1, may be religious beliefs that divorce is immoral, unacceptable behavior. Thus, those with stronger religious beliefs may be more likely to feel that divorce is thought of negatively by others. Still another basis for feelings of stigma is the shift in financial status often associated with divorce. This, in turn, may produce the feeling or the actuality of being treated differently because of the divorce.

The Stigma Scale

To explore these ideas, 15 questions developed by Lopata (1973, 1979) to assess widows' feelings of restriction in relationships with others because of the death of their spouses were modified for use with the divorced. The items themselves were the same as Lopata's, but in each case the word "widowed" was changed to "divorced." They were scored on a scale from 1 ("agree strongly") to 4 ("disagree strongly"). The divorced were asked the questions at both the second and the third interviews.

Eight of the items clustered to produce a scale with an alpha reliability of .70. A low score on the scale indicated a high sense of stigma. Substantial numbers of respondents agreed or strongly agreed with these eight items (Table 10.2). The level of agreement about the

TABLE 10.2. Feeling Stigmatized as a Divorced Person: Frequency Distribution and Means for Suburban Divorced Sample at Second and Third Interviews

Feelings about being divorced	% replying at second interview					Means at second and third interviews	
	Agree strongly	Agree	Disagree strongly	Disagree	Total	Second interview (n)	Third interview (n)
Divorced women are constantly sexually propositioned even by the husbands of their friends	13.8	38.6	37.9	9.7	100.0	2.4 (145)	2.7 (113)
One problem of being a divorced person is feeling like a "fifth wheel"	10.1	24.5	37.9	18.2	100.0	2.7 (159)	2.6 (129)
People take advantage of you when they know you are divorced	2.5	21.7	51.6	24.2	100.0	3.0 (157)	2.9 (130)
Most divorced people prefer having other divorced people as friends	3.2	20.1	61.7	14.9	99.9	2.9 (154)	2.8 (130)
Women lose status when they become divorced—they lose respect	4.5	25.6	52.6	17.3	100.0	2.8 (156)	2.8 (130)
Divorced men are expected to act like carefree bachelors	9.9	35.8	45.7	8.6	100.0	2.5 (151)	2.5 (127)
Of the men/women I have dated, I have most in common with those who are divorced	5.7	31.4	45.7	17.1	99.9	2.7 (140)	2.6 (120)
Other people gossip a lot about a person who's been divorced	14.9	47.3	31.8	6.1	100.1	2.3 (148)	2.4 (122)
Total scale score						23.3 (150)	22.9 (116)

statements varied from a low of 23.3% for the statement "Most divorced people prefer having other divorced people as friends" to a high of 62.2% for "Other people gossip a lot about a person who's been divorced." For six of the eight items, a third or more of the respondents agreed or strongly agreed with the statements. Furthermore, for seven of the eight items, these feelings did not abate but became stronger with more experience as a divorced person. Although the means for the individual items in Table 10.2 were virtually the same at the second and third interviews, and the scores were correlated ($\tau_b = .35$, $p < .001$), in fact the direction of the relationship indicated a stronger sense of being stigmatized at the third interview, not a weaker one. When the frequency distributions for the stigma scales at the second and third interviews were divided into thirds and cross-classified, more of those with low or moderate stigma scores at the second interview shifted to a stronger sense of stigma by the third interview than shifted to a weaker one. Among the 43 respondents with a moderate sense of stigma at the second interview, 69.8% still felt this way at the third interview, with 25.6% reporting a higher sense of stigma and only 4.7% reporting a lower one. For the eight subjects with a low sense of stigma at the second interview, only one still felt this way at the third interview; half had shifted to a moderate degree of stigma, and three to a high sense of stigma. Among the 58 subjects with a high degree of stigma at the second interview, 69.0% continued to score high on the scale at the third interview, 31.0% moved to a moderate sense of stigma, and none reported low stigma.

Thus, these data indicate that many divorced persons still feel a sense of being treated differently, or stigmatized, because of their marital status. If, as some think, the stigma of divorce is less than it previously was, these data nevertheless illustrate the continued strength of such impulses. Although the widowed also feel stigmatized, comparisons of widowed and divorced women using these same items indicated that the divorced were even more likely to feel this way than the widowed (Kitson, Lopata, Holmes, & Meyering, 1980). Although the applicability of these results may be limited by the fact that the data were collected in different communities (Chicago and Cleveland) and by age differences of the widows and divorcees (which were controlled for statistically), the findings suggest that divorce may be even more stigmatized than widowhood. For divorced women, their "devalued status" is presumably of their own making, whereas for widows the change is seen as "not their fault." Part of the sense of stigma experienced by the widowed may also be attributable to ageism, not to their marital status. Marital status itself makes a bigger contribution for the divorced.

Correlates of a Sense of Stigma

As part of the effort to determine which of the divorced respondents were most likely to feel stigmatized, Pearson's zero-order correlations, were computed between scores on the stigma scale and the demographic and attitudinal variables hypothesized above to be related to such feelings.

At the second interview, feeling stigmatized was not associated with higher scores on subjective distress or the illness contacts index, but was significantly associated with lower self-esteem ($r = -.22$, $p < .05$) and stronger feelings of attachment ($r = -.19$, $p < .05$). As expected, non-whites were less likely than whites to feel stigmatized ($r = .19$, $p < .05$). This association may be related to the greater likelihood of divorce in the black community. When more persons have been divorced, divorce may be less likely to be viewed negatively. As seen above, this is not the same as approving of divorce, because there were no significant differences in approval or disapproval of the decision to divorce by race. Rather, the greater frequency of divorce may produce the feeling that divorce is a regrettable necessity, but one whose participants should not be stigmatized. In other words, wider experience with others who have been divorced may make divorce seem less unacceptable.

At the second interview, stigma was not associated with gender, generational differences, social attitudes, or religious beliefs. Women were no more likely than men to feel stigmatized. Similarly, there were no differences in stigmatization for those who were older or those who had been married longer. These findings suggest that although the sense of stigma associated with being divorced may have decreased from that of earlier generations, there was still a certain shared ethos about the importance of marriage and the family among the respondents that was not generational. Measures of reported family approval or disapproval of the divorce were not associated with stigma. The various measures of religiosity—the influence of religion on daily life, church attendance, and belonging to a religious denomination—were also not associated with stigma. Furthermore, there was no association between having sought mental health help or between having been hospitalized for mental illness and stigma.

Those with higher income were less likely to feel stigmatized ($r = .24$, $p < .01$). Income itself may serve as a resource in softening disapproval, as in the old saw about the late popular pianist Liberace, "He laughed all the way to the bank." The findings that stigma was associated with continued contacts with the ex-spouse ($r = -.22$, $p < .05$) and with attachment suggest that part of the sense of stigma experienced by the divorced may be attributable to the loss of a partner—even a partner who was, at best, ambivalently regarded. This interpretation is supported by the lack of association between who suggested the divorce and stigma. Although having suggested the divorce may make adjustment somewhat easier, it does not diminish the sense of social unacceptability of the event itself. Those who were remarried or cohabiting were less likely to feel stigmatized ($r = .16$, $p < .05$), suggesting that for some the shift in marital status is the basis of a greater sense of stigma.

By the third interview, some of the significant relationships reported at the second interview were no longer so important, while others had strengthened. Those with higher subjective distress scores now had higher scores on feeling stigmatized ($r = -.20$, $p < .05$). The causal order of the association is unclear. Feelings of anxiety and depression may make a person feel discriminated against, or loss of status and lack of respect may make a person feel more uncomfortable.

Attachment and self-esteem were still associated with stigma (r's $= -.19$ and $-.22$, respectively; p's $< .05$ for both), but the illness contacts index remained unassociated. Race also continued to make a difference, with nonwhites less likely to feel stigmatized than whites ($r = .20$, $p < .05$). In addition, at the third interview men were significantly less likely to feel stigmatized than women ($r = -.20$, $p < .05$). Their mean score on the scale was 23.8 versus 22.0 for women. This finding emphasizes that it is still more important for women to be married than for men.

Those who reported that their families did not approve of the divorce were now more likely to feel stigmatized ($r = -.19$, $p < .05$), as were those who reported having sought mental health help during their marriages or in the year prior to the first divorce interview ($r = -.27$, $p < .01$). Marital status, either as measured at the second interview or as newly assessed at the third, was no longer associated with stigma. Reported income at the second or at the third interview was not associated with stigmatization at the third.

These data suggest that the divorced felt stigmatized because of the change in marital status, the loss of the partner, and (to some extent) the loss of economic status. Because of these changes, many of those who had divorced felt that others treated them differently—and less well—than when they were married.

CONTINUING TIES WITH THE EX-SPOUSE

Love, Hate, or Pity for the Ex-Spouse

Divorce legally breaks the bonds between spouses, but the psychological bonds are less easily broken. Different aspects of the couple's continuing relationship were assessed at all three interviews to see what kinds of links divorced spouses maintained with each other. For example, at the second and third interviews, the respondents were specifically asked about their feelings of love or hate for their ex-spouses, with seven choices from "I love him/her" to "I don't love or hate him/her, I feel sorry for him/her;" At the second interview, when the median time since separation was 18 months and the average was 2 years, one-third of the divorced still "loved" or "liked" their ex-spouses, followed by a quarter who said that they did not "feel much of anything" for them. A little over a fifth said they neither loved nor hated their ex-spouses, but rather "felt sorry for" them. This was perhaps the most damning reaction of all, since few subjects at either interview wanted to believe that their former partners felt sorry for them (Table 10.3). The differences between what respondents felt for their ex-spouses and their perceptions of their ex-spouses' feelings for them were especially revealing: Loving feelings were more commonly ascribed to the ex-spouses. At the same time, 26.2% of the ex-spouses were reported to "hate" or "both love and hate" their former partners, as opposed to 8.3% of the respondents who reported these responses. At the third interview, fewer respondents reported such feelings (2.4%), and fewer, although still substantially more (18.9%), ascribed them to their ex-spouses.

TABLE 10.3. Feelings about the Ex-Spouse Reported by the Divorced for Themselves and Their Ex-Spouses at Second and Third Interviews: Suburban Divorced Sample

Feelings now about ex-spouse (or his or her feelings about respondent)	% replying at second interview		% replying at third interview	
	Respondent's feelings	Spouse's feelings	Respondent's feelings	Spouse's feelings
Love	7.0	22.1	7.2	16.0
Still like, but don't love	26.8	25.5	26.4	30.2
Don't feel much of anything	25.5	17.9	34.4	30.2
Don't like much any more	9.6	5.5	4.0	3.8
Hate	3.2	9.0	1.6	6.6
Both love and hate	5.1	17.2	0.8	12.3
Don't love or hate, feel sorry for	22.9	2.8	25.6	0.9
Total	100.0	100.0	100.0	100.0
(n)	(157)	(145)	(125)	(106)

In Ambert's (1989) Toronto study, in which each ex-spouse in a divorced couple was interviewed about his or her feelings about the other and perceptions of the other's feelings about him or her, 3 in 10 accurately assessed the ex-spouse's feelings. A respondent was more likely to claim ignorance of the ex-spouse's feelings when he or she was actually indifferent or antagonistic. These data illustrate that what their ex-spouses think still matters to many divorced persons.

Anger at the Ex-Spouse

Anger at the ex-spouse is another hallmark of divorce. On a scale from 1 ("not at all my feelings") to 5 ("very much my feelings"), at the first interview 46 people, or 22.7% of 202 replying, had strong anger (indicated by scores of 4 or 5) in reply to the question "I'm angry at my (ex-)-husband/wife." Those with low anger represented 64.3% of the sample. There were no differences by gender in mean scores. By the second interview the numbers with high and low anger had gone down slightly—to 18.6% and 68.3%, respectively, ($n = 161$). The majority of those with low scores at the first interview remained low on anger at the second, whereas more than a quarter of those with scores of 3, or moderate anger, moved to high anger at the second interview. Among those with high feelings of anger at the first interview ($n = 31$), 35.5% reported low anger at the second interview and 16.1% moderate anger, while 48.4% continued to have high scores. By the third interview much of the anger had dissipated. None of those with low or moderate scores at the first interview reported high anger at the third interview, and only about one in three of those with high anger initially ($n = 23$) still reported moderate scores (8.7%) or high scores (21.7%) at the third interview. At the end of the study only five people, or 4% ($n = 118$), had high scores on anger; another six, or 5%, had moderate scores.

These proportions seem too low, given what is known about continuing conflict among the divorced. In retrospect, more questions should have been asked about anger. In an effort to remedy this problem in the 1985–1986 marital transition study, a nine-item scale to assess "anger at the loss" was developed. Of the 173 divorced women replying, 40.5% reported low anger at the first interview, 39.9% moderate anger, and 19.7% high anger (Kitson, Zyzanski, & Roach, 1991). By the second interview (approximately 13 months after filing for divorce), 13.7% still reported high anger, 38.4% moderate anger, and 40.5% low anger ($n = 146$). As in the suburban divorced sample, some respondents continued to have the same degree of anger, whereas others increased or decreased their scores. Overall, scores did go down somewhat as time passed. Of those with high anger at the first interview, 44.4% continued to report it at the second interview ($n = 27$), with only three persons, or 11.1%, shifting from high to low anger. The remaining 44.4% moved to more moderate levels of anger (Kitson, 1991a). Although these figures are still probably underestimates, given people's general unwillingness to acknowledge anger, they seem more realistic estimates of the level of continuing anger in divorce.

Studies focusing on more difficult divorces indicate that some as yet unknown proportion of ex-spouses or couples continue in corrosively hostile relationships. Although they comprise a minority of divorcing couples, they make up much of the court docket for contested divorces, problematic dissolution agreements, and continued postdivorce litigation (Hauser, 1985; Isaacs, Montalvo, & Abelsohn, 1986; Johnston & Campbell, 1988).

Contacts with the Ex-Spouse

What about continued contacts with the ex-spouse? At the second and third interviews, the suburban divorced respondents were asked whether they had been in contact with their ex-spouses "in the past few weeks" in any of the following ways: talked by telephone, talked in person, received or sent a letter, heard reports from others, saw but did not converse, or went out (i.e., went on a date) with the ex-partner. At the second interview, 52.3% ($n = 158$) of the divorced had talked with their ex-spouses by telephone; 41.6% ($n = 126$) reported this at the third interview. Two in five at both interviews had heard about their ex-spouses through friends or their children, and 35.4% at the second interview and 31.7% at the third interview had spoken to them in person within the past few weeks.

One in six, or 16.1%, had seen their ex-spouses but not spoken to them at the second interview, and 6.4% had done so at the third interview. At the second interview (1 year after divorce), 9.4% had gone out on dates with their ex-partners, and at the third interview (2–3 years after divorce), 4.0% had done so. So few subjects had communicated with their ex-spouses by letter at either interview that this measure was dropped from further analysis. When the scores for the other six contact measures were summed, every divorced person on the average had had some form of contact with the ex-spouse in the several weeks preceding the interview. The mean number of contacts at the second interview, an average of 2 years after separation, was 1.4; at the third interview, an average of 4 years after separation, the mean was 1.2. This, of course, is somewhat misleading, because some had no contact at all and others had multiple contacts. For example, at the second interview, 26.1% of the respondents reported no contacts, while

31.0% indicated one contact, 24.2% two, 15.5% three, and 3.1% four or more contacts. There were no significant differences in the number of contacts between ex-spouses by race at either the second or the third interview.

When the divorced were asked whether they would like to have "more, less, or about the same amount of contact" with their ex-spouses, the majority, 61.8%, indicated they would prefer to have less contact, whereas 29.9% wanted the same amount and 8.3% would have liked more contact.

Although ex-spouses with children were significantly more likely to keep in contact at both the second and third interview (Table 10.4), somewhat surprisingly, childless ex-spouses fairly often continued to see or hear about each other: 65.4% reported some form of contact in the past several weeks at the second interview, and 32.5% did so at the third interview. For these ex-partners, there was no reason to keep in contact except for continued bonds to each other.

For those with children, contacts also varied depending on the age of the children. The preschool years may be the developmental period in which it is most difficult for children to handle separations from their parents (Bowlby, 1973; Kalter, 1990; Wallerstein & Kelly, 1980). Despite the potential psychological toll on such children, this was one of the two periods, along with the stage in which one or more children were aged 18 or over, in which parents were least likely to report two or more contacts in the past few weeks. For those with preschoolers, 46.2% reported contacts at the second interview ($n = 26$), compared to 63.3% of those with grade-school-age children ($n = 30$), 53.9% of these with teenagers ($n = 13$), and 41.5% of those with at least one child aged

TABLE 10.4. Number of Contacts with the Ex-Spouse and Presence of Children at the Second and Third Interviews: Suburban Divorced Sample

Number of contacts with ex-spouse	% replying at second interview[a]		% replying at third interview[b]	
	No children	One or more children	No children	One or more children
None	34.7	22.3	67.5	26.9
One	42.9	25.9	20.0	17.2
Two	14.3	28.6	12.5	35.5
Three or more	8.2	23.2	—	20.4
Total	100.1	100.0	100.0	100.0
(n)	(49)	(112)	(40)	(93)

[a]$\chi^2 = 12.1$, $df = 3$, $p < .01$.
[b]$\chi^2 = 25.3$, $df = 3$, $p < .001$.

18 or older ($n = 41$). At the third interview, couples with preschoolers were the least likely group of those with children to remain in contact. Only 36.4% reported contacts ($n = 11$), compared to 53.3% of those with grade-school-age children ($n = 30$), 58.3% of those with teenagers ($n = 12$), and 52.3% of those with at least one child aged 18 or older ($n = 44$). A preschooler is perhaps more difficult to handle in a visiting situation, because there are relatively few activities the parent and child can share. In addition, a marriage may have been disintegrating or a spouse may have already left at the point at which bonds with a young child would normally have strengthened. Younger ex-spouses are also more likely to remarry, and ties to their children sometimes attenuate further after remarriage, as Furstenberg et al. (1983) have reported. These may be among the reasons why divorce when the child is young has a severe initial impact. The child is developmentally at an emotional disadvantage, which is compounded by the likelihood that the noncustodial parent's ties to or ability to handle a young child are weaker. In the suburban divorce study, contacts were most frequent when children were between the ages of 6 and 12 at the second interview, and when these children had moved into the teenage years at the third. In such families, the noncustodial parents and their children were likely to have developed strong ties before the divorce.

What can be concluded about continued contacts between the ex-spouses? The present data and those of Jacobson (1983) and Spanier and Thompson (1984) indicate that a number of ex-spouses maintain contact even when no children are present, at least in the early years after the divorce. Ambert (1989) found 6 years after the divorce that these contacts were quite infrequent for those with no children.

These data suggest that the ties between marital partners are not easily broken, as indicated by the positive feelings many subjects reported about their ex-spouses and the continued contacts in person, by telephone, or through friends and family, even when no children were present. In the next section, the focus shifts to some of the feelings the divorced respondents reported about the divorce process. These dislocations may make continued contacts with the ex-partner more appealing than might be expected.

POSITIVE AND NEGATIVE ASPECTS OF THE DIVORCE

Difficult Adjustments

The difficulties of the divorce process are reflected in the replies of the suburban divorced sample to a series of questions about the positive and negative aspects of the divorce. Although the majority of the subjects felt that the divorce was generally an unpleasant experience, some of the unpleasantness faded with time, and the benefits of the decision became clearer. For example, at the first interview, only one-sixth of the respondents reported no difficulties in reply to a question about "the most difficult kinds of adjustments for you to make since the decision to divorce." With an average of 1.9 difficulties mentioned by women and 1.6 by men, there were no significant differences in the mean number of difficulties mentioned by gender. Whites, with a mean of 1.9, were significantly more likely than nonwhites, with a mean of 1.4, to report difficult adjustments ($t = 3.3$, $df = 197$, $p < .001$).

Men and women, however, differed significantly in the types of difficulties they experienced (Table 10.5). Although the difficult adjustments most frequently mentioned by both genders were related to

TABLE 10.5. Percentages of Divorced Men and Women Reporting Difficult Adjustments and Harder versus Easier Adjustments to Divorce at First and Third Interviews

| | % reporting at first interview: Difficult adjustments[a] | | % reporting at third interview | | | |
| | | | Harder than thought[b] | | Easier than thought[c] | |
	Male ($n = 99$)	Female ($n = 103$)	Male ($n = 60$)	Female ($n = 72$)	Male ($n = 60$)	Female ($n = 72$)
Nothing	16.2	15.5	50.0	40.3	66.7	41.7
Everything	—	—	1.7	1.4	—	—
Living alone	42.4	71.8	18.3	20.8	28.3	38.9
Taking on new roles	35.3	32.0	21.7	30.6	6.7	34.7
Finances	14.1	34.0	6.7	9.7	6.7	15.3
Divorce-related feelings	20.2	24.3	8.3	6.9	—	2.8
Making new relationships	24.2	13.6	18.3	6.9	6.7	6.9
Children's well-being	20.2	8.7	1.7	2.8	1.7	1.4

Note. Replies do not total 100% because of multiple responses.
[a]$\chi^2 = 22.1$, $df = 6$, $p < .01$.
[b]$\chi^2 = 7.3$, $df = 7$, n.s.
[c]$\chi^2 = 16.2$, $df = 6$, $p < .05$.

"living alone" and "taking on new roles," women were substantially more likely to mention problems in "adjusting to independence" "and being a single parent" as specific problems within these two areas. The remaining concerns for men in order of ocurrence were "making new relationships," "divorce-related feelings." and "children's well-being," with "finances" as of the least concern. For women, "finances," "divorce-related feelings," and "making new relationships" were their next most pressing concerns, with "children's well-being" the least frequently mentioned concern. These difficulties were also associated with subjective distress: Those reporting more difficulties reported greater distress.

Racial differences emerged in several categories. Nonwhites were more likely than whites to report no difficult adjustments (26.9% vs. 12.4% of whites). At the same time, nonwhites were more likely to mention "taking on new roles" as being problematic (23.1% vs. 9.0% of whites). Whites were much more likely to spontaneously mention the "stigma of the divorce" (15.9% vs. 1.9% of nonwhites).

Pleasant and Unpleasant Changes

At the second interview, the respondents were asked about some of the pleasant and unpleasant changes associated with the divorce. Only 11.2% said that there were no pleasant changes, and although there were no significant differences by gender, nonwhites were significantly more likely to report pleasant changes than whites ($\chi^2 = 14.3$, $df = 6$, $p < .05$). Nonwhites were more than twice as likely as whites to report a "greater sense of peace of mind" (26.3% vs. 12.2% for whites). Forty-two percent of the nonwhites reported "more freedom," as opposed to 32.5% of the whites who reported this; 18.7% of the whites and none of the nonwhite respondents reported "personal growth" as a pleasant outcome of the divorce.

Unpleasant changes also differed significantly by race but not by gender, with 42.1% of the nonwhite subjects reporting no unpleasant changes, compared to 26.0% of the whites ($\chi^2 = 11.4$, $df = 5$, $p < .05$). Whites reported somewhat more difficulty with adjusting to "being alone without others to date" (17.9% vs. 10.5% for nonwhites); they also had more concerns about "stigma of the divorce" and "adjusting to the fact of the divorce" (13.0% vs. 5.3% of nonwhites). These data suggest— as noted earlier in this chapter and in Chapter 6 on psychological adjustment—that at least in the first several years of the divorce process, the suburban nonwhites surveyed found that the divorce brought fewer changes and fewer negative changes than did the whites studied.

Easier Adjustments Than Expected

At the third interview, the respondents were asked, "Were there any things that surprised you or that you had not anticipated about being divorced? For example, were there things that were easier to do or learn than you had thought they would be?" Women were significantly more likely than men to report that things were easier than they had anticipated (56.9% vs. 32.8%, respectively; ($\chi^2 = 7.2$, $df = 1$, $p < .01$). There were no significant differences by race in activities that were easier, and no differences by gender or race for things that were harder to do.

To facilitate comparisons of perceptions of how difficult it was to adjust to the divorce over time, replies to this question at the third interview were categorized in a similar manner to those at the first interview (Table 10.5). For activities that were reported as difficult at the first interview, some by the third interview had faded in importance with experience, such as "living alone"; however, women continued to report "taking on new roles" and "adjusting to independence" as problems. Males, on the other hand, reported at the first interview that "making new relationships"—finding women to date and making new friends—was harder than anticipated. By the third interview, this was less frequently mentioned as a concern. Thus, some of the problems that the divorced respondents faced when they were initially interviewed, although realistic issues at that point, were concerns that for the most part had faded in importance by the third interview as they dealt with them successfully. Furthermore, those things that were perceived as difficult adjustments at the second and third interviews were not associated with subjective distress, as they had been at the first interview. In addition, the higher adjustment scores of nonwhites as reported in Chapter 6 were reflected in fewer problems and difficulties after the divorce and more frequent reports of pleasant changes as a result of the decision to end their marriages.

Activities That Helped in Coping

Given the frequency with which the divorced mentioned difficulties at the first interview, the question arises: What, if anything, can be done to alleviate such problems? To address this issue, at the second interview the subjects were asked, "Are there any particular activities that have especially helped you to cope with things?" Slightly over half of the 154 who replied said that nothing really helped. For the remaining 71, however, "keeping busy" with either outside activities (mentioned by 35.2%) or work (33.8%) helped the most, followed by "dating and friends" (23.9%). There were no statistically significant differences in replies by gender or race.

The reasons given to explain why these activities were helpful focused on "keeping busy" and enhancing self-esteem. More than half (60.6%) of the 66 persons who gave explanations said that the activities helped because they took their minds off the divorce. Enhancement of social opportunities by getting out to meet others was the next most frequent reply (mentioned by 30.3%), with the remainder saying that the activities helped them to gain independence (19.7%) or self-awareness (9.1%).

The data presented so far again illustrate the processual nature of adjustment to divorce. Divorce in its earlier phases is a blow to a person's social and psychological self. The adjustment process is made more difficult by the quite commonly reported feeling that others do not approve of the decision to divorce, and therefore make the divorced person feel that he or she is treated poorly because of being divorced. Such feelings grow with experience as a divorced person instead of diminishing. Old roles and attitudes have to be shed; new ones must be tried out and perhaps discarded, and still others assumed. Many of the divorced had continuing ties with their ex-spouses, as indicated by their remaining in contact after the divorce.

ATTITUDES ABOUT THE LEGAL PROCESS

Although the suburban divorce respondents did not spontaneously mention it as a source of difficulties, it is often thought that the legal system itself contributes to the difficulties that divorced persons experience. When no-fault legislation was proposed, it was thought that the institution of this new option would lessen acrimony and decrease psychological distress among those facing the dissolution of their marriages (R. Phillips, 1988; Weitzman, 1985). The reasoning behind these expectations was that having to prove "guilt" and "innocence" in a fault-based divorce was thought to make the legal process more adversarial, and therefore more psychologically upsetting. This view ignores the matrix of contradictory feelings experienced by the divorced. Nevertheless, the legal system could add to the turmoil.

As noted in Chapters 2 and 5, Ohio has a mixed system of divorce laws allowing "fault-based" and "no-fault" divorce. This section examines the satisfaction of the suburban divorced respondents with their legal experiences, as well as the impact of no-fault divorce provisions on these attitudes.

Questions Asked about the Legal Process

At the second interview, when the divorced had recently received their decrees, they were asked to reply to a series of questions about various aspects of their experiences. The first of these was "From your point of view, do you feel there was a lot of conflict in your divorce or was it friendly?", with replies from 1 ("a lot of conflict") to 5 ("friendly"). They were also asked, "Overall, do you think the legal process increased the amount of conflict in your divorce, or did it make it easier to divorce without a lot of conflict?", with replies from 1 ("increased the conflict") to 5 ("decreased the conflict").

Several other questions asked about satisfaction with various aspects of the legal process. These items were scored on a scale from 1 ("very dissatisfied") to 5 ("very satisfied") and included satisfaction with the way their attorneys handled the cases. Three items—satisfaction with the divorce settlement; satisfaction with the division of property; and satisfaction with "the whole legal process—including the law, the judges, and the lawyers"—were combined into a single scale with an alpha reliability of .75 and a range of scores from 3 to 15.

The Impact of No-Fault Divorce on Satisfaction with the Legal Process

As noted above, it has been assumed that no-fault divorces should decrease conflict and make the divorce a friendlier process. The data support these assumptions. The 58 people in the suburban study who reported that their marriages were ended by dissolution of marriage (the true no-fault provision in Ohio, as opposed to living separately for 2 years, which is known legally in Ohio as "no-fault") were significantly more likely than the 100 who used the fault-based provision to consider their divorces friendlier, with a mean of 3.4 for no-fault and 2.9 for fault-based divorces ($t = 2.1$, $df = 156$, $p < .005$). Similarly, those who used no-fault provisions were significantly more likely to feel that the legal process decreased conflict, with a mean of 4.0 as opposed to 3.3 for those who used the fault-based system ($t = 3.6$,

$df = 151$, $p < .0005$). There was, however, no significant difference between the two groups in satisfaction with the legal process as measured by the composite satisfaction scale, and no difference in satisfaction with the respondent's attorney.

Only one relationship each was significant by gender and race for the questions assessing attitudes toward the legal process. Men were significantly more likely than women to feel that the divorce was friendly, with means, respectively, of 3.4 and 2.8 ($t = 2.6$, $df = 158$, $p < .01$). Nonwhites, with a mean of 12.1, scored significantly higher on the composite satisfaction scale than did whites, with a mean of 10.6 ($t = 2.2$, $df = 158$, $p < .05$).

In states such as Ohio, with a mixed system of fault-based and no-fault divorce, it is thought that the choice of one type or the other depends on the reasons for the divorce and the number of assets. With more assets or more grievous complaints, the fault-based system might produce an outcome that would be more advantageous to one or the other partner. In the suburban divorce sample, however, there were no differences in the type of legal action filed depending on whether "expressive," "instrumental," or "serious" marital complaints (see Chapter 5) were mentioned by the respondents as reasons for the divorce. There were also no differences in the type of divorce obtained by income or length of marriage. Younger persons were, however, significantly more likely to obtain no-fault divorces. The average age of no-fault recipients was 30.4, as opposed to 34.5 for those who obtained fault-based divorces ($t = 2.5$, $df = 157$, $p < .005$). Thus, although those with more assets might have been expected to "seek a better deal" through a fault-based divorce, this was not the case. Younger persons, however, were apparently more amenable to using a newer legal option. Thus, with these data collected early in the period of experience with no-fault divorce in Ohio, there were few differences in who chose which type of legal option.

Differences in Adjustment by Type of Decree?

The impact of the legal system on psychological adjustment has been little studied (Kitson & Morgan, 1990). In the suburban divorce study, those who obtained fault-based divorces were significantly *less* likely to report symptoms of subjective distress: Their mean distress score was 2.1, compared to a mean of 3.0 for those who obtained no-fault (dissolution) decrees ($t = 2.5$, $df = 157$, $p < .005$). There were no differences in attachment, illness contacts, or self-esteem scores by type of decree.

At the first interview in the county-wide marital transition study, there was no statistical difference in depression as measured by the Zung Self-Rating Depression Scale (Zung, 1965) by type of decree. There was also no difference between the two types of decrees on the "anger at the loss" scale described above. The reasons for finding less psychological distress among those who obtained fault-based divorces compared to those who obtained dissolutions, or no difference in scores—both of which are contrary to expectations—are unclear. It would seem, however, that the type of legal system and any ensuing reductions in legal animosities would be unlikely to outweigh the impact of the contradictory emotions and feelings that the end of the marriage itself engenders. In support of this view, serious marital complaints in the suburban divorce survey were associated with more conflictual divorces ($r = -.21$, $p < .01$).

Seeking Postdivorce Legal Help

Two to three years after receiving their decrees, 15% of the suburban divorced sample reported at the third interview that their ex-spouses had gone back to their lawyers at least once "for help or for changes" in the settlement. There were no significant differences by gender in who sought help. Most of these requests (72%) involved money or property—an increase or decrease in money, enforcement of child support and alimony payments, or the return of personal property ($n = 25$). The remaining concerns involved changes in custody or visitation, or enforcement of visitation.

In about a quarter of these instances, the lawyer advised the respondent either to forget about their concerns or to ignore the spouse's request. In the remaining instances, the lawyer recommended complying with the spouse's request (35.0%) or seeking court action (40.0%). Only 5 of the 131 respondents, or 3.8%, reported that they or their ex-spouses actually went back to court. All of these instances involved money or property. In each instance, the judge was reported to have ordered action (the return of property, the making of support or alimony payment, or a decrease in payments). Thus, in this study postdivorce legal actions were relatively rare. Nevertheless, if 5% of the 1,175,000 divorces granted in 1990 required further legal action, this would produce an additional 58,750 court appearances (a figure duplicated in other years as well, to produce an even larger number of postdivorce legal actions).

These data provide support for the hypothesis that no-fault divorce should decrease acrimony and conflict. There is, however, little support for the theory that no-fault divorce should decrease psychological distress. In fact, in these data, distress was greater for those in the suburban study who obtained no-fault divorces. Relatively few of the divorced sought additional legal assistance in the first years after the divorce.

REAFFILIATION: REMARRIAGE, COHABITATION, ENGAGEMENT

Marital Status of the Divorced at the Second and Third Interviews

Although it is frequently not the objective of the decision to divorce, one common outcome is the decision to begin dating again and possibly to remarry. Feeling bruised and wary because of their previous experiences, many in the suburban divorced sample nevertheless decided to begin to look for a new love interest. It is not that they necessarily disliked being married; they just did not like the persons to whom they had been married. This section looks at some of these new relationships. Data from the U.S. Bureau of the Census indicate that the majority of the divorced remarry; estimates range from two-thirds to three-quarters (Glick & Lin, 1986; Norton, 1991; Norton & Moorman, 1987). Remarriages are more common among younger than older divorced persons and among men than women.

Only a few divorced subjects reported being remarried or cohabiting at the first interview, with only four men and no women being remarried and six men and four women cohabiting. However, at this first interview, remarriage and cohabitation were only noted if the respondent mentioned them, not in response to a direct question; this may have produced underestimates, especially for cohabitants.

By the second interview ($n = 160$), a year after the decree was granted, men were significantly more likely to have remarried than women (19.2% vs. 4.6%; $\chi^2 = 7.1$, $df = 1$, $p < .01$). There were no significant differences in remarriage rates by race, with 11.5% of the whites and 10.5% of the nonwhites remarrying. There were also no differences by gender or race in cohabiting: 10% of the men versus 6.8% of the women, and 8.1% of the whites versus 10.5% of the nonwhites, were cohabiting. When cohabitants and the remarried were combined, males were still significantly more likely than females to be reaffiliated (30.1% vs. 11.4% of the women ($\chi^2 = 8.9$, $df = 1$, $p < .01$).

At the third interview, 43.6% of the 133 subjects reported being remarried (28.6%), cohabiting (8.3%), or being engaged without a full-time living arrangement (5.3%). One person had remarried, divorced, and remarried again since the initial interview, and another had remarried, had divorced, and was now cohabiting. A few persons (4.5%) who had either been cohabiting or remarried since the beginning of the study had seen these new relationships end in separation or divorce. A slight majority (51.9%) reported being single. There were no statistically significant differences in marital status by gender or race, regardless of how marital status was examined—that is, the married compared to all others, or the married and those who were cohabiting (with or without the engaged) compared to the single.

Two persons (1.5%) were living with, and four (3.0%) had remarried, the persons from whom they were separated or divorced at the first interview. Briscoe et al. (1973) reported that 3% of their St. Louis divorced respondents had remarried their ex-spouses within 2 years of the divorce. These percentages are some of the few pieces of empirical data on the phenomenon of remarriage to the same spouse after divorce; they are similar to Glick's (1985) estimate that 4% of divorced individuals remarry their ex-spouses.

Theories about Who Reaffiliates

As discussed earlier in this book, various theories have been used to explain why people divorce and what happens to them after divorce. Although predicting who will marry the first time is difficult, can the theories about the reasons for divorce be used to help predict which of the divorced are likely to find new partners fairly rapidly? It would seem likely that if certain characteristics are associated with the likelihood of divorce, they should also play some role in the desire to remarry. That is, if people evaluate certain characteristics as important in deciding to divorce, these characteristics should also be important in deciding to remarry. The theories to be examined here to address this idea are the pathology, crisis, exchange, and social role models. The pathology model suggests that the psychological problems of a divorced person account for his or her inability to live harmoniously with a partner. Indicators of these problems include parental divorce, hospitalization for mental problems, or the seeking of outpatient therapy. These same problems may also make the divorced person especially psychologically needy and unable to live alone happily; as a result, it may be such a person who is most likely to rush into remarriage. An alternative explanation is that seeking therapy, is a sign of strength and health rather than a sign of disability. Therapeutic intervention can help individuals obtain an understanding of their problems, thereby making them better able to cope with new relationships. In this case, the period when the therapy occurred may make a difference. Therapy received before the marriage ended, or therapy reported at the first or second interview, might serve as an indication of having dealt with problems. Continuing therapy or therapy reported at the third interview might suggest ongoing problems, a decision to address issues that were not dealt with previously, or the advent of new stressors.

Regardless of the individual's predivorce psychological status, the crisis model states that the adaptations required by the divorce in and of themselves produce disturbance in health. As time passes, the symptoms of health disturbance should decrease as attachment to the former spouse diminishes, new roles are learned, self-esteem is enhanced, and new social ties are developed. This model would suggest that those who have adjusted most successfully are able to consider remarrying. One problem in assessing the accuracy of this model is the difficulty of disentangling the greater sense of well-being produced by a new relationship from the individual's psychological status before it occurred.

The exchange model of divorce states that people divorce when the reward-cost ratio of continuing a relationship is such that it is more psychologically and socially costly to stay in a relationship than it is to get out of it (Becker, 1981; Kitson, Holmes, & Sussman, 1983; Levinger, 1976; Nye, White & Frideres, 1973). Levinger (1978) has arrayed these factors into "material," "symbolic," and "affectional" rewards and costs that make the relationship attractive to maintain, serve as barriers to ending it, or are alternative attractions to the relationship. Principles such as these may also come into play in the decision to remarry. On the affectional level, the reasons for the divorce—the type of needs unmet by the relationship—may differentially lead people to seek out new partners. One symbolic resource that is valued in our society is youth, especially for women. For men age seems to be less of a problem, but men with high incomes are more highly valued than those with low incomes. The exchange model also suggests other possibilities for the likelihood of remarriage, particularly for women with minor children and low income. For such women, the social, emotional, and economic costs of attempting to manage small children on their own with limited economic resources may make remarriage look more attractive. An important benefit of income maintenance programs such as Aid to Families with Dependent Children is to forestall the possibility of such hasty marriages, as Ross and Sawhill (1975) have demonstrated. In the suburban divorce study, few were on welfare, so it might be anticipated that younger women with children and low incomes and younger women without children should remarry more rapidly. Alternatively, the exchange model could lead to the prediction that on the remarriage market being a male of any age is an asset, whereas being a female, particularly an older female with children, is a liability. (For a discussion of this perspective on remarriage, see Mueller & Pope, 1980.)

A fourth explanation involves social roles. It states that whereas marriage seems to be more beneficial in promoting men's physical and psychological well-being than it is women's, the single status is more detrimental to men because they have fewer social supports and resources (Bernard, 1972; Gove, 1972a, 1972b). If this is the case, then those with fewer social supports should be more likely to remarry. This should include proportionately more men than women.

Who Reaffiliated?

Since life is often more complicated than our theories or models, the indicators for the various theories are examined first individually and then jointly. In testing the theories, a first issue to determine is how marital status should be defined among the divorced. Because attitudes about living together outside of marriage have changed, and because of the large number of cohabitants in the sample, it seems too restrictive to look only at those who had legally remarried. But then, what about those who were engaged and not living together for various reasons? Such reasons might include work commitments, unbreakable leases, the feeling that minor children should not live in a household with unmarried cohabiting adults, or other moral or social reservations about living with a member of the opposite sex outside of marriage. These possibilities argue for comparing the single to the reaffiliated or repartnered—that is, those who had a stable, committed relationship with a member of the opposite sex, as indicated by engagement without living together, cohabitation, or remarriage. Although the engaged would be unlikely to pool resources (as the remarried and sometimes the cohabiting would do), any common characteristics associated with finding a new partner should apply to the engaged as well as the others. To test this hypothesis, Table 10.6 displays two sets of Pearson's correlations each for men and women: for the remarried and cohabiting compared to the single and engaged; and for the engaged, cohabiting, and remarried compared to the single. In both cases, the category including the single was coded 0, and the category for the reaffiliated was coded 1.

A second issue is how to measure the various indicators being examined, since, as has been seen, people found their new partners at

TABLE 10.6. Characteristics Associated with Finding New Partners by Gender and Race: Pearson's Zero-Order Correlations

| | Sex and marital status measures[a] | | | |
| | Male | | Female | |
Indicators of marital status	Engaged, cohabiting, remarried vs. single	Cohabiting, remarried vs. single, engaged	Engaged, cohabiting, remarried vs. single	Cohabiting, remarried vs. single, engaged
Types of marital complaints				
Stable over time	.20	.19	.06	−.07
Serious	.03	.07	−.12	−.06
Expressive	.31*	.24	.06	−.05
Instrumental	.12	.12	.12	−.11
Social class position	−.30**	−.30**	−.18	−.14
Change in income	.02	.15	.47***	.53***
Income at third interview	.40**	.52***	.43***	.47***
Number of children living with respondent	−.27*	−.24	−.32**	−.35***
Race	−.05	−.01	−.07	−.21
Age	−.18	−.11	−.33	−.27*
Health and psychological status, third interview				
Attachment	−.20	−.15	−.14	−.19
Illness contacts	−.15	−.17	−.02	−.08
Self-esteem	−.10	−.11	.02	.09
Subjective distress	−.09	−.17	.01	−.02
Mental health help				
Hospitalization	−.06	−.05	−.03	.02
Prior to last year of marriage	−.12	−.15	.29*	.32**
In last year of marriage	.07	.11	−.03	−.01
At second interview	−.06	−.03	.18	.13
At third interview	.04	.07	.01	.00
Ever mentioned	−.05	−.05	.23	.23
Confidants	−.12	.00	−.10	−.10
Number of relatives	−.06	−.05	.07	.04

[a]0 = single; 1 = reaffiliated as defined above.

*p < .05.
**p < .01.
***p < .001.

different times. With the exception of income, there were few differences among the background indicators by time period; those who were the youngest at the beginning of the study were obviously still the youngest at the end, although they were older. The physical and mental health measures were examined across time periods. Using change measures made it possible to assess whether those who reaffiliated had improved in health status more rapidly than the others. Neither set of health measures distinguished among the subjects. Thus, with the exception of the income indicators, for which multiple measures of the same concept were available, replies at the third interview were used. Income was measured in two ways. First, income at the third interview was determined; for the married and cohabiting, this was likely to include the income of both partners, so that the variable did not measure the possible role of income in deciding to remarry. As a result, a measure was also included to assess the change in income from the first to the second and from the second to the third interviews for those who married between these periods.

For the most part, neither method of looking at marital status was correlated with many of the indicators; in general, however, the associations were somewhat larger when the engaged were grouped with the cohabiting and remarried. For the income measures, the correlations were somewhat smaller when all three partnership groups were included, since engaged couples were probably less likely to pool their incomes; still, the income associations were so strong that the decrease in the size of the correlations was tolerable. Also, the change-in-income measure was a better predictor of reaffiliation for women than was income at the third interview. For men, the change-in-income measure was not associated with either measure of marital status, whereas income at the third interview was: Men with new partners had higher family incomes. Because men generally have higher incomes than women, these data suggest that income for males was a stronger predictor of becoming repartnered than was change in income.

Among the other variables used to test the exchange model, the associations between social class and reaffiliation were not significant for women, but they were for men. Men who were higher in social class position were more likely to reaffiliate when either marital status measure was used. There were no associations between race and marital status for men or women. Although the relationship between age and marital status was not significant for men, it was for women: Older women were less likely to be reaffiliated. For women when both marital status measures were used, and for men when the measure that included the engaged was used, becoming repartnered was more likely for respondents without children living with them. This means that women having no children, or at least fewer children, were more likely to have found another partner. For men, it means that those few men who had their children living with them were less likely to have found another partner. Women may be less likely to want to marry men with ready-made families, and the men themselves may have been so committed to making things work with their children that their interest in finding new partners may have been less.

Men who were repartnered at the third interview—that is, engaged, cohabiting, or remarried—were significantly more likely to have made expressive complaints about their old marriages at the first interview. For the whole sample, just over half of the repartnered (51.7%) reported three or more expressive complaints, as opposed to 25.3% of those who were not repartnered ($\tau_b = -.16$, $p < .01$). Thus, the types of complaints made about the breakup of their marriages may have made some of the repartnered especially ready to seek out others. There were no differences in being repartnered for the other types of complaints (instrumental, serious, or stable).

In terms of specific individual marital complaints, the repartnered were apparently more ready to look for others to fill some of their affectional and companionship needs because of the reasons for the breakup of their marriages. For example, among the specific marital complaints, the repartnered were significantly more likely to report the following: "change in interests or values" (29.3% vs. 14.7%; $\tau_b = .18$, $p < .05$); "overcommitment to work" (19.0% vs. 5.3%; $\tau_b = .21$, $p < .01$); and "jealousy" (15.5% vs. 2.7%; $\tau_b = .23$, $p < .05$). There were, however, no significant differences in whether the respondents were reaffiliated for the complaint of "extramarital sex" as a problem of the marriage.

At the same time as they were perhaps more desirous of companionship, those who were remarried, cohabiting, or engaged may have been less "burned" by their previous marriages; that is, the complaints they had about their relationships may not have been the type from which it was particularly difficult to recover. Among the latter, for example, those who reported "alcohol" as a problem in the marriage were less likely to be repartnered ($\tau_b = -.17$, $p < .05$). Similarly, none of the five who reported "actual physical abuse" as a problem were repartnered ($\tau_b = -.17$, $p < .05$). None of the subjects who reported Conflicts over the Children (Factor 1) were repartnered ($\tau_b = -.15$, $p < .05$).

Those who found new partners may have had more need to do so, and therefore may have been more willing to seize available opportunities. Whether this is "needy" behavior that leads to bad choices is another issue. With only one exception, therapeutic help for women, the indicators of pathology were not associated with marital status. Those who scored as the most physically or psychologically needy were not the ones who sought out new partners. None of the psychological or health status measures was strongly associated with marital status. In particular, there was no significant association between hospitalizations for mental illness and marital status.

As noted above, seeking help from therapists was measured in several ways: whether any therapy had ever been sought, and then when it was received (in the earlier years of the marriage, in its last year, or after the marriage ended), as assessed at the second or third interview. None of the correlations between therapy and marital status was statistically significant for men, and only one was for women: Women who reported having obtained help from a psychiatrist/psychologist, marriage counselor, or social worker prior to the last year of the marriage were significantly more likely to have found new partners. These data indicate that the most psychologically needy were not the ones who reaffiliated first.

Finally, neither of the measures of social roles was significantly associated with marital status. Those with confidants and those who reported seeing more relatives at least monthly were no more or less likely than those who did not report such contacts to have become repartnered.

This analysis indicates that the reaffiliated or repartnered should include the engaged, as well as the remarried and the cohabiting. Furthermore, the analysis shows that relatively few of the measures examined were associated with the decision to reaffiliate. To determine whether variables fit into a pattern that more strongly represented one or the other of the models discussed above, the indicators hypothesized to be associated with marital status were entered into a stepwise multiple regression. Two versions of the regression were run: one using change in income as the measure of economic situation, because this was a stronger predictor for women, and another using income at the third interview, because this was a stronger predictor for men.

For women, when the change-in-income variable was used, three variables accounted for 33% of the variance in the likelihood of being remarried: the degree to which income changed as a result of the decision; a smaller number of children living with the respondent; and seeking therapeutic help before the last year of the marriage (respectively, $\beta = .27$, $p < .01$; $\beta = -.32$, $p < .05$; and $\beta = .39$, $p < .05$). When total income at the third interview was used instead of the change-in-income variable, 2% more variance was explained ($R^2 = .35$ compared to $R^2 = .33$). Being repartnered was associated with higher income at the third interview, being younger, and having no or few children in the household (respectively, $\beta = .32$, $p < .01$; $\beta = -.34$, $p < .01$; $\beta = -.29$, $p < .05$).

For men, when the change-in-income variable was used, only one variable entered the equation: having affective complaints about the marriage ($\beta = .31$, $p < .05$). Those who had more affective complaints were more likely to have found new partners. But only 10% of the variance was explained by this variable, with the change-in-income variable contributing nothing. When income at the third interview was used instead of the change-in-income measure, more variables entered the equation and 21% more variance was explained. Men who had higher incomes, who had fewer or no children in the household, and who were younger in age were more likely to have found new partners (respectively, $\beta = .47$, $p < .01$; $\beta = -.30$, $p < .05$; and $\beta = -.25$, $p < .05$; final $R^2 = .31$). These are the same variables that entered the second (total income at the third interview) equation for women.

In summary, then, it is possible to make predictions about which divorced men and women were most likely to be engaged, cohabiting, or remarried 4 years after separation. Income at the third interview seemed to be a better predictor of finding a new partner than change in income, because more variables entered the equation for men and more variance was explained for both men and women when the income variable was used. Having more income made it easier for men to consider finding new partners, and apparently made men more attractive to women. In addition to income, other variables associated with the exchange model explained more of the variance than those from other models. In fact, for men, only indicators of the exchange model made significant contributions when either income measure was used: expressive complaints, income, number of children living in the household, and age. For women, income, number of children, and age entered one of the equations and explained a similar amount of variance (35% compared to 31% for the men). Thus, relative youth, money, and freedom from child care responsibilities (or at least having fewer children to care for) are resources that make it easier for both men and women to find new partners. Having obtained therapy prior to the last year of marriage entered the regression when the change-in-income measure was used. It may be that those who obtained therapeutic help before the end of their marriages had a clearer sense of why they ended their relationships and what they wanted in new ones.

Although variables associated with the exchange model were the best predictors of which divorced persons were most likely to have found new partners, it should be noted that only about a third of the variance in reaffiliation was explained by them. Statistically, the results of the multiple regressions are fairly impressive; substantively, however, a number of other factors that have not been explored go into the decision to reaffiliate. Such factors are hard to explore. People consciously or unconsciously seek out certain characteristics in new partners, even if they are not always willing or able to articulate them. These difficulties are illustrated by replies to a question asked of those who were not remarried at the second interview: "If you were to remarry, how do you think this marriage would differ from your previous one?" Of the 132 who answered, 60.6% said that the relationship would be different expressively; that is, there would be better communication, more interests in common, and more sharing. Close to a third (31.8%) said that the spouses' role performance would be different, with some saying the husband should be more dominant and others that there should be more equality. Finding a partner with a different personality was mentioned by 30.3%. Only 6.8% mentioned that they wanted to find someone who was more financially stable, followed by 4.5% who said that a new spouse had to be someone they "liked"; that is, the relationship should be based on friendship. Finally, 15.2% said they had no idea or did not intend to remarry. (The percentages do not total 100% because of multiple replies.) These data reflect the same problem that data on reasons to divorce do. The multiple-regression analyses above indicate that finding a new partner was not a random event, and that certain characteristics such as money and youth were apparently important in making that decision. Yet only one of the factors that the divorced said would be important in finding a new mate—wanting a more expressive relationship, as represented by marital complaints reflecting expressive concerns—entered any of the regressions. What people say about relationships is not necessarily the same thing as what they do.

Describing the New Relationships

The next issue to be explored is what the new relationships of the repartnered respondents were like. Those individuals who reported cohabitation or remarriage were asked a series of questions about their new relationships. In retrospect, these questions should have been asked of the engaged as well, but they were not.

Being remarried or cohabiting after a divorce was not without its problems, as indicated by the lack of difference in the associations of marital status with the various measures of health status. The fact that these men and women felt this pressure was indicated by their replies to the question, "Do you ever feel that having been divorced makes it harder for you in this marriage (relationship)?" Forty-three percent of those queried ($n = 51$) said that the divorce had indeed made the new relationship harder, with no differences in reply by gender. However, among the 36 people who added explanations, the answers were skewed more toward the pluses than toward the minuses of the divorce. This suggests that despite the problems, the difficulties were felt to be surmountable. The most frequent reply, given by 58.3%, was that if a person could learn from his or her mistakes the divorce could be an advantage. Another 27.8% said the divorce made them bring along some problems that otherwise would not be there, while 11.1%, or four people, said that because of their experiences they hoped to anticipate problems in the new relationship before they became serious. Finally, one woman said that the divorce had created problems with her new partner's family because the family's religion did not approve of divorce.

When the subjects were asked what they liked best about being remarried or living together, 54.3% mentioned companionship; 30.4%, security or love; 8.7%, compatibility; and the remaining 6.5%, a variety of reasons.

The vast majority of the subjects considered their new marriages or relationships happy. The mean score in reply to a question asking about happiness, using a 6-point scale with 1 meaning "very unhappy" and 6 "very happy," was 5.2 ($n = 50$). Only one person said that the relationship was "very unhappy" and two others that it was "somewhat unhappy." The average score of 5.2 was the same score that the continuously married gave to this question at their second interview ($n = 135$). In general, then, those of the divorced who were remarried or cohabiting felt that the divorce had produced some difficulties and concerns for them in their new relationships; despite the difficulties, however, the majority were as happy in their new relationships as the married comparison subjects were in their old ones.

THE SINGLE

It was certainly not the case that all of those without new partners had lost interest in the opposite sex, although in some cases they seemed suspicious and somewhat leery of entering new relationships. Among those who were not remarried or cohabiting, the majority reported some dating. At the second interview, 19.5% reported dating "seldom or never," with 71.7% dating "at least two or three times a month." By the third interview some of the dating had tapered off, with 23.4% ($n = 75$) dating "seldom or never" and 67.1% dating "at least two or three times a month." With no significant differences by gender, the majority of the single (58.5%) were satisfied with the frequency with which they were dating, whereas 32.9% wanted to date more and 8.5% less. Even fewer (15.9%) reported little social activity with friends or dates. There were no significant differences by race at the second or third interview in the frequency of dating or visiting with friends.

Virtually no one reported being without social contacts. Those who did not date or see friends visited with relatives. Only 5 out of 82 persons at the third interview, or 6.1%, saw neither friends nor relatives in the area at least monthly.

Ways of Meeting Others

Re-entering what has variously been called "the meat market" or "the singles scene," with its proliferation of fern-bedecked singles bars, is difficult for many of the divorced; this is particularly so for those who have been married and out of circulation during the period of substantial change in dating and sexual behavior in the past few decades. To explore how individuals launched themselves back into the dating scene, at the third interview the divorced respondents were asked what they thought were the best ways to meet others, and how they had actually met the people they had dated. What the repartnered said they did was then compared to what those who were still single reported. These questions explored "acceptable" or socially desirable ways of meeting others, as opposed to what people actually did.

The data suggest either that those who found new partners were luckier than those who had not, or that the single chose less appropriate places to look for dates. The remarried, cohabiters, and single all considered friends the best source of meeting people, perhaps because the interests and values of those with friends in common should be similar (Table 10.7). The repartnered differed from the single in their evaluation of the work place as a good location for meeting others. The repartnered ranked the work place as the second best way in which they met partners, whereas the single ranked it behind parties, tied for third with three other items considered poorer ways of meeting others. Few of the reaffiliated met their partners in singles groups. Although the single reported meeting few dates in singles groups, they rated such groups as the third best way to meet people. Parties were ranked as the second most *frequent* way in which the single met their dates and also the second *best* way to meet dates, whereas the repartnered ranked parties as the sixth most frequent way of meeting their partners. The repartnered were apparently more willing to take a chance in meeting others than were those who were still single; more of the former reported meeting people at the laundromat, during grocery shopping, or during other such encounters, which

TABLE 10.7. How Remarried, Cohabiting, and Single Persons Met Partners and Dates, and Best Method of Meeting Dates for the Single

| Method of meeting | How new partner/date was met | | | | | |
| | Cohabiting/ remarried (n = 50) | | Single (n = 76) | | Best method for singles (n = 70) | |
	%	(Rank)	%	(Rank)	%	(Rank)
Through family	2.0	(7)	23.7	(6)	4.3	(5)
Through friends	26.0	(1)	71.1	(1)	38.6	(1)
At a party	8.0	(6)	61.8	(2)	25.7	(2)
At a bar	12.0	(5)	40.8	(5)	4.3	(5)
At a singles group	2.0	(7)	21.1	(7)	11.4	(3)
At work	18.0	(2)	55.3	(3)	4.3	(5)
Through church	2.0	(7)	11.8	(9)	4.3	(5)
Knew before divorce	16.0	(3)	52.6	(4)	7.1	(4)
Chance meeting	14.0	(4)	15.8	(8)	NA[a]	
Total	100.0		[b]	100.0		

[a]Not asked.
[b]Percentages do not total 100.0 because of multiple replies.

may require more initiative in starting a conversation. This may be similar to the role of marital complaints in becoming reaffiliated, in that it may be related to being more cautious and less willing to take a chance, because of the serious nature of the problems in the marriage that had just ended.

When those who were single were asked at the third interview, "Do you think you will marry again?", 26.8% said "no," 15.9% were ambivalent or just did not know, and 57.3% said "yes"; there were no significant differences by gender. The most frequent reason given for being uncertain or saying "no," mentioned by a third of the subjects, was uncertainty about meeting the right person. This was followed by not wanting the problems and responsibilities of marriage; feeling wary, burned, or untrusting because of the marriage that failed; feeling that one's needs could be met without remarriage, and feeling that "You don't have to marry just for the sake of marrying." One woman reported that no one could replace her lost love, and one man said that his religious beliefs prohibited remarriage.

Expectations for Partners

The single were asked at the third interview to name the first and second most important of six expectations for a marital partner. The most important for both men and women was that the person be a "helpmate/partner," mentioned by 55.1% of the women and 53.6% of the men. For women, this was followed by "someone to talk things over with" (mentioned by 51.0%), whereas this ranked third for men (46.4%) behind "sexual partner" (50.0%). "Sexual partner" ranked last for women (14.3%). "Parent" and "provider" were tied for women, with 30.6% choosing each of these, whereas these two items were ranked last by men, with only 7.1% mentioning "parent" or "home-maker." For women, "leisure-time companion" ranked fifth, with only 18.4% mentioning it as their first or second choice; for men this ranked fourth, with 35.7% mentioning it. The differences in rankings by gender are quite striking, and reflect what the multiple-regression analysis has also indicated: Women who were repartnered looked for good provid-ers. Although the married and cohabiting said (as noted above) that the most important part of their new relationship was companionship, apparently companionship was easier with a solid financial base.

Because they were either more demanding, more wary, or less lucky in finding persons to date, the single reported more problems in having their expectations met in their current relationships than was true for the remarried and cohabiting. A question about whether there were any problems in partners' or friends' meeting expectations in the six marital roles was asked of all the divorced respondents. Although the numbers are small, several trends are apparent. First, as was true both for divorced respondents describing their earlier marriages and for married respondents describing their current ones (see Chapter 4), sin-gle, remarried, and cohabiting women all reported more complaints about men than men did about women. For single and remarried/cohabiting women, the most frequent problem area was "parent" (men-tioned, respectively, by 28.6% and 33.3%). The most problematic area for remarried/cohabiting men was likewise "parent" (20.2%), whereas slightly more single men mentioned "someone to talk things over with" (19.2%) than "parent" (18.2%) as the most problematic area. The least often cited problem role for single women and men was "sexual partner" (mentioned, respectively, by 11.9% and 11.5%), whereas 4.5% of the remarried/cohabiting women and 3.6% of the men ranked "leisure-time companion" as the least problematic area.

These findings may mean that women who divorce are especially critical of their partners, which might also have been one reason for their divorces. However, this explanation seems unlikely, because the women in the married comparison group were also more critical of their husbands than the husbands were about their wives (see Chap-ter 4). Alternatively, this finding may mean that women are more likely to assess the "emotional temperature" of a relationship than are men (see also Weiss, 1990, on this point). Second, the rank order of complaints differed for men and women. Among men, those who were still single had more complaints than those who were remarried or cohabiting, whereas the total differences in complaints were negligible between the two groups of women. Among the men, the single reported substantially more concerns about the roles of "leisure-time companion" and "someone to talk things over with" than did those with new partners (respectively, 15.4% and 3.7% for "leisure-time companion" and 19.2% and 3.6% for "someone to talk things over with"). But in neither case were men's concerns about these issues as great as they were for single women (19.0% for "leisure-time companion" and 23.8% for "someone to talk things over with") and for the remarried (22.7% for "someone to talk things over with"). Thus, companionship and having a partner with whom it was possible to talk were substantial problems both for many persons in their previous marriages and for the continuously married; they continued to be problems for the single in looking for new relationships and for the repartnered in establishing new ones. Those who were still single seemed to be taking care in finding new partners.

CONCLUSION

In this chapter, some of the experiences and problems of the suburban divorced sample after the divorce was granted have been explored. Many respondents reported that they felt stigmatized by others as a result of the divorce. A scale assessing a sense of stigmatization reflected a greater sense of stigma for whites than for nonwhites. It is unclear whether the sense of being stigmatized is the result of "real" reactions from others or a projection of the divorced respondents' own sense of marital failure.

Many of the divorced—even those without children—continued to maintain contacts with their ex-spouses. These contacts and the continuing anger with their ex-spouses reflect the ambivalence of the divorced about their former partners.

Virtually all of the subjects reported some difficulties taking on new tasks and establishing themselves after the divorce, but for the most part these difficulties faded with time. Nonwhites (here, predominantly blacks) seemed to have fewer difficulties adjusting than whites. Because of the high divorce rate in the black community, divorce may seem a less unusual event, and thus adjustment may be less difficult.

Those who sought divorces under no-fault provisions felt that the divorce was friendlier and less conflictual, but there were no differences in satisfaction with the legal process. In the suburban study, those who obtained fault-based divorces were less psychologically upset than those who used no-fault provisions. In the marital transition study, there were no differences in depression or anger by the type of decree. Thus, no-fault provisions do not seem to lessen psychological distress in divorce. Relatively few respondents returned to the court for postdivorce legal actions; when they did, the court appearances involved money or property.

By the time of the third interview, 4 in 10 of the subjects were remarried, cohabiting, or engaged; many of the remaining respondents were dating. Thus, a number of the divorced were interested in re-establishing relationships. Men with higher incomes, and those of both sexes who were younger and had no or fewer children were more likely to be reaffiliated by the third interview, 2–3 years after divorce.

Only a very few of the single appeared to be isolated (6%). Most were involved in dating, going out with friends, or visiting with relatives. Those who had found new partners seemed less wary in their choice of new partners than those who remained single. They more often found them at work and through casual contacts.

For those who had not yet found a new partner, concerns about their children or the presence of children from a potential partner's previous marriage seemed to be factors. In new relationships, as in their former marriages, the most problematic areas in terms of having marital expectations met were the roles of "leisure-time companion" and "someone to talk things over with." These data and the similar findings reported for the married in Chapter 4 highlight the pre-eminence of these concerns in relationships today.

CHAPTER 11

Adjustment to Divorce: Cross-Sectional and Longitudinal Patterns

The ceremony was elaborate but tasteful. I wore black and was attended by my lawyer, his paralegal, two uniformed clerks, one stenographer, and the judge, who avoided my gaze the way doctors do in intensive care units. In six months and one day, he advised me, we would be free to marry again, and with any luck, repeat the entire episode.

Two weeks later, I visited my lawyer to discuss a bill and reminisce. "You look much better since your divorce," he told me. "You look much better since my divorce," I told him, realizing with sudden clarity that this was a dangerously attractive man. But even if he were single and I had more chrome, I was too eroded by divorce to relish an opportunity.

"Don't confuse me," he said, "or I'll put your papers in someone else's file."

"If you do, I'll wind up divorced from the wrong man."

He looked up from his memos. "I would hope you already are."

—Barron (1985, p. 20)

At the first interview, as discussed in Chapter 6, a substantial number of the suburban divorced sample had heightened scores on the measure of subjective distress, low scores on self-esteem, heightened scores on the illness contacts inventory, and high scores on attachment. For many, this distress decreased with time, but what characteristics or experiences helped? What distinguished those whose distress scores did not improve from those whose scores did? In this chapter, patterns of adjustment to divorce are examined both cross-sectionally and across time, in order to determine differences and similarities in outcome for men and women, whites and non-whites.

Even when an attempt is made to simulate a longitudinal design by interviewing people at varying lengths of time after a divorce (Goode, 1956), much research on divorce has been cross-sectional, looking at individuals only once (Albrecht et al., 1983; Spanier & Thompson, 1984). Because much of what is known about divorce is based on such designs, the question arises of what can be learned from one such look. The data from one time period are clearly useful, but do patterns observed at one point continue over time, or do they change? Is it realistic, as is often done, to describe "the process of adjustment to divorce" on the basis of such data? The present chapter addresses this issue by examining which factors are associated with better and worse adjustment scores cross-sectionally and then longitudinally, to determine whether these factors can "predict" adjustment across time. A question to be addressed is this: If certain variables are associated with better or worse adjustment scores at the first interview, what do these associations explain about adjustment at the second or third interview? If there are uniformities and stability in results across time, then these analyses will provide a sense of greater confidence in the findings of cross-sectional studies. If they do not, then the risks of attempting to generalize beyond the period of time covered in a cross-sectional study are clearer. In addition, this chapter explores what set of factors and which of two models of the process of adjustment to divorce provide the most information about coping with divorce.

MODELS OF ADJUSTMENT TO DIVORCE

As has been noted, adjustment to divorce has less often been a focus for research than have the causes or correlates of the decision to divorce. Relatively little is known about what makes adjustment to a divorce more or less difficult. In this section, some of the leading explanations or models for exploring adjustment to divorce that have been described earlier in the book are briefly reviewed.

The Pathology Model

Marital separation and divorce have repeatedly been shown to be associated with high rates of physical and psychological mortality and morbidity, but why? One explanation stresses the role that pathology and selectivity play: Those who divorce are thought to be somehow less fit to be married because of their psychological or social characteristics. The psychological problems of one or both partners are believed to produce the divorce, and these problems are thought to make postdivorce adjustment difficult as well. Although such a model is commonly invoked as an explanation, there are few cross-sectional or longitudinal studies that explore its implications (for some exceptions, see Blumenthal, 1967; Briscoe et al., 1973; Briscoe & Smith, 1973, 1974, 1975; Ilfeld, 1978). This model is not directly examined in this chapter except as part of the loss model, to be discussed below.

The Life Events Model

Another approach to the study of the divorce process looks at adjustment as a response to a stressful life event (Holmes & Rahe, 1967; Myers et al., 1972). Individuals have to cope with the dislocations in accustomed patterns of thinking and acting brought about by the end of their marriages. With time, resources, and help from others, individuals are able to regain the level of functioning they had prior to the marital breakdown. This approach could also be called the "crisis model," but the length of time involved in coping with the event makes this a less useful descriptor.

According to the life events approach, the event itself creates the disturbance in functioning, not prior characteristics or circumstances (Ahrons & Rodgers, 1987; Bloom, Hodges, et al., 1985; Buehler et al., 1985–1986; Ensel, 1986; Myers et al., 1972; Raschke, 1977; Spanier & Thompson, 1984; Tschann et al., 1989). As Bloom et al. (1978) suggest, this stress or life events approach can also include attention to roles by stating that certain social roles, particularly gender roles, may create different risks of distress for individuals as they enter or leave different marital statuses. The life events approach, as it is used to study divorce, often leaves out the meaning of the event for the participants. In fact, the definition of the event may account for many of the adjustment difficulties experienced in divorce.

The Loss Model

A third approach attempts to link the crisis and pathology models. It views divorce as an event involving not only change, but also loss. It sees divorce as a negative or exit-related event (Dohrenwend et al., 1978; Simos, 1979). According to this approach, certain individuals may well have greater difficulty adjusting to the breakdown of their marriages because of prior losses or psychological vulnerabilities. A substantial body of research on adjustment to the death of a spouse has taken such an approach. It stretches back to the work of Erich Lindemann (1944) describing the reactions of survivors of the 1942 Cocoanut Grove nightclub fire (see also Bornstein, Clayton, Halikas, Maurice, & Robins, 1973; Clayton, 1979; Clayton, Desmarais, & Winokur,

1968; Parkes, 1972; Parkes & Weiss, 1983; Raphael, 1983; Windholz, Marmar, & Horowitz, 1985; Zisook & Shuchter, 1986). In fact, similar factors may affect adjustment in widowhood and divorce (for a review, see Kitson et al., 1989).

The Loss Hypothesis

As described in Chapter 6, the impact of negative or loss-related life events such as the sequelae of divorce can have a long-lasting impact on health status. A loss model incorporates elements of pathology, selectivity, or vulnerability, while also examining characteristics of the relationship that may make adjustment difficult. According to this approach, part of the distress the divorced experience may be related to the losses sustained prior to the divorce, and part of it to issues occurring at the time of the marital dissolution, coupled with the highly ambivalent state in which divorced persons find themselves afterward. It is often hard for a divorced person and those around him or her to understand that it is possible to be simultaneously glad to be out of a bad marriage, grieving for the end of the relationship, pining for the ex-spouse, and angry at him or her. In addition, although divorce is certainly a more common and acceptable solution for marital distress than it was in earlier years, being divorced is still to some extent considered a stigmatized status, even by those who divorce. Thus, the loss of status represented by the shift from being married to being single, the loss of a once and possibly still loved partner, and the economic and other losses associated with the end of a marriage may help account for the heightened distress of the divorced. If a person has experienced other losses prior to the divorce and additional losses since the divorce, he or she may be in an especially hazardous situation. Taking such losses into account may explain more about the difficulties in adjustment associated with marital dissolution than a more traditional life events or crisis approach may.

　　To test this loss hypothesis, two models of divorce adjustment are examined in this chapter to determine which accounts for more of the distress experienced by the divorced. The first is the life events model, and the second is the loss model. It is hypothesized that the loss model should be a more powerful approach for examining divorce adjustment than the crisis model should be.

Characteristics of the Loss Model

The loss model of adjustment to divorce being used is based upon the work of Colin Murray Parkes (1972, 1975, 1982, 1986) in predicting bereavement outcome after the death of a spouse. Parkes divides outcome predictors into three sets of factors: "antecedent," "concurrent," and "subsequent."

Antecedent factors are those events or experiences that may predispose an individual to a more severe reaction to a loss. These include losses of significant others in childhood or adulthood; previous mental illness; the occurrence of other life events at about the time of the new loss; the timing of the event; and the importance, strength, and degree of ambivalence of the individual's relationship with the lost partner.

Concurrent factors include sociocultural background characteristics such as age, race, social class, and religion. Among other social and cultural factors thought to influence a person's ability to handle losses are social expectations. For example, some social groups may not tolerate open expressions of distress, and therefore may inhibit adjustment to difficult experiences for their members. There may also be, as noted above, a covert or not so covert expectation that people should be married and living with their spouses; those who are not may be stigmatized.

Other factors that are predicted to influence adjustment to a loss are subsequent events or opportunities that are available to or open up for an individual. These include the person's degree of social involvement or isolation (and new opportunities or activities arising from social involvement), secondary stresses (such as the presence of children), employment opportunities, and money problems.

Steps Taken to Test the Models

Because the loss model includes a number of factors—in fact, many of the factors examined in the preceding chapters—the remainder of this chapter proceeds in several steps. First, correlations between the indicators of the concepts hypothesized to influence adjustment are examined, to determine which are associated with the indicators of adjustment (subjective distress, attachment, self-esteem, and illness contacts) and with two independent variables that have repeatedly been associated with differences in adjustment, gender and race. Then, those variables that are significantly associated with at least some of the dependent variables are entered into multiple regressions to test the loss and life events models. The following questions are explored: (1) Which model (life events or loss) is more closely associated with better adjustment cross-sectionally? (2) Which model better predicts adjustment across time?

HOW THE VARIABLES IN THE MODELS
WERE MEASURED

This section describes the way in which the variables were constructed to assess the models. Items that were asked at several interviews were coded in the same manner across the various time periods. Many of the items in the two models are the same; the models differ in the inclusion of measures of loss in the loss model.

Antecedent Variables

Several measures of prior losses were developed. First was a measure of childhood loss, based on whether the parental home was disrupted by death of a parent or divorce before the respondent was aged 11. With more subjects, death or divorce of parents would be examined individually as types of loss, but here a combined measure was used: No parental loss was coded as 0, and parental loss was coded as 1. A previous marriage for the respondent that ended in either divorce or death of the spouse, and having previously been hospitalized for a mental illness, were two more measures of loss. In each case, no occurrence of the event was coded as 0, and occurrence was coded as 1.

Three measures of life events were used: the total number of life events that occurred in the year prior to the first interview; the weighted total of life events; and the weighted total of negative life events, a loss measure. (See Chapter 6 for a description of these items.)

Having sought mental health help from a psychiatrist or psychologist, marriage counselor, or social worker within the last year for personal problems was another item likely to influence adjustment. The more inclusive measure of any mental health help received by the respondent was used, rather than whether the help was received alone or with others, because in these analyses any help received by the respondent was more strongly associated with the dependent variables than was either help received alone or help received jointly.

Measures of the marital relationship and its quality included (1) whom the respondent blamed for the divorce, which was coded 0 for the respondent or a joint decision and 1 for the spouse; (2) the combined causes for divorce variables, "instrumental" and "serious" marital problems, treated as dummy variables, with "expressive" problems as the criterion category (see Chapter 5 for a description of these variables); (3) continued anger with the (ex-)spouse, with 1 meaning "not at all my feelings" and 5 "very much my feelings" (see Chapter 10); (4) a variable counting the number of ways the respondent felt the couple grew apart (see Chapter 4); and (5) who suggested the divorce, coded as 0 for the respondent or a mutual decision and 1 for the spouse.

Although the questions were only asked at the second interview, the scale for the variable of reasons for hesitating to divorce (see Chapter 4 for a description) has been used even in analyses for the first interview, because the items asked for retrospective recall of why the divorce might have been delayed. Hesitating to divorce has been defined as a loss variable, because the reasons for hesitating involve loss of status, income, and so forth. Finally, an indicator of the recency of the divorce decision was how long ago the divorce was suggested. Length of the marriage until the couple separated was also included as a measure.

Concurrent Variables

The concurrent or sociocultural factors affecting adjustment included the respondent's age and social class (i.e., his or her own ranking on the Index of Social Position [Hollingshead, 1957] where this was available). For those who were not employed at the first interview, generally women, the husband's social class position was used. For later interviews, the variable was recomputed for those whose occupation and education had changed. Religion was assessed through church attendance; the extent to which religion influenced the respondent's daily life; and religious denomination, which was coded as a series of dummy variables (Roman Catholic versus all others; Jewish; and all Protestants, subdivided into main-line Protestants and fundamentalist Protestants). The category "none" was used as the criterion variable. Help from friends or the (ex-)spouse's or respondent's family was classified into help with finances, services, and information; in each case, no help, was coded as 0 and the number of help sources (friends, ex-spouse's family, and respondent's family) was coded from 1 to 3.

Postdivorce Variables

Variables that might influence adjustment after the event included the level of income the respondent anticipated in the year after the first interview and his or her actual level of income at the third interview. Employment status was coded 0 for no employment and 1 for full- or part-time employment. The variable of hours worked was coded as follows: 0 for no hours of employment, 1 for part-time work, 2 for full-time work, and 3 for both full- and part-time employment.

Several variables were included concerning children: the number of children born of the marriage, the number living with the respondent, and a set of life-cycle-related variables. The presence of children in the household was coded as 0 for no children and 1 for one or more children. For those with children, the life cycle stage of the family was coded with a series of dummy variables for preschool children, children in grade school, and teenage children. "Empty nest" families, with all children over the age of 18, constituted the criterion category. As a measure of secondary stress associated with the children, a variable for no help with the children was based on whether the parent reported help with the responsibilities of "disciplining the children" and "helping the children with homework" (see Chapter 9). No help with either activity was scored as 2, and help with one was scored as 1.

Measures of the respondent's social opportunities included the number of friends with whom he or she talked confidentially, frequency of dating, and the number of solitary leisure-time activities ("reading," "watching TV, listening to records/radio," and "social drinking in bars"; see Chapter 9). Although "social drinking in bars" could obviously be done either alone or with others, its pattern of associations fit with these solitary activities.

FACTORS INFLUENCING ADJUSTMENT: CORRELATION COEFFICIENTS

Table 11.1 displays zero-order Pearson's correlation coefficients between the series of variables designed to measure concepts in the life events and loss models on the one hand, and gender, race, and the dependent variables of subjective distress, attachment, self-esteem, and the illness contacts index on the other. Because of the size of the correlation matrix that would be produced if all the correlations were reported, only the factors significantly associated with better or poorer adjustment at the first interview are displayed. Dummy variables were used for gender and race, with males and whites coded 0 and females and nonwhites coded 1.

Among the correlations of the antecedent factors hypothesized to influence adjustment, nonwhite respondents were significantly more likely than whites to report that their parents' marriages ended in the death of a parent or in divorce before they themselves reached the age of 11. The only variable with which the life events measures were associated was the illness contacts measure, with those with more life events reporting more illnesses. All three of the life events measures

TABLE 11.1. Pearson's Correlations of Dependent Variables (Subjective Distress, Attachment, Illness Contacts Index, Self-Esteem), Gender, and Race with Independent Variables (Antecedent, Concurrent, and Postdivorce Characteristics): Suburban Divorced Sample at First Interview

Independent variables	Dependent variables					
	Attachment	Subjective distress	Self-esteem	Illness contacts index	Gender	Race
	Antecedent variables					
Total number of life events	.00	.04	−.06	.18*	−.10	−.13
Weighted total life events	.01	.07	−.04	.24***	−.11	−.10
Weighted negative total life events (L)	.07	.12	−.02	.26***	−.12	−.05
Previously divorced or widowed (L)	−.06	.09	−.03	−.02	.03	.10
Parents' marriage ended (L)	−.09	−.16*	.05	−.04	−.12	.24***
Anger at (ex)-spouse (L)	.24***	.21**	.11	.12	.11	−.15*
Reasons for hesitating to divorce (L)	.11	.13	.11	−.04	.21*	.03
Couple grew apart	−.24***	−.06	−.08	.17*	.05	−.07
Any mental health help in last year of marriage	.17*	.22**	.08	.15*	.13	−.17*
Ever any mental health hospitalization (L)	.09	.14*	−.08	.25***	.15*	.00
Who suggested divorce	.30***	.02	.11	−.11	−.32***	−.07
Who is to blame for divorce	.03	.01	−.11	.10	.29***	.13
Serious marital complaints	.09	.17*	.01	.04	.26***	−.11
Instrumental marital complaints	−.03	.05	.06	−.02	.13	−.07
How long ago divorce suggested	−.18*	−.15*	.03	−.03	−.05	.10
How long separated	−.14*	−.21**	.07	.07	−.05	.25***
Length of marriage	−.08	.02	−.02	−.02	−.16*	−.01

298

Concurrent variables

Age	.02	−.04	−.02	−.04	−.24***	.05
Respondent's social class position	.05	.04	.00	.12	−.01	.12
Financial support	−.05	.02	.08	.09	.21**	−.11
Service support	.04	.03	.07	.03	.17*	.04
Information support	.10	.05	.11	−.01	.15*	−.09
Roman Catholic	.20**	.15*	.02	.10	.10	−.23***
Protestant (all denominations)	−.04	−.16*	−.08	−.08	.11	.28***
Jewish	−.06	−.04	−.04	.01	−.08	−.13
Protestant (fundamentalist)	−.07	−.14*	−.04	−.11	.00	.45***
Protestant (main-line)	.01	−.06	−.06	.00	.12	−.05
Church attendance	−.03	.03	−.01	.06	−.12	−.20*
Influence of religion	−.04	.08	.04	−.05	−.05	−.18**

(continued)

TABLE 11.1. (*Continued*)

Independent variables	Dependent variables					
	Attachment	Subjective distress	Self-esteem	Illness contacts index	Gender	Race
	Postdivorce variables					
Estimated income coming year	.01	–.11	–.03	–.17*	–.49***	–.03
Employment status	–.08	–.05	–.07	–.20**	–.20**	–.04
Number of hours worked	–.08	–.03	–.04	–.18**	–.23***	.00
Number of confidants	.11	.10	.00	.04	.17*	–.31***
Number of children with respondent	.01	.04	–.03	.14*	.34***	.01
Number of children born to union	.06	.00	.06	.07	.01	.04
No children	.05	.00	–.07	–.02	.03	.19**
Preschool-age children	.07	.01	.02	–.03	.13	.09
Grade-school-age children	.03	.08	–.09	.00	.07	.07
Teenage children	–.10	–.17*	–.08	–.06	–.11	.04
Solitary activities	.00	.03	–.11	.14*	–.02	–.11
No help with children	–.02	.05	.01	.07	.35***	.01

Note. (L) indicates a variable included in the loss model.
  *$p < .05$.
 **$p < .01$.
***$p < .001$.

300

were associated with the illness contacts inventory, but the strongest correlation was with the weighted negative events score. Having been hospitalized for mental illness was associated with illness contacts, with subjective distress, and also with gender (more women than men reported such hospitalizations). Those with higher subjective distress scores, higher levels of attachment, and higher illness contacts scores at the first interview were more likely to have sought mental health help for problems in the year prior to the first interview.

Women were more likely than men to report having hesitated to divorce because of various kinds of losses or other reasons, but the variable was not associated with the dependent variables. Reporting that the couple grew apart was associated with higher scores on attachment and the illness contacts measure. None of the dependent variables or race, was significantly associated with length of marriage. Women reported shorter marriages than men did.

Women were more likely to blame their husbands for the divorce than were men their wives. Instrumental complaints were not associated with any of the adjustment variables or with race or gender. Serious marital complaints, however, were positively associated with subjective distress and with being female. Anger with the spouse was associated with higher levels of subjective distress and greater attachment. The more recently the divorce had been suggested, the higher the amount of subjective distress and the greater the attachment to the (ex-)spouse. Similarly, those who had more recently separated reported more subjective distress. Nonwhites reported significantly longer separations than did whites.

Virtually all of the independent variables measuring antecedent factors were associated with the dependent variables of gender or race. Although self-esteem was strongly associated with the other adjustment variables, as indicated in Chapter 6, none of the independent variables was significantly associated with it.

Among the concurrent factors, the respondent's age and social class were not associated with any of the dependent variables, but age was associated with gender (women were younger than men). Women were more likely to receive help from others (with finances, services, and information) than were men. Neither church attendance nor the influence of religion was associated with the dependent variables, but whites were less likely than nonwhites to report attending church frequently or to feel that religion influenced their daily lives. Roman Catholics had higher scores on attachment and subjective distress while those of any Protestant denomination had lower scores on subjective distress.

Among the postdivorce variables, having lower income, not being employed, and being employed fewer or no hours were associated with more illness contacts and with being female, but not with any of the other indicators.

Few of the measures of the presence, age, or number of children were significantly associated with the outcome measures. Nonwhites were more likely to report children being present, and those with more children living with them were more likely to have high scores on the illness contacts index. Only one indicator of the life cycle stage of the children was associated with any of the adjustment measures: Having anything but teenage children was associated with more distress. Women were also more likely to report having no help with the children. Solitary activities were associated with higher scores on the illness contacts index.

In summary, virtually all of the independent variables were associated with some of the dependent variables or with race or gender. This means that it was difficult to winnow out variables to exclude from the multiple-regression analyses. A large number of variables in such an analysis has an impact on how strong a relationship needs to be before it becomes significant: When more variables are entered into a regression equation, the degrees of freedom are increased, as is the strength of the correlation needed to reach significance.

MULTIPLE CORRELATIONS FOR ADJUSTMENT AT THE TIME OF FILING FOR THE DIVORCE

In this section, the findings about the combinations of factors playing the most important role in making adjustment more difficult at the time of the first interview, or at the time the divorce was filed, in the suburban divorced sample are discussed. The statistical technique employed in these analyses was stepwise multiple regression (R^2). After all of the variance in the dependent variable under study that could be explained by the independent variables was accounted for, the other three dependent variables were entered to see whether any of them added to the amount of variance explained in the dependent variable being examined. The dependent variable of attachment was itself a measure of loss, but this approach made it possible to see what, if any, additional contribution attachment would make to each of the other regression equations with and without the addition of other loss variables. Only those correlations significant at the .05 level are considered here. Because so many of the scores for the dependent variables differed by race and gender, the results for men and women and whites and nonwhites are examined separately. For those analyses conducted by gender, race was entered as an independent variable, and for those analyses done by race, gender was entered as an independent variable.

The results are displayed with and without the addition of the loss variables. To recapitulate, the loss variables were as follows: hesitating to divorce, being angry with the (ex-)spouse, having been married previously, having experienced negative life events in the past year, having been hospitalized for an emotional or mental illness, and the parents' marriage having ended by death or divorce before the respondent was aged 11. The expectation is that the loss variables should contribute significantly to an understanding of the adjustment process.

There are several points to be made about the regression analyses displayed in Tables 11.2 (for gender) and 11.3 (for race). First, there was relatively little overlap in the independent variables that entered the equations for men and women and for whites and nonwhites. Second, more variance was explained for women than for men and for whites than for nonwhites; thus, these data indicate more about the factors influencing initial adjustment for women and for whites. In one sense, as the analyses in Chapter 6 illustrate, women and whites had more adjustment difficulties than men and nonwhites, so there was more variance to explain, and yet there is little indication in these cross-sectional data of what might make adjustment easier for some men and for some nonwhites than for others. Third, the loss model explained more variance than did the life events model; thus, coping with the losses that the divorce brought was an important part of adjustment for many. Fourth, even though a substantial and significant amount of variance was explained, anywhere from two-thirds to one-half of the variance was not explained. This means either that other factors that were not explored influenced the respondents' adjustment or that the size of the sample restricted the complexity of the analyses that could be done. Both of these explanations are likely to be true. Fifth, the other dependent variables added to the variance explained after the independent variables explained what they could. This reconfirms that adjustment is best considered a multidimensional phenomenon. The following sections examine the specific findings for each of the adjustment measures by gender and race.

Gender Differences

In testing the life events model for the adjustment variable of subjective distress for men (see Table 11.2), only one of the independent variables entered the equation, race: White men expressed more distress than nonwhite men, as indicated by the negative standardized beta coefficient (−.24). With an R of .24, only 6% of the variance in

TABLE 11.2. Life Events and Loss Models for Adjustment at the First Interview by Gender: Multiple Correlations

Dependent adjustment variables, model tested, and independent variables	Males (n = 102)			Females (n = 107)		
	R	R^2	β	R	R^2	β
Subjective distress: Life events						
Race	.24	.06	−.24*	—	—	—
Estimated income coming year	—	—	—	.25	.06	−.25*
Roman Catholic	—	—	—	.34	.11	.23*
Self-esteem	.46	.21	.39***	.60	.36	.26*
Attachment	.56	.31	.33***	.55	.30	.43***[a]
Illness contacts index	—	—	—	.65	.42	.24*
Subjective distress: Loss						
Previously divorced or widowed	.27	.07	.27*	—	—	—
Anger at (ex-)spouse	—	—	—	.34	.11	.34**
Race	.38	.14	−.27*	—	—	—
Reasons for hesitating to divorce	—	—	—	.43	.19	.27*
Attachment	.53	.28	.38***	.55	.30	.36**
Illness contacts index	—	—	—	.62	.38	.29***
Self-esteem	.62	.38	.32***	.66	.44	.27*
Attachment: Life events						
Couple grew apart	—	—	—	.33	.11	−.33**
Roman Catholic	.34	.11	.34*	—	—	—
Any mental health help in last year of marriage	—	—	—	.41	.16	.24*
Preschool-age children	.48	.24	.35*	—	—	—
Who first suggested divorce	.54	.29	.23*	—	—	—
Subjective distress	.65	.42	.37***	.57	.32	.40***
Attachment: Loss						
Roman Catholic	.34	.12	.34*	—	—	—
Anger at (ex-)spouse	—	—	—	.25	.06	.25*
Preschool-age children	.48	.24	.35	—	—	—
Who first suggested the divorce	.54	.29	.23*	—	—	—
Subjective distress	.65	.42	.37***	.47	.22	.42***
Self-esteem: Life events						
Subjective distress	.37	.14	.37***	.44	.19	.44***
Self-esteem: Loss						
Reasons for hesitating to divorce	—	—	—	.30	.09	.30*
Financial support	—	—	—	.40	.16	.28*
Subjective distress	.37	.14	.37***	.58	.31	.40***
Illness contacts index: Life events						
Solitary activities	.38	.14	.38***	—	—	—
Who suggested the divorce	.43	.18	−.21***	—	—	—
Any mental health help in last year of marriage	—	—	—	.26	.07	.26*

(continued)

TABLE 11.2. (*Continued*)

Dependent adjustment variables, model tested, and independent variables	Males (n = 102)			Females (n = 107)		
	R	R^2	β	R	R^2	β
Employment status	—	—	—	.34	.12	−.22*
Subjective distress	—	—	—	.46	.21	.32***
Illness contacts index: Loss						
Solitary activities	.38	.14	.38***	—	—	—
Weighted negative total life events	—	—	—	.46	.21	.46***
Subjective distress	—	—	—	.56	.31	.35**

^aFor display purposes, the statistics for the attachment measure for women are out of order and should, in terms of the statistics, precede self-esteem.
*p < .05.
**p < .01.
***p < .001.

subjective distress was accounted for, as indicated by the R^2 of .06. Twenty-five percent more variance was explained by allowing the other dependent adjustment variables to enter. Self-esteem and attachment each made a contribution, with low self-esteem and higher attachment associated with higher distress.

The loss model explained somewhat more variance than the life events model for men before the other dependent variables were entered, with an R^2 of .14 versus an R^2 of .06. The most strongly associated measure was one assessing previous losses: Men who were previously married were more distressed, while race again entered the equation. In this equation, as opposed to the life events model, attachment entered the equation before self-esteem. Overall, with an R^2 of .38, the loss model explained 7% more variance that did the life events model, with an R^2 of .31.

In the test of the life events model for subjective distress for women, more variance was explained than was true for men before the dependent variables were entered. Women who anticipated lower incomes in the year following the first interview and who were Roman Catholic were more distressed. All three of the dependent variables also made significant contributions to the explained variance, with attachment making the greatest, followed by self-esteem and the illness contacts inventory. Thus, some of the anxiety and depression experienced was accounted for by continued attachment to the (ex-)spouse, low self-esteem, and the illness contacts index. The variables that made a significant contribution to the subjective distress score for women in the life events model explained 42% of the variance.

Eight percent more variance was explained by the independent variables in the loss model of subjective distress for women ($R^2 = .19$ vs. $R^2 = .11$ in the life events model), and 2% more variance was explained overall, with an R^2 of .44 versus .42. The independent variables in the loss model accounted for some of the variance that would otherwise be accounted for by the other dependent adjustment measures. Only two independent measures of loss entered the equation: Distress was higher for those who were angry with their partners and who were more hesitant to divorce. The other three adjustment variables also made contributions, with the greatest being made by attachment. High scores on subjective distress were associated with high scores on attachment and the illness contacts index, and a low score on self-esteem.

When the attachment measure was used as the dependent variable, more variance was explained for men than for women in both models. This was the only variable of the various gender-based multiple-regression analyses at the first interview for which this was true. In the life events model, Catholic men were more attached than non-Catholics, as were men who reported that their wives wanted the divorce. Men who had preschool-age children were also more attached. Only one of the dependent variables entered the equation, subjective distress, but it almost doubled the amount of explained variance (from .19 to .36).

None of the loss variables entered the equation for men. Only two of the three independent variables that appeared in the life events model entered the loss model for subjective distress: being Roman Catholic and reporting that the wife suggested the divorce. Higher subjective distress was also associated wth higher attachment scores.

For women in the life events model, two of the independent variables and one of the other adjustment measures made significant contributions to the attachment score. Those who reported having grown apart from their spouses were less likely to be attached at the first interview, whereas higher attachment scores were associated with having sought mental health help. It is possible that the distress of separation anxiety led to the seeking of therapeutic help. Similarly, higher subjective distress was also associated with higher attachment.

Only one independent variable made a contribution to the loss model for women: Anger with the (ex-)spouse was associated with higher attachment. Subjective distress was also associated with higher attachment scores.

For the self-esteem variable, none of the independent variables made a significant contribution for men or women in the life events model, or for men in the loss model. In each equation, however, the adjustment variable of subjective distress explained a significant amount of the variance; high subjective distress was associated with low self-esteem. For women in the loss model, two independent variables were significantly associated with self-esteem: Those who were more hesitant to divorce because of fears about the future and those who received financial help from friends or family were more likely to have low self-esteem. It is difficult to disentangle cause and effect in cross-sectional data, but it is plausible that one reason for hesitating to divorce may be lack of confidence in one's ability to cope without one's partner. Similarly, being unable to cope financially as an adult without having to turn to others for help, regardless of the severity of the circumstances, is also likely to erode confidence.

The life events model for the index of illness contacts was associated with more solitary activities for men. These activities may have been the result of illness, or both illness and the choice of these activities may have resulted from the events of the divorce. Men who reported that the suggestion to divorce was their own or was a joint decision were less likely to report illness symptoms. None of the dependent variables entered the life events or loss models. In the loss model, only the number of solitary activities explained any of the variance.

For women in the life events model, problems with physical health were associated with having sought mental health help in the past year and lack of employment. Problems requiring counseling and being unemployed were associated with more illness contacts. Psychological distress can affect physical health, and vice versa; similarly, physical health problems may make it harder to be employed, or problems in finding employment may make health problems loom larger. Subjective distress also increased the amount of variance that was explained: Illness problems were exacerbated by feeling anxious and depressed.

When the loss variables were entered, only one variable made a significant contribution—negative life events in the year prior to the interview—but this one variable explained as much variance as did the whole life events model ($R^2 = .21$). With the addition of the variance accounted for by the adjustment variable of subjective distress, the total variance explained was .31.

Perhaps the most striking finding in this analysis is the lack of overlap in the variables that influenced adjustment by gender. At the same time, however, fairly consistent findings concerning the relationship of the other dependent variables were obtained. Although women were generally affected more severely than men, both were troubled by symptoms of anxiety and depression, continued attachment to the ex-spouse, low self-esteem, and illnesses.

Race Differences

The data on race indicate that few of the independent or dependent variables made contributions for nonwhites, whereas more variance was explained for whites (Table 11.3). As discussed in Chapter 6, the nonwhite respondents initially exhibited less distress than whites. The independent variables assessed in these analyses did not account for much variance in the distress of those nonwhites having a more difficult time adjusting at the first, or time-of-filing, interview.

The independent variable that made the first contribution to explaining the subjective distress levels of whites in the life events model was having sought mental health help in the previous year. Having sought help may have produced the distress, or, as is more likely, those who were distressed sought help. Having teenagers in the home was associated with less distress, as was a higher social class position. Although being the parent of teenage children brings its own tribulations, apparently rearing younger children produces even greater distress in the initial stages of a divorce. This is presumably because smaller children require more constant, active supervision, a task that is generally not shared with others. Low self-esteem was associated with high distress, as were high scores on attachment and the illness contacts inventory.

Adding the loss variables increased the amount of variance explained by the independent variables from .11 to .14. The first two variables to enter the equation were, again, having sought mental health help and having teenagers in the home. These were followed by two loss measures, having previously been married and being angry with the (ex-)spouse, both of which were associated with heightened distress. Having had a previous marriage end (generally by divorce) was associated with increased anxiety and depression concerning the end of the study marriage. It was probably harder for a respondent to feel that he or she had made a mistake in choosing a partner if two or more marriages had failed; instead, the person may have had to think more about his or her own contribution to the failure. Anger itself is often tied to depressive affect; this perhaps accounts for the association displayed here.

All three of the dependent variables again contributed to the explained variance. The independent variables in the loss model did not make as much of a contribution as those in the life events model; they did, however, allow 3% more variance to enter the model overall. Among nonwhites, only attachment made a contribution to explaining the level of subjective distress at the first interview, and only in the life events model, not the loss model.

TABLE 11.3. Life Events and Loss Models for Adjustment at the First
Interview by Race: Multiple Correlations

Dependent adjustment variables, model tested, and independent variables	Whites (n = 153)			Nonwhites (n = 56)		
	R	R²	β	R	R²	β
Subjective distress: Life events						
Any mental health help in last year of marriage	.19	.04	.19°	—	—	—
Teenage children	.28	.08	−.20°	—	—	—
Respondent's social class position	.33	.11	.18°	—	—	—
Self-esteem	.52	.27	.41°°°	—	—	—
Attachment	.57	.33	.27°°°	.31	.10	.31°
Illness contacts index	.61	.37	.20°°°	—	—	—
Subjective distress: Loss						
Any mental health help in last year of marriage	.19	.04	.19°	—	—	—
Teenage children	.28	.08	−.20°	—	—	—
Previously widowed or divorced	.33	.11	.18°	—	—	—
Anger at (ex-)spouse	.37	.14	.16°	—	—	—
Self-esteem	.53	.28	.39°°°	—	—	—
Attachment	.59	.35	.29°°°	—	—	—
Illness contacts index	.63	.40	.22°°	—	—	—
Attachment: Life events						
Who suggested divorce	.29	.08	.29	.34	.11	.34°
Couple grew apart	.37	.14	−.24°°	—	—	—
Any mental health help in last year of marriage	.41	.17	.18°	—	—	—
Roman Catholic	.44	.19	.15°	—	—	—
Subjective distress	.55	.30	.34°°°	.49	.24	.36°
Attachment: Loss						
Who suggested divorce	.29	.08	.29°°	—	—	—
Couple grew apart	.37	.14	−.24°	—	—	—
Subjective distress	.53	.28	.37°°°	—	—	—
Self-esteem: Life events						
Couple grew apart	—	—	—	.35	.12	−.35°
Subjective distress	.45	.20	.45°°°	—	—	—
Self-esteem: Loss						
Subjective distress	.45	.20	.45°°°	—	—	—
Illness contacts index: Life events						
Couple grew apart	.22	.05	.22°°	—	—	—
Serious marital complaints	.29	.08	.19°	—	—	—
Respondent's social class position	—	—	—	.34	.12	.34°
Number of children with respondent	—	—	—	.47	.22	.34°
Subjective distress	.40	.16	.28°°°	—	—	—

(*continued*)

TABLE 11.3. (*Continued*)

Dependent adjustment variables, model tested, and independent variables	Whites (n = 153)			Nonwhites (n = 56)		
	R	R²	β	R	R²	β
Illness contacts index: Loss						
Weighted negative total life events	.30	.09	.30**	—	—	—
Ever any mental health hospitalization	.36	.13	.19*	—	—	—
Subjective distress	.43	.18	.23*	—	—	—

*p < .05.
**p < .01.
***p < .001.

For the attachment variable in the life events model for whites, the spouse's having suggested the divorce was associated with heightened longing for him or her, but citing more reasons why the couple grew apart was associated with less attachment. Presumably, when a respondent could see more reasons for the end of the relationship, bonds with the ex-partner had already been more clearly severed. Mental health help in the past year was associated with continued attachment to the former partner, as was being Catholic. None of the loss measures contributed to the multiple regression, and the only one of the dependent variables that explained any of the variance was subjective distress. Attachment apparently assessed a unique, nonoverlapping amount of the variance, so that dependent variables other than subjective distress had nothing else to contribute at the first interview.

Among nonwhites in the life events model, as with whites, attachment was higher if the spouse suggested the divorce. In the situation in which the partner suggested the divorce, the respondent may have felt no choice in the matter but to have agreed to the divorce, but may have wanted nevertheless to remain with his or her partner, as indicated by the continued attachment. Attachment was also associated with greater subjective distress. No variables entered the loss model of attachment for nonwhites.

None of the independent variables contributed to explaining variance in self-esteem for whites, and among the dependent variables, only subjective distress was associated with self-esteem in either the life events model or the loss model. For nonwhites, by contrast, reporting more reasons the couple grew apart was associated with higher self-esteem. Apparently, such persons felt confident that they did not have to stay in bad relationships but could strike out on their own.

Two independent variables were associated with the illness contacts inventory for whites: Those who reported more reasons for growing apart and those with more serious marital complaints had higher illness contacts scores. Living in a relationship that felt as if it were deteriorating—and, furthermore, deteriorating because of serious marital complaints such as threatened or actual violence or alcohol use—may have had a greater impact on illness. Although each of these independent variables made a significant contribution, subjective distress doubled the amount of explained variance from an R^2 of .08 to one of .16.

When the loss variables were allowed to enter, they explained more variance than the life events model (13% vs. 8%), with negative life events in the past year and previous mental hospitalizations being associated with more illness symptoms. Having had other negative life events (e.g., a job loss, moving to a poorer-quality neighborhood, etc.) within the year of filing for divorce constituted an additional stressor. By the same token, having been hospitalized for emotional or mental problems made adjustment more difficult. Again, subjective distress made a contribution, but not as great a one. The total explained variance was slightly lower ($R^2 = .18$ vs. .20 in the life events model).

Among nonwhites, two independent variables made a contribution to the life events model of adjustment to illness: The lower the social class position of the respondent and the greater the number of children, the higher the illness contacts score. Caring for children itself constitutes a stressor; at the same time, children also bring illnesses into the home, increasing the illness rates for all members of the family, as Dingle, Badger, and Jordan (1964) demonstrated.

MULTIPLE CORRELATIONS FOR ADJUSTMENT A YEAR AFTER THE DECREE WAS GRANTED

As will be recalled from Chapter 6, the major decrease in adjustment difficulties for the divorced occurred between the first interview (conducted at the time of filing for divorce) and the second interview (conducted, on the average, 2 years after separation and a year after the divorce or dissolution of marriage was granted). What might account for this decrease? Which individuals adjusted with more difficulty? Can some predictions be made about which factors might influence

adjustment longitudinally? Would loss continue to play a role in adjustment, as was shown at the first interview, or would the role of loss
variables become less important as time passes? In this section, the
question to be addressed is this: Can the level of adjustment at the
second interview be predicted from scores on the independent variables at the first interview?

In addition to comparing outcomes with and without using the
loss model, a second issue explored here is whether the scores on
the dependent variables at the first interview might influence scores at
the second interview. It is possible that those who had more difficulty
adjusting initially would continue to have more difficulty over time.
In order to test this possibility, in the regression analysis for each of
the adjustment variables, the values at the first interview for the
dependent variable being examined were entered into the multiple-
regression equation *before* the independent variables. If the initial
values of the dependent variable indeed affected later values, this
would suggest that the findings of cross-sectional studies on divorce
can be interpreted as providing at least some indication of the adjustment levels that might have been found if those studies had been
longitudinal. After the effects of the dependent variable at the first
interview and of the independent variables were explored, the other
dependent variables were allowed to enter, to see whether any more
variance would be explained. The findings are again reported by
gender and race.

Several conclusions can be drawn from the analyses. First, the
level of adjustment (as measured by subjective distress, attachment,
self-esteem, and the illness contacts index) at the first interview
affected adjustment at the second interview: Those who had higher
scores initially still had higher scores a year later. Second, the factors
that influenced the level of adjustment continued to differ for men and
women and for whites and nonwhites. Third, for the dependent variables of subjective distress, attachment, and self-esteem, controls for
the other dependent variables at the second interview added explained variance over what was known before the values of these
variables were accounted for. Fourth, in general, the loss model
explained more variance than the life events model.

Gender Differences

At the first interview, more of the variance in adjustment scores was
explained for women than for men. At the second interview, the
opposite was the case: With the exception of the subjective distress

variable, as much as or more of the variance in the 72 divorced men's scores on attachment, self-esteem, and the illness contacts index was accounted for in the multiple regressions than was true for the 88 women in both the loss and the life events models. Bloom and Caldwell (1981) reported differences in the rates of adjustment by gender, with women in several samples they studied reporting more retrospectively assessed symptoms of health distress early in the divorce process (before separation), whereas distress was greater for men in the months following separation (see also Wheaton, 1990). In this study the symptom levels of women were better explained at the time of filing, and those of men were better explained a year after the decree was granted.

For both men and women, for the dependent variable of subjective distress, only two variables entered the life events model; the subjective distress score at the first interview (for men and women, respectively, $\beta = .33$, $p < .05$, and $\beta = .73$, $p < .001$) and self-esteem at the second interview for men, $\beta = .49$, $p < .001$; for women, $\beta = .35$, $p < .001$). Those with higher subjective distress at the first interview and lower self-esteem at the second were more likely to have symptoms of anxiety and depression at the second interview. Although the loss variables contributed no added explanatory power for men ($R^2 = .33$ for both models), for women in the loss model, the variable of weighted negative life events made a contribution ($R^2 = .67$ vs. .64 for the life events model). Those women who reported more negative life events in the year *prior* to the divorce filing still had higher subjective distress scores a year after the decree was granted ($\beta = .21$, $p < .05$). These events, coupled with the divorce itself, apparently continued to require adjustment.

For men, substantially more variance in attachment was explained by the loss than by the life events model ($R^2 = .74$ vs. .58, a 16-point increase). For women, there was no improvement in prediction when the loss model was used ($R^2 = .56$ for both models). In both models, women who had high attachment scores at the first interview reported higher levels of attachment at the second interview ($\beta = .62$, $p < .001$). Among the independent variables affecting adjustment, attachment was higher for women who felt that religion did not influence their daily lives ($\beta = .22$, $p < .05$); for those who attended church less frequently ($\beta = -.28$, $p < .05$); and for those who reported having more confidants ($\beta = .25$, $p < .05$). Thus, the lack of religious beliefs and activities apparently made adjustment more difficult for women, as did having a *larger* network of friends. At least some of the literature on social support suggests that having friends helps with adjusting to difficult events, but here there is additional evidence that they do not necessarily do so.

For men in the life events model, in addition to the fact that those who had high attachment scores at the first interview still had higher levels of attachment at the second ($\beta = .58, p < .001$), those who were older ($\beta = .31, p < .05$), who felt stigmatized ($\beta = -.26, p < .05$), and who had lower self-esteem ($\beta = .32, p < .01$) were more likely to have higher attachment scores. When the loss variables were entered, those with higher attachment scores at the first interview had higher scores at the second. Attachment scores were also higher for those who were previously hospitalized for mental illness, who reported fewer negative life events as having occurred in the year prior to filing for the divorce, who had higher stigma scores, who were older, and who had higher scores on subjective distress at the second interview (respectively, $\beta = .58$, $p < .001$; $\beta = .33$, $p < .01$; $\beta = -.37$, $p < .01$; $\beta = -.26$, $p < .05$; $\beta = .21$, $p < .05$; and $\beta = .28$, $p < .01$). Because the questions about stigma were first asked at the second interview, it is difficult to determine whether stigma predicted low self-esteem or whether those with low self-esteem were more likely to feel that others picked on them and treated them differently because of their change in marital status. The data from the third interview should shed more light on this issue.

For the dependent variable of self-esteem for men in the life events model, in addition to the contribution of the self-esteem score at the first interview ($\beta = .47$, $p < .001$), those who had a stronger sense of being stigmatized by others because of their marital status were more likely to have low self-esteem ($\beta = -.29, p < .05$). Subjective distress and attachment at the second interview also made contributions $\beta = .44$, $p < .001$, and $\beta = .33$, $p < .01$, respectively). With the addition of previous hospitalization for mental illness ($\beta = .26$, $p < .05$), more variance was explained by the independent variables before the other dependent adjustment variables were entered in the loss model—37% of the variance, versus 30% in the life events model. Those men who reported such a hospitalization were more likely to have low self-esteem. The final R^2 values for the two models, however, differed little after the effects of subjective distress and attachment at the second interview were entered: The R^2 for the life events model was .58, and for the loss model it was .59.

For the self-esteem variable for women, only the other dependent variables accounted for the scores with and without the loss variables. These included the self-esteem score at the first interview and subjective distress and the illness contacts index at the second interview (respectively, $\beta = .29, p < .001$; $\beta = .43, p < .001$; $\beta = -.23, p < .05$;

$R^2 = .50$). Those with higher subjective distress and lower illness contacts scores had lower self-esteem.

For the illness contacts index variable for men in both models, the illness index score at the first interview entered the equation ($\beta = .44, p < .05$). No other variables entered for the life events model ($R^2 = .20$). Mental hospitalization played much the same role in the loss model for illness contacts as it did for self-esteem: Those men who had previously been hospitalized for an emotional illness were more likely to have high illness contacts scores ($\beta = .32, p < .05$; $R^2 = .28$).

For women, in addition to the illness contacts score at the first interview ($\beta = .17, p < .05$), those who reported that the decision to divorce was the woman's or was a joint decision were less likely to be physically ill ($\beta = -.28, p < .05$). When the spouse was blamed as the cause of the divorce at the first interview, scores were higher on the illness contacts index at the second interview ($\beta = .26, p < .05$; final $R^2 = .17$). When the loss variables were allowed to enter, the illness contacts scores at the first interview and who suggested the divorce made the same contributions as in the other model, and the negative life events score made a slight difference ($\beta = .30, p < .05$; $R^2 = .18$). These data illustrate the impact that a pileup of events and the feeling of being out of control of events can have in fostering illness. A divorced person who felt that the divorce was foisted upon him or her by the spouse and/or who experienced a number of other life events at about the same time as the divorce was more likely to report health problems such as days lost to illness, doctor visits, and hospitalizations at the second interview.

To summarize the gender-related multiple-regression findings for the impact of the respondents' characteristics at the time the divorce was filed upon their adjustment a year later, more independent variables entered the equations for three of the four adjustment variables, and more variance was explained for men than for women. Two variables, feeling stigmatized and having been hospitalized for mental illness, were especially important for men: Those men who felt stigmatized and those who had been hospitalized felt worse. Although it might be expected that the sense of being stigmatized would be more important for women because of the greater importance marital status has for them, it did not contribute to the multiple regressions for them, but it did for men. Although both mental illness and the sense of being stigmatized made independent contributions, the sense of failure, or feeling treated differently because of the divorce, may have been stronger for those men whose emotional problems contributed to the decision to divorce. Alternatively, such men may have had a greater sensitivity to the feelings of others or a sense of paranoia that made them feel that people were treating them differently, whether or not they actually were.

Race Differences

In the racial comparisons, the first-interview predictors of the adjustment variable scores at the second interview were stronger for nonwhites on all four of the adjustment variables than they were for whites. For the 123 whites, neither the independent variables in the life events model nor those in the loss model made much contribution; among the 38 nonwhites, the addition of the loss variables generally increased the predictions—that is, more of the adjustment difficulties reported by subjects at the second interview were accounted for by including indicators of loss. These data suggest a lag in adjustment for nonwhites as compared to whites. These same variables had little or no impact on adjustment at the time the divorce was filed for nonwhites, but were associated with adjustment difficulties for whites at that time. Few other studies have explored this racial difference in the timing of divorce adjustment.

For whites, none of the independent variables in the life events or loss models made a contribution to the prediction of subjective distress. Only subjective distress at the first interview and self-esteem at the second entered the equation (respectively, $\beta = .58$, $p < .001$, and $\beta = .42$, $p < .001$, $R^2 = 50$). Among nonwhites, the life events model overall produced stronger predictions ($R^2 = 70$) than did the loss model ($R^2 = .62$) for subjective distress. In both models, subjective distress at the first interview entered the equations ($\beta = .40$, $p < .01$). In the life events model, having experienced more life events in the year prior to the divorce and having higher attachment and illness contacts scores at the second interview made contributions (respectively, $\beta = .52$, $p < .05$; $\beta = .53$, $p < .01$; $\beta = .32$, $p < .05$). In the loss model, those who reported more negative life events in the year before the divorce was filed ($\beta = .58$, $p < .01$), and those who reported having been hospitalized for an emotional or mental illness ($\beta = .35$, $p < .05$), were more likely to be distressed at the time of the second interview. Attachment also added explained variance in the loss model for nonwhites ($\beta = .36$, $p < .05$), but the addition of the loss variables accounted for variance that was explained by the illness contacts index in the life events model.

For nonwhites, more variance was explained by the addition of the loss variables in the multiple regression for the attachment variable ($R^2 = .74$) than was explained in the life events model ($R^2 = .52$), whereas there were no differences in the two models for whites ($R^2 = .46$). For whites in both models, only one independent variable made a contribution, the respondent's social class ($\beta = -.20$, $p < .05$): Those with higher social status were more attached. A person may mourn the loss of a partner and a lifestyle as well. The initial attachment score ($\beta = .58$, $p < .001$) and self esteem at the second interview ($\beta = .30$, $p < .001$) also made contributions, with those who were more at-tached initially still being so at the second interview and those with lower self-esteem being more attached.

For nonwhites in the life events model, in addition to the attach-ment score at the first interview ($\beta = .60$, $p < .01$), the only variable that made a contribution was sources of financial support ($\beta = -.41$, $p < .01$). Those who reported fewer such sources of financial support were more attached to their ex-spouses. One of the hallmarks of attachment is that anxiety can increase attachment (Bowlby, 1975). For the divorced, having few or no persons who were able to provide backup in case of financial need may have increased attachment feelings. Alternatively, their relationships with their ex-spouses may have been so amicable that such persons felt that they could rely on their ex-partners when financial support was needed. As a result, they may have felt less need to turn to others when or if financial problems occurred. In the loss model, in addition to the continued contribution of the initial attachment score and the financial support variable, nonwhites who reported prior mental hospitalizations ($\beta = .40$, $p < .01$) and who reported more reasons for hesitating to divorce ($\beta = .30$, $p < .05$) exhibited higher continued attachment scores at the second interview. These data suggest that certain vulnerabilities were associated with higher attachment, making a person more likely to pine for his or her ex-partner.

For the self-esteem variable among whites in the life events model, the only sources of variation in the score were the other dependent variables ($R^2 = .51$). The largest contribution (32% of the variance) was made by the initial self-esteem score ($\beta = .56$, $p < .001$), with the remainder due to scores on subjective distress, attachment, and the illness contacts index at the second interview (respectively, $\beta = .40$, $p < .001$; $\beta = .19$, $p < .05$; $\beta = -.18$, $p < .05$). Thus, with more anxiety and depression, higher attachment, and more illness contacts, self-confidence was lower. In the loss model, however, even with the continued substantial contribution of the other dependent variables, the explained variance increased by 6% to an R^2 of .57. Self-esteem at the second interview was lower for those who were more hesitant about divorcing; for those who attended church less frequently at the time the divorce was filed; for those whose parents' marriages had ended prematurely; and for those who felt more stigmatized (respectively, $\beta = .20$, $p < .05$; $\beta = .21$, $p < .05$; $\beta = .18$, $p < .05$; $\beta = -.20$, $p < .05$). Even after these variables were entered, higher subjective distress and attachment scores at the second interview made an added contribution to lower self-esteem ($\beta = .32$, $p < .001$, and $\beta = .16$, $p < .05$, respectively).

Among non-whites in the life events model for the self-esteem measure, those who had lower self-esteem initially ($\beta = .32$, $p < .05$) and who reported more life events initially had lower self-esteem at the second interview ($\beta = .49$, $p < .05$). In the loss model for self-esteem, after self-esteem at the first interview was entered, the negative life events variable was the only independent variable that made a contribution. Those who reported more negative life events had lower self-esteem ($\beta = .47$, $p < .05$). This equation accounted for 2% less variance ($R^2 = .32$) than did the life events equation ($R^2 = .34$).

For the illness contacts index for both whites and nonwhites, none of the independent or other dependent adjustment variables entered either the life events model or the loss model. Furthermore, the contribution of the initial illness contacts score to the equations was only significant for whites ($\beta = .27$, $p < .05$).

In summary, more variance in adjustment scores for nonwhites was explained by predicting scores from the first to the second interview than by looking at adjustment cross-sectionally at the first interview. This means that at the time the divorce was filed, various social and psychological characteristics measured by the independent variables did not have much effect on the level of adjustment for nonwhites. However, adjustment at the second interview, a year after obtaining the decree, was affected by many of these factors. Furthermore, issues involving loss did make adjustment to a divorce more difficult for some individuals, even 2 years after separating.

MULTIPLE CORRELATIONS FOR ADJUSTMENT FROM TIME OF FILING TO 2–3 YEARS AFTER THE DIVORCE

In this section, predictors of adjustment from the first interview to the third interview are reported. At the third interview, the subjects had been separated from their spouses, on the average, for 4 years, and their divorces or dissolutions of marriage had been granted 2-3 years earlier. By this time, the subjects had generally adjusted fairly well; some subjects were doing less well than others, however. In this section, characteristics or experiences measured at the first interview that might have influenced adjustment 3-4 years later are identified. The role of loss might be less if vulnerabilities and the losses associated with the divorce were to become less important in predicting adjustment with the passage of time. Because changes over such a relatively lengthy period of time were explored, a number of unmeasured events or characteristics that had little or nothing to do with the divorce or that were not asked about at the end of the marriage may have intervened. The ability to explain any of the variance over this length of time should suggest certain continuities in adjustment.

The analyses described in this section were similar in format to those for assessing adjustment from the first to the second interview. The scores for the dependent variables at the first interview were controlled for in each of the multiple regressions, because the scores at the third interview might have been affected by the scores at the first interview. Next, the independent variables in the life events and loss models were entered. Finally, once these variables had explained all the variance they could, the other dependent adjustment variables were allowed to enter, to see whether they accounted for any more of the variance.

Several conclusions can be drawn from these analyses. First, scores on the adjustment variables at the time the divorce was filed still explained a substantial amount of variance in the subsequent values of these variables 3-4 years later. This means that although there were variations in the patterns of adjustment, those who were more distressed by the divorce to begin with continued to be more distressed as time passed. A second conclusion is that even over a 3- to 4-year period, the loss model of divorce continued to show some advantage in its ability to explain difficulties in adjustment over a model that did not treat divorce as an event involving loss. The differences between the models were not so great as in the earlier analyses, so it does appear that losses and vulnerabilities slow adjustment but that their effects are lessened somewhat with the passage of time. Third, few independent variables in either the life events model or the loss model played a pre-eminent role in adjustment. The variables that entered the equations differed for men and women and for whites and non-whites. A fourth conclusion is that the other dependent adjustment variables continued to add explained variance, indicating that adjustment is a multidimensional phenomenon.

Gender Differences

There was no improvement in the predictions of subjective distress at the third interview for either men ($n = 61$) or women ($n = 72$) when the loss model rather than the life events model was used. For both genders, those with higher subjective distress scores at the first interview were also more distressed at the third interview (for men, $\beta = .44$, $p < .01$; for women, $\beta = .43$, $p < .01$). For men, the only independent variable that entered the equations was that of instrumental marital complaints ($\beta = -.32$, $p < .05$). Those men who reported that the marital breakup was caused by disagreements over or poor performance of basic tasks (e.g., "disagreements over money," "general neglect of household duties") were less likely to be distressed at the third interview. Presumably, it was possible to learn how to do or to make other arrangements for the performance of instrumental tasks without a great deal of long-term difficulty, as compared to adjusting to the end of a marriage in which expressive or serious marital complaints were the issues. Among the other dependent variables, self-esteem then entered the equation for men. Low self-esteem at the final interview was associated with greater anxiety and depression ($\beta = .39$, $p < .01$; final $R^2 = .43$).

For women, after the effects of subjective distress at the first interview were accounted for, the only other variable to enter the life events and loss models was the independent variable of the length of time between the separation and the third interview ($\beta = .35$, $p < .01$; final $R^2 = .30$): The longer the time period, the greater the distress. This finding was surprising, because at the first interview those who had experienced separations more recently had greater distress. Presumably, however, the longer periods of separation were the result of reluctance to divorce, either for structural reasons such as religious edicts against divorce or for personal reasons (e.g., fear of being on one's own, or anger at or love of the spouse). The limbo of being neither married nor divorced can increase anxiety and depression if the delay is the spouse's, or even if it is one's own. In epidemiological studies, the separated often have the highest levels of distress, as compared to the divorced, single, married, and/or widowed (Somers, 1979; Verbrugge, 1979). It is often assumed in such studies that those who are separated have only recently become so, and that recency explains this distress. The data presented here suggest that this may not be the case.

For the attachment variable for men in both the life events and loss models, none of the independent variables as measured at the first interview predicted the level of attachment 3–4 years later. The degree of attachment at the first interview explained almost a quarter of the variance at the third interview ($\beta = .48$, $p < .01$), and self-esteem explained another 10% ($\beta = .34$, $p < .05$; $R^2 = .33$). If attachment levels were high at the first interview, they still were high 3–4 years later. Those at the third interview who were still attached to their spouses were also more likely to have low self-esteem.

For the attachment variable for women in both models, several variables entered the equation in addition to the variance explained by the attachment score at the first interview ($\beta = .51$, $p < .001$). The loss model explained more variance than did the life events model ($R^2 = .55$ vs. .50). In the life events model, those who had sought help from a mental health counselor before the first interview were still more distressed 3–4 years later than those who had not sought such help ($\beta = .31$, $p < .01$). This distress may have been the result of reluctance to divorce a partner to whom the person was still attached, or of the person's own psychological problems that antedated the divorce and/ or that were produced by the deteriorating marriage. Respondents who reported fewer solitary activities were less attached to their ex-spouses ($\beta = -.30$, $p < .01$); conversely, the more time a woman reported spending in solitary leisure-time pursuits, the more attached she was to her ex-spouse. Subjective distress also contributed to the equation, with higher attachment associated with higher subjective distress ($\beta = .26$, $p < .05$).

In the loss model for women, the independent variables mentioned above continued to explain the same amount of variance and were joined by the variable assessing whether the respondent had been married previously. By the time of the third interview, women who had been married previously were less likely to be attached to the ex-partner from the study marriage ($\beta = -.24$, $p < .05$). An explanation for this finding comes from Cherlin's (1979) work. He has suggested that a previous marriage makes a woman chary of giving up employment in a new one. Similarly, in the present study a woman who was married previously may also have been more reluctant to commit herself fully to a new relationship; conversely, her inability to make such a commitment may have been a contributant to the study divorce. Subjective distress also made a contribution, with heightened attachment associated with higher distress at the third interview ($\beta = .25$, $p < .05$).

The independent variables in the life events model explained no variance in men's self-esteem scores, with only the initial self-esteem and final attachment scores making contributions (respectively, $\beta = .52$, $p < .001$, and $\beta = .36$, $p < .05$; $R^2 = .39$). However, in the loss model, after the initial effects of self-esteem were again accounted for, those who had been hospitalized for a mental illness were more likely to suffer from low self-esteem at the final interview ($\beta = .30$, $p < .05$). Attachment at the third interview continued to make a contribution ($\beta = .36$, $p < .05$; final $R^2 = .44$).

For women, there was no difference between the life events and loss models for the self-esteem variable ($R^2 = .39$). In both models, in addition to the impact of the initial self-esteem score ($\beta = .44$, $p < .01$), those who reported little or no help with their children's homework or discipline had lower self-esteem ($\beta = .26$, $p < .05$). Those with lower self-esteem also had higher subjective distress scores at the third interview ($\beta = .36$, $p < .01$). It is as if those who had little or no help with caring for their children had less confidence in their ability to do the job, perhaps because they could not discuss their decisions or problems with someone else.

For men, the only variable that predicted illness contacts scores at the third interview in either the life events or loss model was the illness contacts score at the first interview ($\beta = .35$, $p < .05$; final $R^2 = .12$): Those with higher scores initially had higher scores later. Thus, the illness problems were chronic. For women, in addition to the impact of the illness contacts variable at the first interview ($\beta = .39$, $p < .01$), church attendance also influenced adjustment at the third interview ($\beta = -.26$, $p < .05$): Attending church more frequently at the first interview was associated with lower illness contacts scores at the third interview. Religious participation, then, helped with adjustment. In the loss model, respondents who were married previously had higher scores on the illness contacts index ($\beta = .29$, $p < .05$). The addition of this loss variable added 8% more explained variance ($R^2 = .30$ vs. .22 for the life events model). None of the other dependent adjustment variables added any explained variance to the equation for the illness contacts index in either model for men or women.

To summarize the gender-related results of the analyses using data from the first interview to predict adjustment at the third, there was no clear pattern of superiority in predicting adjustment for men or women. Slightly over a fifth to a little over a half of the variance was explained by these data. More variance was explained in the attachment and illness variables for women, whereas more variance was explained for men in the subjective distress and self-esteem variables. The loss variables added some explained variance compared to the life events model, but the impact of losses on adjustment was attenuated in these longer-term predictions.

Race Differences

Although it was possible to explain the adjustment scores for whites at the end of the study on the basis of their characteristics at the first interview, among nonwhites relatively little variance was explained in this manner. The lack of significant correlations was partly the result of the relatively small number of nonwhites still in the study at the third interview (29, compared to 104 whites); however, it was not *simply* the result of this, because it was possible to explore correlates of adjustment more successfully among nonwhites cross-sectionally at the third interview (see below). These somewhat tentative findings, like the cross-sectional data on adjustment at the first interview, suggest that other intervening events and experiences since the first interview played a greater role in predicting adjustment for nonwhites than for whites.

For all four of the dependent adjustment variables for nonwhites, other than the contribution of the initial value of these same adjustment variables in each of the equations, only one independent variable made a contribution for one of the dependent variables. Furthermore, none of the adjustment scores at the third interview had anything to add to the understanding of the patterns of adjustment. Thus, the R^2 values for attachment, self-esteem, and the illness contacts index were, respectively, .02, .10, and .51. The only independent variable that made a difference was the number of hours worked at the first interview for the subjective distress variable: Those who worked no hours or only part-time at the time the divorce was filed were more likely to have high subjective distress scores at the third interview ($\beta = -.50$, $p < .05$; $R^2 = .36$).

Among whites, those with higher subjective distress scores at the beginning of the study also had higher distress scores at the end ($\beta = .42$, $p < .001$). When instrumental marital complaints were reported at the first interview, distress was lower at the third interview ($\beta = -.23$, $p < .05$). If a partner could not perform even the rudimentary functional tasks needed to make a success of a marriage, it was presumably less upsetting, even perhaps a relief, to be out of such a relationship. Among the other dependent adjustment variables, both self-esteem and attachment at the third interview made contributions to the subjective distress score: Those with lower self-esteem and higher attachment were more distressed (respectively, $\beta = .38$, $p < .001$, and $\beta = .23$, $p < .05$). No additional variables entered the loss of life events models, with an R^2 of .39 for both.

After the influence of attachment at the first interview was accounted for ($\beta = .59$, $p < .001$), only one independent variable helped to explain the level of attachment for whites at the third interview—the respondent's social class ($\beta = -.21$, $p < .05$). As social class went down in status, so did attachment; that is, those with higher social class positions were more attached. The importance of the loss of the partner was apparently enhanced if status was also lost. No additional variance was explained by the loss model, and none of the other dependent adjustment variables added any explained variance in either model for attachment ($R^2 = .47$ for both models).

For the self-esteem variable, those with lower self-esteem at the first interview continued to have low self-esteem at the third ($\beta = .50$, $p < .001$). Respondents who received no help from others with finances at the time the divorce was filed had higher self-esteem than those who received assistance ($\beta = -.21$, $p < .05$). Regardless of its utility or the manner in which it was proffered, it was apparently somewhat degrading to receive financial assistance from others. Subjective distress at the third interview was also associated with self-esteem ($\beta = .35$, $p < .001$; final $R^2 = .40$). In the loss model, those who reported that their parents' marriage had ended by divorce or death had lower self-esteem ($\beta = .25$, $p < .01$). Parental marital disruption may influence self-esteem by fostering a sense of failure, because the offspring are following in the footsteps of their parents. Events surrounding the divorce of the parents may also have affected the respondents' sense of themselves early in their lives. Such children are said to be less likely to be supervised in their activities, more likely to have poor parental role models, and more likely to marry young, thereby increasing their chances of making poor marital choices (McLanahan & Bumpass, 1988; Mueller & Pope, 1977). With the addition of subjective distress at the third interview ($\beta = .34$, $p < .01$), the final R^2 for the loss model was only 1 percentage point higher than the life events model ($R^2 = .41$).

For the illness contacts index in the life events and loss models, the initial illness contacts score made a contribution, with those who reported higher illness levels at the beginning of the study still reporting them at the end ($\beta = .26$, $p < .05$). In addition, those who reported more frequent church attendance at the beginning of the study were less likely to report high illness contacts scores at the end ($\beta = -.26$, $p < .05$; final R^2 for both models = .14). It is possible that those with fewer difficulties with their health were more able to get out regularly to activities such as church. Similarly, they may have been less preoccupied with their health if they were able to be out and around.

These data suggest that loss still plays some role in adjustment even as long as 4 years after separation, or 2–3 years after the divorce was granted. Furthermore, more of the adjustment difficulties of whites than of nonwhites could be explained over this length of time.

MULTIPLE CORRELATIONS FOR ADJUSTMENT 2-3 YEARS AFTER THE DIVORCE: CROSS-SECTIONAL ANALYSES

Thus far, this chapter has addressed the questions of what variables were associated with adjustment cross-sectionally at the first interview; what variables predicted adjustment from one interview to another; and whether a model including loss variables is superior in its predictive ability to a life events model. The findings have shown that it is possible to explain anywhere from a third to three-quarters of the variance in adjustment scores from knowledge of an individual's initial score on the same adjustment variable; indicators of his or her attitudes, feelings, or experiences at the time of the first interview; and his or her scores on the other adjustment measures. This gives greater confidence in the results of cross-sectional studies and suggests a certain continuity in adjustment. Furthermore, a loss model does add to the understanding of adjustment, particularly in the early stages of the divorce process.

The final issue to be explored is this: Can anything more be learned from a cross-sectional look at the correlates of adjustment at the end of a longitudinal study—in this case, approximately 4 years after separation, or 2-3 years after the divorce was granted? How do these findings compare to the results indicating the impact of the variables measured at the first interview upon adjustment 3-4 years later?

In the analyses presented in this section, the scores for variables that were assessed at the third interview were used wherever possible. For some of the loss variables (such as mental hospitalizations or the end of the parents' marriage), however, only earlier indicators were available, because the impact of events that may have happened many years before the divorce was being explored.

Some variables that were not included in the earlier analyses were introduced here. These included marital status, with engaged, cohabiting, or married coded as 0 and single coded as 1. The number of contacts with the ex-spouse at the time of the third interview was also included. Finally, the three-item scale assessing satisfaction with the legal settlement, described in Chapter 10, was also included.

Because the analyses were cross-sectional, meaning that the independent variables were generally measured at the same time as the adjustment variables, it is not possible to predict the adjustment scores; that is, it is not clear what "caused" what. Some ideas or hints may have been provided by the longitudinal analyses, but instead of predictions, the question here is this: What factors appeared together or were associated or correlated? Because what happened at just one time period was being assessed, it was not necessary to control for initial values of the dependent variables being examined. By the same token, however, adjustment was still viewed as a multi-dimensional phenomenon, so that the other dependent variables were given an opportunity to enter the multiple-regression equations after the independent variables, to see whether they would explain any more of the variance. As the following discussion indicates, in some cases (as in the analyses presented earlier in this chapter), the other dependent variables explained more variance than the independent variables.

Gender Differences

For men, more variance was explained by the life events model than by the loss model, both before ($R^2 = .36$ vs. .33) and after ($R^2 = .50$ vs. .42) the other dependent adjustment variables were allowed to enter, because of the different mix of variables that entered the two models and the amount of overlapping variance that the loss variables explained. In other words, the independent contribution of each of the variables in the loss model was less than in the life events model. In the life events model, men who had higher subjective distress scores at the third interview were more likely to report having recently received information or guidance from family or friends; were more likely to have experienced a number of life events in the year prior to the third interview; and were less likely to be the fathers of grade-school-age children (respectively, $\beta = .43$, $p < .05$; $\beta = .34$, $p < .05$; $\beta = -.27$, $p < .05$). Those respondents whose children were older than toddlers were more likely to stay in contact with their children (see Chapter 10), and apparently maintaining those contacts was less distressing than not doing so. Among the other adjustment variables, lower self-esteem was associated with greater depression and anxiety ($\beta = .40$, $p < .001$). In the loss model, three of the variables remained the same for men: having received information or guidance, having grade-school-age children, and having lower self-esteem (respectively, $\beta = .43$, $p < .01$; $\beta = -.29$, $p < .05$; $\beta = .35$, $p < .05$). Instead of the life events variable, however, having been hospitalized previously for mental illness entered the multiple regression ($\beta = .28$, $p < .05$). Men who had been hospitalized were more likely to be distressed 3–4 years after the divorce was granted.

For women, more variance was explained by the loss model than by the life events model, both before and after the other adjustment variables were introduced. An additional 5% of the variance was explained for the independent variables ($R^2 = .38$ vs. .32 for the life events model), with an increase in variance of 10% (from an R^2 of .30 to one of .40) when the other adjustment variables were allowed to enter. In both models, four of the independent variables (the length of time between separation and the interview, having sought mental health help in the year prior to the third interview, having children of any age from the marriage that ended in divorce, and claiming any religious affiliation other than Protestant) and two of the adjustment variables (self-esteem and attachment) were the same. In the life events model, subjective distress was higher for those who had been separated longer; who had sought mental health help; who had children; and who were Catholic, were Jewish, or reported no religious denomination (respectively, $\beta = .32$, $p < .05$; $\beta = .31$, $p < .05$; $\beta = -.26$, $p < .05$; $\beta = -.23$, $p < .05$). In addition, low self-esteem and high attachment to the ex-spouse were associated with greater subjective distress in both the life events and loss models (respectively, $\beta = .31$, $p < .01$, and $\beta = .29$, $p < .05$ in the life events model; $\beta = .29$, $p < .05$, and $\beta = .26$, $p < .05$ in the loss model). These data point up the stressfulness of caring for children; they also indicate that individuals belonging to religious traditions with a strong focus on family or with strong sanctions against divorce, as well as those not belonging to any religious tradition, were more likely to be distressed. Those who were experiencing difficulties were seeking help, or, alternatively, the help being sought increased difficulties. In general, it is more likely that people seek therapy when they are distressed, but it is also likely that exploration of the issues that lead a person to seek therapy may "keep the pot boiling" and increase distress in the short run.

In the loss model for women, the only variable that was added was anger with the ex-spouse, which helped, perhaps, to explain their continued distress despite the long period of separation ($\beta = .25$, $p < .05$). It entered before the variable of any religious affiliation other than Protestant ($\beta = -.24$, $p < .05$). These may have been women whose self-esteem was battered, who were simultaneously angry with and pining for their ex-spouses, and who were saddled with the primary responsibility for the children. Their anger may have even led to a longer separation period. Alternatively, they might have been angry because their spouses went ahead with the divorce against their wishes or stalled the divorce action when they themselves wanted to proceed. At the same time, these women apparently recognized that things were not going as well as they should be, as evidenced by their efforts to seek mental health help.

With the attachment variable, the same pattern was found of lower explained variance for men with the loss model ($R^2 = .30$) than with the life events model ($R^2 = .39$). The variable of receiving information and guidance again made a contribution, with attachment being higher for men who had turned to more sources ($\beta = .30$, $p < .05$). Those who reported greater dissatisfication with the legal settlement at the second interview were more distressed at the third interview. Dating less frequently, having no children, and being Jewish—a set of items suggesting the importance of a family that was no longer there—were associated with greater attachment to the ex-spouse (respectively, $\beta = .32$, $p < .05$; $\beta = .27$, $p < .05$; $\beta = .24$, $p < .05$).

In the loss model for the attachment variable, none of the variables mentioned in the preceding paragraph entered the equation for men. Instead, only two entered: Anger with the ex-spouse and lower self-esteem were associated with greater attachment (respectively, $\beta = .36$, $p < .05$, and $\beta = .41$, $p < .01$). Although the total variance explained was lower in the loss model, the anger variable accounted for as much variance as did the variables of dating, support, dissatisfaction with the legal settlement, and having children in the life events model. Apparently some men's anger with their ex-spouses is so great as to color all of their activities (see also Johnston & Campbell, 1988; Wallerstein, 1986; Wallerstein & Kelly, 1980).

Among women, the loss model variables made no added contribution to explaining the level of attachment at the third interview (R^2 for both models = .53). The variables that entered the life events and loss models for attachment were the same. Attachment was associated with having been separated from the spouse for a longer period of time; having been married for more years before filing for divorce; having more friends with whom to talk over confidential matters; reporting serious marital complaints; having more children from all unions; and having help with child care tasks (respectively, $\beta = .39$, $p < .01$; $\beta = .31$, $p < .01$; $\beta = .28$, $p < .05$; $\beta = -.24$, $p < .05$; $\beta = .27$, $p < .05$; $\beta = .24$, $p < .05$). Among the other adjustment variables, subjective distress explained an additional 4% of the variance, with greater subjective distress associated with greater attachment ($\beta = .24$, $p < .05$). The direction of these relationships is unclear; that is, did these dimensions foster attachment, or vice versa? It does, however, seem possible that a woman might be less likely to go through with a divorce when she continued to be attached to her spouse, and that a long marriage was likely to have good as well as bad times, thereby fostering attachment. Similarly, serious marital complaints such as alcoholism and threatened or actual abuse often made it harder to pull away from the spouse. With a longer marriage it was also more likely that a couple would have more children and that the ex-spouse might be a source of help for them, in part because of the continuing bonds between the two spouses.

For men's scores on the self-esteem variable, again slightly less overall variance (3% less) was explained with the loss model ($R^2 = .36$) than with the life events model ($R^2 = .39$), but the independent variables explained more variance ($R^2 = .21$ vs. .11 in the life events model). Furthermore, the loss variable that entered the equation suggested a possible reason for the lowered self-esteem: Men who reported seeking financial help from family or friends in the year before the interview ($\beta = .33$, $p < .05$) had lower self-esteem, and higher subjective distress and attachment scores as well (respectively, $\beta = .46$, $p < .001$, and $\beta = .30$, $p < .05$). In the loss model, the first variable to enter the equation for self-esteem was having previously been hospitalized for emotional or mental illness ($\beta = .33$, $p < .05$). This was followed by having received financial help in the past year ($\beta = .32$, $p < .05$). Subjective distress still accounted for additional variance after these two variables were entered ($\beta = .41$, $p < .01$). Thus, those who had been hospitalized may have been more vulnerable because of lower income, fewer employment opportunities, or difficulty in maintaining employment, and may have been more affected by the need to seek financial help from others.

For women in the life events model for self-esteem, the only independent variable to enter the equation was the length of time between separation and the interview; a longer separation was correlated with lower self-esteem ($\beta = .30$, $p < .05$). Such women were also more likely to be anxious and depressed, as indicated by their higher subjective distress scores ($\beta = .38$, $p < .01$). The sense of being in limbo because of the long separation may have affected self-esteem, or, alternatively, the lack of self-esteem may have made it difficult to make the final break in the relationship.

In the loss model, only one independent variable entered: Being more hesitant to divorce was associated with lower self-esteem ($\beta = .13$, $p < .01$). Such women may have doubted their ability to manage on their own. Higher subjective distress was also associated with low self-esteem ($\beta = .41$, $p < .001$). Overall, more variance was explained with the loss model ($R^2 = .30$ vs. .22 for the life events model).

Among men, for the illness contacts index, there was no difference in the variables that entered the two models. Men who had higher illness contacts scores were more likely to have sought information and guidance from family and friends and were less likely to have been employed (respectively, $\beta = .46$, $p < .001$, and $\beta = -.40$, $p < .01$; final $R^2 = .37$). For women, the only variable that was associated with the illness contacts index in either model was age: Older women were more likely to have high scores on the index ($\beta = .29$, $p < .05$ final $R^2 = .09$). Chronic illnesses are associated with being older (Verbrugge, 1979, 1985).

These data confirm what earlier analyses showed—namely, that the importance of different dimensions of adjustment varied for men and women. More variance was explained for the self-esteem and illness contacts variables for men, whereas more variance was explained for subjective distress and attachment for women. Reactions to a divorce thus differed by gender. Loss variables did make some contribution, even an average of 4 years after separation, but less for men than for women. Although a substantial amount of variance was explained in some of the equations, this still left almost half of the variance to be explained by other factors that were not assessed in this study.

Race Differences

Generally, in these cross-sectional analyses, a higher amount of variance was explained for nonwhites than for whites, but fewer variables entered the equations. This was, in part, the result of the number of cases in each group—29 nonwhites and 104 whites. Even with the small number of nonwhites, the findings can suggest directions for future research. Among whites in the life events model, higher subjective distress was associated with having more friends with whom to talk over confidential matters; having sought mental health help in the year prior to the interview; complaining about marital problems other than instrumental ones; and having low self-esteem and higher continued attachment to the ex-spouse (respectively, $\beta = .26$, $p < .05$; $\beta = .22$, $p < .05$; $\beta = -.21$, $p < .05$; $\beta = .49$, $p < .001$; $\beta = .21$, $p < .05$). Having confidants and seeking mental health counseling were consistently associated with adjustment difficulties across the various time periods in this study. The relationships do not follow the view that support aids adjustment; in these analyses, both professional help and personal support were associated with more distress. The reasons for such associations are unclear. Friends may have sensed that a person was in distress and tried to help out, but apparently without much effect in reducing distress or anxiety; this may have led to frantic friendship activity (see also Greene & Feld, 1989). One possible explanation for this association has been identified by Patterson and Forgatch (1990) in a study of single mothers. Women who were irritable and depressed had confidants who were also irritable and sad, leading to poor problem solving for the single mothers. Thus, if the only support a distressed woman is able to obtain is that from another woman with a similar outlook the feeling of "ain't it awful" can feed on itself, fueling more distress. In addition, as discussed above, counseling may itself exacerbate distress in the short run.

The loss model explained another 6% of the variance before the other dependent adjustment variables entered ($R^2 = .21$ vs. .15), and explained 3% more of the overall variance than the life events model ($R^2 = .46$ vs. .43). Higher subjective distress scores were associated with being angry with the ex-spouse, experiencing negative life events in the year prior to the interview, and having more confidants (respectively, $\beta = .30$, $p < .01$; $\beta = .25$, $p < .05$; $\beta = .24$, $p < .05$). Low self-esteem ($\beta = .47$, $p < .001$) and high attachment ($\beta = .21$, $p < .05$) were also associated with higher anxiety and depression.

Among nonwhites, there was no difference in the variables that entered the life events and loss models ($R^2 = .54$). In both models, those who sought mental health help during the marriage or since were more likely to be distressed, as were those with more children living in the household (respectively, $\beta = .64$, $p < .01$, and $\beta = .38$, $p < .05$; final $R^2 = .54$).

As for the attachment measure, only two variables—one independent and one dependent—entered the life events model for whites: More contacts with the ex-spouse in the weeks prior to the third interview and higher subjective distress were associated with higher attachment (respectively, $\beta = .31$, $p < .01$, and $\beta = .41$, $p < .001$; final $R^2 = .27$). In the loss model, attachment was associated with more contacts with and anger with the ex-spouse, as well as with higher levels of subjective distress (respectively, $\beta = .31$, $p < .01$; $\beta = .21$, $p < .05$; $\beta = .38$, $p < .001$; final $R^2 = .28$). It thus appears that the mixed situation of being angry and attached, a sign of greater ambivalence about the relationship, was more distressing and volatile than that of only being attached.

For nonwhites, in the life events model assessing attachment, only one variable entered the equation: Greater length of marriage was associated with greater attachment ($\beta = .44$, $p < .05$). In the loss model, two variables entered, and the amount of variance explained doubled from an R^2 of .20 to .40. These variables were a prior mental hospitalization ($\beta = .48$, $p < .05$) and hesitating to divorce ($\beta = .43$,

$p < .05$), with those who had been hospitalized and those who were more hesitant being more attached.

In the life events model, none of the independent variables influenced self-esteem for whites, with only subjective distress making a contribution ($\beta = .38$, $p < .001$; $R^2 = .26$): Low self-esteem was associated with high subjective distress. In the loss model, self-esteem was lower for those whose parents' marriages had ended by divorce or death and for those with a greater sense of being stigmatized by the divorce (respectively, $\beta = .24$, $p < .01$, and $\beta = -.22$, $p < .05$). Subjective distress and self-esteem were, however, more strongly associated than were the independent variables ($\beta = .45$, $p < .001$; final $R^2 = .30$). The direction of the association is unclear. The discouragement of depression may have made a person feel unable to cope; on the other hand, feeling incompetent may also have made a person feel depressed and anxious. Because these data are cross-sectional, it is also not possible to determine whether feeling stigmatized led to low self-esteem or whether low self-esteem led to a feeling that one was being stigmatized by others.

Among nonwhites, only one variable entered the life events and loss model equations for self-esteem: Those who belonged to a Protestant fundamentalist denomination were more likely to have low self-esteem ($\beta = .47$, $p < .05$; $R^2 = .22$). Such denominations help people to cope by shifting the focus from the concerns of this world to those of the next, but the various restrictions and edicts of the groups may also have made respondents belonging to them feel incompetent in their ability to meet these demands, especially since divorce is frowned upon in many fundamentalist groups.

For the illness contacts variable among whites in both the life events and loss models, only one variable entered the equation: Roman Catholicism was associated with higher scores on the illness contacts index ($\beta = .27$, $p < .05$; $R^2 = .07$). Among nonwhites, three variables entered the life events model: Having had more life events occur, being older, and dating less frequently were associated with higher illness contacts scores (respectively, $\beta = .56$, $p < .01$; $\beta = .47$, $p < .01$; $\beta = .40$, $p < .01$). In the loss model, the character of the life events that occurred was revealed to be negative, as the negative life events variable entered the equation ($\beta = .54$, $p < .01$). This was followed by age and total income, with those who were older and who had lower income having higher illness contacts scores (respectively, $\beta = .50$, $p < .01$; $\beta = -.42$, $p < .01$). The loss model explained more variance than did the life events model ($R^2 = .73$ vs. .68).

In summary, the cross-sectional analyses approximately 4 years after separation, or 2–3 years after the divorce, indicate several things.

First, more variance in adjustment was explained by gender than by race. Second, more variance in adjustment was explained for women than for men and for nonwhites than for whites. Third, the life events model was generally a somewhat better approach for understanding men's adjustment difficulties at the third interview, whereas the loss model still showed some small advantage for women, nonwhites, and whites. The role of loss, however, was more pronounced in the earlier than in the later stages of the divorce process. Fourth, somewhat more variance was explained with a cross-sectional model that took more proximal measures into account than with an approach attempting to predict responses at the third interview from those at the first interview, in part because other events not assessed or assessable at the first interview intervened in the meantime; some of these events complicated adjustment, and others made it easier. Finally, although marital status was added to the equation at the third interview, in no case did it contribute to adjustment. This suggests that the repartnered and the single faced many of the same issues.

CONCLUSION

A problem with statistical techniques such as zero-order correlation and multiple regression is that they indicate that a variable accounts for a statistically significant amount of the variance explained. This, however, as noted previously, is not necessarily the same thing as a meaningful amount of variance. In trying to understand what factors influence adjustment to divorce, it is useful to know which variables make statistically significant contributions; this information helps map or describe what is happening. It is, however, even more useful to be able to account for a significant and meaningful amount of the variance. Although the amount of variance explained in the multiple-regression analyses displayed above was in some cases low, in other instances from half to three-quarters of the variance was explained. This means that a substantial amount of the difficulty in adjustment was accounted for by the variables being examined. As a result, if certain characteristics of individuals are known, there is a better than 50-50 chance of being able to anticipate whether these persons will have difficulties in adjusting to divorce.

A second point about statistically significant relationships is that it is possible to lose sight of the relative importance of the findings. One factor may affect many individuals and another only a few; yet each may make a significant contribution in distinguishing between high and low scores on the adjustment variables. A prime example is that of the variable of previous mental hospitalization. Men and nonwhites who had been hospitalized for a mental or emotional illness were more likely to have difficulty in adjusting. Overall, only 12.4% of the divorced sample had been hospitalized for a mental or emotional illness. More women (17.3%) than men (7.4%) had been hospitalized. More of the men's admissions were in the year prior to filing for the divorce (5 of 7 admissions vs. 10 of the 17 admissions for women). Thus, although a history of illness requiring mental hospitalization was a factor associated with greater adjustment difficulties for some, it was not a common event among the divorced; in fact, for women, more of whom had been hospitalized than men, it made no difference in adjustment. It is this same kind of issue that makes community-based research on adjustment to divorce, such as the present research, important. Those in the community who are *not* having difficulties adjusting are likely to be missed, because the picture of the problems people have in adjusting to divorce is based upon the situations of those who have sought help from various agencies and professionals. This is not to downplay the significant, serious, and continuing problems some individuals have in adjusting to divorce, but only to say that theirs is just part of the picture. Many other people, with time, cope quite admirably with a situation that presents them with a myriad of difficulties.

The overall findings are varied, Table 11.4 summarizes them and illustrates the roles played by gender and race. Only a few variables affected adjustment for men, women, whites, and nonwhites. These inclusive variables were weighted total negative life events (a loss variable), who suggested the divorce, and financial support. Adjustment difficulties were greater when other negative events happened at the time of the divorce; when the spouse suggested the divorce (except for women, in which case the relationship was the opposite); and when a divorcing person's economic situation was such that he or she needed financial help from others. For both genders such help increased distress, but by race it did not; because of limitations in the number of cases, it was not possible to look at this relationship in more detail. More variables affected adjustment for three of the four groups. Greater adjustment difficulties were associated with being Catholic; having received mental health help in the last year of the marriage; being older; having ever been hospitalized for a mental illness; being angry with the ex-spouse; and hesitating to divorce (these last three items were loss variables). Fewer adjustment difficulties were reported when instrumental marital complaints were made and when the couple had grown apart. Finally, for men and whites, having been previously married (a loss variable) increased adjustment difficulties,

TABLE 11.4. Influences on Adjustment by Gender and Race

Influences on adjustment	Male	Female	Nonwhite	White
Protestant (all denominations)		−		
Protestant (fundamentalist)			+	
Roman Catholic	+	+		+
Jewish	+			
Church attendance		−		
Influence of religion		+		
Instrumental marital complaints	−	−		−
Serious marital complaints		+		+
Who suggested the divorce	±	−	+	+
Who is to blame for the divorce		+		
Couple grew apart		−	−	−
Dissatisfaction with divorce settlement	−			
Financial support	+	+	−	−
Information support	+			
Any mental health help in last year of marriage		+	+	+
Length of marriage		+	+	
Age	+	+	+	
How long separated		+		
Parents' marriage ended (L)				+
Previously divorced or widowed (L)	+	−		+
Ever any mental health hospitalization (L)	+		+	+
Anger at ex-spouse (L)	+	+		+
Reasons for hesitating to divorce (L)		+	+	+
Weighted negative total life events (L)	+	+	+	+
Total number of life events	+		+	
Stigma	−			+
Solitary activities	+	−		
Number of confidants		+		+
Dating	+		+	
Number of contacts with ex-spouse				+
Number of hours worked (fewer)			+	
Employment status (underemployed)	+	+		
Income (low)		−	+	
Respondent's social class position			±	+
Race (white)	+			
Gender				
Number of children with respondent			+	
Number of children born to union		+	+	
No children	+	±		
Preschool-age children	+			
Grade-school-age children	−			
Teenage children				−
No help with children		+		

Note. (L) indicates a variable included in the loss model. A plus sign (+) means that the more of the characteristic, the more the adjustment problems; a minus sign (−) means that the less of the characteristic, the less the adjustment problems.

but it decreased them for women. These two lists include all but one of the loss variables—parents' marriage ending by death or divorce.

The loss model does provide additional clarification of what makes adjustment harder versus easier. The dependent variable of attachment was itself a measure of coping with loss; it played an important role in many of the analyses. Those who were more attached to their (ex-)spouses and who had experienced prior losses or additional losses near the time of the divorce were more vulnerable and had more difficulty coping with their change in marital status, both initially and over time, than those who did not suffer such losses. The impact of prior losses was generally greater earlier in the adjustment process. The majority of individuals, however, seemed to be able to cope over time with the changes divorce brought to their lives.

A greater variety of variables were associated with adjustment outcomes for women; often, more variance was accounted for than was true for men or for either racial group. This may be related to the fact that more studies in the past have focused on women, so that there is a greater fund of information from which to draw. Few studies have looked at differences in adjustment for men or by race. The findings for men and for nonwhites (here, mostly blacks) also highlight that although divorce constituted a crisis to which respondents adjusted, other stressors also occurred after the divorce itself, and these made their own contribution to the difficulties respondents experienced. More variance in adjustment for whites than for nonwhites was explained initially, whereas more variance was explained for nonwhites at the time of the second interview and in the cross-sectional data at the third interview. These findings are, however, only suggestive because of the relatively small number of nonwhite respondents in the study. These data highlight the need for more longitudinal analyses that include both men and women, as well as subjects from different ethnic groups.

The data also indicate the importance of taking a multidimensional approach to the concept of "adjustment." Subjective distress, attachment, self-esteem, and illness contacts all contributed to an understanding of the adjustment process, but these different dimensions had varying importance for men and women and for nonwhites and whites. Subjective distress and attachment generally played a greater role in adjustment difficulties than did self-esteem and illness contacts. The illness contacts measure (in contrast to self-esteem) was not as strong a measure psychometrically, with a lower alpha reliability (which may have accounted for its lower scores). It is likely that lingering attachment is the source of much of the heightened psychological distress experienced by the divorced (Kitson, 1991a). On the other hand, the losses and changes that occurred at the time of and subsequent to the divorce contributed to heightened psychological symptoms, both initially and overtime.

The longitudinal data presented here have clearly added richness and complexity to the findings; they have enhanced our understanding of how the divorce process differs by gender and race. These differences would not have been as clear if only cross-sectional data had been used. On the other hand, a person's initial adjustment score continued to contribute to his or her later adjustment at the second interview, a year after the divorce, as well as at the third, 2-3 years after the divorce; thus, various dimensions of adjustment remained stable in their importance across time. This suggests that although the issue of time must be taken into account, cross-sectional findings are at least somewhat indicative of longer-term outcomes as well.

CHAPTER 12

Conclusions, or Where Do We Go from Here?

Dr. and Mrs. Alexander Goodman
have the honour of announcing
the divorce of their daughter
Barbara Jane
from
Ronald Melvin what's his name
in the year of our Lord
nineteen hundred and seventy
Superior Court
Los Angeles, California

—Lewis (1983, p. 76)

This book has attempted to link the pathology and crisis models of adjustment to divorce by viewing adjustment as a process that is made more difficult for certain people who have experienced previous losses and who have certain kinds of vulnerabilities. The present research represents one of a handful of longitudinal studies about adjustment to divorce, as well as one of the few studies based solely on interviews with subjects drawn from divorce court records. Adjustment has been examined here as a multidimensional phenomenon that includes subjective distress, continued attachment to the former spouse, self-esteem, and illness contacts.

The primary sources of data were a sample of suburban divorced persons drawn from divorce court records in Cuyahoga County, Ohio (metropolitan Cleveland) who were interviewed three times beginning in 1974–1975, and a comparison sample of married persons drawn from the same city blocks as the divorced, who were interviewed twice. Findings have also been reported from several other metropolitan Cleveland surveys. The first was a survey of suburban Cleveland respondents (selected from the same communities as those in the suburban longitudinal divorce survey) who had filed for divorce and then withdrawn their petitions. A second county-wide probability sample looked at the frequency of marital separations among people who separated but may not necessarily have filed for divorce. A third study reported on results of a 1985–1986 county-wide survey of marital transition among divorced and widowed women. In this book, the divorced respondents in the marital transition study have been compared and contrasted with the suburban divorced sample; for the most part, the two sets of divorced subjects replied similarly. This is important for several reasons. First, it provides greater confidence in the results of the suburban divorced study, which could have been called into question because of the time that has passed since that survey was completed in 1979. The dynamics of divorce adjustment do not appear to have changed over this period. Second, replication of study results is important as a goal in research; it enhances confidence that the results reported did not occur by chance.

This book has begun with a series of questions about how men and women and blacks and whites adjust to divorce, and how the attitudes and behaviors of people who divorce differ from or resemble those of people who remain married. In the following section, some of the findings relating to these questions are reviewed.

SOME KEY POINTS ABOUT THE DIVORCED AND DIVORCE ADJUSTMENT

Background Characteristics

Even though the suburban divorced and married samples were selected from the same city blocks, so that they would be as similar as possible in background characteristics, the divorced differed in a number of ways from the married. The divorced were more likely to have characteristics that have been found to place people at greater risk for divorce. They were more likely to have been divorced previously; to have come from different ethnic and religious groups than their ex-spouses; to have no religious affiliation; to have conceived a child out of wedlock or to have no children; to have made a suicide attempt at some point; to have been hospitalized for mental or emotional problems; and to be more likely to report that their ex-spouses had psychological problems. It is difficult to determine whether some of these differences or problems existed before the marriage or developed after it. It is also not clear whether these issues were precipitants of the divorce or were the results of the turmoil of the marriage. Nevertheless, these risk factors were more common among the divorced than the married persons studied, and they made adjustment to the divorce harder for those who had them.

Estrangement

Despite the greater legal ease of obtaining a divorce today, the studies reported upon here suggest that many couples still think long and hard before entering the divorce courts. In fact, there is some evidence from the marital transition study that the decision period is lengthening. More than two-fifths of the suburban divorced sample and over half of the marital transition sample had initiated a trial separation before the one that led to the divorce decision. Many of these people sought help from therapists, and, with or without the help of therapists, spouses negotiated with each other to change problematic areas of their relationships (eg., disagreements over gender roles; use of leisure time; and alcohol, other drug abuse, and gambling). In the study of couples who filed for divorce and changed their minds, such negotiations were most successful when the partners were able to keep the promises they had made; otherwise, the reconciliations broke down.

At the same time that couples attempted to work out solutions to their problems before divorcing, a not insubstantial number of people found their situations so unacceptable as to file for divorce but then, for whatever reasons, withdrew their divorce petitions or separated without necessarily filing for divorce. Such people do not appear in divorce statistics, but they represented close to a quarter of the relationships surveyed in the Cleveland area. This indicates that a sizable subgroup of people are not satisfied with their marital relationships, but remain in them.

Divorce has apparently become an option that individuals are increasingly likely to consider at some point. Both the suburban married and divorced samples acknowledged that they had thought about ending their marriages and about various reasons that made them hesitate to divorce. These reasons (including financial, social, and personal issues) were most commonly thought about by those who eventually divorced, but virtually every respondent in both samples had thought about some of these reasons. Couples often reported protracted periods of dissatisfaction with the marriage before making a break.

Marital Complaints

The present data also tell something about the nature of relationships today: Women are still the keepers of relationships. They are more aware than men of the "emotional temperature" of their relationships, and they seem to have clearer expectations about what they want from these relationships. Despite increases in the number of men who file for divorce since the institution of no-fault divorce, women remain more likely to file for a divorce or dissolution. Women, for the most part, also have better-worked-out explanations for the reasons for the breakdown of their marriages than do men. In the present research, men often began trying to explain the breakdown of their marriages by saying, "I don't know what happened."

The changes in the wider society that have made it acceptable for women to be employed and to receive a decent wage (although still often lower than that of men) have increased the acceptability of divorce as a solution to marital problems. Women now have the social and economic means to end marriages. They no longer have to remain in relationships that they find unsatisfactory because of extramarital affairs, alcoholism, drug abuse, or violent behavior on the part of their partners.

Marital complaints change as social and legal situations change. For example, the complaints made in William Goode's (1956) survey of Detroit women in 1948 differed quite substantially from those made in metropolitan Cleveland in the mid-1970s; however, complaints changed little between the 1970s and 1980s in the Cleveland data. In turn, laws change because people's perceptions of what is acceptable change. It is these changes in perceptions that have led to the world-wide shift in divorce laws in the past quarter of a century.

The importance of affection and companionship in relationships today is highlighted in the data from both the suburban divorced and the married samples. Both groups yearned for more communication with and support and concern from their partners. Many respondents reported that their spouses fulfilled the more instrumental roles of the marriage ("provider/homemaker," "parent") satisfactorily. Their dissatisfaction stemmed especially from their spouses' performance in the role of "someone to talk things over with," and to a lesser extent in those of "helpmate/partner" and "leisure-time companion." The expectations for these dimensions of relationships are harder to meet and maintain, and are more easily eroded by slights, hurts, and inattention. There appears to be a growing recognition that such relational complaints are acceptable grounds for ending a marriage. This was also illustrated by the reports of the suburban divorced respondents that they and their spouses had grown apart.

Certain kinds of marital complaints were easier to adjust to than were others. Complaints of "extramarital sex" and others that reflected on a person's self-esteem were harder to adjust to than instrumental complaints. Complaints also varied over the course of the study. Some complaints (such as "arguing all the time," "joint conflict over roles," and "out with the boys/girls") reflected the heat of the earlier stages of the marital breakdown. Other complaints remained stable over time (such as "alcohol," "actual physical abuse," and "lack of communication or understanding"), whereas others increased in frequency of mention between the time of filing and 2–3 years after the divorce (such as "different backgrounds; incompatible," "change in interests or values," and "emotional/personality problems").

Adjustment

In these data, the divorce experience was associated with heightened subjective distress, continued attachment to the ex-spouse, lowered self-esteem, heightened scores on an illness contacts index, economic problems, changes in social networks, and a welter of other life events (many of which were associated with or resulted from the divorce). After a period of upset, which for many decreased substantially within a year of obtaining the divorce decree, the divorced was able to cope quite admirably. By the end of the study, an average of 4 years after separation, most of the divorced sample differed little in terms of psychological functioning from the married sample. On only one indicator, subjective distress, were their scores significantly higher than those of the married. Adjustment did not represent a simple decrease in symptoms, however. Some individuals' symptoms increased between the first and second or second and third interviews, and those with more psychological vulnerabilities as represented by prior losses and changes had greater difficulty adjusting.

The findings on adjustment difficulties were not just statistically significant, but substantively so. Thirty to forty percent of the divorced initially experienced moderate to high symptoms of subjective distress and feelings of attachment to their ex-spouses.

Economic Issues

In divorce, women are more likely to have custody of the children; they find that the amount of child support provided is often limited and alimony rarely awarded; and they generally experience a substantial reduction in income. In this study, their income decreased by 37.4% between the first and second interviews—a figure somewhat higher than Hoffman and Duncan's (1988) national estimate of an income decrease of 33.3%, but lower than Weitzman's (1985) dramatic projected decline of 73%. To their credit, many of the women in the suburban divorced sample recognized their need for additional education and training (presumably to strengthen their occupational positions) and sought it, with the result that approximately 40% had obtained such training by the end of the study. One in four of the women had increased their occupational status, compared to fewer than 1 in 10 men. Income began to improve for everyone by the time of the third interview; however, women with children made the least improvement (an increase of 33.8%).

Parents' Perceptions of Children's Adjustment

Despite (or perhaps because of) their own high levels of distress, divorced parents did not report much distress or change in their children that they attributed to the divorce. The distress levels observed in children differed little for the divorced and the comparison married groups. These findings fly in the face of data on the often serious initial impact of divorce on children (Hetherington et al., 1989; Krantz, 1988). Parents were apparently often unaware of changes in their children, particularly their young children, despite evidence from studies of children of divorce that chronicle heightened distress (Kalter, 1990). It is likely that some parents found it too threatening to acknowledge that their actions in ending the marriage caused their children distress. In a few cases, a parent may have felt that the children were better off without the other parent, regardless of the problems the marital breakup caused. Moreover, some parents were likely to have been so wound up in their own distress as to be unable to see the distress of their children. It is also possible (but unlikely) that the children, unlike their parents, were indeed little affected by the end of their parents' marriage. There is some evidence from data in the 1985–1986 marital transition study that with more discussion of these issues in the media and elsewhere, parents are more aware of the potential distress their children can experience. In discussing difficult kinds of adjustments, 28% of the mothers in the marital transition study mentioned concerns about their children, compared to only 9% of the mothers in the suburban divorced study. Even so, the vast majority of the mothers surveyed did not mention any such concerns. These data suggest the need for more public awareness programs to help divorcing parents recognize and handle the potential distress of their youngsters more appropriately.

Social Support

Although social support is thought to aid adjustment to distressing events, the divorced were no more likely than the married to have received help from their own families or from friends or coworkers, and less likely to have received help from their spouses' families. Divorce fragmented support networks. It was important for the divorced to establish a supportive network early on, as the support network was further reduced with time. Some types of help actually increased distress, particularly receiving financial support and advice from the same help source. It is likely that such a relationship increased a person's sense of being obligated to listen to the advice because the financial assistance was needed. Services, such as assistance with tasks, were helpful.

Therapy

Therapy was most helpful when a respondent received it with the partner before the divorce was obtained. Either such couples were more cooperative, or conjoint therapy helped them to reframe the issues of the divorce in such a way as to make adjustment easier. With few other data available on the extent to which divorcing individuals in a community sample seek psychotherapy, this study indicates that substantial numbers of people seek such help. Forty-five percent of the respondents in the suburban sample had sought such assistance at some point in their marriages from therapists (psychiatrists/psychologists, marriage counselors, or social workers), compared to 12.4% of the married sample.

Issues in the Postdivorce Period

Many of the divorced felt that others treated them less well because of their divorced status. It is difficult to ascertain whether this sense of stigma was the result of the respondents' own feelings of failure or of others' disapproving reactions. Both reactions, however, mean that divorce is still seen as unacceptable behavior. Blacks (who constituted the vast majority of the nonwhite sample in this study) reported less sense of stigma and less disapproval of the divorce decision by others than did whites. The greater frequency of divorce in the black community may have contributed to the easier adjustment blacks in this study experienced, compared to whites.

By 2-3 years after the divorce, more than two out of five of the suburban divorced respondents were repartnered—either remarried, cohabiting, or engaged. Men with higher incomes were more likely to be repartnered, as were women who were younger and who had few or no children. These data support an exchange perspective on the factors leading to being repartnered fairly quickly after a divorce.

A Model of Divorce Adjustment

Finally, a model of divorce adjustment that is multidimensional and includes losses explains more about the ease and difficulty of adjustment than an approach that simply looks at divorce as a crisis or life events stressor. Initial scores on the adjustment measures continued to influence adjustment even 2–3 years after the divorce. Those who were more distressed at first continued to have higher scores. Attachment and subjective distress were more powerful variables than were self-esteem and illness contacts in explaining adjustment over time. Certain individuals had experienced losses and had vulnerabilities that made adjustment more difficult for them. These included experiencing other negative life events, having been hospitalized for a mental illness, being angry with the ex-spouse, hesitating to divorce, and having been previously married.

It was possible to understand more about the correlates of adjustment for women and whites at the time of filing, and for men and blacks a year later, at the second interview. Thus, the impact of the divorce event for some respondents became more apparent after other events and experiences intervened.

WHAT ABOUT DIVORCE IN THE FUTURE?

How much can what has been learned here about the divorce process suggest about divorce in the future? This section examines some of these societal and public policy issues.

Divorce Rates

Although there has been a long-term upward trend in divorce rates, in the past 30 to 40 years divorce rates have gone up astronomically—not just in the United States, where the rates are the highest in the world, but in other industrial and industrializing societies (R. Phillips, 1988). Although the rates in the United States appear to have stabilized, with even some recent decreases, they have "stabilized" at a high rate. What does this mean for marriages in the future? Demographers continue to project high divorce rates, with estimates that from two in five to three in five recently contracted marriages will eventually end in divorce (Glick, 1988; Bumpass, 1990; Norton, 1991; Norton & Moorman, 1987; however, see Kemper, 1983, who argues for a downturn in divorce rates).

On the other hand, now that greater attention is being paid to the social, psychological, economic, and parenting problems associated with divorce, more couples seem at least to be thinking longer about the decision to divorce. At the same time, however, divorce rates among older persons are increasing (Uhlenberg, Cooney, & Boyd, 1990). Even with these countervailing trends, unless there is a serious multiyear economic downturn like the Great Depression of the 1930s, it seems likely that divorce rates will remain high. The marriage rate is decreasing (reducing the numbers eligible to become divorced); nevertheless, several associated trends support the prediction of continued fairly high divorce rates. First, individuals are more likely to live together before marriage than in the past (and some of these cohabitants end their relationships without ever appearing in divorce statistics). Spouses who have lived together before marrying are more likely to divorce than those who have not (Bennett, Blanc, & Bloom, 1988; Bumpass & Sweet, 1988). As a result of these experiences and the greater frequency of divorce, many people's views concerning the longevity of relationships have changed. Relationships are more often seen as endable and replaceable. Second, the importance and difficulty of maintaining the relationship dimensions of affection and companionship have been documented in the data presented here. With fewer structural restraints to keep marriages intact, people's expectations about the kind of role that intimate relationships should have in their lives is also likely to increase. This can set people up for disappointment.

A third factor associated with heightened marital instability is the premarital conception rate, which continues to be high (Norton & Moorman, 1987). Although women are more willing to have babies out of wedlock today, many pregnant women still marry, and those marriages are at greater risk for termination. If, as seems likely, efforts to tighten abortion rights continue in the United States, and sexual practices remain as they are, this too may produce even greater pressure on people to marry precipitously and to be susceptible to divorce.

Around the world, there appears to be a long-term trend toward divorce rates that reflect those in Western societies. This has led in some societies to decreases in divorce rates and in others to increases. It seems likely that these trends will continue, and thus that rates will continue to become similar across societies (Goode, 1963, 1984).

Adjustment Difficulties

If divorce stays at high rates, will adjustment to it become easier than it is now for many people? The answer depends, in part, on one's perspective concerning the meaning of divorce. If divorce becomes increasingly viewed as simply a civil or legal matter—a shedding of an outdated relationship, like the shedding of an outmoded coat—then its emotional impact should become less. For this to be the case, however, attitudes about the importance and sanctity of marriage as a "rite of passage" for adults need to be changed. Instead, there is an increasingly conservative trend toward restrictions in individual and family choice. In fact, members of a coalition of conservative Republicans and moderate and liberal Democrats have recently pressed for a 9-month waiting period before a divorce becomes final (Holmes, 1991). It seems unlikely that these attempts will be successful, but restrictions in divorce have occurred in the recent past in societies such as Iran and the former Soviet Union (Aghajanian, 1986; Moskoff, 1983). Many of these restrictions, however, were subsequently lessened, with a rebound in divorce rates.

It is likely that divorce will continue to be distressing for individuals because of several characteristics of the process. First, if marriage continues to be held up as an ideal, and people find that they are unable to live up to that ideal, then those who "fail" at this important task are likely to be upset at their failure, and others will continue to be upset with and for them. Second, to have chosen a partner so poorly makes a person question his or her judgment and feel like a fool for having been sucked in by this unworthy partner. It is also hard for the person to be found wanting in his or her own eyes or in the eyes of another. Such discoveries are upsetting and shake the person's self-confidence. These psychological verities are likely to continue to make divorce an upsetting event for most of those who experience it.

Third, even if it is true, as Price and McKenry (1989) and Ahrons and Rodgers (1987) state, that divorce is becoming a "normal" part of the family life cycle, other "normal" changes (e.g., marriage, the birth of children, and retirement) require adjustment and can elicit significant distress from those experiencing them. Thus, divorce can continue to do so as well for many of those going through it. Fourth, marriages rarely end without acrimony, whether this takes the form of arguments and disagreements or of cold, distant withdrawal. Acrimony, too, takes it emotional toll.

Fifth, many people going through divorce are extremely ambivalent about it. A spouse, after all, was originally selected because he or she seemed a good choice. Not all of the marriage was bad, nor (usually) was the partner without any redeeming features. It is often hard for a divorcing individual to understand that he or she can simultaneously be glad to be out of a relationship and yet still feel tugs back to that person and that relationship. In fact, the dislocations of the divorce can disconcertingly make a person want the old familiar partner back to assuage the distress. Such tangled feelings of longing coupled with various degrees of loathing increase adjustment difficulties for divorced and widowed women (Kitson, Babri, & Dyches, 1990).

Sixth, divorce entails not only the loss of an (at best) ambivalently regarded person, but also, for many, loss of lifestyle, status, income, and often friends and family. Families tend to split along bloodlines into "his" and "hers." People thought to be part of a person's network, it becomes clear, were not; they were "his" or "her" friends. Even those divorced people who maintain links with generally couple-based social networks may find that they have less in common with their married friends. With less income, it may also be harder to find the cash to share a dinner, movie, or sporting event, so that contacts decrease. Still others may offer unsolicited advice or treat the divorced person differently because of the change in marital status. Such changes and losses are also distressing.

Seventh, breaking up a marriage means breaking a number of other ties. Divorced spouses often have to change apartments or sell their homes and move to smaller or at least different quarters. A woman who was not employed before may start working; children with whom a custodial parent usually had some real (or at least perceived) help before may now become a sole and unrelenting responsibility. All of this may be occurring at a time when an individual may want time and space to explore new interests and relationships. A man may find himself experiencing reduced contacts with his children and taking on new household and social responsibilities. Each partner finds changes in his or her economic situation, with these changes more likely to be substantial decreases in income for women. These changes too can add to the strain of marital breakdown. Thus, divorce is not a break simply in one relationship, but in a set of relationships; these changes require restructuring, which also requires adjustment.

Unless spouses are able to end their relationship without ending any of the other links that marriage entails, it seems likely that divorce will continue to produce a fairly major upheaval in many people's lives, and that this upheaval will be experienced with anxiety, depression, anger, restlessness, sleeplessness, and inability to concentrate. The experience of the blacks in this study illustrates, however, that in a culture in which divorce is more frequent, adjustment may be eased. As has been seen, it was not that the blacks in this study who divorced were without distress, because blacks who divorced had greater distress than those who remained married; nevertheless, their distress was lower than that of the whites studied. Other studies are reporting similar results (Fine, McKenry, & Chung, in press; Gove & Shin, 1989).

It is important to remember that in certain social circles, divorce has been a relatively uncommon occurrence until recently. This means that for an event that still carries a baggage of moral, social, and psychological disapproval, there were few divorced people to observe and few cues to follow from others (and a devil one does not know is worse than a devil one knows). But, as this situation changes, and people gain more experience with divorced people in their neighborhoods, at work, and at church, the "differentness" of the divorced status may be lessening. At least, this is what appears to have happened among blacks in this study. Thus, although divorce is likely to remain a distressing event for many who experience it because it entails breaking the bonds of a once intimate and important relationship, that distress may well be less than it has been if current trends continue.

Economic Issues

Within the decade of the studies reported upon here, the economic resources of divorced women actually decreased. When a constant-dollar formula was applied to the average income of the divorced women in two time periods in the same community, the more recently divorced group (1985–1986) actually had lower incomes than the group who had divorced earlier (1974–1975). Both amounts were low, but the point is that after close to two decades of change in divorce laws that were designed to increase equity and (presumably) to produce greater awareness of inequity, income actually decreased for women. This has serious implications both for individuals and for the society. The key concern is the adequacy of financial resources for minor children. As a result of such shortfalls, their life chances may be hampered. If children who might otherwise have received education or training to fill leadership positions are not able to do so because their parents have divorced, this hurts not only them but also the society.

To avoid any more such problems, other options need to be considered for ensuring an adequate financial base for women and children, such as requiring more fathers to pay more child support. For example, in 1986, only 61.3% of mothers with minor children in the home without fathers present were awarded child support payments. Of those awarded payments, only 76.0% received at least some of the payments, and a mere 50.5% received all of the payments due them (U.S. Bureau of the Census, 1987b).

Under three different child support standards already in place in Wisconsin, Colorado, and Delaware, Garfinkel and Oellrich (1989) demonstrated that the yearly amount of money paid in child support, estimated at \$6.8 billion in 1983, could be increased to as much as \$24 billion to \$29 billion. This would mean that more fathers would pay at least some support, and many would pay at least two and a half times as much as they are legally required to do now. In the present research, divorced women's incomes decreased substantially while men's decreased only slightly. The institution of more realistic schedules of child support payments would redress this imbalance. Each parent would continue to be responsible for the maintenance of his or her child. In addition, cost-of-living increases in child support payments would be pegged to the rate of inflation. If a couple with a child were to divorce when that child was aged 5, child support payments would continue for 13 years, until that child reached age 18. The rate of payment would need to keep pace with salary increases of the noncustodial parent, as well as with inflation. Agreements concerning post-secondary education for children should be written more routinely into decrees.

Other proposals for improving child support payments include standardizing the amount of the award, guaranteeing a minimum level of child support, and increasing government benefits to single mothers by providing child care subsidies and work-welfare programs (McLanahan & Booth, 1989). Other societies provide a family supplement for those with children. France also has a system of free or low-cost child care and medical programs, which can be particularly beneficial to low-income single mothers (Bergmann, 1990). Social security payments are made for minor children in the United States in the form of Survivors' Insurance when one of the child's parents dies before the child is aged 18 and the deceased has worked long enough to be eligible for benefits (Lopata & Brehm, 1986). At a time when divorce has surpassed death as the major reason for the premature ending of marriages, such steps may need to be taken for the divorced as well. One possibility is automatically deducting support payments from the noncustodial parent's paycheck. Efforts must also continue to enforce payment of the child support that has been awarded. The issue of the adequacy of provisions for child support payments is a public problem with implications for the whole society, not just a private issue involving those who divorce.

Legal Issues

After the revolution in divorce laws, legislatures have continued to tinker with the legal system. Case law continues to expand and clarify the meaning of the new laws (Freed & Walker, 1988; Kay, 1990). In fact the courts have been asked to examine custody and visitation issues in homosexual relationships (Margolick, 1990), and civil cases have been filed to obtain damages for emotional duress in divorce (C. Phillips, 1988). More such legal extensions can be expected as people explore the meaning of the shift to the dissolution of marriage as a contractual relationship.

Under the option of no-fault divorce and its contractual focus, some couples are unable to come to agreements about assets and custody. Mediation is increasingly being mandated for such couples, and courts are being required to establish mediation services. This trend is likely to continue.

As Weitzman (1985) and others have established, under the guise of equality divorce laws have actually become less fair for women, who still bear the brunt of child custody and child-rearing expenses. The problems include inequities in the amount of support provided and the length of time for which it is provided, compared to the standard of living during the marriage. Among other issues (see also Kay, 1990), the option of rehabilitative support, or alimony, needs to be explored more fully. The data presented here suggest that women who received this support were able to upgrade their occupations, incomes, and self-confidence more readily than those without this option. Efforts also need to be expanded to better understand the "new marital property"—pensions, professional degrees, and the "goodwill" associated with a business—in order to establish more equitable property settlements (Wishik, 1986).

Human Service Needs

The present research also raises issues about professional help sources. A community-based survey such as this provides information often not otherwise available to therapists about the proportions of the divorced who seek help. The numbers who sought help in these studies were substantial.

When asked about programs or services that would have helped them, most of the divorced respondents mentioned programs similar to those already in place, at least in metropolitan Cleveland. Respondents were not necessarily aware of these services, however, or the programs available were restricted to those on welfare, focused on those of certain religious faiths, limited to certain areas of the county, or out of respondents' financial reach. In a time of reduced resources, new programs may not be needed as much as greater awareness of what is available. In addition, more efforts need to be made to help working- and middle-class people to afford these services, not simply those who are the poorest. Many private therapists are priced out of the market for those whose incomes are relatively limited, but not so limited as to push them into poverty and the availability of Medicaid programs. For those entering or returning to the labor force or those in low-paying jobs, insurance benefits may be nonexistent, delayed for a probationary period, or limited to the employed persons. When only the workers themselves are covered, their wages may be so low that they may not be able to afford insurance coverage for their children. Such persons might be able to pay for services on a sliding fee scale, which would help offset program costs.

Many people are ambivalent about special groups or programs for divorced persons, but some of the divorced respondents suggested the idea of a divorced-person-to-divorced-person program. Mutual help groups are available for widows (Silverman, 1980; Silverman, Mac-Kenzie, Pettipas, & Wilson, 1974). Such programs might be helpful for divorced persons as well.

FUTURE RESEARCH DIRECTIONS

Some future directions for research are highlighted by what has been learned from, and what has become apparent in the course of doing, the present studies. These include some characteristics that new research on divorce should incorporate, as well as some areas of research need.

Research Characteristics

Theory

The data presented here indicate that neither of the two leading "schools" of divorce adjustment—the pathology approach or the crisis/life events approach—adequately explains what occurs as people adjust to divorce. There are some people whose adjustment is hampered by psychological problems, and there are some people who rapidly recover from the divorce experience. For the remainder, however, the event and its sequelae become a series of chronic stressors. Adjustment is not easy or quick, and is slowed by having to cope with this event on top of other concurrent or preceding losses and vulnerabilities. But, more importantly, most people appear to adjust fairly well over time to the changes divorce brings to their lives. Thus, the process of adjustment seems to include elements from both schools of thought. The loss model examined here encompasses elements of both approaches, but researchers should continue to examine adjustment in more detail, to see whether another approach can explain the events of divorce in a more parsimonious manner. For example, divorce "trajectories"—the paths that different individuals take to end their marriages and cope with the changes that ensue—need to be explored.

Researchers taking a more clinical approach are linking the systems theory perspective to developmental theory. They see divorce as an event requiring the negotiation of developmental tasks (Ahrons & Rodgers, 1987; Carter & McGoldrick, 1988). This approach seems particularly suited for examining children's adjustment (Emery, 1988; Hodges, 1986; Kalter, 1990), but little empirical work with adults or families has taken this tack. It would be a useful, if complicated, endeavor to do so.

Sampling Issues

A key issue in new research on divorce will be the quality of the samples from which conclusions are drawn. To the extent that divorce records are public information, researchers engaged in basic research should seek to use such records in drawing their samples. Public records with data available on the characteristics of the couples and their children help to establish the representativeness of the portion of the sample selected that was actually interviewed. In locations in which access to such records is limited by law, researchers need to make more efforts to demonstrate the representativeness of their divorce samples, compared to the samples used in other published studies or to other publicly available data on the characteristics of those who divorce in their communities. Researchers engaged in prevention and intervention studies need to consider what types of programs and samples will most appropriately address the issues they wish to explore (see Pillow, Sandler, Braver, Wolchik, & Gersten, in press, for a call for interventions on high-risk samples). It is only through attention to these sampling issues that a good-quality, generalizable body of information about the characteristics of those who divorce and the process through which they move as they adjust to the decision to end their marriages can be developed.

Measures

Although replication of previous research findings in new settings with various modifications and additions is important and useful work, more effort needs to be expended in developing new measures that more appropriately explore the elements involved in the process of divorce. The measures developed for the present research, such as the scales assessing hesitancy to divorce, a couple's growing apart, attachment, stigma, satisfaction with the legal process, and a couple's contacts after divorce, help in this process, but more such efforts are needed. These efforts include modifications and extensions of already developed measures to increase their internal consistency, as well as attempts to develop new measures. Such new measures can make explicit the unoperationalized concepts that are used to explain the statistical associations that are found. For example, when it is said that divorce is distressing because people are still attached to their partners, it helps immeasurably to develop measures to assess this "attachment." It is important to use the best-quality measures, not simply ones that have been used before. Only in this way will it be possible to continue to move forward.

Longitudinal Studies

Aside from the present research, there have been relatively few longitudinal studies of adjustment to divorce. Here, an argument is made to stretch the concept of "longitudinality" even further by looking at the preseparation period, divorce adjustment, and remarriage.

The Preseparation Period. Researchers need to look at the preseparation period in greater detail, to begin to pinpoint potential problem areas in relationships. Such studies can better address the role of psychiatric illness as a precipitant or result of marital distress. In a sense, however, this can become an infinite regress, because events may occur even earlier in a marriage than the point at which a study begins, or even before the marriage itself takes place. Nevertheless, as Menaghan (1985), Menaghan and Lieberman (1986), and Booth et al. (1985) have demonstrated, such studies can clarify some of the issues related to divorce timing and adjustment difficulties. These efforts may also lead to the development of intervention programs. Divorce is a better solution than staying in a bad marriage, but a better goal is to reduce the number of bad marriages. In a 5½-year follow-up study, Markman (1981) found that couples who rated their premarital communication patterns as positive were more satisfied with their relationships at the second testing than were those who rated the interactions as negative; he therefore suggested that deficits in communication precede the development of marital distress. In an attempt to test these ideas, Markman and his colleagues have found that couples who engaged in a Premarital Relationship Enhancement Program had better communication skills, greater marital satisfaction, and lower divorce rates as much as 4 years later (Markman, Floyd, Stanley, & Lewis, 1986; Markman, Floyd, Stanley, & Storaasli, 1988). Levenson and Gottman (1985) found physiological cues in marital relationships that predicted deterioration in marital satisfaction at a second testing 3 years later. Gottman and Krokoff (1989) found that conflictual marital interaction patterns of whining, stubbornness, and withdrawal, especially for the husband, were predictive of deterioration in marital satisfaction at a 3-year follow-up. Studies such as these are often small in scale, and involve convenience samples and very detailed microcoding of interactions. These characteristics limit the generalizability of the findings and the ability of others to replicate the results easily, but more such efforts are needed. The steps couples go through as their relationships deteriorate, and what (if anything) can be done to prevent or remediate these processes, need to be specified in greater detail.

Divorce Adjustment. As noted throughout this book, little research has taken a long view of adjustment. In the suburban divorce study, changes in adjustment were still apparent at the third interview (approximately 4 years after separation). Bloom, Hodges, et al. (1985) also found long-term changes and instituted a 4-year follow-up to continue to assess them. Wallerstein and her colleagues found such changes as well and have reported upon adjustment at 5, 10, and 15 years after divorce (Wallerstein, 1991; Wallerstein & Blakeslee, 1989; Wallerstein & Kelly, 1980). Hetherington (1989) and Chiriboga et al. (1991) have likewise found long-term problems in adjustment.

Divorce leaves a long trail; as a result, studies need to take a longer view. There are several impediments to this, however. First, research funding generally comes in blocks of up to 5 years, so with time for startup and data analysis, most studies can only describe 3½ or 4 years of experience at most. Second, many studies of divorce adjustment use small samples, so that subject attrition becomes a problem. This detracts from efforts to seek another round of funding because subject-to-variable ratios become inadequate to justify further funding. These problems mean that it is difficult to maintain continuity in longitudinal projects. Nevertheless, such efforts will clarify many of the remaining issues in divorce research.

Remarriage. There has also been relatively little research following couples through the divorce process and into remarriage (Ahrons & Wallisch, 1987; Furstenberg & Spanier, 1984; Hetherington, 1989). Many studies do not include a large enough sample of divorcing persons to be able to examine remarriage in much detail. In addition, because of the growth of the literature and the special issues that each area involves, the field of divorce research is unfortunately beginning to fragment into those who look at "causes," "consequences," and "remarriage." This is reflected by literature reviews on these three topics in the 1990 decade review of the *Journal of Marriage and the Family* (Coleman & Ganong, 1990; Kitson & Morgan, 1990; White, 1990). In the 1980 decade review, there was only one review that covered all three aspects (Price-Bonham & Balswick, 1980); in the 1970 issue, divorce was only touched upon in a review of marital happiness (Hicks & Platt, 1970). In a countervailing trend, the *Journal of Divorce* recently recognized the continuity of adjustment processes by changing its title effective with Volume 14 to the *Journal of Divorce and Remarriage*. More efforts need to be made to look at the whole process of divorce.

This book has examined remarriage to some extent, but it has not been a major focus. A number of issues need further exploration. What are the social and psychological characteristics of those who marry again? Do those who remarry rapidly differ from those who remarry more slowly or who do not remarry at all? What does remarriage do to relationships with the children and ex-spouse(s) of the new partners? Do people select new partners similar to those they divorced? What is the adjustment process like in such marriages? Does adjustment differ from that in first-time marriages? Do communication patterns in second marriages resemble those of first marriages? Does therapy either before or after remarriage aid adjustment in the new marriage? What makes the redivorce rate in remarriages high?

Research Needs

Despite the substantial body of literature that has developed on the topic of divorce, several issues need further examination. Some of these are discussed below.

Gender Differences

More research needs to look at gender differences in adjustment. Women (both married and divorced) had higher symptom rates than men in the present research, and this has been borne out in other reports (Albrecht, 1980; Bloom, Hodges, et al., 1985; Chiriboga et al., 1991; Farnsworth, Pett, & Lund, 1989; Riessman, 1990). Other studies have reported few differences in adjustment by gender (Gove & Shin, 1989; Weiss, 1975), and one (Diedrick, 1991) has found greater predivorce difficulties for women and greater postdivorce difficulties for men. Epidemiological data report higher morbidity rates for divorced men than for divorced women (Riessman & Gerstel, 1985). These differences need to be reconciled. The types of measures used may explain a substantial portion of the difference. Measures focusing on anxiety and depression and on verbal description of affect are not as appropriate for men as for women, but such measures are often used in research (Dohrenwend & Dohrenwend, 1976). Women are generally better able to recognize and label their emotions than are men. Briscoe et al., (1973) found antisocial, acting-out behavior more salient for divorcing men, and anxiety and depression more salient for women (see also Riessman, 1990, on this point).

The timing of distress may also be another gender-based issue. The present data indicate that women had more difficulties (or that their difficulties were better assessed) at the time of filing for divorce. For men and blacks, adjustment was better understood within the first year after divorce.

Biological Issues in Adjustment

Illness contacts (measured as episodes of illness severe enough to require bed rest, doctor visits, and hospitalizations) were more common among the divorced than the married in the suburban study. Morbidity and mortality among the divorced need to be explored more fully. Recently, advances have been made in several other dimensions of physical and psychological illness that need to be kept in mind.

Genetic Vulnerabilities. Psychiatric research is increasingly exploring the role of the family of origin in the transmission of mental illness. There is increasing evidence that affective disorders, schizophrenia, alcoholism, and drug abuse may have a genetic component—that is, that such illnesses can be traced through family trees and that genetic propensities may make people more likely to be affected by these illnesses (Nelson & Charney, 1980). In Briscoe and Smith's (1973) work, more of the first-degree relatives of the divorced than of the married were described as having affective disorders. Research reporting on such relationships expands the definition of "intergenerational transmission of divorce" (or, perhaps more appropriately and even less felicitously, "intergenerational transmission of behaviorally, socially, and psychologically troubled relationships") to include a genetic propensity to affective disorders, susceptibility to problems with alcohol, schizophrenia, and so forth. This brings the old "nature versus nurture" argument into new high relief.

Immunological Functioning. In efforts to specify the mechanisms by which stress can adversely affect health status, researchers are linking psychological, social, and physiological measures to highlight the increased risk of illness because of suppressed immunological functioning in stressful conditions such as divorce and bereavement (Ader, Cohen, & Felten, 1990; Calabrese, Kling, & Gold, 1987; Geiser, 1989). In a study of separated, divorced, and married women, Kielcolt-Glaser et al. (1987) found that the married with poor-quality marriages had poorer immunological functioning, as did the divorced who had been separated from their spouses for shorter periods of time and who were more attached to them. Further study of the link between psychological and physiological functioning may help to explain the heightened health disturbance of the separated and divorced, and may also provide another way to examine the impact of the decision to divorce on health status.

Ethnic Differences

In these data, adjustment difficulties differed for whites and non-whites, with nonwhites (almost all of whom were blacks) generally having fewer problems. Efforts to understand adjustment difficulties were better for blacks at approximately a year after the divorce was granted and for whites at the time of separation. Other issues intervened after the divorce occurred that complicated adjustment for some (see also Chiriboga et al., 1991). The issues of potential differences in the difficulty and timing of adjustment need to be explored not only with blacks, but also with Hispanic- and Asian-Americans. Except for Chiriboga et al.'s (1991) small subsamples, there are virtually no studies of divorce adjustment among Hispanic- and Asian-Americans. As Laosa (1988) notes, divorce rates vary within these ethnic groups, but such groups are treated as undifferentiated masses—and again, are virtually ignored in divorce research.

A Multidimensional View of Adjustment

More research needs to take a broader view of, and to examine different dimensions of, adjustment. As has been shown here, adjustment encompasses a number of domains, with differences by gender and race in the importance of the various dimensions. Research taking a multidimensional approach requires a large sample and more complicated analysis plans, but understanding of the concept of adjustment has reached the point at which more complex models and techniques for assessing changes over time are needed.

The research reported upon here has looked primarily at dimensions of psychological adjustment as the dependent variables, but dimensions of social adjustment need to be explored as well (De-Garmo & Kitson, 1990; Kitson & Roach, 1989). Still others have looked at specific roles in greater detail, such as parenting (Ahrons & Wallisch, 1987; Buehler et al., 1985-1986). More specific and systematic efforts to explore what the concept "adjustment" means are needed.

Psychiatric Symptoms among the Divorced

There has been an undercurrent in much divorce research (even though it is usually described as the "bad" other view) suggesting that psychiatric problems of one or both of the marital partners "produce" the divorce and "cause" problems in adjustment. However, little research has examined these issues in any detail; more information is needed. The data presented here suggest that such issues do influence adjustment for some people, but still better measures are needed than those used here. A state-of-the-art assessment of the role of such factors in adjustment is needed.

Although it might be tempting to replicate the findings of this study with the measure of subjective distress used here, it would be more useful to couple this effort with the use of newer, more sophisticated measures such as the Derogatis Brief Symptom Inventory or the Symptom Checklist 90, both of which assess a number of dimensions of psychological functioning and can provide norms for comparisons with normal and psychiatric patients (Derogatis, 1977). Measures such as the Diagnostic Interview Schedule (Robins, 1986) can provide not just symptom levels but psychiatric diagnoses. The problem with many of these measures is their length, but sections that seem especially appropriate can be singled out for inclusion in surveys. Measures of this sort are much better, more detailed indicators of distress than the often-used Bradburn (1969) Affect Balance Scale, and should be considered instead. At the time the suburban divorce study was designed, the choice of items from the Psychiatric Status Schedule (Spitzer et al., 1970) was a good one, but there are better measures available now to explore these areas of interest.

Cross-National Research

Much of the knowledge available about divorce adjustment is primarily restricted to Western nations, particularly the United States, Great Britain, and the major British Commonwealth countries (Canada, Australia, and New Zealand). To some extent this is the result of language restrictions, but it is also a result of different orientations to research; there is a stronger focus on macrosocietal, structural relations in other societies. This has led to a body of literature on causes and correlates of divorce in other societies that may or may not be quantitative (Amoateng & Heaton, 1989; Bilge & Kaufman, 1983; Chester with Kooy, 1977; Cseh-Szombathy, Koch-Nielsen, Trost, & Weda with Bak & Tamasi, 1985; Goode, 1963; Platte, 1988; Trent & South, 1989). On the other hand, in the United States (and in Great Britain, to a lesser extent), there has been a more quantitative focus, as the references throughout this volume attest.

Research in other societies, particularly developing societies, would foster understanding of the relative importance of structural factors (the ease or difficulty of obtaining a divorce and the acceptability of divorce) versus interpersonal factors in adjustment. If attachment, loss, and a sense of failure are associated with divorce in other societies, then divorce should be psychologically distressing there as well. To the extent that structural conditions remain more disapproving of divorce as an option for one or the other gender, these dimensions may work together to produce even greater adjustment difficulties than in the United States. On the other hand, distress may be less apparent for one gender or the other, or the society may be such that divorce is not seen as unacceptable. Such analyses would clarify the relative role of structural versus emotional factors in adjustment.

Interventions

The research reported upon here identifies behavioral and demographic risk factors that are more common among those who divorce, as does the observational research of Markman et al. (1986, 1988) and Gottman and Krokoff (1989). More effort needs to be focused on evaluating preventive interventions that attempt to counteract or ameliorate these risk factors. Although attempts to restrict access to divorce as an option in unhappy marriages are misguided, any efforts to improve marital and family interaction in order to avoid the need to end problem marriages should be encouraged.

There are various programs designed to help the divorced adjust through group settings (based in part on Robert S. Weiss's educational support groups; see Weiss, 1975) and through individual and conjoint therapy. However, there have been relatively few attempts to evaluate the effectiveness of these programs (Bloom, Hodges, & Caldwell, 1982; Budman & Clifford, 1979; Sprenkle & Storm, 1983; Wertlieb, Budman, Demby, & Randall, 1984). Social service agencies around the country provide therapeutic help, but the effectiveness of these efforts has rarely been evaluated.

There have been more efforts to assess the impact of mediation on the settlement of divorces and on adjustment (Emery, 1988; Emery & Wyer, 1987a, 1987b; Folberg & Milne, 1988; Kelly, 1989), perhaps in part because mediation involves the application of a new approach to the area of divorce. Generally, evaluations of the effects of mediation have reported positive results.

The data presented here indicate that substantial numbers of divorcing people seek help. The impact of this help on their well-being is less clear. The suburban divorced respondents who sought help were generally more distressed, both initially and at the end of the study. Conjoint marital therapy before the marriage ended seemed to help more than individual therapy. Yet the divorced who had sought counseling, for the most part, felt that therapy was one of the things that helped them to cope and was also an area in which more help was needed for others. These findings suggest that there is still a great deal to be learned about how or whether professional and informal help sources aid adjustment to divorce. Clearly, many divorced persons can profit and have profited from professional assistance, but more information is needed about which kinds of programs are most effective for which types of people under what conditions.

Couple- and Family-Based Research

More studies need to look at both partners to the divorce and, when there are children, to include them in these analyses. The interaction (or noninteraction) of family members contributes to the situation to which people are trying to adjust. Better assessments of this are needed from the perspective of the various family members, not just one reporter.

There are obviously problems in obtaining cooperation from both parties to the divorce and from their children, as the research of Ahrons and Wallisch (1987), Ambert (1989), Fulton (1979), Jacobson (1987), and Masheter (1991) attests. Nonetheless, more studies of families from whom complete data are available need to be designed. Most efforts to date have focused on cooperative couples in which both partners (and sometimes their new partners) were in contact, and therefore were perhaps more willing to participate in the research (Ahrons & Wallisch, 1987; Jacobson, 1987). Efforts need to be extended to look at the whole array of families, not just the cooperative ones, and to leave in the research those from whom only partial cooperation was obtained.

There are other methodological problems in such work as well. These include the problem of deciding whether or how to count replies from several children in the same family. Families with more children can count more heavily toward the total, if individuals as opposed to family groups are assessed. Family members are likely to have similar replies (Kalter et al., 1989), so that scores may be skewed by larger family groups (Furstenberg et al., 1983; Wallerstein & Kelly, 1980). Another problem is that of how to combine the data from different perspectives, because the replies are likely to be at least somewhat correlated (Thompson & Walker, 1982). Even with these difficulties, more studies are needed that attempt to address these problems and look at the divorcing family as a system.

Children, like their parents, need to be directly assessed. Many studies now use the Child Behavior Checklist (Achenbach & Edelbrock, 1983), which asks parents and sometimes teachers to assess a child's functioning. As has been seen, parents may not be especially good reporters of their children's behaviors. Other, more objective measures of children's adjustment are needed.

This book has taken a comprehensive approach to the study of divorce by examining the process of marital breakdown from estrangement to 2–3 years after the divorce was granted. It has put these data in the context of a decade of research in one urban area. A great deal has been learned about how divorce affects adjustment, but there is still more to learn. This portrait of divorce is drawn as fully as has been possible. Perhaps the most important point is that despite the difficulties and setbacks that occur along the way, most people, with time, are able to adjust quite well to this major event in their lives.

Survey Instruments for the Suburban Divorced and Married Samples

To save space, the surveys are not reproduced in their entirety here and are not formatted as they would normally appear in an interview schedule. Instead, questions discussed in the text are listed by the time period or periods at which they were asked, with an indication of the study samples to which they apply—divorced, married, or both. The questions are also not displayed in the order in which they were asked in the surveys, because some items were only asked at one time period and were interposed with items asked several times. Furthermore, not all of the transition statements used to switch topics, or all of the directions to the interviewers and reply categories, are included. These decisions were necessitated by the number (five) and length of the interviews conducted (from 20 minutes for the second telephone interview with the married to 1-1½ hours for the in-person interviews); the repetition of items because of the longitudinal nature of the study; and space limitations.

[CARD] indicates that the respondent was handed a response card with the scale categories or choices from which he or she was to choose an answer.

FIRST INTERVIEW WITH DIVORCED

1a. Let's start right out talking about the divorce. The public court records indicate that __you filed __your husband/wife filed __both of you filed for __a divorce __a dissolution of the marriage. Is this correct? __Yes __No

1b. (*If no, specify*)

(*If dissolution of marriage*) For the remainder of the interview, when I use the word "divorce," I also mean "dissolution of marriage," as is true in your case.

2a. Thinking back, did you or your husband/wife first suggest the idea of divorce? __Respondent __Spouse __Mutual

2b. How long ago was that (*weeks, months, years*)?

3. Later on, which of you continued to insist more on a divorce? __Respondent __Spouse __Mutual

4a. (*If court record*) The court records indicate that this is your (*insert number*) marriage. Is this correct? __Yes __No

4b. (*If no*) How many times were you married previously?

4c. (*If no court record*) Is this your first marriage? __Yes __No

4d. (*If no*) How many times were you married previously?

4e. (*If any previous marriages*) Did your previous marriages end in death or divorce? (*Specify for each marriage*)

(*Questions repeated for [ex-]spouse*)

5. (*If spouse not living with respondent*) When did you and your husband/wife separate (*weeks, months, years*)?

6. How did your child(ren) react to the decision to divorce? (*Probes*: What did they say or do? Have they given you any advice about the decision to divorce? Have the children asked any questions about the decision to divorce?)

7. What caused your marriage to break up?

8a. It's hard, I know, to pinpoint this, but when would you say things started to go bad in your marriage?

8b. Could you tell me about that?

Now I'd like to talk with you about other people's reaction to the decision to divorce and the kinds of help or assistance people have given you recently.

9a. Was there anyone you hesitated to tell about the plan to divorce? __No __Yes

9b. (*If yes*) Who was that? Why did you feel that way?

10a. Did anyone in your family or your husband's/wife's family encourage you either to stay married or get divorced from your husband/wife? __No __Yes

10b. (*If yes*) Who was that? Why did he/she/they feel that way?

11. What have been the most difficult kinds of adjustments for you to make since the decision to divorce?

12a. (*If information available from court records*) I would like to verify some information from the divorce court records. The records indicate that you were married on (*insert date and year*). Is this correct? __Yes __No

12b. (*If no*) When were you married?

12c. (*If no court information available*) When were you and your husband/wife married (*date and year*)?

13a. (*If information available from court records*) The court records indicate that you were born on (*insert date and year*). Is this correct? __Yes __No

13b. (*If no*) When were you born?

13c. (*If date of birth not indicated from court records*) When were you born (*date and year*)?

(*Questions repeated for* [*ex-*]*spouse*)

Now I have a few questions about any changes that the decision to divorce may have made in your money situation.

14a. How much is your husband/wife contributing in child support for each of the children a week?

14b. How often does he/she pay this amount? __Always __Usually __Once in a while __Seldom __Never

15. During the past year have you done any reading or seen or heard any discussions that have had an influence on the decision to divorce? __No __Yes

FIRST INTERVIEW WITH DIVORCED AND MARRIED

1a. How many people live here with you?

1b. (*If any*) Would you please tell me their first names and their relationship to you? (*For children, specify when born—date and year*)

2. Some people's attitudes about marriage and divorce are changing. Here are some reasons that have been given by people in describing their divorces (marriages). Would you please look at this list and tell me if any of these are true in your case? (*Hand respondent* CARD *and read list simultaneously; answers: yes and no*) (1) Our interests grew (have grown, for the married) further and further apart; (2) Our relationship was (is) boring; there were (are) no real "lows" but no "highs" either; (3) Our relationship didn't (doesn't) let me and/or my spouse grow as a person; (4) I wasn't (am not) and/or my spouse wasn't (isn't) ready to assume all the responsibilities that marriage requires; (5) I wanted (want) the freedom that being single allows; (6) My work and the people I met (meet) through my work became (are becoming) more important to me than my marriage; (7) It seemed (seems) that the outside world had (has) more to offer me than my marriage did (does); (8) When I saw (see) what other people my age were (are) doing with their lives, it made (makes) me realize that I've been missing something important.

3. During the past year, have you or your husband/wife turned to any of the following people for help? [CARD: (1) clergyman, priest, or rabbi; (2) physician; (3) lawyer; (4) psychiatrist or psychologist; (5) marriage counselor; (6) social worker] (*Check who consulted and by whom: respondent, spouse, or both*)

4a. (*If any professional help in the past year*) You mentioned that you turned to (*specify source*) for guidance during the past year. At any other time in your marriage, did you or your husband/wife turn to any of the people listed on this card for help with marital problems? [CARD as above] __No __Yes (*specify*)

4b. (*If no professional help in the past year*) At any other time in your marriage, did you or your husband/wife turn to any of the people listed on this card for help with marital problems? [CARD as above] __No __Yes (*specify*)

5a. What are the main things you do in your spare time? Would you please give me the numbers of the activities you spend time at? [CARD: (1) going to movies; (2) watching TV, listening to records/radio; (3) attending sporting events as spectator; (4) going dancing; (5) taking part in sports (tennis, bowling, etc.); (6) attending concerts; (7) social drinking in bars; (8) attending plays; (9) visiting with relatives; (10) visiting with friends; (11) attending organization meetings (*specify*); (12) self-improvement activities (school, physical, dance, etc.); (13) groups for divorce (e.g., Parents Without Partners, etc.); (14) going for drives in car; (15) reading; (16) playing cards/games; (17) traveling (vacations); (18) playing musical instruments; (19) art/handicrafts (sewing, painting, etc.); (20) volunteer work (hospitals, etc.) (*specify*); (21) entertaining in your home; (22) other (*specify*)]

5b. (*For divorced*) Are you doing anything *differently* in your spare time *now* than you did before the decision to divorce?

6. In general, how much would you say your religious beliefs influence your daily life? [CARD: (1) very much; (2) quite a bit; (3) to some extent; (4) slightly; (5) not at all]

7a. May I ask in what religious faith you grew up? (*If Protestant, specify specific denomination: e.g., American Baptist, Southern Baptist, etc. If Jewish, specify Orthodox, Conservative, Reform*)

7b. To what religious faith do you now belong?

(*Questions repeated for* [*ex-*]*spouse*)

8a. I'd like to talk a little bit about some of the expectations married people have for their spouses concerning various areas of their marriages. During your marriage, how well did (has) your husband/wife live(d) up to your expectations in each of these areas? [CARD: (1) very badly to (5) very well]: (1) as a parent; (2) (male) as provider; (female) as a homemaker; (3) as a sexual partner; (4) as helpmate/partner; (5) as leisure-time companion; (6) as someone to talk things over with.

8b. (*For divorced*) Did your husband's/wife's behavior in any of these areas we have just talked about have any influence on the decision to divorce? (*Check all that apply*)

8c. (*For married*) Have any of these been a problem in your marriage?

9a. I'm going to read you a list of different kinds of household responsibilities. Would you please tell me who had full, major, or equal responsibility for each of these tasks during the last year (of your marriage)?: (1) (*if children*) helping the children with homework; (2) maintaining relationships with parents, in-laws, and other relatives; (3) taking care of the lawn; (4) taking out the garbage; (5) cleaning house; (6) cooking meals; (7) doing laundry; (8) (*if children*) disciplining the children; (9) doing dishes; (10) shopping for household items; (11) handling financial affairs; (12) (*if children*) playing with the children; (13) (*if owns car*) washing and taking care of the car; (14) painting and repair work around the house; (15) (*if children*) taking care of the children; (16) shoveling the snow; (17) maintaining social activities (e.g., inviting people over, making arrangements to go out; (18) dealing with groups or individuals outside of the family, such as (a) (*if children*) the school; (b) the church or YMCA/YWCA; (c) neighbors; (d) the authorities, such as the police, government officials, inspectors.

9b. (*For divorced*) Who is responsible for this task now?

10. I'm going to read some comments that people have made about marriage and divorce in general (*for divorced*: and about their reaction to their own divorces in particular). Would you please give me the number on the card that is closest to how you feel about these things? [CARD: (1) strongly disagree to (5) strongly agree] (1) The main purpose of marriage is to make each partner happy; (2) Couples are able to get divorced far too easily today; (3) (*if children*) Children are usually better off if their parents get divorced than if the parents stay together only for the children's sake; (4) The legal provisions for the division of property are fair; (5) Marriage is for life, even if the couple is unhappy; (6) The legal provisions for alimony are fair; (7) (*if children*) The legal provisions for child custody are fair; (8) Divorce is wrong except in the case of adultery; (9) (*if children*) The legal provisions for child support are fair; (10) It is all right for a couple to decide to divorce if a marriage isn't really bad but is boring; (11) It is all right for a couple to feel that if their marriage does not work out they can always get a divorce.

11. What was the last year of school you finished? __None; __Less than 7th grade; __7th to 9th grade; __10th to 11th grade; __Completed high school; __Noncollege training beyond high school; __Some college; __Completed college; __Some graduate or professional training beyond college; __Received advanced degree (*specify*)]

(*Questions repeated for* [*ex-*]*spouse*)

12a. Did you receive any of your education since you have been married to your husband/wife? __No __Yes

12b. (*If yes*) Would you tell me what this has been?

(Questions repeated for [ex-]spouse)

13. What is (was) your father's occupation? (*Specify industry, also, list former occupation/industry if retired or deceased*)
14. How much education does (did) your father have?

(Questions repeated for respondent's mother and [ex-]spouse's parents)

15a. Which number on this card best describes the total income for your family for the last year of your marriage (before taxes)? [CARD: (1) under $1,000; (2) $1,000 to $1,999; (3) $2,000 to $2,999; (4) $3,000 to $3,999; (5) $4,000 to $4,999 (6) $5,000 to $5,999; (7) $6,000 to $6,999; (8) $7,000 to $7,999 (9) $8,000 to $9,999; (10) $10,000 to $14,999; (11) $15,000 to $19,999; (12) $20,000 to $29,999; (13) $30,000 or over]
15b. What do you think your income is likely to be in the coming year (before taxes)? [CARD as above]
16. Race: __White __ Black __Oriental
17. Sex: __ Male __Female
18a. Did you have (have you had) any health problems during your marriage that affected your relationship with your husband/wife: __Yes __ No
18b. (*If yes*) What were these and how did they affect your relationship?

(Questions repeated for [ex-]spouse)

SECOND INTERVIEW WITH DIVORCED AND
FIRST INTERVIEW WITH MARRIED

1. (*For divorced*) Here are some reasons why people may hesitate to divorce. Thinking back to when you were married to your former husband/wife, would you please tell me if you ever thought of any of these in terms of your own marriage?
(*For married*) Many married people have at one time or another thought of ending their marriage even though they don't go ahead and do it. Would you please tell me if you have ever thought of any of these in terms of your own marriage?
(a) It's easier to stay married than to change my whole way of life; (b) (*if male*) The alimony and child support payments I can afford to pay aren't enough for my wife to live on; (*if female*) The alimony and child support payments my husband can afford to pay aren't enough for me to live on; (c) I couldn't make enough money to support myself if I were divorced; (d) Another marriage probably wouldn't be any better than this one; (e) I like the security of being married; (f) Divorce is too risky with the way the economy is today; (g) Getting divorced would mean a lower standard of living for me; (h) (*if male*) Getting a divorce would hurt my

career; (*if female*) Getting a divorce would hurt my husband's career; (i) I think I expected too much from marriage; (j) Because my parents' marriage wasn't very happy, I've probably tried harder in mine.

2a. (*For divorced*) I'd like to ask you some questions about your last marriage. Before the final separation, did you and your former husband/wife ever separate because of disagreements? __No __Yes

2b. (*If yes*) How many times did you separate?

2c. Could you tell me about it?

3a. (*For married*) Thinking back, have you or your husband/wife ever seriously suggested the idea of a divorce? __No __Yes

3b. Why did it come up at that time?

3c. Did you or your husband/wife file for divorce? __No __Yes

3d. Have you and your husband/wife ever separated because of disagreements? __No __Yes

3e. (*If yes*) How many times have you separated?

4a. Do you feel a part of any ethnic or nationality group? __No __Yes

4b. (*If yes*) What ethnic or nationality group is that?

4c. (*If more than one*) To which do you feel closest?

(*Questions repeated for* [*ex-*]*spouse*)

5a. Is your natural father living now? __No __Yes

5b. (*If no*) How old were you when your father died?

(*Questions repeated for respondent's mother and* [*ex-*]*spouse's parents*)

6a. Are/were your natural parents divorced or separated from each other? __Yes, divorced __Yes, separated __No

6b. How old were you when this happened? __(Separated) __(Divorced)

7. (*For all respondents*) How happy would you say your natural parents' marriage is/was (before the divorce/separation; before your father/ mother died)? Would you say it was __very happy __somewhat happy __not too happy?

8a. Knowing what you know now, if you could live your life again, would you marry the same person, marry a different person, or not marry at all?

8b. Why is that?

FIRST, SECOND, AND THIRD INTERVIEWS WITH DIVORCED AND FIRST INTERVIEW WITH MARRIED

1. During the past year, what kinds of help listed on the card did you receive from __your (ex-)husband's/wife's family __your family __your friends or coworkers __(*if children*) your children? [CARD: (1) none; (2) financial support (such as money, gifts, food, or housing); (3) service

support (such as babysitting, driving you places, errands, invitations to social events, dates); (4) information, guidance, or counseling (such as someone to talk things over with, teaching new tasks, moral support)]

2. How often do you get together with your (ex-)husband's/wife's relatives to visit at your house or theirs or to go out? (Specify which relatives)? __No relatives in metropolitan area __Daily __Almost every day __Once a week __Several times a month __Monthly __Less than monthly

(Question repeated for respondent's relatives)

3. How many friends do you have that you occasionally talk over confidential matters with?

4a. *(If any religious preference)* How often do you attend services? __More than once a week __Once a week __Two or three times a month __Once a month __A few times a year __Only on holidays __Never

4b. *(IF EVER ATTEND)* (For divorced: During this period of the divorce,) *(For married:* During the past few months,) would you say you are attending church/temple more or less frequently or about the same as before?

5a. In general, has anything about your health been bothering you? __No __Yes

5b. *(If yes)* What do you think is wrong?

5c. Is this something you've told a doctor about? __No __Yes

5d. *(If yes)* What does the doctor say is wrong?

6a. Do you worry much about your health? __No __Yes

6b. *(If yes)* What do you worry about?

7. Have you had any of these conditions in the past year? __Asthma __Allergies __Headaches __Backaches __Indigestion __Nervous stomach __Irregularity __Trouble with menstrual periods *(for women)* __Pain in chest

8. Looking back, how many times in the past year have you been ill enough to have to stay in bed at least a day? __None __One __Two __Three __Four __Five __Six __Seven or more

9a. Have you seen any doctors in the past year about your health? __No __Yes

9b. *(If yes)* How many times did you see the doctor(s)? __1 to 3 times __4 to 5 times __6 to 10 times __11 to 15 times __16 to 20 times __21 times or more

10a. Have you been hospitalized for an operation or illness in the past year? __No __Yes

10b. *(If yes)* How many separate times did you stay in the hospital? __Once or twice __Three or four times __Five times or more

11a. Have you been hospitalized for an emotional or mental illness in the past year? __Yes __No

11b. (*If no*) Have you ever been hospitalized for an emotional or mental illness? __No, never __Yes, prior to last year

12. How is your appetite for food? How often do you eat during the day?

13. How is your memory?

14. How are you at making decisions?

15a. What kinds of things do you worry about?

15b. (*If any mentioned*) How much do you worry about these things?

16a. Are there things or situations you are afraid of? __No __Yes

16b. (*If yes*) What are they?

17a. How often do you feel anxious or tense?

17b. (*If tense or anxious at all*) What causes this?

18a. How often do you feel sad, depressed, or blue?

18b. (*If ever*) When you feel sad, depressed, or blue, how long does it usually last?

19. How easily do you get upset or irritated?

20a. How often do you find yourself just thinking? __Very often __Fairly often __Sometimes __Once in a while __Never

20b. What kinds of thoughts do you have that other people wouldn't understand? Do you get thoughts that don't make sense, that you can't get rid of or put out of your mind? (*Probe*: Would you tell me about this?)

20c. (*If respondent is preoccupied, daydreams a great deal, or has bothersome thoughts*) How does this affect your daily routine, or what you do?

21. Sometimes people think about suicide. Have you thought about this even if you would not really do it?

22. Have you ever reached the point where you seriously considered taking your life or perhaps made plans on how you would go about it?

23. Have you ever made an attempt to take your own life? (*Probe*: How did you do this? Were you unconscious or hurt? Were you hospitalized?)

24. Do you ever have much trouble getting to sleep or staying asleep? __Nearly all the time __Pretty often __Not very often __Never

25. Many people have some problem with sex. Is there anything about your sex life or sexual feeling that is troubling you now?

26. In general, how do you feel things will work out for you in the future?

27. (*For all*) Here is a list of possible sources of income. Tell me the numbers of those that apply for you. [CARD: (1) own job; (2) (ex-)spouse contributes for general expenses; (3) (ex-)spouse contributes for child support; (4) help from family; (5) help from friends; (6) welfare; (7) savings; (8) income from child's job; (9) other (*specify*); (10) present spouse's job]

28a. Does anyone feel that you use poor judgment in handling money? __Yes __No

28b. (*If yes*) Why does he/she think that?

28c. Is there any truth to that? __No __Yes

29. Which number on this card best describes the total income for you/your

family for this year (before taxes)? [CARD: (1) under $1,000; (2) $1,000 to $1,999; (3) $2,000 to $2,999; (4) $3,000 to $3,999; (5) $4,000 to $4,999; (6) $5,000 to $5,999; (7) $6,000 to $6,999; (8) $7,000 to $7,999; (9) $8,000 to $9,999; (10) $10,000 to $14,999; (11) $15,000 to $19,999; (12) $20,000 to $29,999; (13) $30,000 or over]

While I am checking over the interview to make sure we have not left anything out, would you please fill out this sheet? (*Hand respondent self-esteem questions and pencil*)

30. (*On sheet*) Would you please indicate whether you agree or disagree with these statements? Circle one number for each question: 1 (strongly agree) to 5 (strongly disagree).

(a) I feel I'm a person of worth, at least on an equal basis with others; (b) I feel I have a number of good qualities; (c) All in all, I am inclined to feel that I am a failure; (d) I am able to do things as well as most other people; (e) I feel I do not have much to be proud of; (f) I take a positive attitude toward myself; (g) On the whole, I am satisfied with myself; (h) I wish I could have more respect for myself; (i) I certainly feel useless at times; (j) At times I think I am no good at all.

31. (*After respondent finishes sheet*) Since we would like to talk with you again in the coming months, would you please tell me the names and addresses of two people who will always know where you live? In case you move, we would like to be able to reach you. We will, of course, only contact them after we have made every effort to contact you ourselves, and will not tell them the subject of the study. (*Get name, address, city, state, and telephone number; note: do not take* [ex-] *spouse as a source*) (*Time at end of interview:* ———)

32. May I have your telephone number in case my office wants to verify this interview?

FIRST, SECOND, AND THIRD INTERVIEWS WITH DIVORCED AND FIRST AND SECOND INTERVIEWS WITH MARRIED

1. (*Questions 1a–1j are all answered "no" or "yes"*) (a) During the past several weeks, have you felt that things have been going your way? (b) Have you been pleased about having accomplished something? (c) During the past several weeks, have you felt bored? (d) Have you felt depressed or very unhappy during the past several weeks? (e) Have you felt proud because someone complimented you on something you had done? (f) During the past few weeks, have you felt on top of the world? (g) During the past few weeks, have you felt very lonely or remote from other people? (h) During the past few weeks, have you felt upset because

someone criticized you? (i) Have you felt particularly excited or interested in something in the past few weeks? (j) Lately, have you had such periods of restlessness that you couldn't sit long in a chair?

Before we finish the interview, in this last section, I'd like to ask you some background questions about you and your family.

2. What is your current employment situation? (*For second and third interviews*: The last time we (I) spoke with you, you were: __Currently employed full-time __Currently employed part-time __Currently unemployed but looking for work __Currently unemployed but not looking for work __Homemaker __Full-time student

3a. (*If currently employed*) What kind of work do you do (*occupation and industry*)?

3b. Is this the same job you had during most of your marriage? __Yes __No

3c. (*If no*) What was your usual occupation (*Specify industry also*)?

3d. (*Refer to job held during most of the marriage:*) About how many hours a week do/did you work on this job?

3e. Do you have any other jobs that you get paid for? __No __Yes

3f. (*If yes*) What kind of work do you do in your part-time job (*occupation and industry*)?

4a. (*If currently unemployed*) What kind of work do you usually do (*occupation and industry*)?

4b. About how many hours a week did you work on this job?

4d. When did you stop working (*year*)?

5a. (*If homemaker or full-time student*) What kind of work did you do on the last job you held (*occupation and industry*)? __Never worked

5b. What is (was) your usual occupation (*Specify industry also*) __Same as last job held

5c. About how many hours a week did you work on this job?

5d. When did you stop working (*year*)?

(*Questions repeated for* [*ex-*]*spouse*)

FIRST, SECOND, AND THIRD INTERVIEWS WITH DIVORCED

1. I am going to read some statements. For each statement, I'd like to know in what way it expresses your feelings about the divorce. For each one, would you please pick the number on the card that best reflects your feelings? [CARD: (1) not at all my feelings to (5) very much my feelings] (a) Everything I have to do seems like an effort; (b) I find myself spending a lot of time thinking about my (ex-)husband/wife; (c) I'm

feeling like myself again; (d) Sometimes I just can't believe that we're getting a divorce; (e) I find myself wondering what my (ex-)husband/wife is doing; (f) I have no interest in anything; (g) I'm going ahead with the divorce only because it's what my (ex-)husband/wife wants; (h) I'm angry at my (ex-)husband/wife; (i) I do not feel any guilt about the divorce; (j) I feel as if I've been dumped; (k) Perhaps with all things considered, we should have tried longer; (l) This has been coming for a long time, and I'm glad we've finally made the break; (m) I feel as if this is all a horrible mistake; (n) It isn't an easy decision to divorce your husband/wife, but basically I'm relieved; (o) Although this is the right decision, I know it's hurt my (ex-)husband/wife very badly; (p) I feel I will *never* get over the divorce; (q) I feel a little guilty about the divorce, but it was the right decision for us; (r) Divorce is one of the most tragic things that can happen to a person.

2. (*If respondent asks about a help source,* suggest that he/she : (a) talk with his/her attorney and have him/her make the suggestions. (b) refer the person to the Community Information Service [a local referral service] (*telephone number*). *Check here if respondent asked for help source:* __)

FIRST AND THIRD INTERVIEWS WITH DIVORCED AND FIRST INTERVIEW WITH MARRIED

1. (*For those with children*) Have you noticed any difference in your child(ren's) behavior from what it was before the decision was made to divorce? For example:

    (*For married with children*) Now I'd like to ask about some ways your children may have changed recently. Children change and grow. Have you noticed any differences in your child(ren)'s behavior in the past few months? For example:

    (a) Have you noticed any differences in how happy the child(ren) seem(s)? (*specify*) (b) Any differences in how they (he/she) get(s) along with friends? (c) Any differences in how they (he/she) get(s) along with other family members? (d) Any differences in how well they (he/she) are (is) doing in school? (e) Any differences in the child(ren)'s health? (f) Any differences in the child(ren)'s behavior? (g) Have (Has) the child(ren) gotten into any trouble lately? __No __Yes (*If yes, specify*) Is this different from before?

2a. Until now we've been talking about your everyday behavior and your health. Now let's turn to a number of other common experiences that people have—that is, events that concern everyday life, such as school, the job, and family. I would like to go over with you a number of such events to learn whether any of them have happened to you or to members of your family during the past year. (*Note if needed*) By "family" we mean your immediate family and that of your (ex-)husband/ wife—parents, children, brothers, and sisters. (*If someone else specified as family, write in*)

(*Response categories for questions 1-13:* __No __Self __[Ex-]spouse __New spouse __Other [*specify*])

2b. During the past year, did anyone have any changes or problems in school? (*If yes*) During the past year, did anyone (a) start to school, training program, etc.? (b) graduate from school, training program, etc.? (c) fail at school, training program, etc.? (d) change school, training program, etc.? (e) have any problems in school?

2c. During the past year, did anyone move or do any remodeling of his/her home? (*If yes*) During the past year, did anyone (a) move to same type of neighborhood? (b) move to better neighborhood? (c) move to worse neighborhood? (d) build a new home? (e) do major remodeling of house?

2d. During the past year, did anyone get (a) engaged? (b) married? (c) widowed? (d) divorced (besides self)? (e) separated (besides self)?

2e. During the past year, has anyone had any trouble with in-laws?

2f. During the past year, has anyone entered the Army, Navy, or other armed service?

2g. During the past year, have there been any new additions to the family, or has anyone left? (*If yes*) (a) Was there a birth of a child? (b) If so, was it a first child? (c) Was there an adoption of a child? (d) Did a new person (other than child born above) move into the family or household, or return after a lengthy absence (older person, relative, child returning from armed forces, etc.)? (e) Did a member of the family or household leave home (other than armed forces—e.g., marriage, college)?

2h. During the past year, was there (a) a stillbirth? (b) mental illness? (c) death of a pet?

2i. During the past year, did anyone have any changes in work patterns, for the better or for the worse? (*If yes*) Did anyone (a) start to work for the first time? (b) if change in job, change to same type of job? (c) get promoted or move to a more responsible job? (d) get demoted or change to a less responsible job? (e) get laid off (temporarily)? (f) expand business? (g) return to work? (h) have a business fail? (i) have trouble with a boss? (j) have any trouble or changes at work (e.g., changes in hours or conditions, changes in responsibilities, changes to a different kind of work, transfer to a different department)? (k) remain out of work over a month? (l) get fired? (m) have any big reorganization at work? (n) retire? (o) have any sort of significant success at work?

2l. During the past year, did anyone have (a) a serious physical illness? (b) a serious injury or accident? (c) a death of a loved one (family or close friend)? (d) a pregnancy?

2m. During the past year, was there any change in finances for the better or worse? (*If yes*) (a) Was there a major improvement in financial status (e.g., a lot better off than usual)? (b) Was anyone's financial status a lot worse than usual (e.g., loss of a large amount of money, unusually heavy debts/expenses)? (c) Was there a foreclosure of mortgage or loan (e.g., car, house, furniture)?

2n. During the past year, have there been any legal problems, other than the divorce? (*If yes*) (a) Has anyone been in court? (b) Has anyone been in detention, in jail, or in some other correctional institution? (c) Has anyone been arrested? (d) Did anyone have any lawsuit or legal action?

2o. During the past year, was there (a) a loss of a driver's license? (b) any change in relations with a neighbor, friend, or relatives, such as serious or major disagreement? (c) any vacation (a week or more away from home)? (d) any change in the number of family get-togethers (a lot more or fewer than usual)?

2p. Does anything else come to mind that happened to anyone in your family in the past year? (*If yes, specify*)

SECOND AND THIRD INTERVIEWS WITH DIVORCED

1a. When we were (I was) here earlier, (*check all appropriate categories*) __you, __your, _____, __your _____, __(*insert number*) children _____ (*list names*), and __others _____ (*list names and/or relationships*) were living together (*for the single and childless*: you were living by yourself).

1b. Have any of these people left your household? __No __Yes

1c. (*If someone has left*) Who left? What is his/her/their relationship to you?

1d. Has anyone joined your household? __No __Yes

1e. (*If yes*) Would you please give me their first names and relationship to you? (*For children, specify when born—date and year*)

1f. Since we talked with you in (*month, year*), did anyone live with you for a while who is not doing so now? __No __Yes (*If yes, specify*)

2a. (*For all*) Looking back, what were your general feelings about your family's standard of living when you were married—that is, the kind of house, clothes, car, (*if children*: opportunities for the children,) and so on? [CARD: (1) very dissatisfied to (5) very satisfied] Would you please give me the number that best reflects your feelings?

2b. And how about now—how satisfied are you with your standard of living? [CARD as above] Would you please give me the number on the card?

3. How often do you (does your ex-husband/ex-wife) see the children—the actual, not the legal schedule? __No regular schedule; whenever I (he/she) want(s) __At least twice a week __Once a week __Less than weekly but more than once a month __Once a month __Less than monthly __Never, no visits __Other (*specify*)

4. During the past few weeks, have you done any of the following? __Spoken to your ex-husband/wife by phone __Spoken to your ex-husband/wife in person __Heard from your ex-husband/wife by letter __Written to your ex-husband/wife __Heard about your ex-husband/wife through friends or neighbors __Seen your ex-husband/wife but did not speak to him/her __Gone out with your ex-husband/wife

5. (*For all*) Would you like to have more, less, or about the same amount of contact with your ex-husband/wife? __More __Less __About the same

6. Would you give me the number on the card that describes your feelings toward your ex-husband/wife now? [CARD: (1) I love him/her; (2) I still like him/her, but I don't love him/her; (3) I don't feel much of anything for him/her; (4) I don't like him/her much any more; (5) I hate him/her; (6) I both love and hate him/her; (7) I don't love or hate him/her, I feel sorry for him/her]

(*Questions repeated for ex-spouse*)

7. I'd like your opinion about some statements I'm going to read. These are general statements, and there are no right or wrong answers. Would you give me the number from the card that best reflects your opinion? [CARD: (1) agree strongly; (2) agree; (3) disagree; (4) disagree strongly] (a) A divorced person has to make his/her own life and not depend on others; (b) Married people are jealous of a divorced person when their spouses are around; (c) Many divorced people who remarry are very unhappy in that marriage; (d) Relatives are your only true friends; (e) Divorced women are constantly sexually propositioned even by the husbands of their friends; (f) One problem of being a divorced person is feeling like a "fifth wheel"; (g) People take advantage of you when they know you are divorced; (h) My married friends have not been much help to me; (i) Most divorced people prefer having other divorced people as friends; (j) It is all right for a divorced person to have sexual relations with a person without planning on marriage; (k) Women lose status when they become divorced—they lose respect; (l) Divorced men are expected to act like carefree bachelors; (m) Of the men/women I have dated, I have most in common with those who are divorced; (n) Other people gossip a lot about a person who's been divorced; (o) I feel more independent now than before I became divorced.

8. (*For all singles*) Would you give me the number on the card that best describes how often you go out on dates during an average month?

[CARD: __Three or more times a week __Twice a week __Once a week __Two or three times a month __Once a month __Less than once a month __Seldom or never]

9a. (For those not remarried) And, other than dating, how often do you go out with friends during an average month? [CARD as above]

9b. (For those who are remarried) How often do you go out (without your spouse) with friends during an average month? [CARD as above]

10. (For all singles) Would you say in general that you're satisfied with the frequency with which you go out on dates, or would you like to go out more or less often? __Satisfied as is __More often __Less often

11. (For those with children) Do you see any changes in the child(ren) that you think are related to the divorce? (Probe for each child: How about [child's name]?)

12. When we (I) talked with you last, these are the main things you said you did in your spare time (read items checked from the list). Have there been any changes—things you've stopped doing or new things you've started doing? [CARD: (1) going to movies; (2) watching TV, listening to records/radio; (3) attending sporting events as spectator; (4) going dancing; (5) taking part in sports (tennis, bowling, etc.); (6) attending concerts; (7) social drinking in bars; (8) attending plays; (9) visiting with relatives; (10) visiting with friends; (11) attending organization meetings (specify); (12) self-improvement (school, physical, dance, etc.); (13) groups for divorce (e.g., Parents Without Partners, etc.); (14) going for drives in car; (15) reading; (16) playing cards/games; (17) traveling (vacations); (18) playing musical instruments; (19) art/handicrafts (sewing, painting, etc.); (20) volunteer work (hospitals, etc.) (specify); (21) entertaining in your home; (22) other (specify)]

13. Since (insert date), when we spoke to you last, have you turned to any of the people listed on this card for help with personal problems? [CARD: (1) clergyman, priest, or rabbi; (2) physician; (3) lawyer; (4) psychiatrist or psychologist; (5) marriage counselor; (6) social worker]

14. I'm going to read you a list of different kinds of household responsibilities. In getting these tasks done for yourself now, would you please tell me who has full, major, or equal responsibilities for each? (1) (if children) helping the children with homework; (2) maintaining relationships with parents, in-laws, and other relatives; (3) taking care of the lawn; (4) taking out the garbage; (5) cleaning house; (6) cooking meals; (7) doing laundry; (8) (if children) disciplining the children; (9) doing dishes; (10) shopping for household items; (11) handling financial affairs; (12) (if children) playing with the children; (13) (if owns car) washing and taking care of the car; (14) painting and repair work around the house; (15) (if children) taking care of the children; (16) shoveling the snow; (17) maintaining social activities (e.g., inviting people over, making arrange-

ments to go out; (18) dealing with groups of individuals outside of the family, such as (a) (*if children*) the school; (b) the church or YMCA/YWCA; (c) neighbors; (d) the authorities, such as the police, government officials, inspectors.

SECOND INTERVIEW WITH DIVORCED

Now I'd like to ask some questions about the divorce itself.

1. Some people report that their divorces involved a lot of conflict, and others say their divorces were friendly. From your point of view, do you feel there was a lot of conflict in your divorce or was it friendly? On a scale of 1 to 5, how would you rate your divorce? [CARD: (1) a lot of conflict to (5) friendly]

2. In general, how satisfied are you with the divorce settlement? Would you please give me the number on the card that best reflects your feelings about this now? [CARD: (1) very dissatisfied to (5) very satisfied]

3. We'd like to know how you arrived at the divorce settlement. First, how did you arrive at the division of property? Did you and your ex-husband/ex-wife work it out yourselves; did the lawyer(s) work it out; or was it decided in court? (*Check all that apply on this card.*) [CARD]

4. Next, I want to ask you some questions about property and what happened to it at the time of the divorce. (*As necessary, indicate what percentage each one got or whether items were sold or divided*) (a) First, did you own a house? __No __Yes (*If yes*) Who got it? (b) Did you own (a) car(s)? __No __Yes (*If yes*) Who got it (them)? (c) And what about the furniture? (d) Did you own (a) TV(s)? __No __Yes (*If yes*) Who got it (them)? (e) Did you own a stereo? __No __Yes (*If yes*) Who got it? (f) Did you have any bank accounts? __No __Yes (*If yes*) Who got it (them)? (g) Did you own any stocks or bonds? __No __Yes (*If yes*) Who got them? (h) Did you have a pension? __No __Yes (*If yes*) Who got it? (i) Did your ex-husband/ex-wife have a pension? __No __Yes (*If yes*) Who got it? (j) Did you have a business? __No __Yes (*If yes*) Who got it? (k) Did you have any other major property (*specify*)? __No __Yes (*If yes*) Who got it?

5. How satisfied are you with the court-ordered division of property? Would you give me the number on the card that best reflects your overall feelings? [CARD: (1) very dissatisfied to (5) very satisfied]

6a. What was the court order for alimony? (*Probe:* How much did the court order you [him/her] to pay?)

6b. How often did the court say you (he/she) should pay this amount? __Weekly __Every 2 weeks __Monthly __Other (*specify*)

6c. Do you know if the court said the amount of alimony should be stopped or changed at a later time? __No change __Yes, change __Don't know

6d. (If yes) When is it to be changed?

6e. How much are you to pay (receive) then?

6f. How often are you to pay (receive) this amount then?

6g. How much are you (is he/she) actually paying?

6h. How often are you (is he/she) paying this amount? __Weekly __Every 2 weeks __Monthly __Other (specify)

7. (If any children under age 18) What did the court order for the custody arrangements for the child(ren)? (Probe: What kind of visiting arrangements were set up by the court—the legal, not the actual arrangements?)

8a. What was the court order for child support? (Probe: How much did the court order you (your ex-husband/ex-wife) to pay for child support (amount per child)?

8b. How often are you (is he/she) supposed to be paying this amount? __Weekly __Every 2 weeks __Monthly __Other (specify)

8c. And for how long are you (is he/she) supposed to pay this amount? (Specify number of years, age of child, or event)

8d. How much are you (is your ex-husband/ex-wife) actually paying in child support (amount per child)?

8e. And how often are you (is he/she) actually paying this amount? __Weekly __Every 2 weeks __Monthly __Other (specify)

9a. (If any children age 18 or older) Have any arrangements been made for paying for the child(ren)'s education? __No __Yes

9b. (If yes) What are they?

10. Next, I want to ask you some questions about how the legal process affected your divorce. I'm referring to the whole legal process—that is, the law, the judges, and the lawyers. In terms of your divorce, how satisfied would you say you are with the whole legal process—including the law, the judges, and the lawyer(s)? [CARD: (1) very dissatisfied to (5) very satisfied]

11. Overall, do you think the legal process increased the amount of conflict in your divorce, or did it make it easier to divorce without a lot of conflict? Would you give me the number on the card that best reflects your feelings? [CARD: (1) increased the conflict to (5) decreased the conflict]

12. If you had to assign blame for the failure of the marriage, whom would you blame? [CARD: (1) ex-husband/ex-wife; (2) mostly ex-husband/ex-wife; (3) both of us; (4) mostly myself; (5) myself; (6) neither of us; (7) other (specify)]

13. Did you or your former spouse ever file for divorce or a dissolution of marriage before? __No __Yes, respondent __Yes, ex-spouse __Yes, both (dissolution)

14. (If separated at time 1) Since we last spoke with you, did you try reconciling? __No __Yes

15a. (*If not separated at time 1*) When we talked with you last, you hadn't separated yet. When did you separate (*date*)?

15b. Did you try reconciling after that? __No __Yes

16a. As far as you know, has your former husband/wife been involved with another woman/man since the divorce? __No __Yes, remarried __Yes, engaged __Yes __Don't know

16b. Was your ex-husband/ex-wife involved with (this person or) any other person besides yourself during your marriage? __No __Yes, this one __Yes, this one and other(s) __Yes, another one __Don't know

17a. Were you involved with someone else besides your former husband/wife during your marriage? __No __Yes

17b. (*If yes*) When did this begin?

17c. Are you still seeing this person? __Yes, remarried __Yes, engaged __Yes __No

17d. Are you seeing anyone else at this time? __Yes, engaged __Yes __No

18. Are you presently seeing anyone? __No __Yes, remarried __Yes, engaged __Yes

19. (*If not remarried*) If you were to remarry, how do you think this marriage would differ from your previous one? (*Probe*: What would be your expectations about the way things should be?)

20a. Have you been in a social situation in which you felt someone thought less of you when he or she found out that you were divorced? __No __Yes

20b. (*If yes*) Could you tell me about it?

21a. Thinking back over the period since the divorce was filed, are there any particular activities that have especially helped you to cope with things? __No __Yes

21b. (*If yes*) What are these activities?

21c. How have they been helpful to you?

22a. Since the divorce suit was filed, is there a particular person who has been especially helpful to you in adjusting to the divorce? __No __Yes

22b. (*If yes*) Who is this person and what is his/her/their relationship to you?

22c. (How was he/she) (have they) been helpful?

23. In general, would you say that the members of your family disapprove of the divorce, are neutral, approve, or just do not care? [CARD: (1) they disapprove of the divorce; (2) they are neutral; (3) they approve of the divorce; (4) they don't care; (5) other (*specify*); (6) don't know]

(*Questions repeated for ex-spouse's family*)

24. Divorce affects people in different ways. Using this card, I'd like to know if any of these things have happened to you at any of these times. [CARD with the following choices: (1) before the decision to divorce; (2) at the time of the decision; (3) at the final separation; (4) when first filing for divorce; (5) at final divorce decree; (6) now; (7) never] (*Note: If*

respondent mentions more than one period for an item, check all that apply and ask:) Of these, which *one* would you say was the best (worst)? (*Put an asterisk by that reply*) (a) During which one of these periods do you think your health was the poorest? (b) During which one of these periods do you think your health was the best? (c) When did you have the most difficulty in sleeping? (d) When did you have the least difficulty in sleeping? (e) When did you have the most difficulty in doing your work efficiently? (f) When did you have the least difficulty in doing your work efficiently? (g) During which period did you feel the most lonely? (h) During which period did you feel the least lonely? (i) During any of these periods, did you have an unwanted serious weight change (*specify*)? (j) When did you feel really low or down? (k) When did you feel that you just didn't care about yourself? (l) During which period(s), if any, did you smoke more than usual? (m) During which period(s), if any, did you drink alcohol more than usual? (n) When were you most angry at your ex-husband/ex-wife?

25. Knowing what you know now, if you could live your life again would you marry the same person, marry a different person, or not marry at all? __Same person __Different person __Not marry at all

26a. Some of the changes divorce requires are pleasant and some are unpleasant. What have been some of the pleasant changes?

26b. And what have been some of the unpleasant changes?

27a. Thinking over your experiences, are there any kinds of special programs or assistance that would have made things easier for you when you first separated?

27b. In terms of the future, what kinds of help or assistance do you think would aid you?

28a. In general, what is your opinion of groups for divorced people? Do you think they are a good thing or not? (*Probe:* Why is that?)

28b. Have you ever attended any meetings of groups for divorced people? __No __Yes

28c. (*If yes*) What group was that?

29a. Did you turn to anyone for financial help since the divorce? __No __Yes

29b. (*If yes*) Whom did you turn to? [CARD: (1) own family; (2) ex-husband's/wife's family; (3) church; (4) ex-husband/wife; (5) friends; (6) coworkers; (7) welfare or Aid to Families with Dependent Children; (8) other (*specify*)]

THIRD INTERVIEW WITH DIVORCED

1. (*If not all children living with respondent*) When we first talked with you, you mentioned that you had (*specify number of*) children. Except

for those children living with you (and those/the one we just talked about), with whom do they (he/she) live?

2. How many times have you moved since January 1974?

3a. When we talked with you before, you were __single __engaged __married __living with someone, Are you now (*read all for everyone*) __single __engaged __married __married and separated or divorced __living with someone __widowed?

3b. (*For all engaged, married, or living with someone at time 2 and now*) Is this to (with) the same person you spoke of in (*date of last interview*)? __No __Yes

4a. (*If remarried since time 2, even if now separated, divorced, or widowed*) When did you remarry (*date, year*)?

4b. (*If widowed*) When did your husband (wife) die (*date, year*)?

5. (*If presently remarried or living together*) How did you meet your husband/wife (the person you are living with)? (*Probe for where and how*)

6. All in all, how happy has your present marriage (relationship) been for you? [CARD: (1) very unhappy; (2) unhappy; (3) somewhat happy; (4) somewhat happy; (5) happy; (6) very happy]

(*Also asked of married sample at second interview*)

7a. Do you ever feel that having been divorced makes it harder for you in this marriage (relationship)? __No __Yes

7b. (*If yes*) In what ways?

8. What do you like best about being remarried (living together)?

9a. (*For single*) I'd like to talk a little bit about some of the expectations people have for their partners concerning various areas of their relationships. Which of these areas is most important to you in choosing a partner? Which is next most important? [CARD: (1) as a parent; (2) (male) as a provider; (female) as a homemaker; (3) as a sexual partner; (4) as a helpmate/partner; (5) as a leisure-time companion; (6) as someone to talk things over with]

9b. (*For single*) Thinking about the person you're dating (who has been most important to you), have his/her characteristics in any of these areas been a problem in your relationship? [CARD as above] __No __Yes

10a. (*For remarried/cohabiting*) I'd like to talk a little bit about some of the expectations people have for their partners concerning various areas of their relationships. How well does your husband/wife (friend) live up to your expectations in these areas (see above)? [CARD: 1, very badly to 5, very well]

10b. (*For remarried/cohabiting*) Has your husband's/wife's (friend's) behavior in any of these areas we just talked about been a problem in your marriage/relationship? [CARD as above]

11a. *(For single)* Do you think you will marry again? __No __Yes

11b. *(If no)* Why not?

12a. *(For single)* Here are some places where you might have met someone you dated. Since your separation, have you ever met a date at any of the places listed on this card? [CARD: (1) through your family; (2) through a friend; (3) at a party or social gathering; (4) at a bar; (5) in a singles group; (6) at work; (7) through a church; (8) because you knew him/her before; (9) other *(specify)*]

12b. Which of these seems to be the best way to meet dates? [CARD as above]

13a. *(For single)* Any major event like a divorce may bring about changes in a person. Do you see any changes in yourself as a result of the divorce? __No __Yes

13b. *(If yes)* What kind of changes?

14a. When we talked with you last, you said you __had turned __had not turned to someone for financial help since the divorce. Have you turned to anyone for financial help since then? __No __Yes

14b. *(If yes)* Whom did you turn to? [CARD: (1) own family; (2) ex-husband's/wife's family; (3) church; (4) ex-husband/wife; (5) friends; (6) coworkers; (7) welfare or Aid to Families with Dependent Children; (8) other *(specify)*] *(For each turned to, ask:)* Did they give you any financial help? __No __Yes

15a. Were there any things that surprised you or that you had not anticipated about being divorced? For example, were there things that were easier to do or learn than you had thought they would be? __No __Yes

15b. *(If yes)* What were they?

16a. Were there things that were harder to do or to learn than you thought they would be? __No __Yes

16b. *(If yes)* What were they?

17. Some people report that before they divorced they prepared themselves for it. Did you make any preparations like these before the divorce? __Learn about your legal rights in divorce __Read about the experiences of other people who divorced __Build a nest egg __Get a job __Prepare for a career __Learn to cook __Learn about finances __Get counseling to help with the divorce decision __Anything else *(specify)*

18. Looking back over your marriage, what would you now say caused your marriage to break up?

Now I would like to ask a few questions about your child(ren)

19a. Do you think the divorce has changed your ex-spouse's relationship with the child(ren)? __No __Yes

19b. *(If yes)* In what ways?

(Questions repeated for respondent)

20a. Do you think the children have (child has) changed in any ways as a result of the divorce? __No __Yes

20b. *(If yes)* Who has changed and how has he/she changed?

21a. Now we'd like to ask you about alimony (and child support). When we talked with you last, you indicated that the court __had ordered __had not ordered that you pay (receive) alimony. Are you *currently* paying (receiving) alimony? __No, none ordered and order not changed __No, but should be paying (receiving) __Yes, paying (receiving)

21b. *(If alimony ordered)* How much are you actually paying (receiving) in alimony?

21c. *(If currently paying [receiving] alimony)* How often are you paying (receiving) this amount? __Weekly __Every 2 weeks __Monthly __Payment irregular *(specify below)* __Other *(specify)*

21d. *(If any change in amount or frequency)* When we talked with you before, you were paying (receiving) __more alimony __less alimony __more frequently __less frequently than you are now. Why has there been a change?

22a. *(If any children)* When we last talked, you reported that the court order for child support was *(specify amount for each child)* to be paid __weekly __every 2 weeks __monthly __other *(specify)*. How much are you (is your spouse) *actually* paying in child support *(amount per child)* now?

22b. *(If any)* How often are you (is he/she) *actually* paying this amount? __Weekly __Every 2 weeks __Monthly __Payment irregular *(specify below)* __Other *(specify)*

22c. *(If any change from time 2)* When we talked with you before, you were paying (receiving) __more child support __less child support __more frequently __less frequently. Why has there been a change?

23a. Since the divorce became final, have either you or your ex-spouse gone back to the lawyer to ask for help or for changes in any part of the settlement? __No __Yes

23b. *(If yes)* Who wanted the change or help? __Respondent __Ex-spouse __Both __Don't know

23c. How many times have you (or your ex-spouse) gone back to see the lawyer? *(Specify for each)*

23d. What did you (he/she) want?

23e. What did the lawyer recommend?

24a. Have either you or your ex-spouse gone back to the judge or the referee to ask for help or for changes in any part of the settlement? __No __Yes

24b. Who wanted the change or help? __Respondent __Ex-spouse __Both __Don't know

24c. How many times have you (or your ex-spouse) been before the judge or referee about these matters? (*Specify for each*)

24d. What did you (he/she) want?

24e. What have been the results?

25a. In our first interview with you, you said that the last year of school you had completed was (*specify*). Is this still the case? __No __Yes

25b. (*If no*) What is the situation now?

A P P E N D I X B

Coding for the Subjective
Distress Index

If respondents indicated "no problem" in reply to the items, they received a score of zero. The following replies received scores of 1 or 2 as noted below:

1. Anything about your health bothering you? (1) Indicates numerous aches and pains or physical dysfunctions for which no medical help has been sought or for which doctors can find no organic basis (hypochondriasis).
2. How worried are you about your health? (1) Indicates undue preoccupation with one or more physical complaints or conditions.
3. How is your appetite for food? How often do you eat during the day? (1) Reports appetite is poor or not eating enough. Reports eating little or less than usual.
4. How is your memory? (1) Mentions memory impairment or problems with forgetting things.
5. How are you at making decisions? (1) Reports difficulty in making up mind or in making decisions.
6a. What are things or situations you're afraid of? (1) Indicates fear of losing mind or of losing control of emotions.
6b. (If admits any fears) How much do you worry? (1) Indicates an irrational fear of a particular object or situation, for example, crowds, heights (or some other type of phobia).
7. Are there things or situations you're afraid of? (1) Reports sudden attacks of fear or panic.
8. How often do you feel anxious? (1) Admits often feeling anxious or tense. (2) Admits feeling anxious or tense most of the time.
9. How often do you feel sad, depressed, blue? How long does the depression last? (1) Admits to often feeling sad or depressed. (2) Admits to feeling depressed most of the time.
10a. What kinds of thoughts do you have that others would not understand? (1) Reports recurrent, unwanted thoughts that he/she regards as senseless (obsessions).
10b. How do these thoughts affect your daily routine? (1) Indicates preoccupations, day-dreaming, or bothersome thoughts interfere with the performance of daily routine.

11. Do you have any trouble sleeping? (1) Reports trouble sleeping nearly all the time or pretty often.

12. Anything about your sex life bothering you? (1) Indicates some impairment in the pleasure obtained or performance of sexual intercourse (frigidity, premature ejaculation, etc.).

13. How do you think things will work out in the future? (1) Indicates a negative or discouraged attitude toward future accomplishments or attainments. (1) Mentions feeling aimless or getting nowhere.

14. How easily upset or irritated do you become? (1) Admits some irritability or being easily or very easily upset.

15. What kinds of things do you worry about (If admits to worries: How much do you worry)? (1) Mentions worrying a lot, or that he/she can't stop worrying.

16. Any truth to others' feelings of your poor judgment in handling money? (1) Yes

17. Any thoughts about suicide? (1) Yes

18. Have you ever seriously considered taking your life? (1) Yes

19. Have you ever made an attempt to take your life? (1) Yes

A P P E N D I X   C

The Cleveland Marital Complaint Code for the Question "What Caused Your Marriage to Break Up?"

GENERAL

01 using spouse; demanding
02 lack of communication or understanding; disinterest; lack of love (respect/caring) from spouse
03 change in interests or values; grew apart; personal growth
04 different backgrounds; incompatible; nothing in common
05 sexual incompatibility; complaints; lack of satisfaction or interest; disagreements; wouldn't initiate; infrequent
06 sexual problems due to health (injury, illness, etc.)
07 too young at time of marriage; weren't ready; missed out on things
08 arguing all the time; can't agree on anything
09 sanctification of previous wife by spouse (MT)
10 emotional needs not met; felt alone even with someone else (MT)
11 manipulative; critical (MT)
12 infertility problems (MT)
13 desertion; spouse just left
14 homosexual tendencies (MT)
15 sexual abuse (marital rape, etc.) (MT)

FINANCES AND WORK

20 financially irresponsible; spent money without regard; debts; poor management

Note. (MT) after a coding category indicates that the category was only used in the county-wide marital transition survey (1985–1986), not in the suburban divorce study (1974–1975). Coding categories were numbered 01 to 99 but not all 99 categories were used (e.g., category numbers 16 to 19 are blank and so forth).

21 disagreements over money; how to spend it; who controls it; materialism; spouse interested in material things
22 not a good provider; not enough money
23 unemployment; sporadic employment; financial parasite; not doing fair share
24 overcommitment to work; hours spent working; more interest in work than spouse/family
25 disapproval of type of spouse's employment
26 no support; unwilling to give money
29 other, finances, work

DRUGS, ALCOHOL, GAMBLING

30 drugs (cocaine, marijuana, heroin, etc.)
31 alcohol
32 gambling
33 tranquilizers, barbiturates, downers
34 other, drugs, etc.

ANGER, JEALOUSY, VIOLENCE

35 actual physical abuse; concussion; black eye
36 threatened physical abuse ("he said he'd kill me"); anger; temper (*do not code here if actual physical abuse mentioned*)
37 jealousy; mistrust; suspicion of other adults; suspicion of infidelity but no evidence
38 verbal abuse; puts respondent down; mental abuse
39 other, anger, jealousy

CHILDREN

40 disagreements over child rearing and discipline
41 concern over effect of discord on the child(ren)
42 jealousy or dislike of child(ren)
43 disagreements over having child(ren)
44 premarital pregnancy
45 conflicts with respondent's stepchild(ren) (MT)
46 conflicts with spouse's stepchild(ren) (MT)
47 lack of discipline with child(ren) (MT)
48 child abuse/molestation (MT)
49 other problems, children

PERSONALITY

50 untrustworthy; immature; liar; irresponsible
51 emotional/personality problems; insecure; unstable; mental illness
52 criminal activities; jail; embezzlement
53 inflexible; stubborn; can't accept change
54 self-centered; selfish; egotistical
55 promises made but not kept (MT)
59 other, personality

LACK OF INVESTMENT IN FAMILY

60 out with the boys/girls; staying out; not coming home; carousing but not specific mention of other man/woman; other women (but not specific); "street-type" person
61 general neglect of household duties, responsibilities; poor housekeeper; poor role performance
62 not enough social life together; spouse doesn't take me out; lack of companionship
63 no sense of family; no togetherness; takes respondent/family for granted; no interest/ignores family; spouse not a good parent
64 spouse more concerned with his/her mother than family (MT)
65 open marriage; each free to pursue independent relationships (MT)
66 co-marital sex; swinging expected (MT)
69 other, lack of investment

ROLE CONFLICTS

70 conflict within the individual; desire for freedom or independence or life of one's own; women's liberation; male/female midlife crisis; desire to be single; sense of self stifled by marriage; bored (unhappy) with role
71 joint conflict over roles; disagree over proper role for women/men; sex role conflict; authoritarian; being too controlling; manipulative; judging; paternal/maternal; too many responsibilities with no sharing
73 fear of aging (MT)
79 other, role conflicts

OUTSIDE RELATIONSHIPS

80 extramarital sex; another woman/man
81 problems with in-laws and relatives; didn't get along with his/her parents

82 disagreements over friends; problems with spouse's friends; didn't like my friends

89 other, outside relationships

MISCELLANEOUS

90 external events (death of relative, job change, someone moved in or out, etc.); blame on third party or thing but not infidelity ("It's his/her/its fault; fate")

91 health problems (illness, injury, venereal disease, etc.)

92 illegitimate child of spouse's born (MT)

98 not sure what happened; don't know; don't understand; bewildered; no idea; he/she just left (code here when mentioned but followed by explanation)

99 refuse to discuss or no explanation; don't know (code here when mentioned with no attempt at explanation)

++other, miscellaneous

References

Achenbach, T. M., & Edelbrock, C. S. (1983). *The Child Behavior Checklist and Child Behavior Profile.* Burlington: University of Vermont, Department of Psychiatry.

Adams, A. (Ed.). (1989). *An uncommon scold.* New York: Simon & Schuster.

Ader, R., Cohen, N., & Felten, D. (Eds.). (1990). *Psychoneuroimmunology* (Vol. 2). San Diego: Academic Press.

Aesop. (1965). *Aesop's fables.* New York: Franklin Watts.

Aghajanian, A. (1986). Some notes on divorce in Iran. *Journal of Marriage and the Family, 51,* 749-755.

Ahrons, C. R. (1981). The continuing coparental relationship between divorced spouses. *American Journal of Orthopsychiatry, 51,* 315-328.

Ahrons, C. R., & Rodgers, R. H. (1987). *Divorced families: A multidisciplinary developmental view.* New York: W. W. Norton.

Ahrons, C. R., & Wallisch, L. (1987). Parenting in the binuclear family: Relationships between biological and stepparents. In K. Pasley & M. Ihinger-Tallman (Eds.), *Remarriage and stepparenting: Current research and theory* (pp. 225-256). New York: Guilford Press.

Albrecht, S. L. (1980). Reactions and adjustments to divorce: Differences in the experiences of males and females. *Family Relations, 29,* 59-68.

Albrecht, S. L., Bahr, H. M., & Goodman, K. L. (1983). *Divorce and remarriage: Problems, adaptations, and adjustments.* Westport, CT: Greenwood Press.

Aldous, J. (1969a). Wives' employment status and lower-class men as husband-fathers. *Journal of Marriage and the Family, 31,* 469-476.

Aldous, J. (1969b). Occupational characteristics and male's role performance in the family. *Journal of Marriage and the Family, 31,* 707-712.

Amato, P. R., & Booth, A. (1991a). Consequences of parental divorce and marital unhappiness for adult well-being. *Social Forces, 69,* 895-914.

Amato, P. R., & Booth, A. (1991b). The consequences of divorce for attitudes toward divorce and gender roles. *Journal of Family Issues, 12,* 306-322.

Ambert, A. M. (1989). *Ex-spouses and new spouses: A study of relationships.* Greenwich, CT: JAI Press.

American Statistical Association. (1974). Report on the ASA conference on surveys of human populations. *American Statistician, 28,* 30-34.

Amoateng, A. Y., & Heaton, T. B. (1989). The sociodemographic correlates of the timing of divorce in Ghana. *Journal of Comparative Family Studies, 20,* 79-96.

Anspach, D. F. (1976). Kinship and divorce. *Journal of Marriage and the Family, 38,* 323–330.

Arendell, T. (1986). *Mothers and divorce: Legal, economic, and social dilemmas.* Berkeley: University of California Press.

Bachrach, L. L. (1975). *Marital status and mental disorder: An analytical review* (DHEW Publication No. ADM 75-217). Washington, DC: U.S. Government Printing Office.

Bane, M. J. (1979). Marital disruption and the lives of children. In G. Levinger & O. C. Moles (Eds.), *Divorce and separation: Context, causes, and consequences* (pp. 276–286). New York: Basic Books.

Barron, S. (1985, May 23). *The New York Times,* p. B-20.

Bebbington, P. (1987). Marital status and depression: A study of English national admission statistics. *Acta Psychiatrica Scandinavica, 75,* 640–650.

Beck, D. F. (1976). Research findings on the outcome of marital counseling. In D. H. Olson (Ed.), *Treating relationships* (pp. 433–473). Lake Mills, IA: Graphic.

Becker, G. S. (1973). A theory of marriage: Part I: *Journal of Political Economy, 81,* 813–846.

Becker, G. S. (1974). A theory of marriage: Part II: *Journal of Political Economy, 82,* S11–S26.

Becker, G. S. (1981). *A treatise on the family.* Cambridge, MA: Harvard University Press.

Bell, R. R., Turner, S., & Rosen, L. (1975). A multivariate analysis of female extramarital coitus. *Journal of Marriage and the Family, 37,* 375–384.

Bennett, N. G., Blanc, A. K., & Bloom, D. E. (1988). Commitment and the modern union: Assessing the link between premarital cohabitation and subsequent marital stability. *American Sociological Review, 53,* 127–138.

Bergler, E. (1946). *Unhappy marriage and divorce.* New York: International Universities Press.

Bergler, E. (1948). *Divorce won't help.* New York: Harper.

Bergmann, B. R. (1990, August). *The French child welfare system: An excellent system we could adapt and afford.* Paper presented at the meeting of the American Sociological Association, Washington, DC.

Berkman, L. P., & Syme, S. L. (1979). Social networks, host resistance, and mortality: A nine year follow-up study of Alameda County residents. *American Journal of Epidemiology, 109,* 186–204.

Berman, W. H. (1985). Continued attachment after legal divorce. *Journal of Family Issues, 6,* 375–392.

Berman, W. H. (1988). The role of attachment in the post-divorce experience. *Journal of Personality and Social Psychology, 54,* 496–503.

Bernard, J. (1972). *The future of marriage.* New York: World.

Betzig, L. (1989). Causes of conjugal dissolution: A cross-cultural study. *Current Anthropology, 30,* 654–676.

Bilge, B., & Kaufman, G. (1983). Children of divorce and one-parent families: Cross-cultural perspectives. *Family Relations, 32,* 59–71.

Bishop, J. (1980). Jobs, cash transfers, and marital instability: A review and synthesis of the evidence. *Journal of Human Resources, 15,* 301-334.

Blake, N. M. (1962). *The road to Reno: A history of divorce in the United States.* New York: Macmillan.

Blau, Z. S. (1973). *Old age in a changing society.* New York: New Viewpoints/ Franklin Watts.

Blechman, E. A. (1982). Are children with one parent at psychological risk? A methodological review. *Journal of Marriage and the Family, 44,* 179-195.

Bloch, M. (1973). The long term and short term: The economic and political significance of the morality of kinship. In J. Goody (Ed.), *The character of kinship* (pp. 75-87). Cambridge, England: Cambridge University Press.

Bloom, B. L., Asher, S. J., & White, S. W. (1978). Marital disruption as a stressor: A review and analysis. *Psychological Bulletin, 85,* 867-894.

Bloom, B. L., & Caldwell, R. A. (1981). Sex differences in adjustment during the process of marital separation. *Journal of Marriage and the Family, 43,* 693-701.

Bloom, B. L., Hodges, W. F., Caldwell, R. A. (1982). A preventive program for the newly separated: Initial evaluation. *American Journal of Community Psychology, 10,* 251-264.

Bloom, B. L., Hodges, W. F., Caldwell, R. A., Systra, L., & Cedrone, A. R. (1977). Marital separation: A community survey. *Journal of Divorce, 1,* 7-19.

Bloom, B. L., Hodges, W. F., Kern, M. B., & McFaddin, S. C. (1985). A preventive intervention program for the newly separated: Final evaluations. *American Journal of Orthopsychiatry, 55,* 9-26.

Bloom, B. L., Niles, R. L., & Tatcher, A. M. (1985). Sources of marital dissatisfaction among newly separated persons. *Journal of Family Issues, 6,* 359-373.

Blumenthal, M. (1967). Mental health among the divorced. *Archives of General Psychiatry, 16,* 603-608.

Bohannan, P. (1970). The six stations of divorce. In P. Bohannan (Ed.), *Divorce and after* (pp. 29-55). Garden City, NY: Doubleday.

Bohannan, P. (1985). *All the happy families: Exploring the varieties of family life.* New York: McGraw-Hill.

Booth, A., Johnson, D. R., & Edwards, J. N. (1983). Predicting marital instability. *Journal of Marriage and the Family, 45,* 387-394.

Booth, A., Johnson, D. R., White, L. K., & Edwards, J. N. (1985). Predicting divorce and permanent separation. *Journal of Family Issues, 6,* 331-346.

Booth, A., & White, L. K. (1980). Thinking about divorce. *Journal of Marriage and the Family, 42,* 605-616.

Bornstein, P. E., Clayton, P. J., Halikas, J. A., Maurice, W. L., & Robins, E. (1973). The depression of widowhood after thirteen months. *British Journal of Psychiatry, 122,* 561-566.

Bowlby, J. (1969). *Attachment and loss: Vol. 1. Attachment.* New York: Basic Books.

Bowlby, J. (1973). *Attachment and loss: Vol. 2. Separation: Anxiety and anger.* New York: Basic Books.

Bowlby, J. (1975). Attachment theory, separation anxiety, and mourning. In S. Arieti (Ed.), *American handbook of psychiatry* (2nd ed., Vol. 6, pp. 292–309). New York: Basic Books.

Bowlby, J. (1977a). The making and breaking of affectional bonds: Part I. Aetiology and psychopathology in light of attachment theory. *British Journal of Psychiatry, 130*, 201–210.

Bowlby, J. (1977b). The making and breaking of affectional bonds: Part II. Some principles of psychotherapy. *British Journal of Psychiatry, 130*, 421–431.

Bowlby, J. (1980). *Attachment and loss: Vol. 3. Loss: Sadness and depression.* New York: Basic Books.

Bowlby, J., & Parkes, C. M. (1970). Separation and loss within the family. In E. J. Anthony & C. Koupernik (Eds.), *The child in his family* (pp. 197–216). New York: Wiley.

Bradburn. N. (1969). *The structure of psychological well-being.* Chicago: Aldine.

Brandwein, R. A., Brown, C. A., & Fox, E. A. (1974). Women and children last: The social situation of divorced mothers and their families. *Journal of Marriage and the Family, 36*, 498–514.

Breslau, N., Salkever, D., & Staruch, K. S. (1982). Women's labor force activity and responsibilities for disabled dependents: A study of families with disabled children. *Journal of Health and Social Behavior, 23*, 169–183.

Briscoe, C. W., & Smith, J. B. (1973). Depression and marital turmoil. *Archives of General Psychiatry, 29*, 811–817.

Briscoe, C. W., & Smith, J. B. (1974). Psychiatric illness—marital units and divorce. *Journal of Nervous and Mental Disease, 158*, 440–445.

Briscoe, C. W., & Smith, J. B. (1975). Depression in bereavement and divorce. *Archives of General Psychiatry, 32*, 439–443.

Briscoe, C. W., & Smith, J. B., Robins, E., Marten, S., & Gaskin, F. (1973). Divorce and psychiatric disease. *Archives of General Psychiatry, 29*, 119–125.

Brown, P. (1976). *Psychological distress and personal growth among women coping with marital dissolution.* Unpublished doctoral dissertation, University of Michigan.

Brown, P., Felton, B. J., Whiteman, V., & Manela, R. (1980). Attachment and distress following marital separation. *Journal of Divorce, 3*, 303–317.

Brown, S. D., & Reimer, D. A. (1984). Assessing attachment following divorce: Development and psychometric evaluation of the Divorce Reaction Inventory. *Journal of Counseling Psychology, 31*, 520–531.

Budman, S. H., & Clifford, M. (1979). Short-term group therapy for couples in a health maintenance organization. *Professional Psychology, 10*, 419–429.

Buehler, C. A., Hogan, M. J., Robinson, B. E., & Levy, R. J. (1985–1986). The parental divorce transition: Divorce-related stressors and well-being. *Journal of Divorce, 9*, 61–81.

Bumpass, L. L. (1990). What's happening to the family? Interactions between demographic and institutional change. *Demography, 27*, 483–498.

Bumpass, L. L., & Sweet, J. A. (1972). Differentials in marital stability: 1970. *American Sociological Review, 37,* 754–766.

Bumpass, L. L., & Sweet, J. A. (1988). *Preliminary evidence on cohabitation* (NSFH Working Paper No. 2). Madison: Center for Demography and Ecology, University of Wisconsin.

Burgess, E. W., & Locke, H. J. (1953). *The family: From institution to companionship* (2nd ed.). New York: American Book.

Burr, W. R. (1973). *Theory construction and the sociology of the family.* New York: Wiley.

Calabrese, J. R., Kling, M. A., & Gold, P. W. (1987). Alterations in immunocompetence during stress, bereavement, and depression: Focus on neuroendocrine regulation. *American Journal of Psychiatry, 144,* 1123–1134.

Callan, J. (1986, July 14). Kip Addotta sings about veggies, but he's just arugula guy. *People,* pp. 56, 61.

Carter, B., & McGoldrick, M. (1988). Overview: The changing family life cycle: A framework for family therapy. In B. Carter & M. McGoldrick (Eds.), *The changing family life cycle* (2nd ed., pp. 3-28). New York: Gardner Press.

Carter, H., & Glick, P. C. (1970). *Marriage and divorce: A social and economic study.* Cambridge, MA: Harvard University Press.

Cassel, J. (1976). The contribution of the social environment to host resistance. *American Journal of Epidemiology, 104,* 107–123.

Cassetty, J. (1978). *Child support and public policy.* Lexington, MA: D. C. Heath.

Cherlin, A. J. (1979). Work life and marital dissolution. In G. Levinger & O. C. Moles (Eds.), *Divorce and separation: Context, causes, and consequences* (pp. 151–166). New York: Basic Books.

Cherlin, A. J. (1981). *Marriage, divorce, and remarriage.* Cambridge, MA: Harvard University Press.

Cherlin, A. J., Furstenberg, F. F., Jr., Chase-Lansdale, P. L., Kiernan, K. E., Robins, P. K., Morrison, D. R., & Teitler, J. O. (1991). Longitudinal studies of effects of divorce on children in Great Britain and the United States. *Science, 252,* 1386–1389.

Cherlin, A. J., & Reeder, L. (1975). The dimensions of psychological well-being: A critical review. *Sociological Methods and Research, 4,* 189–214.

Chester, R. (1971). Health and marriage breakdown: Experience of a sample of divorced women. *British Journal of Preventive and Social Medicine, 25,* 231–235.

Chester, R. (1977). Conclusion. In R. Chester with G. Kooy (Eds.), *Divorce in Europe* (pp. 283–316). Leiden, The Netherlands: Martinus Nijhoff.

Chester, R., with Kooy, G. (Eds.). (1977). *Divorce in Europe.* Leiden, The Netherlands: Martinus Nijhoff.

Chiriboga, D. A. (1982). Adaptation to marital separation in later and earlier life. *Journal of Gerontology, 37,* 109–114.

Chiriboga, D. A., Catron, L., & Associates. (1991). *Divorce: Crisis, challenge or relief?* New York: New York University Press.

Chiriboga, D. A., & Cutler, L. (1977). Stress responses among divorcing men and women. *Journal of Divorce, 1,* 95–105.

Chiriboga, D. A., Roberts, J., & Stein, J. A. (1978). Psychological well-being during marital separation. *Journal of Divorce, 2,* 21–36.

Clayton, P. J. (1979). The sequelae of conjugal bereavement. *American Journal of Psychiatry, 136,* 1530–1534.

Clayton, P. J., Desmarais, L., & Winokur, G. (1968). A study of normal bereavement. *American Journal of Psychiatry, 125,* 168–174.

Cobb, S. (1976). Social support as a mediator of life stress. *Psychosomatic Medicine, 38,* 300–314.

Coleman, M., & Ganong, L. H. (1990). Remarriage and stepfamily research in the 1980s: Increased interest in an old family form. *Journal of Marriage and the Family, 52,* 925–940.

Colletta, N. D. (1979). Support systems after divorce: Incidence and impact. *Journal of Marriage and the Family, 41,* 837–846.

Conrad, P., & Schneider, J. W. (1980). *Deviance and medicalization: From badness to sickness.* St. Louis: C. V. Mosby.

Cookerly, J. R. (1976). Evaluating treatment approaches in marital counseling. In D. H. Olson (Ed.), *Treating relationships* (pp. 475–498). Lake Mills, IA: Graphic.

Coombs, L. C., & Zumeta, Z. (1970). Correlates of marital dissolution in a prospective fertility study: A research note. *Social Problems, 18,* 92–102.

Cooney, T. M. (1988). Young adults and parental divorce: Exploring important issues. *Human Relations, 41,* 805–822.

Cooney, T. M., Smyer, M. A., Hagestad, G., & Klock, R. (1986). Parental divorce in young adulthood: Some preliminary findings. *American Journal of Orthopsychiatry, 56,* 470–477.

Cooney, T. M., & Uhlenberg, P. (1990). The role of divorce in men's relations with their adult children after mid-life. *Journal of Marriage and the Family, 52,* 677–688.

Crain, R. L., & Weisman, C. S. (1972). *Discrimination, personality, and achievement: A survey of northern blacks.* New York: Seminar.

Cseh-Szombathy, L., Koch-Nielsen, I., Trost, J., & Weda, I., with Bak, M., & Tamasi, P. (1985). *The aftermath of divorce—coping with family change: An investigation in eight countries.* Budapest: Akademiai Kiado.

Cutright, P. (1971). Income and family events: Marital instability: *Journal of Marriage and the Family, 33,* 291–306.

Davatz, U. (1981). Establishing a therapeutic alliance in family systems. In A. S. Gurman (Ed.), *Questions and answers in the practice of family therapy* (Vol. 1, pp. 46–49). New York: Brunner/Mazel.

Dean, A., & Lin, N. (1977). The stress-buffering role of social supports: Problems and prospects for systematic investigation. *Journal of Nervous and Mental Disease, 35,* 403–417.

Deckert, P., & Langelier, R. (1978). The late-divorce phenomenon: The causes and impact of ending 20-year-old or longer marriages. *Journal of Divorce, 1,* 381–390.

DeGarmo, D. S., & Kitson, G. C. (1990, November). *Adjustment to loss of a spouse: A soft modeling approach.* Paper presented at the meeting of the Gerontological Society of America, Boston.

Demo, D. H., & Acock, A. C. (1988). The impact of divorce on children. *Journal of Marriage and the Family, 50,* 619–648.

Derdeyn, A. (1977). Children in divorce: Intervention in the phase of separation, *Pediatrics, 60,* 20–27.

Derogatis, L. R. (1977). *SCL-90: Administration, scoring, and procedures manual-1 for the revised version and other instruments of the psychopathology rating scale series.* Baltimore: Johns Hopkins University School of Medicine.

Despert, J. L. (1962). *Children of divorce.* Garden City, NY: Doubleday.

Dickson, P. (Ed.). (1981). *Toasts: The complete book of the best toasts, sentiments, blessings, curses, and graces.* New York: Dell.

Diedrick, P. (1991). Gender differences in divorce adjustment. *Journal of Divorce and Remarriage, 14,* 33–45.

Dingle, J. H., Badger, G. F., & Jordan, W. S. (1964). *Illness in the home: A study of 25,000 illnesses in a group of Cleveland families.* Cleveland, OH: Press of Western Reserve University.

Dixon, R. B., & Weitzman, L. J. (1980). Evaluating the impact of no-fault divorce in California. *Family Relations, 29,* 297–307.

Dixon, R. B., & Weitzman, L. J. (1982). When husbands file for divorce. *Journal of Marriage and the Family, 44,* 103–115.

Dohrenwend, B. P., & Dohrenwend, B. S. (1976). Sex differences and psychiatric disorders. *American Journal of Sociology, 81,* 1447–1452.

Dohrenwend, B. S., & Dohrenwend, B. P. (1981). Life stress and illness: Formulation of the issues. In B. S. Dohrenwend & B. P. Dohrenwend (Eds.), *Stressful life events and their contexts* (pp. 1–27). New York: Prodist.

Dohrenwend, B. S., Krasnoff, L., Askenasy, A. R., & Dohrenwend, B. P. (1978). Exemplification of a method for scaling life events: The PERI life events scale. *Journal of Health and Social Behavior, 19,* 205–229.

Dunne, D. (1987). *Fatal charms and other tales of today.* New York: Crown.

Dye, C. J. (1982). Personality. In D. J. Mangen & W. A. Peterson (Eds.), *Research instruments in social gerontology: Vol. 1. Clinical and social psychology* (pp. 77–144). Minneapolis: University of Minnesota Press.

Edwards, J. N., & Booth, A. (1976). Sexual behavior in and out of marriage: An assessment of correlates. *Journal of Marriage and the Family, 38,* 73–81.

Ehrenreich, B., & Piven, F. F. (1984). The feminization of poverty: When the "family-wage system" breaks down. *Dissent, 31,* 162–170.

Elliott, G. R., & Eisdorfer, C. (Eds.). (1982). *Stress and human health: Analysis and implications of research.* New York: Springer.

Emery, R. E. (1988). *Marriage, divorce, and children's adjustment.* Newbury Part, CA: Sage.

Emery, R. E., & Wyer, M. M. (1987a). Child custody mediation and litigation: An experimental evaluation of the experience of parents. *Journal of Consulting and Clinical Psychology, 55,* 179–186.

Emery, R. E., & Wyer, M. M. (1987b). Divorce mediation. *American Psychologist*, *42*, 472–480.

Ensel, W. M. (1986). Sex, marital status, and depression: The role of life events and social support. In N. Lin, A. Dean, & W. M. Ensel (Eds.), *Social support, life events, and depression* (pp. 231–247). Orlando, FL: Academic Press.

Erikson, K. T. (1966). *Wayward puritans: A study in the sociology of deviance*. New York: Wiley.

Espenshade, T. J. (1979). The economic consequences of divorce. *Journal of Marriage and the Family*, *41*, 615–625.

Farnsworth, J., Pett, M. A., & Lund, D. A. (1989). Predictors of loss management and well-being in later life widowhood and divorce. *Journal of Family Issues*, *10*, 102–121.

Fine, M. A., McKenry, P. C., & Chung, H. (in press). Post-divorce adjustment of black and white single parents. *Journal of Divorce and Remarriage*.

Folberg, J., & Milne, A. (Eds.). (1988). *Divorce mediation: Theory and practice*. New York: Guilford Press.

Forehand, R., & McCombs, A. (1988). Unraveling the antecedent-consequence conditions in maternal depression and adolescent functioning. *Behaviour Research and Therapy*, *26*, 399–405.

Forgatch, M. S., Patterson, G. R., & Skinner, M. L. (1988). A mediational model for the effect of divorce on antisocial behavior in boys. In E. M. Hetherington & J. D. Arasteh (Eds.), *Impact of divorce, single parenting, and stepparenting on children* (pp. 135–154). Hillsdale, NJ: Erlbaum.

Fortes, M. (1969). *Kinship and the social order: The legacy of Lewis Henry Morgan*. Chicago: Aldine.

Freed, D. J., & Foster, H. H. (1983). Family law in the fifty states: An overview. *Family Law Quarterly*, *16*, 289–383.

Freed, D. J., & Walker, T. B. (1988). Family law in the fifty states: An overview. *Family Law Quarterly*, *21*, 417–573.

Freidson, E. (1970). *Profession of medicine: A study of the sociology of applied knowledge*. New York: Dodd, Mead.

Freud, S. (1963). Mourning and melancholia. In P. Rieff (Ed.), *General psychological theory: Papers on metapsychology* (pp. 164–179). New York: Collier Books. (Original work published 1917)

Friend, R. C. (1983). The editor at large: Psychiatry and the law. The American family: An endangered species? *Southern California Psychiatric Society Newsletter*, p. 1f.

Frost, R. (1963). The death of the hired man. In *Selected poems of Robert Frost* (pp. 25–30). New York: Holt, Rinehart & Winston. (Original work published 1914)

Fulton, J. A. (1979). Parental reports of children's post-divorce adjustment. *Journal of Family Issues*, *35*, 126–140.

Furstenberg, F. F., Jr. (1976). Premarital pregnancy and marital instability. *Journal of Social Issues*, *32*, 67–86.

Furstenberg, F. F., Jr., Nord, C. W., Peterson, J. L., & Zill, N. (1983). The life course of children of divorce: Marital disruption and parental contact. *American Sociological Review, 48*, 656–668.

Furstenberg, F. F., Jr., & Spanier, G. B. (1984). *Recycling the family: Remarriage after divorce.* Beverly Hills, CA: Sage.

Galligan, R. J., & Bahr, S. J. (1978). Economic well-being and marital stability: Implications for income maintenance programs. *Journal of Marriage and the Family, 40*, 283–290.

Ganong, L., & Coleman, M. (1986). A comparison of clinical and empirical literature on children in step-families. *Journal of Marriage and the Family, 48*, 309–318.

Garbarino, J. (1976). A preliminary study of some ecological correlates of child abuse: The impact of socioeconomic stress on the mothers. *Child Development, 47*, 178–185.

Garfinkel, I., & McLanahan, S. S. (1986). *Single mothers and their children: A new American dilemma.* Washington, DC: Urban Institute.

Garfinkel, I., & Oellerich, D. (1989). Noncustodial fathers' ability to pay child support. *Demography, 26*, 219–233.

Geiser, D. S. (1989). Psychosocial influences on human immunity. *Clinical Psychology Review, 9*, 689–715.

Gerstel, N. (1987). Divorce and stigma. *Social Problems, 34*, 172–186.

Glass, S. P., & Wright, T. R. (1977). The relationship of extramarital sex, length of marriage, and sex differences on marital satisfaction and romanticism: Athanasiou's data reanalyzed. *Journal of Marriage and the Family, 39*, 691–703.

Glenn, N. D., & Kramer, K. B. (1985). The psychological well-being of adult children of divorce. *Journal of Marriage and the Family, 47*, 905–912.

Glenn, N. D., & Kramer, K. B. (1987). The marriages and divorces of the children of divorce. *Journal of Marriage and the Family, 49*, 811–825.

Glenn, N. D., & Supancic, M. (1984). The social and demographic correlates of divorce and separation in the United States: An update and reconsideration. *Journal of Marriage and the Family, 46*, 563–575.

Glick, P. C. (1957). *American families.* New York: Wiley.

Glick, P. C. (1988). The role of divorce in the changing family structure: Trends and variations. In S. A. Wolchik & P. Karoly (Eds.), *Children of divorce: Empirical perspectives on adjustment* (pp. 3–34). New York: Gardner Press.

Glick, P. C., & Lin, S. (1986). Recent changes in divorce and remarriage. *Journal of Marriage and the Family, 48*, 737–748.

Glick, P. C., & Norton, A. J. (1971). Frequency, duration, and probability of marriage and divorce. *Journal of Marriage and the Family, 33*, 307–317.

Glick, P. C., & Norton, A. J. (1979). *Marrying, divorce, and living together in the U.S. today* (Population Bulletin, Vol. 3, No. 32). Washington, DC: Population Reference Bureau.

Goffman, E. (1959). *The presentation of self in everyday life.* Garden City, NY: Doubleday.

Goffman, E. (1963). *Stigma: Notes on the management of spoiled identity.* Englewood Cliffs, NJ: Prentice-Hall.

Goldenberg, I., & Goldenberg, H. (1985). *Family therapy: An overview* (2nd ed.). Monterey, CA: Brooks/Cole.

Goldstein, J., Freud, A., & Solnit, A. J. (1973). *Beyond the best interests of the child.* New York: Free Press.

Goode, W. J. (1956). *After divorce.* Glencoe, IL: Free Press.

Goode, W. J. (1962). Marital satisfaction and instability: A cross-cultural class analysis of divorce rates. *International Social Science Journal, 14,* 507–526.

Goode, W. J. (1963). *World revolution and family patterns.* New York: Free Press.

Goode, W. J. (1974). Comment: The economies of nonmonetary variables. *Journal of Political Economy, 82,* S27–S33.

Goode, W. J. (1984). Individual investments in family relationships over the coming decades. *The Tocqueville Review, 6,* 51–83.

Gottman, J. M., & Krokoff, L. J. (1989). Marital interaction and satisfaction: A longitudinal view. *Journal of Consulting and Clinical Psychology, 57,* 47–52.

Gove, W. R. (1972a). The relationship between sex roles, marital status, and mental illness. *Social Forces, 51,* 34–44.

Gove, W. R. (1972b). Sex, marital status, and suicide. *Journal of Health and Social Behavior, 13,* 204–213.

Gove, W. R. (1973). Sex, marital status, and mortality. *American Journal of Sociology, 79,* 45–67.

Gove, W. R., & Shin, H. (1989). The psychological well-being of divorced and widowed men and women: An empirical analysis: *Journal of Family Issues, 10,* 122–144.

Granvold, D. K., Pedler, L. M., & Schellie, S. G. (1979). A study of sex role expectancy and female postdivorce adjustment. *Journal of Divorce, 2,* 383–393.

Greene, R. W., & Feld, S. (1989). Social support coverage and the well-being of elderly widows and married women. *Journal of Family Issues, 10,* 33–51.

Grief, G. L. (1985). Single fathers. Lexington, MA.: D. C. Heath.

Group for the Advancement of Psychiatry, Committee on the Family. (1980). *Divorce, child custody, and the family.* New York: Mental Health Materials Center.

Guidubaldi, J., & Perry, J. D. (1985). Divorce and mental health sequelae for children: A two-year follow-up of a nationwide sample. *Journal of the American Academy of Child Psychiatry, 24,* 531–537.

Gunter, B. G. (1977). Notes on divorce filing as role behavior. *Journal of Marriage and the Family, 39,* 95–98.

Gurin, G., Veroff, J., & Feld, S. (1960). *Americans view their mental health.* New York: Basic Books.

Hagestad, G. O., & Smyer, M. A. (1982). Dissolving long-term relationships: Patterns of divorce in middle age. In S. Duck (Ed.), *Personal relationships: Vol. 4. Dissolving personal relationships* (pp. 155–188). London: Academic Press.

Halem, L. C. (1980). *Divorce reform: Changing legal and social perspectives.* New York: Free Press.

Hampton, R. L. (1975). Marital disruption: Some social and economic consequences. In J. N. Morgan (Ed.), *Five thousand American families* (Vol. 3, pp. 163–187). Ann Arbor, MI: Institute for Social Research.

Hampton, R. L. (1979). Husbands' characteristics and marital disruptions in black families. *Sociological Quarterly, 20,* 255–266.

Hanks, S. E., & Rosenbaum, C. P. (1977). Battered women: A study of women who live with violent alcohol-abusing men. *American Journal of Orthopsychiatry, 47,* 291–306.

Hannon, M., Tuma, N., & Groenfeld, L. (1977). Income and marital events: Evidence from income-maintenance experiment. *American Journal of Sociology, 82,* 1186–1211.

Hart, N. (1976). *When marriage ends: A study in status passage.* New York: Methuen.

Hauser, B. B. (1985). Custody in dispute: Legal and psychological profiles of contesting families. *Journal of the American Academy of Child Psychiatry, 24,* 575–582.

Henderson, S., Byrne, D. G., Duncan-Jones, P., Scott, R., & Adcock, S. (1980). Social relationships, adversity, and neurosis: A study of associations in a general population. *British Journal of Psychiatry, 136,* 574–583.

Henderson, S., Duncan-Jones, P., Byrne, D. G., & Scott, R. (1980). Measuring social relationships: The Interview Schedule for Social Interaction. *Psychological Medicine, 10,* 723–734.

Hennon, C. B. (1983). Divorce and the elderly: A neglected area of research. In T. H. Brubaker (Ed.), *Family relationships in later life* (pp. 149–172). Beverly Hills, CA: Sage.

Hernandez, D. J. (1988). Demographic trends and the living arrangements of children. In E. M. Hetherington & J. D. Arasteh (Eds.), *Impact of divorce, single parenting, and stepparenting on children* (pp. 3–22). Hillsdale, NJ: Erlbaum.

Herzog, E., & Sudia, C. (1970). *Boys in fatherless homes.* Washington, DC: Children's Bureau, U.S. Department of Health, Education and Welfare.

Hess, R. D., & Camara, K. A. (1979). Post-divorce relationships as mediating factors in the consequences of divorce for children. *Journal of Social Issues, 35,* 79–96.

Hetherington, E. M. (1987). Family relations six years after divorce. In K. Pasley & M. Ihinger-Tallman (Eds.), *Remarriage and stepparenting: Current research and theory* (pp. 185–205). New York: Guilford Press.

Hetherington, E. M. (1989). Coping with family transitions: Winners, losers, and survivors. *Child Development, 60,* 1–14.

Hetherington, E. M., Cox, M., & Cox, R. (1976). Divorced fathers. *The Family Coordinator, 25*, 417–428.

Hetherington, E. M., Cox, M., & Cox, R. (1978). The aftermath of divorce. In J. H. Stevens, Jr., & M. Mathews (Eds.), *Mother-child, father-child relations* (pp. 149–176). Washington, DC: National Association for the Education of Young Children.

Hetherington, E. M., Cox, M., & Cox, R. (1985). Long-term effects of divorce and remarriage on the adjustment of children. *Journal of American Academy of Child Psychiatry, 24*, 518–530.

Hetherington, E. M., & Furstenberg, F. F., Jr. (1989). Sounding the alarm. *Readings, 4*, 4–8.

Hetherington, E. M., Stanley-Hogan, M., & Anderson, E. R. (1989). Marital transitions: A child's perspective. *American Psychologist, 44*, 303–312.

Hicks, M. W., & Platt, M. (1970). Marital happiness and stability: A review of the research in the sixties. *Journal of Marriage and the Family, 32*, 553–574.

Hill, M. S. (1983). Trends in the economic situation of U.S. families and children, 1970–1980. In R. R. Nelson & F. Skidmore (Eds.), *American families and the economy* (pp. 9–58). Washington, DC: National Academy Press.

Hill, R. (1958). Generic features of families under stress. *Social Casework, 39*, 139–150.

Hirschfeld, R. M. A., Klerman, G. L., Gough, H. G., Barrett, J., Korchin, S., & Chodoff, P. (1977). A measure of interpersonal dependency. *Journal of Personality Assessment, 41*, 610–618.

Hodges, W. F. (1986). *Interventions for children of divorce: Custody, access, and psychotherapy.* New York: Wiley.

Hoffman, S. D., & Duncan, G. J. (1988). What *are* the economic consequences of divorce? *Demography, 25*, 641–645.

Hollingshead, A. B. (1957). *Two factor index of social class measurement.* Unpublished manuscript, Yale University.

Holmes, S. A. (1991, May 1). Unlikely union arises to press family issues. *The New York Times*, p. A12.

Holmes, T. H., & Rahe, R. H. (1967). The Social Readjustment Rating Scale. *Journal of Psychosomatic Research, 11*, 213–218.

Houseknecht, S., & Spanier, G. (1980). Marital disruption and higher education among women in the United States. *Sociological Quarterly, 21*, 375–389.

Hunt, M., & Hunt, B. (1977). *The divorce experience.* New York: McGraw-Hill.

Ilfeld, F. W. (1978). Psychologic status of community residents along major demographic dimensions. *Archives of General Psychiatry, 35*, 716–724.

Isaacs, M. B., Montalvo, B., & Abelsohn, D. (1986). *The difficult divorce: Therapy for children and families.* New York: Basic Books.

Jacobson, D. S. (1978a). The impact of marital separation/divorce on children: I. Parent-child separation and child adjustment. *Journal of Divorce, 1*, 341–360.

Jacobson, D. S. (1978b). The impact of marital separation/divorce on children: II. Interparent hostility and child adjustment. *Journal of Divorce*, 2, 3–19.

Jacobson, D. S. (1978c). The impact of marital separation/divorce on children: III. Parent-child communication and child adjustment and regression analysis of findings from overall study. *Journal of Divorce*, 2, 175–194.

Jacobson, D. S. (1987). Family type, visiting patterns, and children's behavior in the stepfamily: A linked family system. In K. Pasley & M. Ihinger-Tallman (Eds.), *Remarriage and stepparenting: Current research and theory* (pp. 257–272). New York: Guilford Press.

Jacobson, G. F. (1983). *The multiple crises of marital separation and divorce.* New York: Grune & Stratton.

Jacobson, P. H., with Jacobson, P. F. (1959). *American marriage and divorce.* New York: Holt, Rinehart & Winston.

Jenkins, D. (1984). *Life its ownself: The semi-tougher adventures of Billy Clyde Puckett and them.* New York: Simon & Schuster.

Johnson, D. R., Booth, A., White, L. K., & Edwards, J. N. (1986). Dimensions of marital quality: Towards conceptual and methodological refinement. *Journal of Family Issues*, 7, 31–49.

Johnston, J. R., & Campbell, L. E. G. (1988). *Impasses of divorce: The dynamics and resolution of family conflict.* New York: Free Press.

Kalter, N. (1977). Children of divorce in an outpatient psychiatric population. *American Journal of Orthopsychiatry*, 47, 40–51.

Kalter, N. (1990). *Growing up with divorce: Helping your child avoid immediate and later emotional problems.* New York: Free Press.

Kalter, N., Kloner, A., Schreier, S., & Okla, K. (1989). Predictors of children's postdivorce adjustment. *American Journal of Orthopsychiatry*, 59, 605–618.

Kaplan, B. H., Cassel, J. C., & Gore, S. (1977). Social support and health. *Medical Care*, 15, 47–58.

Kaslow, F. W. (1981). Divorce and divorce therapy. In A. S. Gurman & D. P. Kniskern (Eds.), *Handbook of marital therapy* (pp. 662–696). New York: Brunner/Mazel.

Kay, H. H. (1970). A family court: The California proposal. In P. Bohannan (Ed.), *Divorce and after* (pp. 215–248). Garden City, NY: Doubleday.

Kay, H. H. (1990). Beyond no-fault: New directions in divorce reform. In S. D. Sugarman & H. H. Kay (Eds.), *Divorce reform at the crossroads* (pp. 6–36). New Haven, CT: Yale University Press.

Kelly, J. B. (1982). Divorce: The adult perspective. In B. Wolman & G. Stricker (Eds.), *Handbook of developmental psychology* (pp. 734–750). Englewood Cliffs, NJ: Prentice-Hall.

Kelly, J. B. (1988). Longer-term adjustment in children of divorce: Conveying findings and implications for practice. *Journal of Family Psychology*, 2, 119–140.

Kelly, J. B. (1989). Mediated and adversarial divorce: Respondents' perceptions of the process and outcomes. *Mediation Quarterly*, 24, 71–88.

Kelly, J. B., & Wallerstein, J. S. (1976). The effects of parental divorce: Experiences of the child in early latency. *American Journal of Orthopsychiatry, 46,* 20–32.

Kemper, T. D. (1983). Predicting the divorce rate: Down? *Journal of Family Issues, 4,* 507–524.

Kessler, R. C., Brown, R. L., & Broman, C. L. (1981). Sex differences in psychiatric help-seeking: Evidence from four large-scale surveys. *Journal of Health and Social Behavior, 22,* 49–64.

Kiecolt-Glaser, J. K., Fisher, L. D., Ogrocki, P., Stout, J. D., Speicher, C. E., & Glaser, R. (1987). Marital quality, marital disruption, and immune function. *Psychosomatic Medicine, 49,* 13–34.

Kinsey, A. C., Pomeroy, W. B., & Martin, C. E. (1948). *Sexual behavior in the human male.* Philadelphia: W. B. Saunders.

Kinsey, A. C., Pomeroy, W. B., Martin, C. E., & Gebhard, P. A. (1953). *Sexual behavior in the human female.* Philadelphia: W. B. Saunders.

Kircheimer, A. (1980, July 9). Divorce: The financial struggle. *The Boston Globe,* p. 21.

Kisker, E. E., & Goldman, N. (1987). Perils of single life and benefits of marriage. *Social Biology, 34,* 135–152.

Kitson, G. C. (1982). Attachment to the spouse in divorce: A scale and its application. *Journal of Marriage and the Family, 44,* 379–393.

Kitson, G. C. (1985). Marital discord and marital separation: A county survey. *Journal of Marriage and the Family, 47,* 693–700.

Kitson, G. C. (1991a, July). *Changes in pining and preoccupation and anger in widows and divorcees.* Paper presented at the meeting of the Third International Conference on Grief and Bereavement in Contemporary Society, Sidney, Australia.

Kitson, G. C. (1991b). *The impact of age on adjustment to widowhood and divorce.* Unpublished manuscript.

Kitson, G. C., Babri, K. B., & Dyches, H. (1990, August). *Adjusting to widowhood and divorce: The role of ambivalent feelings toward the former spouse.* Paper presented at the meeting of the American Sociological Association, Washington, DC.

Kitson, G. C., Babri, K. B., & Roach, M. J. (1985). Who divorces and why: A review. *Journal of Family Issues, 6,* 255–293.

Kitson, G. C., Babri, K. B., Roach, M. J., & Placidi, K. S. (1989). Adjustment to widowhood and divorce: A review. *Journal of Family Issues, 10,* 5–32.

Kitson, G. C., Graham, A. V., & Schmidt, D. D. (1983). Troubled marriages and divorce: A prospective suburban study. *Journal of Family Practice, 17,* 249–258.

Kitson, G. C., Holmes, W. M., & Sussman, M. B. (1983). Withdrawing divorce petitions: A predictive test of the exchange model of divorce. *Journal of Divorce, 7,* 51–66.

Kitson, G. C., & Langlie, J. K. (1984). Couples who file for divorce but change their minds. *American Journal of Orthopsychiatry, 54,* 469–489.

Kitson, G. C., Lopata, H. Z., Holmes, W. M., & Meyering, S. M. (1980). Divorcees and widows: Similarities and differences. *American Journal of Orthopsychiatry, 50,* 291–301.

Kitson, G. C., & Morgan, L. A. (1990). The multiple consequences of divorce: A decade review. *Journal of Marriage and the Family, 52,* 913–924.

Kitson, G. C., & Raschke, H. J. (1981). Divorce research: What we know, what we need to know. *Journal of Divorce, 4,* 1–37.

Kitson, G. C., & Roach, M. J. (1989). Independence and social and psychological adjustment in widowhood and divorce. In D. A. Lund (Ed.), *Older bereaved spouses: Research with practical applications* (pp. 167–183). New York: Hemisphere.

Kitson, G. C., & Sussman, M. B. (1982). Marital complaints, demographic characteristics, and symptoms of mental distress in divorce. *Journal of Marriage and the Family, 44,* 87–101.

Kitson, G. C., Sussman, M. B., Williams, G. W., Zeehandelaar, R. B., Shickmanter, B. K., & Steinberger, J. L. (1982). Sampling issues in family research. *Journal of Marriage and the Family, 44,* 965–981.

Kitson, G. C., & Zyzanski, S. J. (1987). Grief in widowhood and divorce. *Psychiatric Clinics of North America, 10,* 369–386.

Kitson, G. C., Zyzanski, S. J., & Roach, M. J. (1991). *Pining and preoccupation: Measuring attachment in widowhood and divorce.* Unpublished manuscript.

Krantz, S. E. (1988). Divorce and children. In S. M. Dornbusch & M. F. Strober (Eds.), *Feminism, children, and the new families* (pp. 249–273). New York: Guilford Press.

Kraus, S. (1979). The crisis of divorce: Growth promoting or pathogenic? *Journal of Divorce, 3,* 107–119.

Kreisberg, L. (1970). *Mothers in poverty: A study of fatherless families.* Chicago: Aldine.

Kressel, K. (1985). *The process of divorce: How professionals and couples negotiate settlements.* New York: Basic Books.

Kressel, K., Lopez-Morillas, M., Weinglass, J., & Deutsch, M. (1978). Professional intervention in divorce: A summary of the views of lawyers, psychotherapists, and clergy. *Journal of Divorce, 2,* 119–155.

Kulka, R. A., Veroff, J., & Douvan, E. (1979). Social class and the use of professional help for personal problems: 1957 and 1976. *Journal of Health and Social Behavior, 20,* 2–17.

Kulka, R. A., & Weingarten, H. (1979). The long-term effects of parental divorce in childhood on adult adjustment. *Journal of Social Issues, 35,* 50–78.

Kumagai, F. (1983). Changing divorce in Japan. *Journal of Family History, 8,* 85–108.

Kurdek, L. A. (1981). An integrative perspective on children's divorce adjustment. *American Psychologist, 36,* 856–866.

Kurdek, L. A. (1987). Children's adjustment to parental divorce: An ecological perspective. In J. P. Vincent (Ed.), *Family intervention, assessment and theory* (Vol. 4, pp. 1–31). Greenwich, CT: JAI Press.

Kurdek, L. A. (1989). Children's adjustment. In M. Textor (Ed.), *The divorce and divorce therapy handbook* (pp. 77–102). Northvale, NJ: Jason Aronson.

Kurdek, L. A., & Siesky, A. E. (1978). Divorced single parents' perceptions of child-related problems. *Journal of Divorce, 1,* 361–370.

Landers, A. (1984, January 25). Former husband owes much more than child support. *The Plain Dealer* [Cleveland, OH], p. 7-F.

Lang, N., & Pett, M. (1989). *Changes in parent–adult child relations following late-life parental divorce.* Paper presented at the meeting of the Gerontological Society of America, Minneapolis.

Laosa, L. M. (1988). Ethnicity and single parenting in the United States. In E. M. Hetherington & J. D. Arasteh (Eds.), *Impact of divorce, single parenting, and stepparenting on children* (pp. 23–47). Hillsdale, NJ: Erlbaum.

LaRocca, J. M., House, J. S., & French, J. P. (1980). Social support, occupational stress, and health. *Journal of Health and Social Behavior, 21,* 202–218.

Lasch, C. (1977). *Haven in a heartless world: The family besieged.* New York: Basic Books.

Lee, G. R. (1977). *Family structure and interaction: A comparative analysis.* Philadelphia: J. B. Lippincott.

Levenson, R. W., & Gottman, J. M. (1985). Physiological and affective predictors of change in relationship satisfaction. *Journal of Personality and Social Psychology, 49,* 85–94.

Levinger, G. (1965). Marital cohesiveness and dissolution: An integrative review. *Journal of Marriage and the Family, 27,* 19–28.

Levinger, G. (1966). Sources of marital dissatisfaction among applicants for divorce. *American Journal of Orthopsychiatry, 32,* 803–807.

Levinger, G. (1976). A social psychological perspective on divorce. *Journal of Social Issues, 32,* 21–47.

Levinger, G. (1979). Marital cohesiveness at the brink: The fate of applications for divorce. In G. Levinger & O. C. Moles (Eds.), *Divorce and separation: Context, causes, and consequences* (pp. 137–150). New York: Basic Books.

Levitin, T. E. (Ed.). (1979). Children of divorce. *Journal of Social Issues, 32,* 1–186.

Lewis, P. H. (1983). Innovative divorce rituals: Their psycho-social functions. *Journal of Divorce, 6,* 71–81.

Lewis, R. A., & Spanier, G. B. (1979). Theorizing about the quality and stability of marriage. In W. R. Burr, R. Hill, F. I. Nye, & I. L. Reiss (Eds.), *Contemporary theories about the family: Vol. 1. Research-based theories* (pp. 268–294). New York: Free Press.

Lin, N., Simeone, R., Ensel, W., & Kuo, W. (1979). Social support, stressful life events, and illness: A model and an empirical test. *Journal of Health and Social Behavior, 20,* 108–119.

Lindemann, E. (1944). Symptomatology and management of acute grief. *American Journal of Psychiatry, 101,* 141-148.

Litwak, E. (1955). Three ways in which law acts as a means of social control: Punishment, therapy, and education. Divorce law a case in point. *Social Forces, 34,* 217-222.

Litwak, E. (1985). *Helping the elderly: The complementary roles of informal networks and formal systems.* New York: Guilford Press.

Lloyd, S. A., & Zick, C. D. (1986). Divorce at mid and later life: Does the empirical evidence support the theory? *Journal of Divorce, 9,* 89-102.

Locke, H. J. (1951). *Predicting adjustment in marriage: A comparison of a divorced and a happily married group.* New York: Henry Holt.

Loether, H. J., & McTavish, D. G. (1974). *Inferential statistics for sociologists: An introduction.* Boston: Allyn & Bacon.

Lopata, H. Z. (1973). *Widowhood in an American city.* Cambridge, MA: Schenkman.

Lopata, H. Z. (1979). *Women as widows: Support systems.* New York: Elsevier.

Lopata, H. Z., & Brehm, H. P. (1986). *Widows and dependent wives: From social problem to federal program.* New York: Praeger.

Luepnitz, D. A. (1982). *Child custody: A study of families after divorce.* Lexington, MA: Lexington Books.

Macklin, E. D. (1987). Nontraditional family forms. In M. B. Sussman & S. K. Steinmetz (Eds.), *Handbook of marriage and the family* (pp. 317-353). New York: Plenum.

Margolick, D. (1990, July 4). Lesbians' custody fights test family law frontier. *The New York Times,* p. A1, A10.

Markman, H. (1981). Prediction of marital distress: A 5-year follow-up. *Journal of Consulting and Clinical Psychology, 49,* 760-762.

Markman, H. J., Floyd, F. J., Stanley, S. M., & Lewis, H. C. (1986). Prevention. In N. S. Jacobson & A. S. Gurman (Eds.), *Clinical handbook of marital therapy* (pp. 173-195). New York: Guilford Press.

Markman, H. J., Floyd, F. J., Stanley, S. M., & Storaasli, R. D. (1988). Prevention of marital distress: A longitudinal investigation. *Journal of Consulting and Clinical Psychology, 56,* 210-217.

Marris, P. (1974). *Loss and change.* New York: Pantheon.

Masheter, C. (1991). Postdivorce relationships between ex-spouses: The roles of attachment and interpersonal conflict. *Journal of Marriage and the Family, 53,* 103-110.

Masnick, G., & Bane, M. J. (1980). *The nation's families: 1960-1990.* Boston: Auburn House.

Mauldon, J. (1990). The effect of marital disruption on children's health. *Demography, 27,* 431-446.

McCormack, A. (1985). Risk for alcohol-related accidents in divorced and separated women. *Journal of Studies on Alcohol, 46,* 240-243.

McCubbin, H. I., & Patterson, J. M. (1983). Family stress and adaptation to crises: A double ABCX model of family behavior. In D. H. Olson & B. C.

Miller (Eds.), *Family studies review yearbook* (Vol. 1, pp. 87–106). Beverly Hills, CA: Sage.

McDermott, J., Jr. (1968). Parental divorce in early childhood. *American Journal of Psychiatry, 124,* 1424–1432.

McDermott, J., Jr. (1970). Divorce and its psychiatric sequelae in children. *Archives of General Psychiatry, 23,* 421–427.

McLanahan, S. S., & Booth, K. (1989). Mother-only families: Problems, prospects, and politics. *Journal of Marriage and the Family, 51,* 557–580.

McLanahan, S. S., & Bumpass, L. (1988). Intergenerational consequences of family disruption. *American Journal of Sociology, 94,* 130–152.

McLanahan, S. S., Wedemeyer, N. V., & Adelberg, T. (1981). Network structure, social support, and psychological well-being in the single-parent family. *Journal of Marriage and the Family, 43,* 601–612.

McRae, J. A. (1978). The secularization of divorce. In B. Duncan & O. D. Duncan with J. A. McRae (Eds.), *Sex typing and sex roles: A research report* (pp. 227–242). New York: Academic Press.

Menaghan, E. G. (1985). Depressive affect and subsequent divorce. *Journal of Family Issues, 6,* 295–306.

Menaghan, E. G., & Lieberman, M. A. (1986). Changes in depression following divorce: A panel study. *Journal of Marriage and the Family, 48,* 319–328.

Mergenhagen, P. M., Lee, B. A., & Gove, W. R. (1985). Till death do us part: Recent changes in the relationship between marital status and mortality. *Sociology and Social Research, 70,* 53–56.

Milardo, R. M. (1987). Changes in social networks of women and men following divorce: A review. *Journal of Family Issues, 8,* 78–96.

Miller, A. A. (1970). Reactions of friends to divorce. In P. Bohannan (Ed.), *Divorce and after* (pp. 56–77). Garden City, NY: Doubleday.

Moen, P., Kain, E. L., & Elder, G. H., Jr. (1983). Economic conditions and family life: Contemporary and historical perspectives. In R. R. Nelson & F. Skidmore (Eds.), *American families and the economy: The high costs of living* (pp. 213–259). Washington, DC: National Academy Press.

Moore, K., & Sawhill, I. (1976). Implications of women's employment for home and family life. In J. Kreps (Ed.), *Women and the American economy* (pp. 102–122). Englewood Cliffs, NJ: Prentice-Hall.

Morgan, L. A. (1991). *After marriage ends: Economic consequences for midlife women.* Newbury Park, CA: Sage.

Moskoff, W. (1983). Divorce in the USSR. *Journal of Marriage and the Family, 45,* 419–425.

Moynihan, D. P. (1967). The Negro family: The case for national action. In L. Rainwater & W. L. Yancey (Eds.), *The Moynihan report and the politics of controversy* (pp. 39–124). Cambridge, MA: MIT Press.

Moynihan, D. P. (1985). *Family and nation: The Godkin lectures, Harvard University.* New York: Harcourt Brace Jovanovich.

Mueller, C. W., & Pope, H. (1977). Marital instability: A study of its transmission between generations. *Journal of Marriage and the Family, 39,* 83–93.

Mueller, C. W., & Pope, H. (1980). Divorce and female remarriage mobility:

Data on marriage matches after divorce for white women. *Social Forces*, *58*, 726–738.

Murdock, G. P. (1950). Family stability in non-European countries. *Annals of the American Academy of Political and Social Sciences, 272*, 195–201.

Murdock, G. P., & White, D. R. (1969). Standard cross-cultural sample. *Ethnology, 8*, 329–369.

Murstein, B. I. (1974). *Love, sex, and marriage through the ages.* New York: Springer.

Myers, J. K., Lindenthal, J. J., Pepper, M. P., & Ostrander, D. (1972). Life events and mental status: A longitudinal study. *Journal of Health and Social Behavior, 13*, 398–406.

National Center for Health Statistics. (1989). *Advance report of final divorce statistics, 1986* (Monthly Vital Statistics Report, Vol. 38, No. 2, Suppl., DHHS Publication No. PHS 89-1120). Hyattsville, MD: Public Health Service.

National Center for Health Statistics. (1990a). *Advance report of final divorce statistics, 1987* (Monthly Vital Statistics Report, Vol. 38, No. 12, Suppl. 2, DHHS Publication No. PHS 90-1120). Hyattsville, MD: Public Health Service.

National Center for Health Statistics. (1990b). *Annual summary of births, marriages, divorces, and deaths, 1989* (Monthly Vital Statistics Report, Vol. 38, DHHS Publication No. PHS 90-1120). Hyattsville, MD: Public Health Service.

National Center for Health Statistics. (1991). *Annual summary of births, marriages, divorces, and deaths, 1990* (Monthly Vital Statistics Report, Vol. 39, No. 12). Hyattsville, MD: Public Health Service.

Nelson, J. C., & Charney, D. S. (1980). Primary affective disorder criteria and the endogenous–reactive distinction. *Archives of General Psychiatry, 37*, 787–793.

Neugarten, B. L. (1979). Time, age, and the life cycle. *American Journal of Psychiatry, 136*, 887–894.

The New York Times, (1985, October 8). Divorce and the deficit. p. A30.

Norton, A. J. (1983). Family life cycle: 1980. *Journal of Marriage and the Family, 45*, 267–275.

Norton, A. J. (1991, April). Marriage behavior of women: 1990 and beyond. Banquet speech at a symposium in honor of P. C. Glick, *The American family on the eve of the twenty-first century: A demographic perspective*, Tempe, AZ.

Norton, A. J., & Glick, P. C. (1979). Marital instability in America: Past, present, and future. In G. Levinger & O. C. Moles (Eds.), *Divorce and separation: Context, causes, and consequences* (pp. 6–19). New York: Basic Books.

Norton, A. J., & Moorman, J. E. (1987). Current trends in marriage and divorce among American women. *Journal of Marriage and the Family, 49*, 3–14.

Nuckolls, K. B., Cassel, J., & Kaplan, B. H. (1972). Psychosocial assets, life crisis, and the prognosis of pregnancy. *American Journal of Epidemiology*, *95*, 431-441.

Nye, F. I. (1979). Choice, exchange, and the family. In W. R. Burr, R. Hill, F. I. Nye, & I. L. Reiss (Eds.), *Contemporary theories about the family: Vol. 2. General theories/theoretical orientations* (pp. 1-41). New York: Free Press.

Nye, F. I., White, L., & Frideres, J. (1973). A preliminary theory of marital stability: Two models. *International Journal of Sociology of the Family*, *3*, 102-122.

O'Brien, J. E. (1971). Violence in divorce prone families. *Journal of Marriage and the Family*, *33*, 692-698.

Oldham, J. T. (1981). Property division in a Texas divorce of a migrant spouse: Heads he wins, tails she loses? *Houston Law Review*, *19*, 1-53.

O'Neill, W. L. (1973). *Divorce in the progressive era*. New York: New Viewpoints/Franklin Watts.

Oster, S. M. (1987). A note on the determinants of alimony. *Journal of Marriage and the Family*, *49*, 81-86.

Parkes, C. M. (1971). Psychological transitions: A field for study. *Social Science and Medicine*, *5*, 101-115.

Parkes, C. M. (1972). *Bereavement: Studies of grief in adult life*. New York: International Universities Press.

Parkes, C. M. (1975). Determinants of outcome following bereavement. *Omega*, *6*, 303-323.

Parkes, C. M. (1982). Attachment and the prevention of mental disorders. In C. M. Parkes & J. Stevenson-Hinde (Eds.), *The place of attachment in human behavior* (pp. 295-309). New York: Basic Books.

Parkes, C. M. (1986). *Bereavement: Studies of grief in adult life* (2nd American ed.). Madison, CT: International Universities Press.

Parkes, C. M., & Weiss, R. S. (1983). *Recovery from bereavement*. New York: Basic Books.

Parsons, T., & Bales, R. F. (1955). *Family, socialization, and interaction process*. New York: Free Press.

Patterson, G. R., & Forgatch, M. S. (1990). Initiation and maintenance of process disrupting single-mother families. In G. R. Patterson (Ed.), *Depression and aggression in family interaction* (pp. 209-245). Hillsdale, NJ: Erlbaum.

Petiet, C. A. (1982). *Grief in divorcees and widows: Similarities, differences, and treatment implications*. Unpublished doctoral dissertation, California School of Professional Psychology.

Phillips, C. (1988, February 2). Divorce case marks first time a spouse wins civil award for emotional distress. *The Wall Street Journal*, p. 39.

Phillips, R. (1988). *Putting asunder: A history of divorce in Western society*. Cambridge, England: Cambridge University Press.

Piercy, F. P., & Sprenkle, D. H. (1990). Marriage and family therapy: A decade review. *Journal of Marriage and the Family*, *52*, 1116-1126.

Pillow, D. R., Sandler, I. N., Braver, S. L., Wolchik, S. A., & Gersten, J. C. (in press). Theory-based screening for prevention: Focusing on mediating processes in children of divorce. *American Journal of Community Psychology*.

The Plain Dealer [Cleveland, OH]. (1986, July 19). 12% of families control 38% of wealth, report says. p. A6.

The Plain Dealer [Cleveland, OH]. (1987, January 15). Estranged husband wounds his wife, shoots self on bus. p. B1.

The Plain Dealer [Cleveland, OH]. (1988, July 1). Her subtle humor is difference. Friday! section p. 3.

Platte, E. (1988). Divorce trends and patterns in China: Past and present. *Pacific Affairs, 61*, 428-445.

Pope, H., & Mueller, C. W. (1976). The intergenerational transmission of marital instability: Comparisons by race and sex. *Journal of Social Issues, 32*, 49-66.

Price, S. J., & McKenry, P. C. (1989). Current trends and issues in divorce: An agenda for family scientists in the 1990s. *Family Science Review, 2*, 219-236.

Price-Bonham, S., & Balswick, J. O. (1980). The noninstitutions: Divorce, desertion, and remarriage. *Journal of Marriage and the Family, 42*, 959-972.

Public Health Service Act, §301(d), 42 U.S.C. 241(d) as added by Pub. L. No. 100-607, 163 (November 4, 1988).

Raphael, B. (1983). *The anatomy of bereavement*. New York: Basic Books.

Raschke, H. J. (1977). The role of social participation in post separation and postdivorce adjustment. *Journal of Divorce, 1*, 129-139.

Raschke, H. J. (1987). Divorce. In M. B. Sussman & S. J. Steinmetz (Eds.), *Handbook of marriage and the family* (pp. 597-624). New York: Plenum.

Rasmussen, P. K., & Ferraro, K. J. (1979). The divorce process. *Alternative Lifestyles, 2*, 443-460.

Rheinstein, M. (1972). *Marriage stability, divorce, and the law*. Chicago: University of Chicago Press.

Riessman, C. K. (1990). *Divorce talk: Women and men make sense of personal relationships*. New Brunswick, NJ: Rutgers University Press.

Riessman, C. K., & Gerstel, N. (1985). Marital dissolution and health: Do males or females have greater risk? *Social Science and Medicine, 20*, 627-635.

Riley, G. (1991). Divorce: An American tradition. New York: Oxford.

Roach, M. J., & Kitson, G. C. (1989). The impact of forewarning on adjustment to widowhood and divorce. In D. A. Lund (Ed.), *Older bereaved spouses: Research with practical applications* (pp. 185-200). New York: Hemisphere.

Roberts, T. W., & Price, S. J. (1985-1986). A systems analysis of the remarriage process: Implications for clinicians. *Journal of Divorce, 9*, 1-25.

Robins, L. N. (1986). The development and characteristics of the NIMH diagnostic interview schedule. In M. W. Weissman, J. K. Myers, & C. E. Ross (Eds.) Community surveys of psychiatric disorders (pp. 403-427). New Brunswick, NJ: Rutgers University Press.

Rosenberg, M. (1965). *Society and the adolescent self-image*. Princeton, NJ: Princeton University Press.

Rosengren, A., Wedel, H., & Wilhelmsen, L. (1989). Marital status and mortality in middle-aged Swedish men. *American Journal of Epidemiology, 129*, 54–64.

Rosenthal, K. M., & Keshet, H. F. (1981). *Fathers without partners: A study of fathers and the family after marital separation*. Totowa, NJ: Rowman & Littlefield.

Ross, C. E., & Mirowsky, J., II. (1979). A comparison of life-event weighting schemes: change, undesirability, and effect-proportional indices. *Journal of Health and Social Behavior, 20*, 166–177.

Ross, H. L., & Sawhill, I. V. (1975). *Time of transition: The growth of families headed by women*. Washington, DC: Urban Institute.

Rossi, A. (1986, April 27). Destitution is just a divorce away. *The New York Times Book Review*, p. 13.

Ro-Tack, G. K., Wellisch, D. K., & Schoolar, J. C. (1977). A family therapy outcome study in an inpatient setting. *American Journal of Orthopsychiatry, 47*, 514–522.

Rushing, W. A. (1979). Marital status and mental disorder: Evidence in favor of a behavioral model. *Social Forces, 58*, 540–556.

Sager, C. J., Brown, H. S., Crohn, H., Engel, T., Rodstein, E., & Walker, L. (1983). *Treating the remarried family*. New York: Brunner/Mazel.

St. Petersburg Times. (1984, February 26). *People*. p. 3A.

Schlesinger, B. (1978). *One parent families* (4th ed.). Toronto: University of Toronto Press.

Schoen, R., Greenblatt, H., & Mielke, R. (1975). California's experience with non-adversary divorce. *Demography, 12*, 223–243.

Schoenborn, C. A., & Marano, M. (1988). *Current estimates from the National Health Interview Survey*: United States, 1987 (Vital and Health Statistics, Vol. 10, No. 166, DHHS Publication No. PHS 88-1594). Washington, DC: U.S. Government Printing Office.

Schultz, M. (1984). Divorce in early America: Origins and patterns in three north central states. *Sociological Quarterly, 25*, 511–526.

Schultz, S. J. (1984). *Family systems theory: An integration*. New York: Jason Aronson.

Segraves, R. T. (1982). *Marital therapy: A combined psychodynamic–behavioral approach*. New York: Plenum.

Shanas, E., & Sussman, M. B. (1981). The family in later life. In R. W. Fogel, E. Hatfield, S. B. Kessler, & E. Shanas (Eds.), *Aging:: Stability and change in the family*. New York: Academic Press.

Sidel, R. (1986). *Women and children last*. New York: Viking.

Silverman, P. R. (1980). *Mutual help groups: Organization and development* (Sage Human Services Guide No. 16). Beverly Hills, CA: Sage.

Silverman, P. R. (1981). *Helping women cope with grief* (Sage Human Services Guide No. 25). Beverly Hills, CA: Sage.

Silverman, P. R., MacKenzie, D., Pettipas, M., & Wilson, E. (1974). *Helping each other in widowhood.* New York: Health Sciences.

Simos, B. G. (1979). *A time to grieve: Loss as a universal human experience.* New York: Family Service Association of America.

Smith, J. C., Mercy, J. A., & Conn, J. M. (1988). Marital status and the risk of suicide. *American Journal of Public Health, 78,* 78-80.

Somers, A. R. (1979). Marital status, health, and use of health services. *Journal of the American Medical Association, 41,* 1818-1822.

Spanier, G. B., & Anderson, E. A. (1979). The impact of the legal system on adjustment to marital separation. *Journal of Marriage and the Family, 41,* 605-613.

Spanier, G. B., & Casto, R. F. (1979). Adjustment to separation and divorce: A qualitative analysis. In G. Levinger & O. C. Moles (Eds.), *Divorce and separation: Context, causes, and consequences* (pp. 211-227). New York: Basic Books.

Spanier, G. B., & Thompson, L. (1984). *Parting: The aftermath of separation and divorce.* Beverly Hills, CA: Sage.

Speagle, L. E., & Kitson, G. C. (1982, May). *Life events: Their demography and associations for divorced and intact family respondents.* Paper presented at the meeting of the North American Primary Care Research Group, Columbus, OH.

Spicer, J. W., & Hampe, G. D. (1975). Kinship interaction after divorce. *Journal of Marriage and the Family, 37,* 113-119.

Spitzer, R. L., Endicott, J., Fleiss, J. L., & Cohen, J. (1970). The Psychiatric Status Schedule: A technique for evaluating psychopathology and impairment in role functioning. *Archives of General Psychiatry, 23,* 41-55.

Sprenkle, D. H., & Storm, C. L. (1983). Divorce therapy outcome research: A substantive and methodological review. *Journal of Marital and Family Therapy, 9,* 239-258.

Sprey, J. (1979). Conflict theory and the study of marriage and the family. In W. R. Burr, R. Hill, F. I. Nye, & I. L. Reiss (Eds.), *Contemporary theories about the family: Vol. 2. General theories/theoretical orientations* (pp. 130-159). New York: Free Press.

Stephens, W. N. (1963). *The family in cross-cultural perspective.* New York: Holt, Rinehart & Winston.

Sterin, G., & Davis, J. M., with McGraw, R. E. (1981). *Divorce awards and outcomes. A study of pattern and change in Cuyahoga County, 1965-1978.* Cleveland, OH: Federation for Community Planning.

Stone, L. (1990). *Road to divorce: England 1530-1987.* New York: Oxford University Press.

Suchman, E. A. (1965). Social patterns of illness and medical care. *Journal of Health and Human Behavior, 6,* 2-16.

Sussman, M. B., & Burchinal, L. (1962a). Kin family network: Unheralded structure in current conceptualizations of family functioning. *Marriage and Family Living, 24,* 232-240.

Sussman, M. B., & Burchinal, L. (1962b). Parental aid to married children: Implications for family functioning. *Marriage and Family Living, 24*, 320–331.

Thompson, A. P. (1983). Extramarital sex: A review of the research literature. *Journal of Sex Research, 19*, 1–22.

Thompson, L., & Spanier, G. B. (1983). The end of marriage and the acceptance of marital termination. *Journal of Marriage and the Family, 45*, 103–113.

Thompson, L., & Walker, A. J. (1982). The dyad as the unit of analysis: Conceptual and methodological issues. *Journal of Marriage and the Family, 44*, 889–900.

Thornton, A. (1985). Changing attitudes toward separation and divorce: Causes and consequences. *American Journal of Sociology, 90*, 856–872.

Thurnher, M., Fenn, C. B., Melichar, J., & Chiriboga, D. A. (1983). Sociodemographic perspectives on reasons for divorce. *Journal of Divorce, 6*, 25–35.

Trent, K., & South, S. J. (1989). Structural determinants of the divorce rate: A cross-sectional analysis. *Journal of Marriage and the Family, 51*, 391–404.

Trovato, F., & Lauris, G. (1989). Marital status and mortality in Canada, 1951–81. *Journal of Marriage and the Family, 51*, 907–922.

Tschann, J. M., Johnston, J. R., & Wallerstein, J. S. (1989). Resources, stresses, and attachment as predictors of adult adjustment after divorce: A longitudinal study. *Journal of Marriage and the Family, 51*, 1033–1046.

Uhlenberg, P., Cooney, T., & Boyd, R. (1990). Divorce for women after midlife. *Journal of Gerontology: Social Sciences, 45*, S3–S11.

U.S. Bureau of the Census. (1972a). *1970 census of the population: General social and economic characteristics* (Final Report No. PC(1)-C37, Ohio). Washington, DC: U.S. Government Printing Office.

U.S. Bureau of the Census. (1972b). *1970 census of the population: General social and economic characteristics* (Final Report No. PC(1)-C1, United States summary). Washington, DC: U.S. Government Printing Office.

U.S. Bureau of the Census. (1972c). *1970 census of population and housing: Census tracts* (Final Report No. PHC(1)-45, Cleveland, Ohio SMSA). Washington, DC: U.S. Government Printing Office.

U.S. Bureau of the Census. (1972d). *1970 census of the population: Marital status* (Final Report No. PC2-4C). Washington, DC: U.S. Government Printing Office.

U.S. Bureau of the Census. (1975). *Historical statistics of the United States, colonial times to 1970* (Bicentennial edition, Part I). Washington, DC: U.S. Government Printing Office.

U.S. Bureau of the Census. (1976). *Statistical abstract of the United States: 1976*. Washington, DC: U.S. Government Printing Office.

U.S. Bureau of the Census. (1980). *Families maintained by female householders: 1970–1979* (Current Population Reports, Special Studies, Series P-23, No. 107). Washington, DC: U.S. Government Printing Office.

U.S. Bureau of the Census. (1981). *1980 census of the population: Vol. 1.*

General social and economic characteristics (Final Report No. PC80-1-C37, Ohio). Washington, DC: U.S. Government Printing Office.

U.S. Bureau of the Census. (1983). *Child support and alimony: 1981, advance report* (Current Population Reports, Special Studies, Series P-23, No. 124). Washington, DC: U.S. Government Printing Office.

U.S. Bureau of the Census. (1984). *1980 census of population and housing: Census tracts* (Final Report No. PHC80-2-123, Cleveland, Ohio SMSA). Washington, DC: U.S. Government Printing Office.

U.S. Bureau of the Census. (1985). Statistical abstract of the United States: 1985. Washington, DC: U.S. Government Printing Office.

U.S. Bureau of the Census. (1987a). *Marital status and living arrangements: March 1986* (Current Population Reports, Series P-20, No. 418). Washington, DC: U.S. Government Printing Office.

U.S. Bureau of the Census. (1987b). *Child support and alimony: 1985, advance data from March–April 1986 current population surveys* (Current Population Reports, Series P-23, No. 152). Washington, DC: U.S. Government Printing Office.

U.S. Bureau of the Census. (1990). *Marital Status and living arrangements: March 1989* (Current Population Reports, Series P-20, No. 445). Washington, DC: U.S. Government Printing Office.

Verbrugge, L. M. (1979). Marital status and health. *Journal of Marriage and the Family, 41,* 267–285.

Verbrugge, L. M. (1985). Gender and health: An update on hypotheses and evidence. *Journal of Health and Social Behavior, 26,* 156–182.

Veroff, J., Douvan, E., & Kulka, R. A. (1981). *The inner American: A self-portrait from 1957 to 1976.* New York: Basic Books.

Veroff, J., Kulka, R. A., & Douvan, E. (1981). *Mental health in America: Patterns of health seeking from 1957 to 1976.* New York: Basic Books.

Walker, L. E. (1979). *The battered woman.* New York: Harper & Row.

Waller, W. (1967). *The old love and the new: Divorce and readjustment.* Carbondale, IL: University of Southern Illinois Press. (Original work published 1930).

Waller, W., & Hill, R. (1951). *The family: A dynamic interpretation.* New York: Dryden Press.

Wallerstein, J. S. (1983). Children of divorce: The psychological tasks of the child. *American Journal of Orthopsychiatry, 53,* 230–243.

Wallerstein, J. S. (1986). Women after divorce: Preliminary report from a ten-year follow-up. *American Journal of Orthopsychiatry, 56,* 65–77.

Wallerstein, J. S. (1991). The long-term effects of divorce on children: A review. *Journal of the American Academy of Child and Adolescent Psychiatry, 30,* 349–360.

Wallerstein, J. S., & Blakeslee, S. (1989). *Second chances: Men, women, and children a decade after divorce.* New York: Ticknor & Fields.

Wallerstein, J. S., & Corbin, S. B. (1986). Family–child relationships after divorce: Child support and educational opportunity. *Family Law Quarterly, 20,* 109–128.

Wallerstein, J. S., & Huntington, D. S. (1983). Bread and roses: Nonfinancial issues related to fathers' economic support of their children following divorce. In J. Cassetty (Ed.), *The parental child-support obligation: Research, practice, and social policy* (pp. 135-155). Lexington, MA: Lexington Books.

Wallerstein, J. S., & Kelly, J. B. (1974). The effects of parental divorce: The adolescent experience. In E. J. Anthony & C. Koupernik (Eds.), *Children at psychiatric risk* (Vol. 3, pp. 479-505). New York: Wiley.

Wallerstein, J. S., & Kelly, J. B. (1975). The effects of parental divorce: Experiences of the preschool child. *Journal of the American Academy of Child Psychiatry, 14,* 600-616.

Wallerstein, J. S., & Kelly, J. B. (1976). The effects of parental divorce: Experiences of the child in later latency. *American Journal of Orthopsychiatry, 46,* 256-269.

Wallerstein, J. S., & Kelly, J. B. (1977). Divorce counseling: A community service for families in the midst of divorce. *American Journal of Orthopsychiatry, 47,* 4.

Wallerstein, J. S., & Kelly, J. B. (1980). *Surviving the breakup: How children and parents cope with divorce.* New York: Basic Books.

Wan, T. H. (1982). Use of health-services by the elderly in low-income communities. *Milbank Memorial Fund Quarterly, 60,* 82-107.

Weiss, R. L. (1981). Resistance in behavioral marriage therapy. In A. S. Gurman (Ed.), *Questions and answers in the practice of family therapy* (pp. 155-159). New York: Brunner/Mazel.

Weiss, R. S. (1973). The contributions of an organization of single parents to the well-being of its members. *The Family Coordinator, 22,* 321-326.

Weiss, R. S. (1975). *Marital separation.* New York: Basic Books.

Weiss, R. S. (1976). The emotional impact of marital separation. *Journal of Social Issues, 32,* 135-145.

Weiss, R. S. (1979). *Going it alone: The family life and social situation of the single parent.* New York: Basic Books.

Weiss, R. S. (1982). Attachment in adult life. In C. M. Parkes & J. Stevenson-Hinde (Eds.), *The place of attachments in human behavior* (pp. 171-184). New York: Basic Books.

Weiss, R. S. (1984). The impact of marital dissolution on income and consumption in single-parent households. *Journal of Marriage and the Family, 46,* 115-127.

Weiss, R. S. (1990). *Staying the course: The emotional and social lives of men who do well at work.* New York: Free Press.

Weitzman, L. J. (1985). *The divorce revolution: The unexpected social and economic consequences for women and children in America.* New York: Free Press.

Weitzman, L. J., & Dixon, R. B. (1980). The alimony myth: Does no-fault divorce make a difference. *Family Law Quarterly, 14,* 141-185.

Wertlieb, D., Budman, S., Demby, A., & Randall, M. (1984). Marital separation and health: Stress and intervention. *Journal of Human Stress, 10,* 18-26.

Wheaton, B. (1990). Life transitions, role histories, and mental health. *American Sociological Review, 55,* 209-223.

Wheeler, M. (1974). *No fault divorce.* Boston: Beacon Press.

White, L. K. (1990). Determinants of divorce: A review of research in the eighties. *Journal of Marriage and the Family, 52,* 904-912.

Wilcox, B. L. (1981). Social support, life stress, and psychological adjustment: A test of the buffering hypothesis. *American Journal of Community Psychiatry, 9,* 371-386.

Williams, A. W., Ware, J. E., & Donald, C. A. (1981). A model of mental health, life-events, and social supports applicable to general populations. *Journal of Health and Social Behavior, 22,* 324-336.

Wilson, C. (1982). Division of marital property on divorce: What does the court deem "just and right"? *Houston Law Review, 19,* 502-525.

Winch, R. F. (1971). *The modern family* (3rd ed.). New York: Holt, Rinehart & Winston.

Winch, R. F., with Blumberg, R. L., Garcia, M. P., Gordon, M. T., & Kitson, G. C. (1977). *Familial organization: A quest for determinants.* New York: Free Press.

Windholz, M. J., Marmar, C. R., & Horowitz, M. J. (1985). A review of the research on conjugal bereavement: Impact on health and efficacy of intervention. *Comprehensive Psychiatry, 26,* 433-447.

Wiseman, R. S. (1975). Crisis theory and the process of divorce. *Social Casework, 56,* 205-212.

Wishik, H. R. (1986). Economics of divorce: An exploratory study. *Family Law Quarterly, 20,* 79-107.

Yuzawa, Y. (1990). Recent trends of divorce and custody in Japan. *Journal of Divorce, 13,* 129-141.

Zaslow, M. J. (1988). Sex differences in children's response to parental divorce: 1. Research methodology and postdivorce family forms. *American Journal of Orthopsychiatry, 58,* 355-378.

Zaslow, M. J. (1989). Sex differences in children's response to parental divorce: 2. Samples, variables, ages, and sources. *American Journal of Orthopsychiatry, 59,* 118-141.

Zisook, S., & Shuchter, S. R. (1986). The first four years of widowhood. *Psychiatric Annals, 16,* 289-294.

Zung, W. W. K. (1965). A self-rating depression scale. *Archives of General Psychiatry, 12,* 63-70.

Author Index

Subject Index